THE SOVIET WORKER

THE
SOVIET WORKER

AN ACCOUNT
OF THE ECONOMIC, SOCIAL AND
CULTURAL STATUS OF LABOR
IN THE U.S.S.R.

JOSEPH FREEMAN

HYPERION PRESS, INC.
WESTPORT, CONNECTICUT

Library of Congress Cataloging in Publication Data

Freeman, Joseph, 1897-1965.
  The Soviet worker.

    Reprint of the ed. published by International
Publishers, New York.
    Bibliography: p.
    1. Labor and laboring classes—Russia.
2. Russia—Economic conditions—1918-1945.
3. Russia—Social conditions—1917-   I. Title.
HD8526.F7 1973   301.44'42'0947   73-841
ISBN 0-88355-036-9

Published in 1932
by International Publishers, Inc., New York.
Copyright 1932
by Joseph Freeman.

First Hyperion reprint edition 1973

Library of Congress Catalogue Number 73-841

ISBN 0-88355-036-9

Printed in the United States of America

PREFACE

THE Soviet system was established in 1917 as a "dictatorship of the proletariat." Behind this designation is the theory developed by Karl Marx and V. I. Lenin regarding the decisive rôle of the working class in the transition of society from capitalism to communism. According to this theory, it is the historic mission of the working class to be the leader in the profound social transformation which marks the epoch in which we live. The Soviet system is organized on the presupposition that the proletariat leads the other laboring classes of the population towards a communist society.

In view of the avowed aims of the Soviet régime, the status of the worker is of the utmost importance in gauging events and achievements in the Soviet Union. It may even be said to be, in some ways, the touchstone of the entire system.

Regardless of their attitude toward the validity of the theories upon which the Soviet system is founded, observers of Soviet life agree that the worker's status in Soviet society has no precedent in history and no parallel in the contemporary world. Yet this theme has been given the least attention in American literature dealing with the Soviet Union.

This book is an attempt to collate some of the more important material dealing with Soviet labor. Part of this material exists in English. The extraordinary interest of the American reading public in Soviet affairs, due, in part, to the success of the Five-Year Plan, has resulted in the publication of numerous books and articles on various aspects of Soviet life. But since relatively little of this material deals directly with the Soviet worker, I have resorted to a large extent to material published in Russian in the Soviet Union. Most of the statistics in this book are from official Soviet sources.

In addition to Soviet material, I have availed myself of material published by American and British students of the Soviet régime. A year spent in the Soviet Union, during which I attempted to become acquainted with the general principles of the Soviet system, helped me greatly in the assimilation and analysis of the material on which this study is based.

The first three chapters of the book do not deal directly with the status of the Soviet worker; but I have felt it necessary to include them for the purpose of giving the setting of contemporary Soviet labor conditions. The first chapter, which attempts to describe the status of the Russian worker under the Czarist régime, offers a basis of comparison between pre-revolutionary and post-revolutionary labor conditions. The second and third chapters, outlining the development of Soviet economy and the Soviet planning system, are intended to delineate the background against which Soviet labor conditions can best be understood. The remainder of the book seeks to describe the actual circumstances under which the worker labors and lives in the Soviet Union.

At a number of points I have cited theoretical utterances by Soviet economists and statesmen. These theories shed light on the principles of Soviet labor legislation and have therefore seemed to me pertinent to the general theme of the book. I have attempted to present such theories as an integral part of the objective situation described here on the assumption that the aims of the Soviet régime are among the determining factors of its actions.

Four appendices have been inserted in back of the book for the purpose of clarifying, by means of original documents hitherto unpublished in English, some of the major problems affecting Soviet labor. The first of these is the complete text of a Soviet labor agreement; the second is the text of the instructions issued jointly by the All-Union Central Council of Trade Unions and the State Planning Commission (Gosplan) concerning the participation of workers and engineering and technical personnel in the preparation of the second five-year plan; and the third consists of excerpts from the resolution of the Ninth Congress of Trade Unions held in April 1932 summarizing the present policies, activities, and plans of the Soviet trade unions. These three appendices shed considerable light upon the status of the Soviet worker and his rôle in the economic, social and political system of the Soviet Union. The fourth appendix contains a typical budget of a Leningrad workers' family in 1932.

I am greatly indebted to various persons who have been generous with assistance and advice in the course of getting this book together, notably Dr. Hyman Rosen for his aid in research. I also avail myself of this opportunity to thank the Information Department of the Amtorg Trading Corporation, particularly its director, Mr. Samuel S. Shipman, for statistical and other material placed at my disposal.

JOSEPH FREEMAN

NEW YORK CITY,
June 7, 1932.

CONTENTS

THE
SOVIET WORKER

CHAPTER I

THE OLD REGIME

FEUDALISM continued to exist in Russia into the latter half of the nineteenth century. Until the emancipation of 1861 Russian peasants were serfs attached to the soil and were bought, sold and bartered by their landlords. Nevertheless, the factory system appeared in Russia as early as in any European country. During the reign of Peter the Great (1672-1725) there already existed some large factories, especially in the mining regions. As part of his policy of industrial development and "westernization" Peter granted the right to establish factories and to employ serfs from government estates to members of the feudal nobility, merchants and foreigners who were willing to undertake factory production. He was especially anxious to foster large-scale industry for the manufacture of arms and munitions, cloth, linen and sail-cloth, so as to equip his army and navy with domestic products. In his desire to emancipate Russia from its dependence on western European industry, he created the so-called "proprietary" factory established with funds advanced by the government, and supplied with conscripted labor. Serfs and workers were conscripted and handed over to the private individuals privileged to run these factories. Peasants on the government estates were conscripted for work in those factories and bound to them for life as they were formerly bound to the soil. The labor supply of the "proprietary" factories was supplemented from other sources. Manufacturers were granted the right to conscript for factory service beggars, criminals, wives of soldiers on active service, and children in poor-houses and foundling homes. At the same time, foreign specialists were engaged to organize and supervise the infant industries of Russia.[1]

Between 1750 and 1770 the government issued decrees limiting the purchase of serfs to the purchase of land. As a result, the ownership of factories passed into the hands of the feudal nobility which possessed the bondage right. Despite this change there were in 1780 at least 75,000 peasants who had been allotted to work in the "proprietary" factories.

In addition there were thousands of peasants working in the "votchinal" type of factory, so-called from the Russian word "votchina," meaning "patrimonial estate." This type of factory developed among landowners who found they could supplement their agricultural revenue and make more profitable use of the labor of their serfs by conducting industrial enterprises on their estates, such as sugar refining, tobacco growing, mining or distilling. The "votchinal," like the "proprietary" factory, employed only serf labor. In neither type of factory did the industrial serf receive wages.

Early in the nineteenth century a class of free workers began to develop due to the fact that Russian serfs could obtain their freedom from bondage by paying the landowner a monetary tribute (obrok) in lieu of feudal services. The growth of this practice stimulated the development of factories employing wage labor since peasants freed by the "obrok" created a reserve of cheap labor for capitalist manufacturers who could now compete on equal terms with the feudal factory owners and their large supply of serf labor.

It laid the basis for the development of an industrial working class legally detached from the soil and dependent for its livelihood on the ability to sell its labor power. This class steadily increased in numbers so that in 1804 free labor constituted 48 per cent of all factory labor in Russia and in 1825 54 per cent. Nevertheless, many of these workers were still close to the village and retained much of their peasant psychology. They left the mine or factory during the summer

[1] M. I. Tugan-Baranovski, *The Russian Factory*, St. Petersburg, 1898.

months to work in the fields, resuming their industrial occupations in late autumn. However, when power machinery was introduced into Russia in 1846, the factory definitely became a work center and began to develop along modern lines.

National economy was revolutionized by the emancipation of the serfs and the formal abolition of feudalism. Russia's defeat in the Crimean War (1853-1856), which revealed her inferiority to the other Powers, stimulated a general movement of protest against the system of serfdom as a barrier to economic progress. On February 19, 1861 Czar Alexander II issued a decree abolishing this system.

The reform was forced upon the government by political and economic necessity. Landowners could no longer compete on the world grain market because they were handicapped by the low productivity of serf labor. At the same time, merchant capitalism was developing. The nobles, pressed for money, raised loans by mortgaging their serfs. By 1859 about 65 per cent of the serfs had been mortgaged in this manner. The demand for the abolition of serfdom thus had support among certain landowners as well as among the middle classes. Furthermore, the intolerable conditions of serfdom drove the peasants to sporadic revolts which threatened to assume general proportions and led the Czar himself to observe that it would be better to emancipate the serfs "from above" since there was danger that emancipation "will begin of itself from below."

Among the factors which determined the actual results of the "emancipation" of the peasants were the landowners' need of money, cheap labor, and sometimes land. The government therefore decided that the peasants were to receive their personal liberty nominally without paying their masters any compensation. In practice, however, such compensation was paid. The landowners were to turn over to the peasants the plots of land which they had been cultivating. For these plots the peasants were to pay the landowners, but since the peasants had no money and the landowners needed money urgently, the government was to advance the compensation to the landowners and the peasants were to pay it off in annual installments.

The emancipation proclamation did not stipulate the amount of land to be turned over to the peasant and the landowners handed over only part of the land which they had formerly cultivated, usually the least fertile and often only an enclosure. This was inadequate to maintain the peasant, his family and his cattle, so that he was compelled to work for the landowner at low wages.

In practice, therefore, the "emancipated" peasant was as dependent on his landlord as when he was a serf. For the land which he received he paid rent wholly or partly in kind or contracted to pay part of his harvest as rent. To the government the peasant paid annual installments on the compensation money advanced to the landowners, as well as taxes on his land. In order to prevent any individual peasant from evading payment, "collective responsibility" was placed on the village as a whole. Consequently, the peasant could not leave the village unless he paid all that was exacted from him which, in his impoverished condition, was extremely difficult. This restriction of the peasant's movements assured the landowners the necessary supply of cheap labor. Accordingly the "emancipation" of 1861 resulted in a dual system of rural labor. There was the capitalist régime of the small proprietor based on free wage labor, and a modified form of feudal servitude.

The peasantry itself broke up into various classes. There were well-to-do peasants who could add to their land holdings and pay rent in money. This enabled them to collect considerable stocks of grain which they could sell in domestic or foreign markets. Poor peasants, on the other hand, paid rent in labor fixed at low prices. Peasants unable to live on their poor plots of land were often compelled to abandon the village altogether, to enter factories as wage workers and out of their meager wages to pay their rural obligations. Between these two extremes were the great majority of peasants who managed to make a poor living on their small farms but were overwhelmed by the burden of annual payments, high taxes and other disabilities.

The abolition of serfdom and the change in the status of the peasants had marked results on the factory system. The "proprietary" factory had disappeared with the growth of capitalism when the government abandoned its manufacturing activities to private entrepreneurs. The "votchinal" factory disappeared with the abolition of serfdom, when the peasant-workers deserted the factories of the landowners, who found themselves unable to reorganize their factories along capitalist lines. One of the immediate effects of the "emancipation," therefore, was a decline in industry, particularly the iron industry, which had relied to a great extent on serf labor. In addition, Russia suffered from the general economic crisis then prevailing in Europe. These factors affected Russian industry adversely for ten years or more. There was a decline in the number of factories and the number of workers.

However, during the seventies the Donetz Basin was opened, the power loom was introduced, and the industrial revolution was definitely under way in Russia. The rise of steel plants, oil wells and textile mills and the expansion of railways was accompanied by the rapid growth of the urban population in the last three decades of the century. In 1863 the number of cities with a population over 50,000 totaled thirteen; by 1897 this number had risen to 44. The population of this class of cities grew from 1,741,900 to 4,266,300.[2]

The rapid expansion of Russian industry was reflected in all the key industries. During the decade ending in 1898 cast iron production nearly trebled. Russia began to manufacture machinery, including steam-boilers, steam-engines, weaving looms, apparatus for flour mills, etc. Railway construction increased rapidly; mileage doubled between 1890 and 1897, with corresponding increases in locomotives and passenger and freight cars. Water transportation expanded, as did the construction of ships for civil and naval use. The production of coal, iron

[2] Lenin, *Development of Capitalism in Russia* [Russian], p. 436, in 1926 edition of Lenin's Collected Works, Vol. III, Gosizdat, Moscow.

ore, oil, lumber, bricks, cement and glass increased rapidly.
Street car systems were laid out; telephones and electric lights
installed; water and sewage systems constructed. The value
of the total production of Russian industry and mining in
1887 was 1,300,000,000 rubles; by 1897 this had risen to
2,800,000,000 rubles.

Up to the world war this industrial expansion continued
amidst survivals of feudalism. Nearly 87 per cent of Russia's
170,000,000 inhabitants lived in the rural districts. Of these
75 per cent were engaged in agricultural pursuits. The feudal
nobility continued to play a dominant rôle. On the eve of the
reform of 1861 the 103,000 big landowners of Russia owned
187 million acres of land, an average of 1,817 acres per landowner; while 9,795,000 peasants who employed no labor held
96,603,338 acres, an average of 9.72 acres per peasant.[3] Toward
the end of the eighties the rising middle classes obtained some
influence in the government, which began to show marked
partiality toward the development of industry. Between 1892
and 1901 indirect taxes were increased 50 per cent to relieve
industrialists of some direct taxation; and in 1893, 1900 and
1903 protective tariffs were adopted.

From the time Peter the Great sought to "westernize"
Russia, foreign technicians, managers and capital played a
significant rôle in the development of Russian industry. This
rôle grew in importance as industry expanded. Between 1894
and 1900 a total of 800,000,000 rubles was invested in Russian
industry, of which 500,000,000 were foreign capital. The number of foreign companies operating in Russia increased from
three in 1894 to forty in 1900.[4] For twenty years prior to the
war Russia financed her expanding volume of imports by
borrowing abroad at an average of 210,000,000 rubles a year.
The total foreign capital invested in Russian industry before
the war was estimated at 2,200,000,000 gold rubles. In addition,
some 5,400,000,000 rubles of foreign capital were invested in

---

[3] N. N. Vanag and S. Tomsinsky, *The Economic Development of Russia*,
Gosizdat, Moscow, 1928; p. 38.
[4] *Ibid.*, p. 209.

state and municipal guaranteed loans, making a total of 7,600,000,000 rubles.[5]

The increase in the number of factories which had been going on prior to 1861 continued at an even greater rate after the industrial revolution was well under way. In 1815 there were throughout Russia 4,189 enterprises with 173,000 workers. By 1861 there were 14,148 enterprises with 522,500 workers. The census of 1897 reported 19,396 industrial establishments in the census industries employing a total of 1,880,000 workers. The expansion of industry was marked by a growth in the number of large factories. In 1890 there were 108 factories employing 1,000 or more workers with a total of 226,000 workers; in 1902 the number of such factories had risen to 261 and the total number of their employees to 626,500. There were huge steel plants, like the "Hughes" and "Pugatchev" works in the Donetz Basin, employing 10,000 workers each. By 1894 there were eight textile mills employing 5,000 workers each.

In his pioneer work on the development of Russian capitalism Lenin estimated that toward the close of the nineteenth century the empire contained about 13,000,000 wage-earners of various kinds, including employees in mercantile establishments, civil and domestic servants and the like.[6] The ranks of the industrial proletariat were swelled from time to time by acute agricultural crises. Thus during the "black year," 1891, famine drove many peasants to the cities where they sought employment in the factories. In some cases two-thirds to three-fourths of the entire population of a village would migrate to the cities, increasing the supply of cheap labor.[7] Such crises also tended to transform handicraft workers into industrial workers. The growth of the working class continued so rapidly that between 1897 and 1913 the number of wage-earners in census industries increased 70 per cent and in the

[5] Maurice Dobb, *Russian Economic Development Since the Revolution,* E. P. Dutton & Co., New York, 1928, p. 71.

[6] Lenin, *op. cit.,* p. 393.

[7] M. S. Balabanov, *An Outline of the History of the Working Class in Russia,* Vol. III, "Capitalist Russia," p. 37.

domestic craft industries—50 per cent. The number of workers in transportation increased correspondingly, reaching 975,000 in 1913.

The rapid expansion of industry was not accompanied by a corresponding improvement in the lot of the wage-worker. Data collected by government factory inspectors in 1900-1901 regarding the conditions of 1,275,000 workers employed in 12,702 industrial enterprises revealed that the average earnings of a male adult worker were 242 rubles a year or 20 rubles a month, i.e., about $2.50 a week. Factory inspectors reported instances of girls employed in cigarette case factories at wages ranging from two to four rubles a month, while cigarette makers earned a maximum of nine rubles a month. As a result the workers were nearly always in debt.

In 1905 the most skilled workers in Russia averaged 30 rubles a month. The average wages of all workers in large-scale industry in 1913 were 25 rubles a month. Even these low wages were not paid on time. The government factory inspectors did not enforce timely payment, and the workers could not sue in court since that would mean instant dismissal and the blacklist.

With low wages went long hours. Prior to 1861 the average working day in Russian industry was 12 to 18 hours. Often workers began to work at 1 A.M. on Monday and 3 or 4 A.M. on other days, working steadily with two recesses for meals until 9 P.M. In 1889 out of a total of 5,027 enterprises investigated by government factory inspectors, the workers in 3,581 enterprises, or 71 per cent of the total, worked from 5 A.M. to 9 P.M., with 2.5 to 3 hours intermission for lunch and supper. In 1889 the average length of the working day in industry was 13 to 13.5 hours; [8] in 1904 the average was 10.7 hours; and in 1913 the average was 9.87.[9]

Among the worst sufferers of these conditions were women and children employed in various industries, notably the textile

[8] *Ibid.,* Chapter IV.
[9] *Social Economic Planning in the U.S.S.R.,* I.R.I., The Hague, 1931, p. 139.

factories, where women's wages were far below those of men engaged in the same occupations. In 1897 the textile plants of Vladimir paid women workers 10.56 rubles a month; in other occupations women averaged 9.88 rubles a month, while men in the same occupation earned 29 to 32 per cent more.[10] As industry expanded the number of women workers increased, so that by 1913 of the total number of workers in industry 62.7 per cent were men and 26.6 per cent women.

At the same time the disregard of laws regulating the use of child labor resulted in the widespread employment of children of 12, 13 and 14 for twelve hours a day. Factories were required by law to maintain schools for young workers, but this law was a dead letter. Government inspectors reported in 1898 that out of 19,292 factories only 446 maintained schools for young workers, or one school for every 43 factories. The total enrollment in these schools amounted only to about two per cent of the total number of juvenile workers.[11]

Working conditions in industry were extremely backward. An official report in 1900 stated that Russian mines had no proper ventilation, no regular water pumping, and no arrangements for drying the workers' clothes. Safety devices were rare. Many Ural mines had no man-hoists. The miners lived in barracks. This was the case also in factories outside the cities and sometimes even in the cities. Tugan-Baranovski's study of the Russian factory describes conditions as follows:

"The sanitary and hygienic conditions of the Russian factory are horrible. Only a few factories have dormitories for their workmen and what kind of dormitories! Men, women and children sleep side by side on wooden benches, in damp, sultry and crowded barracks, sometimes in cellars, often in rooms without windows. Most of the factories have no dormitories at all. After a workday of twelve, thirteen or fourteen hours, the workmen lie down to sleep in the workshop itself, on stands, bench-boards, or tables, putting some rags under their heads. This is often the case even in shops where dyes and

[10] Balabanov, op. cit., Chapter VI.
[11] Ibid., p. 152.

chemicals are used which injure the worker's health even when he is working." [12]

Workers living in barracks or in the factory itself were entirely dependent on their employers who could not only dismiss them from their jobs but could deprive them of a roof over their heads. They often received wages not in money but in kind at stores owned by the employer. Those workers who lived outside the barracks and had "homes" of their own were not much better off. In 1899 the municipal authorities of Moscow investigated 15,922 flats in the industrial sections of the city. There were 174,622 persons living in these flats, an average of 11 persons per flat. About four-fifths of these flats—12,650 of them—consisted of one room. Many tenants rented a "stall," a section of a room separated by a partition which did not reach the ceiling. Others rented corners, single beds and hallway space. "Stalls" rented for 5.93 rubles per month on an average; single beds for two or three rubles. An official investigator describing one of these flats reported:

"The air is hot and stale. The rooms are incredibly crowded. The flat is damp and exceedingly dirty. The rooms are totally dark. The ceiling is very low; a tall man can hardly stand upright. The odor is foul." Another investigator reported: "The sight of the flat is horrifying. The plaster has crumbled down, the walls are full of holes which are stuffed with rags. Everything is filthy. The stove is a wreck. The place swarms with cockroaches and bedbugs. It is cold. The toilet is in a dangerous place and the children are permitted to go there. All the flats in the house are in a similar condition." A third investigator reported: "The air is suffocating. The exhalations of the people, the evaporations of wet clothes and filthy linen fill the air. When it rains, the water covers the floor two inches deep." [13]

These rooms were occupied by persons earning their living at some legal occupation. They included the families of factory

12 Tugan-Baranovski, *op. cit.*, p. 407.
13 K. A. Pazhitnov, *The Working Class in Russia*, Vol. II, Leningrad, 1924-25, pp. 87-123.

workers, artisans and their apprentices, cabmen, laborers, petty merchants, store clerks, domestic servants, and railway workers.

The revolution of 1905 compelled the government to discuss plans for better housing of the workers, but these plans resulted in little change. An investigation in St. Petersburg in 1908 revealed that 70 per cent of the unmarried workers lived in corners, having no separate rooms of their own but sharing one room with a number of other workers. Only 28.5 per cent of workers with families occupied separate apartments, but even the great majority of these—75 per cent of them—took in boarders to help pay the rent. Most of the flats had little furniture except beds, and the rent often amounted to 50 per cent of the worker's earnings. Similar conditions prevailed in other industrial centers.

From the beginning of the factory system, the Russian peasant turned industrial worker struggled to ameliorate the onerous conditions imposed upon him. During the second half of the eighteenth century there were numerous strikes of bonded serfs, especially in the Ural iron works. These reached a climax in the revolt led by Pugatchev (1773-1774) to which the peasants and workers rallied and which was suppressed by the government. Strikes and uprisings compelled the autocracy to seek compromises. As early as 1722 Peter the Great had issued a decree reducing the working day to 10 hours in winter and 13 hours in summer. A decree issued by one of his successors in 1774 regulated certain labor conditions and attempted to establish a commission of three to supervise factories. In 1845 a decree was issued prohibiting nightwork for children under twelve. But all legislation which might have improved the conditions of the Russian workers was nullified by the fact that there was neither the desire nor the administrative machinery to enforce it.

On the other hand, laws designed to protect employers were strictly enforced. Such was the case, for instance, with the decree issued in 1845 ordering the imprisonment of strikers for terms ranging from three weeks to three months, and more stringent penalties for strike leaders. Despite such measures, the workers were driven by the conditions of their existence to strike. A strike involving thousands of workers broke out in the Nevsky cotton factory in St. Petersburg in 1870. The fact that the leaders of this strike were exiled to Siberia did not deter other workers from striking. There were a number of large strikes in the next two decades, some of them suppressed by the police and militia only after many workers had been killed.

It was under the pressure of such protests that the autocracy from time to time issued labor decrees of one kind or another. In 1878 it sought to prevent strikes and disturbances by issuing a decree permitting the police and the gendarmes to enter factories in order to "make search and arrests for the prevention of disturbances." [14]

The first important legal concession to the workers was the law of June 1, 1882 which prohibited the labor of children under twelve and nightwork by children under fifteen. The decree also provided for government factory inspection. For this purpose the empire was divided into nine districts in charge of twenty inspectors. The provision for factory inspection was the first gesture which the autocracy had made in the direction of enforcing such isolated labor laws as existed on the statute books. For two years this provision was inoperative owing to the strenuous opposition of the factory owners. But in 1884 an Institute of Factory Inspection was set in motion. It functioned until the beginning of the world war. By 1913 the Institute had a personnel of 273 of whom 193 were district inspectors.

The first factory inspectors were chiefly members of the liberal intelligentsia and included economists, lawyers and physicians. They made a number of valuable investigations of working class conditions, and gathered and published statistical data regarding these conditions. These activities aroused the opposition of the employers who compelled the government

[14] George M. Price, *Labor Protection in Soviet Russia*, International Publishers, New York, 1927, p. 26.

to change the personnel and the methods of factory inspection. Count Tolstoi, Minister of the Interior, urged that the "inspectorial force should be connected with the police department and should be in one department, the duty of which should be to guard internal order and peace in industry." The necessary changes were effected to connect the Factory Inspection with the police, and in April 1889 the inspectors were ordered to persuade workers that they had nothing to gain from strikes. They were further instructed to prevent any improvement in the conditions of workers while they were on strike even if the strike were justified. As a result of this change, factory inspectors virtually became gendarmes who took little or no trouble to enforce such labor legislation as existed on the statute books. Few cases were brought to court and most of these were dismissed; a few employers were asked to pay trivial fines. The failure of the Factory Inspection to enforce labor legislation was a logical consequence of its supervision in each province by the governor and a so-called labor commission which he appointed consisting of the public prosecutor, the chief of the gendarmerie, the district engineer, the chief factory inspector, and four representative employers.

The failure of the factory inspectors to enforce the law did not deter the government from issuing decrees from time to time regulating labor conditions in so far as they affected women and minors. Decrees issued in 1884-1885 prohibited nightwork by workers under seventeen and by women in the cotton-spinning industry. In 1886 this law was extended to include other textile factories and to forbid the employment of minors and children in certain hazardous occupations. Such laws were decreed following protests by the workers, especially manifested in a series of strikes in the provinces of Moscow and Vladimir. An official report to the Imperial State Council stated: "The disturbances among the factory workers in the Moscow and Vladimir provinces have shown many unpleasant sides of factory conditions and also that the causes of the disturbances were due to the abnormal relations between factory workers and owners. The irritation of the workers against the owners, with the difficulty which ignorant people have in finding legal ways of protecting their rights, led the workers to attempt to obtain their rights by means of strikes, sometimes accompanied by violence and destruction." [15]

With the events of Moscow and Vladimir fresh in mind, the government issued a set of regulations on June 3, 1886 governing the signing of labor contracts and their abrogation, prohibiting payment in kind, and fixing pay days. The decree required employers to give workers account books in which the labor contract had to be recorded, as well as the time of employment, the wages to be paid, and the fines to be deducted. Company stores were forbidden without special permits. Both the employer and the employee were required to give two weeks' notice before dismissal or resignation. For violation of the last point employers were subject to fines and employees to criminal prosecution. This law, like its predecessors, remained on paper. Neither the Factory Inspection nor the government made any effort to enforce it. The law was modified in 1890 to permit the employment of children in glass factories and for work on Sundays and holidays in all factories where adults were working.

The textile strike which swept St. Petersburg in 1896 was lost after three weeks but left certain definite impressions both on the government and the workers. While punishing workers for striking, the government granted them a concession in the law of June 2, 1897 which limited the working day to 11.5 hours. On August 12 it issued a new decree making strikes illegal. In the same year the government issued a labor code which remained in effect until the beginning of the world war. Although it made some provision for the regulation of labor conditions, it was, like all Czarist labor legislation, nullified by lack of enforcement. Under it the working day in St. Petersburg became longer; nightwork was reduced but not prohibited; the government had the sole right to interpret its provisions; the number of holidays was reduced; and no penalties were provided for the violation of the code.

[15] Kaploun, *Theory and Practice of Labor Protection*, 1927, p. 79.

Imperial law gave the workers no protection. Trade unions were forbidden; strikes were illegal; factory inspectors were police agents; courts were entirely on the side of the employers. The workers felt their position especially keenly in the severe economic crisis of 1899-1903. During this period production declined sharply in all branches of national economy and unemployment was widespread. The crisis was marked by strikes and political disorders. Following the disturbances of February 1901, several professors of the University of Moscow organized the Council of Workers in the Mechanical Trades in Moscow. Many workers joined this organization. It was the first legal trade union in Russia. The workers did not know for some time that its real organizer was Sergius Zubatov, chief of the Moscow Secret Police. Similar police unions were established in Minsk and other centers. Their aim was to provide a safety valve for the dissatisfaction of the workers with their wages and living conditions and their discontent with the autocracy. Ignorant of the part the police was playing in these unions, the masses of workers who joined them in good faith openly voiced their grievances. Indicative of the conditions of the Russian workers under the old régime is the report of the factory inspectors regarding Zubatov's union.

"The result of the establishment of the new organization," the inspectors informed the government, "was a series of strikes far greater in number than any experienced before, with a tremendous unprecedented influx of complaints." On June 3, 1901 the government attempted to allay the dissatisfaction of the workers by allowing them to have representatives of their own, called "monitors," to deal with the employers. The report of the Imperial Council of 1902-1903 makes it clear that the purpose of these "monitors" was to give the workers some mode of expression which would divert them from political activities. However, these "monitors" could be selected only in factories where employers consented to such representation. "Monitors" could be discharged at the employers' will; and workers' meetings and trade unions continued to be strictly forbidden.

The ineffectiveness of labor legislation under the old régime virtually nullified such attempts as were made to provide medical aid, social insurance, and workmen's compensation for employees. The law, for example, required employers to arrange adequate medical aid for their workers. Nevertheless, official reports for 1899 revealed that out of 19,292 factories under the supervision of the Factory Inspection, 15,804 had no arrangements whatever for medical aid; while the remaining 3,488 employed nurses and physicians but did not often give their employees the proper medical care. At a convention in 1903 of physicians from the mining districts, one physician reported: "I saw a mine hospital which looked more like a poorly furnished worker's house. . . . The most important equipment was lacking. . . . A semi-literate army of male nurses are in charge of such hospitals." [16]

Despite these obstacles, there was some progress in medical aid. One Russian economist reports that while in 1897 only 18 per cent of the enterprises provided medical aid for their workers, by 1907 the percentage had risen to 38. In 1897 these enterprises spent 4,000,000 rubles for medical aid; in 1907 such expenditures amounted to 9,000,000 rubles; so that the average per worker rose from 3.9 rubles in 1897 to 6.2 rubles in 1907. [17] Here again, however, improvements followed only after protests by the workers, in this case the revolution of 1905.

Regarding industrial accidents, the government did not keep accurate statistics until the end of the nineteenth century. The subsequent regular publication of such statistics revealed a steady increase in accidents from 4.2 per 100 workers in 1904 to 4.6 per 100 in 1912. The casualty list for mining in 1904 included 556 killed and 66,680 injured; in 1908 there were 1,061 killed and 71,085 injured. Among railway workers 555 were killed and 2,352 injured in 1904, and 848 killed and

[16] Balabanov, *op. cit.*, p. 169.
[17] Pazhitnov, *op. cit.*, Vol. III, p. 113.

5,533 injured in 1913. However, these official figures, drawn up for an exposition in Paris, greatly underestimated the actual state of affairs. Thus they reported for 1910 a total of 593 killed and 3,307 injured; while the medical statistics issued by the government for the same year showed 702 killed and 81,145 injured.[18]

Partial and ineffective compensation laws were introduced in 1901 and 1902. The payment of relief to workers who were ill or disabled was a comparatively rare phenomenon, which was confined to a limited number of industrial enterprises, and made entirely at the discretion of the factory management. A rare exception was the enterprise which had so-called sick funds. Such enterprises were chiefly confined to Poland and the Urals where there were mining companies which operated in connection with government factories. Relief payments usually amounted to 50 per cent of the wages and in some cases to about 33 per cent. Relief was usually paid for a maximum period of six weeks. Of the funds from which relief payments were made, two-thirds were furnished by the workers and one-third by the employers.[19]

Conditions improved somewhat under pressure of the revolutionary movement of 1905-1906, when a number of special agreements were made between workers and employers or groups of employers regarding sick benefits. In 1906 the employees and workers in the lumber industry concluded an agreement whereby the former agreed to pay 50 per cent of the wages in case of sickness for a period not exceeding four weeks. The sickness had to be certified by a physician usually in the employ of the company. Similarly, in the oil and some other industries partial compensation was paid for a period ranging from two weeks to six months. Usually the right to sick relief was granted only to workers employed from six months to two years in the enterprise.[20] Expectant mothers among working women received a lump sum of from three to ten rubles. In some instances the mother was paid for a period of four weeks during confinement; in others she received two weeks' vaca-

---

[18] *Ibid.*, p. 109.   [19] *Ibid.*, p. 115.   [20] *Ibid.*, p. 116.

tion before and three weeks after child-birth with half pay, and in rare instances full pay. A law passed in 1912 provided state insurance for employees in large-scale industry and transportation.

While legislation in favor of the workers was seldom enforced, the employers had a system of their own, with which the law did not interfere, by which they could reduce the workers' wages through a system of fines. The employer had complete discretion in the imposition of fines and the worker no redress. The employer could fine a worker three days' pay for one day's absence; or 3 to 5 rubles for each time he was caught smoking in the factory. The fine system was one of the most drastic ways by which the worker was deprived of legitimate earnings. In addition, the employers practiced regular wage reductions.

The status of the worker under the old régime was affected not only by his economic conditions but by the attitude of the autocracy toward labor activities. By outlawing strikes and trade unions, exiling strike leaders and shooting into crowds of workers demonstrating for higher wages or shorter hours, the government converted economic demands into political protests. The peasant revolts of 1902 in the provinces of Kherson, Bessarabia, Chernigov, Perm, Saratov, Volin, and Ekaterinoslav, were followed in the summer of 1903 by a wave of political strikes involving tens of thousands of workers in southwestern Russia, which developed spontaneously without preliminary organization. The events of 1904, precipitated to a large extent by Russia's military debacle in the war with Japan, led to the episode of January 9, 1905, when the priest Gapon, who with the connivance of the police had established in St. Petersburg a legal trade union similar to Zubatov's in Moscow, marched at the head of 300,000 workers to the Winter Palace to present a petition to the Czar voicing the workers' grievances and praying for remedies. This petition not only revealed the misery of the Russian workers but their faith that the Czar, their "little Father," would ameliorate their difficult conditions. It requested the establishment of general compulsory education, the eight-hour day, the right to organize and strike for improved conditions, freedom of speech and assemblage, and similar liberal measures.

The text of the petition was drafted by Gapon but amended by the workers themselves at mass meetings. On January 9, the 300,000 workers, old and young, men and women, marched to the Winter Palace carrying before them portraits of the Czar and the royal family and singing religious hymns. As the workers approached the palace Square, troops suddenly appeared and fired into the crowd killing more than 500 and wounding nearly 3,000. The events of "Bloody Sunday" agitated the entire country, since the peaceful aims of the demonstration were known to the government in advance. The idea of armed resistance and revolution spread among the workers.

With no legal redress open to them, the workers resorted to strikes which spread throughout the country. Official statistics covering only enterprises under the jurisdiction of the Factory Inspection revealed that in 1905 there were throughout Russia a total of 13,995 strikes involving 2,863,000 workers. These figures, the official reviewer declared, were "unparalleled not only in the strike history of Russia for the last ten years but in the history of the world. The strike movement of Russia was five times greater than that of America or Germany and ten times stronger than that of France." To the factory strikes must be added 333 miners' strikes involving 205,000 miners, making a total of 14,328 strikes during 1905 involving 3,068,000 workers.[21]

This strike movement was not organized by any central body. It was the outcome of the revolutionary activities of the workers, which became more intense during the period between October and December 1905. The strikes and revolutionary activities in the cities had their repercussions among the peasants who intensified their struggle for the land. The defeat

---

[21] D. Koltzov, "Labor in 1905-07," in the *Social Movement*, Vol. II, Part I, p. 253; Pazhitnov, *op. cit.*, p. 146.

sustained by Russia's armed forces at the hands of the Japanese encouraged these revolutionary activities. In this critical situation, the liberal landowners and the manufacturers' associations tended to ally themselves with the autocracy to safeguard the monarchy on condition that the political parties representing these social classes were to participate more closely in the administration of the state. But the workers' activities were directed toward the complete destruction of the monarchy and the fulfillment of the workers' economic demands. The industrialists were unwilling to consider the economic demands of the workers, such as an eight-hour day and the abolition of fines. The workers replied with a general strike in October 1905 which eventually compelled the government to issue the manifesto of October 17, establishing the Duma. Liberals rejoiced at what seemed to be the legal conversion of the government from an absolute to a constitutional monarchy. The new order, however, was ushered in by a series of pogroms and the massacre of many workers by the army and by the Black Hundreds, a private organization to defend the autocracy, subsidized by the government and including among its members the Czar himself.

During the October strike the St. Petersburg workers elected their own representative assembly called the Council of Workers' Deputies. The Russian word for council is *soviet,* and it was this body which was the seed of the Soviets organized in the revolution of 1917, twelve years later. By November 1905 the Council consisted of 562 delegates, representing 281 factories and 16 labor unions.[22] The Social-Democratic Party, one of whose leaders was Lenin, and the Social-Revolutionary Party, one of whose leaders was Kerensky, had special delegates in the Council. Similar councils were established in other cities which followed the lead of the St. Petersburg Council. The latter became the vanguard of all Russian labor, and

[22] *Soviet Russia in the Second Decade.* A Joint Survey by the Technical Staff of the First American Trade Union Delegation to the Soviet Union, edited by Stuart Chase, Robert W. Dunn and Rexford Guy Tugwell; John Day Co., New York, 1928, p. 144.

directed the general strike of October and November. It demanded abrogation of martial law and the convening of a Constituent Assembly. At first the autocracy, impressed by the widespread influence of the Council, negotiated with it; but as the general strike weakened the government instituted a reign of terror which opened with the arrest of the Council's members. At the same time a decree was issued outlawing strikes.

The manifesto of October 17 satisfied the demands of the industrialists for a parliament. Since the autocracy was ready to resist the demands of the workers for economic improvements, the industrialists were ready to come to terms with the autocracy. The government undertook to suppress the revolution by force of arms. Thousands of workers were massacred without trial or warning. At the same time, the autocracy dropped the mask of constitutionalism. The first Duma, which met on April 27, 1906, was dissolved on July 9. The government increased its ruthlessness as army and navy units revolted in Finland, Kronstadt and the Caucasus. Martial law was established throughout the country in the summer of 1906.

Before convening the second Duma, the government issued a decree on November 6, 1906 abolishing communal land-ownership, one of Russia's oldest and most fundamental institutions. Henceforth peasants could detach their plots from the communal area and dispose of it as their private property. The immediate political purpose of this decree was to destroy the idea prevalent in the Russian countryside that the land was the people's; but it had far-reaching economic consequences. The wealthier peasants bought out the poorer peasants, so that the kulak class became stronger, while the poor peasants were reduced to complete poverty. The second Duma met on February 20, 1907. Despite all the government efforts to secure a majority and the exclusion of radical citizens from voting, it could not muster more than 100 out of the 455 deputies, many of whom belonged to the various socialist parties. This Duma was dissolved on June 3, after 100 days of existence. The same day the government, which had been planning dissolution for some time, issued a new electoral law decreasing the representation of workers, peasants, and the poorer urban population, and increasing the representation of the landowners and wealthy industrialists. This law secured the government a third Duma completely obedient to the autocracy.

The end of the revolution and the resumption of absolutism left the workers once more without legal channels for improving their conditions. Until 1917 these conditions remained as oppressive as before 1905. The widespread strikes of 1903-1907 brought little improvement in the sanitary conditions of the factories and medical aid improved but slightly. A study made by the Factory Inspection in 1907, similar to the one made ten years earlier, revealed that most workers still lacked proper medical protection despite a modicum of improvement. Medical aid showed most progress among the railway workers; expenditures for this purpose in 1910 amounted to an average of 9.90 rubles per worker, which was considerably greater than among factory workers.[23]

Improvements in medical aid and payments for illness and disability were affected by the law of June 23, 1912, which legalized the idea of state insurance for workers, advocated for many decades. This law applied to all factories, mills, mines, railways, tramways, and river transportation having a permanent staff of not less than 20 workers and using mechanical power, and to all such enterprises which did not use mechanical power but had a staff of at least 30 workers. The law provided that free medical aid, hospital treatment, drugs and medicines be given to workers who were members of the sick fund—the bulk of whose money came from the workers themselves—on the following conditions: In case the sickness did not result in loss of ability to work, the worker received medical aid for a period not exceeding four months. When members died, the sick funds were required to pay their funeral expenses. In case of injury or disability the worker was to be paid from one-half to two-thirds of his wages if he had de-

23 Pazhitnov, *op. cit.*, pp. 111-114.

pendents; if he had no dependents he was to be paid from one-fourth to one-half of his wages. Payments were to begin from the fourth day of illness and were to continue not more than 26 weeks. In case of repeated illness, the worker could be paid relief for a maximum of 30 weeks in the year. Payment during confinement usually amounted to 50 per cent of the woman worker's wages, and covered a period of two weeks before and four weeks after childbirth.[24]

This law, like other labor legislation under the old régime, failed to reach full effectiveness for lack of the necessary administrative machinery. At best, it affected only one side of the worker's life. His social and political status and his economic position remained unaltered. Low wages and long hours continued. Labor legislation was rare and seldom enforced. Strikes and trade union membership were treated as criminal offenses. The limited social insurance law was promulgated not for the benefit of the workers but to reduce the employers' expenses for medical aid, the workers themselves being compelled to bear the cost of illness and disability. Workers could be dismissed without cause at the whim of the employer. A worker who left his job without notice was severely punished and could even be imprisoned. The system of fines continued; from three to six days' pay was often deducted from the worker's wages for one day's absence; fines, as high as one-third of the worker's wages, could be imposed for "disorderly conduct", such as smoking on the premises, making noise, or disobedience. There were no general rules for safety and sanitation. Nightwork was permitted for women in nearly all industries. After 1912 pregnant women were forbidden to work four weeks before childbirth, but for this period they received no pay unless they belonged to sick benefit societies where they paid dues. Children under twelve were forbidden to work, but there was little restriction on the labor of children over twelve. Minors between 12 and 15 were permitted to work eight hours a day, and in factories employing two shifts of workers, nine hours. Employers who violated

[24] *Ibid.*, pp. 117-118.

labor laws were seldom prosecuted, almost never arrested, and were at worst subject to trivial fines. The factory inspector and other administrators were engaged in safeguarding the interests of the employers, while workers were often arrested, fined, and imprisoned and strike leaders exiled to Siberia.[25]

As a result of the low living standards of the mass of the population, pre-war Russia had a higher death rate than any other European country. The death rate for the European part of Russia from 1911 to 1913 was 28.6 per thousand. The general infant mortality from 1877 to 1909 was lowered only 4 per cent, and in 1913 was 270 per thousand.[26]

The combination of absolute autocracy in government and feudalism-capitalism in economy prevented any fundamental change in the status of Russian labor until 1917. Russia's pre-war economic system rested on a variety of levels, ranging from the pastoral pursuits of nomad races to twentieth century factories with the latest equipment. The empire in parts resembled the undeveloped countries of Asia, and in other parts the advanced countries of western Europe. The bulk of the population was engaged in purely agricultural pursuits which still bore heavy traces of feudalism. Only 15 per cent of Russia's people lived in cities and less than 10 per cent of them were engaged in industry. The domestic and handicraft industries turned out 30 per cent of the empire's total production, and the number of persons engaged in them (4,000,-000) was about double the number in the factories; at the same time, the number of factories employing more than 1,000 hands was almost as great as in the United States. There were 450 such enterprises employing 47 per cent of all factory workers.

Russia on the eve of the world war has been described by one economist as "a country half industrialized, living on foreign capital and managerial personnel, lacking the discipline of modern industrial methods, a part of her proletariat skilled and politically developed while few in numbers, and the rest

[25] Price, *op. cit.*, pp. 32-34.
[26] *Economic Handbook of the Soviet Union,* issued by the American-Russian Chamber of Commerce, New York, 1931, p. 138.

of her workers half-peasant in character and of low efficiency; a country rich in materials, poor in equipment, technique and personnel." [27]

With such handicaps Russia was bound to feel the strain of the world war even more acutely than the more advanced countries of western Europe. The winter of 1916 found her national economy disorganized, with the process of disorganization steadily accelerated by inefficient administration, poor organizing ability, corruption in high places and the partial cessation of imports of manufactured goods and machinery. Under the increasing strain of war and inefficiency, the railway system broke down, aggravating the food crisis in the cities. Finances were disorganized and industry disrupted. Industrial production in 1916-17 was about 70 per cent below the pre-war level. By October 1917 about 30 per cent of the locomotives needed repair; the average daily car loadings were 16,000 as compared with 25,000 in 1915; the pig-iron output had declined rapidly.[28]

This economic collapse, combined with Russia's defeats in the war, unloosed political forces which led to the overthrow of the old régime. Nothing is so essential to an understanding of the status of the worker in present-day Russia as a proper evaluation of the fact that the destruction of the autocratic state and the establishment of the Soviet state was the work of the Russian proletariat. The storm which resulted in the Czar's abdication began with a strike of 25,000 workers in Petrograd on February 28, 1917, followed by a strike at the giant Putilov munitions plant. By March 9 there were 200,000 workers on strike in the capital and on the following day the strike became general. When the Provisional Government was formed it already faced the nucleus of a workers' state in the All-Russian Conference of Soviets, consisting of the elected representatives of the workers and peasants.

The Provisional Government did little to change the status of the workers. It created a Ministry of Labor and appointed various commissions to study the labor laws of the Czarist

[27] Dobb, *op. cit.*, p. 71.   [28] *Ibid.*, p. 83.

régime and to recommend changes. New laws were passed forbidding nightwork for women, the work of minors under seventeen, and the imposition of fines; but no fundamental changes were made, and even the few laws that were passed remained ineffective because many industries, working under pressure of the war, retained the old conditions. The Provisional Government sought to reorganize the factory inspection system, but rejected the demand of the trade unions that factory inspectors be elected. Instead it decreed that inspectors be chosen only from among university graduates or assistant inspectors with four years' experience. Preference was to be given to inspectors of the old régime, and all appointments were to be made on the basis of civil service examinations.

During Kerensky's tenure of office, factory committees of workers had been granted certain powers. In some cases these committees attempted to assume more power than they had been granted. As a result the industrialists demanded the restriction of the committees and the restoration of factory discipline. Disregarding the attitude of the Provisional Government, workers in some cases attempted to exercise control in order to prevent the plants from closing down and the workers from being dismissed. The third conference of trade unions, meeting in 1917 with 220 delegates representing 967 unions with a total membership of 1,475,000, sought to coordinate the attempts of workers' control in industry by urging that the factory committees be subordinated to the trade unions. The conference passed a number of resolutions for the protection of women workers and the unemployed and demanded an eight-hour day, the establishment of conciliation boards, industrial courts and labor secretariats, and improvements in the system of factory inspection.[29]

The employers resisted the eight-hour day and the activities of the factory committees by various forms of sabotage. There was a wholesale closing down of cotton mills in Moscow, Vladimir, and Ivanovo-Voznesensk. Flour mills were also closed, and the number of workers in the metal industry was

[29] *Ibid.*, p. 36; Price, *op. cit.*, p. 47.

greatly reduced. Production declined between 30 and 40 per cent. The summer of 1917 was marked by widespread economic conflicts and general strikes. In August the employers took the offensive at a conference of employers' organizations in Petrograd. The conference represented 2,000 enterprises employing 1,500,000 workers. It organized the "All-Russian League of Manufacturers' Associations" whose aim was to "unite the employers in defense of their interests and to resist the interference of factory committees with factory management." [30]

Under pressure from the manufacturers, the Provisional Government ordered the factory committees not to interfere with the management or in any way to obstruct the owners' conduct of the enterprises. This increased the opposition of the workers to the Provisional Government. The complete collapse of economic life; the nation-wide demand of the Russian people for "bread, land and peace"; and the inability of the Kerensky régime to meet these demands, raised the question of the formation of a workers' state. The Workers' Councils opened their struggle against the Provisional Government with a strike of 500,000 Petrograd workers who demanded "all power to the Soviets." The events of this period culminated in the revolution of November 7, 1917, and the establishment of the Soviet Government.

[30] Price, *op. cit.*, p. 47.

CHAPTER II

THE DEVELOPMENT OF SOVIET ECONOMY

THE formation of the Soviet state marked a transformation in the structure of Russian society. It was
not only a new type of government which had come
into the world, but new economic and social relationships.
The evolution of the new régime, and the status of the worker
in it, can be understood properly only if it is kept in mind
that the revolution which led to its establishment was a
workers' revolution and that the Soviet state is a workers'
state. This state is an integrated whole in which it is difficult
to draw sharp lines between political and social changes on
the one hand, and the changes in the system of production and
distribution on the other. Hence, to clarify the status of the
Soviet worker it is necessary to refer to the system as a whole,
to its aims and purposes, and more especially to the economic
structure which it has evolved.

The Bolsheviks, who came to power in November 1917,
are followers of Karl Marx, one of whose chief contributions
to political and social thought was the conception that capitalist society is based on a class system and consequently torn
by a struggle of antagonistic social classes. This antagonism
is due to the fact that a small minority of the population
exercises what amounts to a monopoly of economic property
and with it a monopoly of political power and social prestige.
The majority of the population, Marx said, is deprived of the
basic instruments of production, and is therefore compelled
to work for wages for the privileged class. Such a system creates a surplus which is taken over by the monopolist class,

and leaves the majority of the population no way of making a living except by hiring itself out for wages. As a result the "free" laborer is under strict economic compulsion much in the same way as a serf or slave, although this compulsion bears a different form.

The far-reaching consequences of the class struggle resulting from this economic system were described by Marx and his disciples in great detail, and they envisaged as its only solution the transference of power to the working class, the abolition of class monopoly and the eventual establishment of a classless society. When the workers assumed political power, according to Marx, they would proceed to abolish class monopoly by nationalizing the means of production and distribution. The precise forms which this process would take neither Marx nor anyone else could foresee, but it is this general idea which underlies the development of Soviet society.

The Soviet state, as its founders conceived it, was to be an instrument of political control in the hands of the workers to bring about the transition of Russia from capitalism to communism. This goal and the basic economic and political policies have remained constant while the methods of their application have undergone change with changing conditions and the progress of the Soviet system. Such adaptations are made because the task of social engineering undertaken by the Soviet state requires the careful calculation of economic, social and political forces. It was in this spirit that the Soviet Government at its inception approached the two leading problems of the nationalization of industry and workers' control in industry. The new economic system was to be predominantly socialist, but the exact forms which socialist industry was to take were to be left to experiment and experience.

It was a thoroughly ruined economy which the Soviet state undertook to reorganize on a socialist base. During the world war the fittest and most skilled workers of Russia had been mobilized for military tasks of one kind or another. In the first three years, some 18,000,000 Russians were engaged in the war, and about 2,500,000 were killed at the front. Pro-

duction declined severely. Practically the whole of industry
was engaged in the output of war materials. The bulk of consumers' goods was supplied to the armies, while the civil
population received an insignificant share. The villages were
compelled to supply the armies with grain. This economic
strain due to the war resulted, before the Soviet régime came
into existence, in interference with the management of
industry from two sources. On the one hand, the imperial government appointed Committees for War Industries which continued to function under the Provisional Government. These
committees had central and local administrative centers, but
their machinery of coördination was weak and their officials
corrupt. They accelerated rather than retarded economic disorganization; nevertheless they furnished a basis for the
future coördination of industry by the Soviet régime. A more
serious form of interference with the private control and
management of industry came from the workers themselves.
Immediately after the formation of the Provisional Government, workers in every large enterprise elected factory committees to represent their interests. Throughout 1917 up to
the establishment of the Soviet state, these factory committees
clashed with the private owners and managers of the enterprises and with the Provisional Government. The factory committee was the chief economic organization of the workers for
securing wage increases and improving labor conditions. In
the big cities, where the workers were politically conscious, the
factory committees sent delegates to the local soviets.

These committees were able, on the first waves of the
revolution during the spring and summer of 1917, to obtain
some wage increases and shorter hours. But the general economic crisis and the attitude of the owners and managers of
the enterprises led to further struggles by the workers. Under
the Provisional Government, the owners and managers retained the attitude toward the workers which characterized
the old régime. They continued to be hostile to the workers'
demands, and brutal treatment of employees was still common.
As a result, the conflict between workers and managers

became acute, and some owners abandoned their plants to the factory committees. In many cases the pressure of the economic crisis and the struggle with the workers was so sharp that owners and managers resorted to sabotage, closing their factories on the ground that they could no longer continue production. This led factory committees to demand the right to control and supervise production and to decide whether or not enterprises should be closed.

On assuming power, the Soviet Government's immediate aim in the economic field was to establish a planned system of production and distribution which would steadily improve the living conditions of the people. It did not, however, plan the immediate nationalization of industry. Lenin looked upon the socialist reorganization of industry as a long and gradual process. The early stages would involve the coördination and control of industry by the workers' state; but the state would at first not take over the actual ownership and management of industry. The workers were to be employed by the old owners and protected by the new state. These ideas were developed by Lenin in a letter to the Petrograd Bolshevik organization which he wrote in October 1917 from Finland. Pointing out the prevailing chaos in production, distribution and transportation, Lenin urged that complete economic catastrophe could be averted only through the centralization of control. Under the pressure of war, he said, capitalist governments had been compelled to adopt measures of control "almost all of which involve the organization of the population." The Czarist government had followed this policy in appointing the Committees for War Industries, but the committees were hampered by their inability to interfere with the interests of the propertied classes. Lenin therefore advocated that in the first week of its existence the revolutionary government should decree "the application of the essential measures of control," which included the nationalization of the banks, the abolition of commercial and business secrets, the obligation of all merchants and industrialists to organize into trusts, and the organization of the people into consumers' coöperatives controlled by the state. This was in line with the resolution of the conference of the Communist Party held in April 1917 which stated that it was not the Party's aim "to achieve socialist reorganization immediately."

Expropriation was to be applied as a penal measure against those who attempted to sabotage the gradual process of nationalization. Such violators of the law were to be imprisoned and their property confiscated. The proletarian state, with the aid of the workers and technicians in each enterprise, was to exercise centralized control over production and distribution. Nationalization was at first limited to the decrees of November 7 and 8, 1917, which transferred all property owned by the Czarist state, including the railways and the State Bank, to the new workers' state, and abolished private ownership in land. The big estates were turned over to local Land Committees and district soviets.[1]

The system of private property was broken up, however, by the pressure of events. The Soviet Government faced the fact that the problem of nationalization was closely bound up with the workers' control in industry. There was an increase in the number of factory owners who suspended production, closed their plants and fled, leaving the workers no alternative but to seize the plant and continue production in order to keep themselves alive. This process was anarchic and for some time the Soviet Government tried to halt it. Lenin discouraged some deputations of workers who came to ask permission to take over plants and factories; he emphasized their lack of training and experience in managing industry. But the danger of counter-revolution and starvation which followed the suspension of production, compelled local soviets and factory committees to take over plants.

To regulate this situation, the Soviet Government on No-

[1] Emile Burns, *Russia's Productive System*, E. P. Dutton & Co., New York, 1931, pp. 13-32. See also Directives of the Communist Party Concerning Economic Questions [Russian]; edited by M. Savelyev and A. Puskrebyshov; Gozsotzekgiz, Moscow-Leningrad, 1931, pp. xxix-xxx.

vember 15, 1917, issued the Decree on Workers' Control.[2] Under this decree the factory committees were granted the right to be consulted regarding the production program in their respective enterprises as well as regarding sale, purchase, and selling price. On these matters, the decision of the factory committee was binding, irrespective of the owner's wishes, although the owner might appeal to the higher economic instances. The factory committee was also given the right to investigate accounts and all the documents of the enterprise. It was charged with the duty of maintaining discipline among the workers in the plant. At the same time, a set of instructions appended to the decree left the owners the exclusive right of giving orders regarding the management of the enterprise. Factory committees were forbidden to interfere with such orders. They were also forbidden to "take possession of the enterprise or to direct it" except by sanction of the higher authorities. The factory committees were to be elected by the manual workers and the clerical and technical staff in each enterprise.

The decree, temporary in character, aimed to solve the problems raised by the system of dual power in industry based on private ownership under the control of the state. The conditions created by this system led many workers to overlook the government regulations and to continue to take over enterprises on their own initiative. The resulting chaos was one of the factors which induced the government to nationalize all large-scale industry. Another important factor was the outbreak of civil war. The Soviet Republic had to concentrate all its energies and resources for defense against counter-revolution and foreign invasion. From 1918 to 1920 some 5,000,000 Russian workers and peasants fought in defense of their new society against the armies of Germany and the Allies; and against Kolchak, Denikin, Wrangel, Yudenich and others, supported, financed and armed by the Allies. War necessitated the complete centralization and control of industry, and to

[2] K. A. Pazhitnov, *Collection of Decrees and Decisions on National Economy*, 1918, pp. 171 *ff.*

this end general nationalization was decreed. The merchant fleet and grain depots were nationalized in February 1918. In May the state took over the sugar industry, the first to be nationalized as a whole. Subsequently it took over the oil industry and declared the production of matches, coffee, spices and yarn to be state industries. Foreign trade was taken over as a state monopoly, and finally, on June 28, 1918, a decree was issued nationalizing all enterprises with a capital of at least 1,000,000 rubles. This decree made it compulsory for the old owner to remain in control and to continue production until the government could set up its own machinery. The owners were permitted to retain the profits until such machinery was functioning.

General nationalization was inaugurated so soon largely because civil war and intervention required greater centralization and control in industry. These factors also resulted in diminishing the power of the factory committees. The period of War Communism had begun. It was a period marked by rigid discipline in the enterprises, the managers of which were given considerable power. The activities of the factory committees were subordinated to the needs of the new state, fighting for its life on seventeen military fronts.

The machinery for coördinating and controlling industry had been outlined in a decree issued on December 1, 1917 which created the Supreme Economic Council. The Council's duties were to organize industry and finance; coördinate all existing economic organizations on the basis of a definite plan; and utilize workers' organizations, such as the factory committees and the trade unions, in the control of production. At first the Council consisted of representatives of all the People's Commissariats (i.e., government departments) and the All-Russian Council of Labor Control, composed of representatives from the trade unions and the factory committees. Later, when the trade unions absorbed the factory committees, and local economic councils began to function in the provinces, the composition of the Supreme Economic Council changed, but it continued to contain a number of members directly representing workers' organizations. Ten of its members were representatives of the All-Russian Central Executive Committee, the central political organization elected by the All-Russian Congress of Soviets; 31 members represented the Central Trade Union Council; there were 20 representatives of the provincial economic councils; two of the coöperatives; and five of the People's Commissariats directly concerned with industry, namely, the commissariats of food, transport, labor, agriculture and trade.[8]

The Supreme Economic Council created several departments, each under a "collegium" or board of seven or nine persons. The first tasks of the various departments of the Supreme Economic Council were to register existing enterprises, gather statistics, appoint managers, and organize production and distribution. They had to control directly those enterprises which had been taken over by factory committees. Prior to general nationalization the departments functioned as directing boards in those industries where most of the enterprises were still in private hands. One of their duties was to see that the various industries carried out government instructions. They also took steps to strengthen workers' control in industry. Factory committees were instructed to elect special control commissions to supervise the management of private industries. The development of the trade unions during this period made it possible to turn over to them the election of the control commissions.

In setting up the administrative machinery for coördinating industry, each department of the Supreme Economic Council appointed a sub-department to direct the actual course of production and distribution for the individual branches of industry or for groups of factories. The most definite form of these sub-departments was the Trust, which included a group of factories operated as a unit and acting more or less independently, but responsible to the board of the department. Thus the Metals Department of the Supreme Economic Council, organized on the basis of the War Industries Committee

[8] Burns, *op. cit.*, pp. 25 *ff.*

in that sphere, divided its work among several Trusts, such as the Machine Construction Trust, the Copper Trust, the Nail Trust, etc.

Workers' control in industry was maintained in various ways in the functions of the Supreme Economic Council. The boards of the departments were appointed by the Council in consultation with the central committee of the trade union involved in the given industry. Similarly, the department board appointed the board for each Trust in consultation with the trade union; and the board of the Trust, in turn, appointed the management board or individual manager of each enterprise on the recommendation of the provincial economic council and the provincial trade union organization. Finally, the provincial trade union based its recommendation on the nomination of the factory committee. In this way the administration of industry, from its highest to its lowest units, was controlled by the workers' economic organizations and, in the long run, by the workers in the enterprises. There were cases where the workers directly chose the managment board of the nationalized industry. For instance, the majority of the board of the Machine Construction Trust, embracing twelve of the leading machinery factories, was elected by a conference of delegates from the factories involved.

The second period of Soviet economic development—the period of War Communism (1918-1921)—was characterized by an emphasis on the change of ownership. For the time being it was of secondary importance whether the new administrative forms were satisfactory for purposes of production in peace-time. Socialism presupposes planned economy, and planning organs were already in existence under the Supreme Economic Council; but civil war, intervention and blockade made the planning of national economy as a whole impossible. Indeed, the Soviet authorities had their hands full coping with further declines in national economy, which had reached such low levels under the old régime as a result of the world war. The occupation of the Donetz Basin by the Germans, following the Brest-Litovsk treaty of March 3, 1918, resulted in a fuel crisis so acute that the railways were operated almost entirely on wood fuel. The fuel crisis was further aggravated by the cutting off of oil supplies from Baku and Grozny. By 1919 the amount of available fuel, exclusive of domestic consumption, fell 50 per cent below the 1917 figure and 60 per cent below the 1916 figure. A similar situation prevailed in regard to pig iron. The Donetz Basin, which supplied 60 per cent of Russia's total output of pig iron in 1913, was in the hands of the Germans; the Urals, which had supplied 19 per cent of the prewar output, were torn by civil war; Poland, which had supplied 10.5 per cent, was an independent republic. As a result, the supply of pig iron almost vanished. The railway system, already considerably disorganized during the world war, was further disrupted under pressure of the acute fuel crisis, the difficulty of repairs, and the requirements of the various military fronts. In 1918-19 about 60 per cent of Russia's railway mileage was controlled by the counter-revolutionary armies, and in 1920 about 80 per cent was within the sphere of military operations. The civil war resulted in the destruction for military purposes of 3,600 railway bridges; 1,122 miles of permanent way, 380 engine depots and railway shops, 3,600 ordinary bridges and 57,090 miles of telegraph and telephone lines.[4] Production as a whole declined to about 20 per cent of the prewar level. City dwellers moved to the villages, where they could obtain food. Consequently, the urban population declined by 30-40 per cent compared with prewar figures. Famine and extreme poverty resulted in epidemics of cholera and typhus which carried off many victims. The national wealth declined more than a third from the prewar level.

To meet these conditions created by civil war and foreign intervention, the government resorted to extraordinary measures. It was able to increase the workers' food rations slightly by requisitioning grain from the peasants. But on the whole the results of the military struggle and the consequent disorganization of industry caused the workers acute suffering. In addition, the requirements of war made it necessary to

[4] Dobb, *op. cit.*, p. 89.

modify the activities of the workers' organizations and to intensify centralized control. By the end of 1920 about 85 per
cent of the enterprises in the Soviet Republic were directed by
individual managers. The factory committee, which in the beginning had participated extensively in industrial control, now
acted as a unit of the local trade union; it confined itself
chiefly to welfare work, to inspection of labor conditions, and
to representing the interests of the workers. It acted as a kind
of advisory committee to the management, and could appeal
against the management's decision through the trade union to
the higher economic organs.

War Communism was in a sense a system of planned
economy, but it was the planned economy of a besieged people.
In order to halt profiteering, the Soviet Government established state monopolies of grain and internal trade. The
private market was entirely abolished. Strict account was kept
of raw materials and articles of consumption. These were
distributed according to military needs and the necessity of
strengthening a state based on the industrial workers in alliance with the peasants. This limited economic planning was
centered in the People's Commissariat of Food Supply, the
Utilization Commission and the planning department of the
Supreme Economic Council. While general long-range planning
was impossible at this time, the government succeeded during
this period in obtaining control of all the economic key positions and in building up the new state apparatus, including the
apparatus for economic administration. Furthermore, the hard-
ships and experiences of the civil war trained sections of the
working class for future leadership in economic activities. In
the last year of the civil war the first steps were taken to develop a general plan for the reconstruction of national economy.
On Lenin's initiative, specialists worked out the State Plan for
the Electrification of Russia (the so-called Goelro Plan). This
plan laid the foundations for the technical and economic reconstruction of the country on the basis of nationwide electrification. It was approved by the Congress of Soviets in

December 1920 and became the starting point for subsequent long-range economic planning.

The immediate task of the government at the conclusion of the civil war was to restore industry as soon as possible to its prewar level. This task required, first of all, a solution of the fuel crisis. Even the negligible pig iron reserves on hand could not be smelted for lack of fuel. The disorganization of the railway system, increased by the fuel shortage, made it difficult to transport reserves of raw cotton which were lying idle in Turkestan or grain from the agricultural sections. One-third of the woolen mills which shut down in August 1921 and 51 out of 64 cotton factories did so for lack of fuel. The fuel crisis was in turn aggravated by the food shortage which compelled many miners in the Donetz Basin to return to the villages in the summer of 1921. Lack of food also caused a reduction in the oil output at Grozny. Underfeeding, starvation and civil war exhausted the workers, and industry suffered the additional strain of an acute shortage of skilled workers.[5]

Because of the hostility prevailing against it at this time, in other countries, Russia could not salvage its economy by resorting to foreign capital, as did Austria in 1922 or Germany in 1924. The policy of granting concessions to foreigners inaugurated under the New Economic Policy brought only about 10,000,000 rubles a year. Ordinary business credits were not obtained until 1924. Russia was therefore compelled to reconstruct its ruined national economy entirely with its own resources and through its own efforts. It concentrated its energies on solving the fuel crisis so that the transportation system could begin to carry raw materials and food to the industrial centers. The arrival of food for industrial workers would stimulate the production of manufactured goods. These, in turn, could be used on the village market as exchange for grain and raw materials. It was necessary to concentrate food and fuel at the most strategic points; accordingly railway workers and coal miners were given precedence in obtaining supplies.

[5] *Ibid.*, pp. 185-6.

It became clear at the end of the civil war that the system of War Communism could not meet the needs of the period of reconstruction which now opened. The disorganized industries could not supply the demands of the peasants for manufactured goods. An immediate increase was necessary in industrial output. The Don Basin, the Baku oil fields, the Turkestan cotton belt and the Trans-Ural wheat belt were again in the hands of the Soviet state, but the economic machinery set up to control industry during the civil war was no longer adequate. Under the system of moneyless economy adopted during War Communism, consumers obtained goods and workers received wages entirely on a ration system. Hence distribution had to be planned by the central government organs whose cumbersome machinery soon became involved in red tape. Many of the central industrial organs were overwhelmed by the amount of business not connected with production which they were compelled to handle. A certain amount of decentralization was imperative. It was also necessary to reëstablish the alliance of the workers and peasants which had been broken by the system of grain requisitions developed for war purposes. The peasants expressed their hostility to the requisitions by reducing the sown area, as a result of which national economy declined still further. This particular problem might have been solved if the government were in a position to reorganize agriculture on the basis of mechanized large-scale production; but such a solution required a vast amount of agricultural machinery and equipment which industry, with its limited resources and extensive disorganization, could not possibly supply. Nor were the peasants ready for large-scale mechanized production; they had to learn from practical demonstrations the superiority of large-scale over individual production. The only possible method at this time of encouraging the peasants to raise the necessary crops and cattle was to restore the private market temporarily.

The new apparatus for managing industry was filled with workers learning the rudiments of administration. They were not equipped to handle all the small industrial and commercial enterprises scattered throughout the country. Yet these had to be managed properly in order to restore the exchange of commodities between city and country. Smaller enterprises which had been nationalized in 1920 were now a burden to the state. Hence, it was necessary to lease these smaller enterprises to private entrepreneurs while the State retained ownership. These entrepreneurs (Nepmen) were to keep the smaller industries running until such time as the State was ready to take over direct control again, and at the same time were to furnish the competition necessary to compel the State enterprises to "learn to trade."

These were some of the factors behind the inauguration of the New Economic Policy (NEP) in 1921. NEP had two important aspects: it fulfilled the need of the rehabilitation period for market relations in a modified form, and it marked a temporary retreat from socialist forms in order that the state might gather strength for another advance. NEP succeeded in restoring and developing market exchange between town and village by abolishing the state monopoly of domestic trade and substituting for grain requisitions a tax in kind. Centralized supply and extreme administrative centralism were abolished. Industrial departments and groups could purchase supplies in the open market. The coöperatives ceased to be agents of the state and began to operate independently. The trade unions were left to function chiefly with their own resources; at the same time they retained their participation in the administration of industry. They served as a link between the workers and their government, educating them, stimulating their initiative and protecting them against state organs which overstepped the bounds of their authority.

NEP, however, did not mean a change in the system of ownership which had been developed during War Communism. The nationalized enterprises continued to be the property of the state. The new policy merely allowed private capital to carry on production for the time being in minor industries and small factories. The number of enterprises which had been nationalized had reached by August 1920 a total of 37,000 employing 2,000,000 workers. By September 1922 some 4,000 enterprises with an average of 18 workers each and altogether involving about five per cent of Russia's total production were leased to private capital.[6]

The reorganization of industry under NEP at first brought hardship to the workers. The government, in its drive to build up basic industry with the limited resources at its command, reduced the supplies of food and materials to the light industries, leaving them to obtain what they needed in the open market. As a result many factories closed down or reduced the number of workers in their employ, with a consequent drop in such light industries as wool, hemp, linen, and paper. The number of railway workers was greatly reduced and the end of 1922 witnessed 500,000 unemployed workers registered throughout the country.[7]

The famine of 1921, comparable to the famine which marked 1891 as the "black year," greatly contributed to making the conditions of the workers worse and to retarding the restoration of the country's productive forces. The death rate in 1922 reached the figure of 60 per 1,000. Nevertheless, the end of 1921 and the beginning of 1922 marked a notable and definite upturn in Soviet economy. The fuel industry was drastically reorganized. The Fuel Distribution Board, the Mining Council and the separate boards for oil, wood and coal were merged into a single organization. This was followed by a reorganization of the mining industry in the Donetz Basin. Food supplies were concentrated in that area and were distributed according to the new system of collective payment on the basis of results. Production was concentrated in the best mines. In January 1921 there were 920 coal mines operating; by the end of the year all resources had been concentrated in 471 mines, and other mines were shut down. The State coal trust, Donugol, was reorganized, a total of 360 mines being left under its control of which 288 were put into immediate operation. By October 1922 Donugol was operating only 202 mines and by October 1923 its resources had been concen-

⁶ *Ibid.*, pp. 188-9.   ⁷ *Ibid.*, p. 190.

trated in 179 mines. Not only did the average number of workers per mine increase greatly under this system of concentration, but the output per miner as well as total production mounted rapidly.[8]

Improvement in the fuel situation made it possible to reorganize the transport system. New engines were imported from Germany and Sweden and labor was concentrated in the railway repair shops. The railways were grouped under regional administrations, and each line was placed under a superintendent with extensive powers. The transportation of fuel improved, enabling textile and other mills to increase production. In November and December 1922 the cotton industry reported for the first time adequate fuel supplies. Cotton spinning trebled the following year and production reached 19 per cent of the prewar figure. The improved harvest of 1922, which reached 60-70 per cent of the prewar level, increased the food supplies in the industrial centers. Real wages rose. By December 1922 the wages of Moscow workers had reached 76 per cent of the prewar average. The country had passed the most critical period of its economic disorganization, and for the first time since 1916 economic conditions showed definite improvement.

Even in this extremely difficult period important steps were taken toward the coördination of industry and the planning of national economy. To begin with, the working class had gained during the period of War Communism considerable experience in managing industry. In 1920 the Supreme Economic Council reported that out of the 1,143 members of the managing boards of factories under its control, 726 were workers, 398 were specialists, (i.e., old-régime experts drawn into the new productive system), and 19 were clerical workers. At the same time the central apparatus for controlling industry was reorganized and new apparatus established for the planning of national economy. Originally the Supreme Economic Council was designed to coördinate the whole of national economy, but the gigantic tasks with which it was confronted compelled

[8] *Ibid.*, p. 191.

it to confine its activities to State industry alone. During the civil war, the government organized the Council of Labor and Defense (STO) for the purpose of coördinating all activities which affected defense. STO developed a subsidiary planning organ, the State Planning Commission (Gosplan), the duty of which was to survey and formulate plans for national economy as a whole. In February 1921 Gosplan was instructed to draw up, on the basis of the electrification (Goelro) plan adopted in the previous year, a general plan for national economy, and to begin to draw up annual economic plans.

The decree of August 9, 1921, which extended NEP, provided that Gosplan was to plan for national economy as a whole. It was to coördinate the needs and resources of industry, agriculture, transportation, food, supplies, etc.; it was to determine which were the most essential industrial enterprises and was to concentrate raw materials, equipment and labor in these enterprises. Gosplan was further charged with the duty of inaugurating a single economic scheme embracing the entire Soviet Union, and to harmonize the schemes of all economic organs, including the government departments. It was to superintend the execution of the plan in general and in detail, while the Supreme Economic Council, which now became the commissariat for industry, was to carry out those portions of the general plan which referred to state action in the sphere of industry.

In 1922-23 Gosplan outlined the principles of an industrial plan 85-90 per cent of which was actually carried out. For this purpose Gosplan examined the plans of all the economic commissariats and the state budget; it drew up plans for export and import and for the restoration of the famine areas. At the same time it drew up the outlines of a five-year plan for the development of national economy for use at the Genoa conference. Gosplan thus became and has remained the central economic and technical advisory body of the government. The planning organs of the various departments are under its guidance and supervision in regard to such matters as organization and method; but Gosplan is not a commissariat, and its decisions, before becoming effective, must be approved by the state. This system ensures the separation of planning functions from administration and avoids dualism of control.

With the inauguration of NEP each enterprise received a wage fund based on its output relative to the minimum number of workers necessary for the production of a standard output under prevailing conditions. Differences were introduced into the wages paid to skilled and unskilled employees by the establishment of a wage-scale consisting of seventeen categories. Roughly speaking, the first nine categories included skilled and unskilled workers and apprentices; the remaining eight included foremen, technical and administrative employees. Employees in the ninth category were paid usually about three times as much as those in the first; while those in the seventeenth were paid one and two-thirds as much as those in the ninth. At the same time piece work and bonus systems were introduced.

Important steps were also taken in the reorganization of the administrative machinery of state industry. In the earlier stages of Soviet economy (1918), the Supreme Economic Council had formed sub-departments called Trusts which consisted of coördinated groups of enterprises. The Trust had independent powers of operating in the market with its own capital both as buyer and seller. The Supreme Economic Council outlined policies and exercised the power of general direction and control; the Trusts were given the power of administration and execution in their own spheres along the general lines mapped out by the Council. The administrative board of the Trust was appointed by the Supreme Economic Council in consultation with the trade union concerned in the given industry. The board, in turn, appointed the managers of the individual factories, who could not buy or sell, but were charged exclusively with the internal administration of the plant. Wages and working conditions were fixed by collective agreements with the trade unions. Production plans for the factories under the Trust's control were arranged by the board of the Trust, but the annual production program of the Trust was subject to the approval of the Supreme Economic Council. The government economic organs retained the power to fix minimum prices when necessary.

A decree issued on April 10, 1923 reformulated the functions, powers and obligations of the Trusts. The latter were not the owners of the enterprises they administered but trusteés of the state, which granted them revokable charters and furnished the capital through the budget of the Supreme Economic Council. The Trust could not dispose of its basic capital, consisting of factories, equipment, etc. Working capital, on the other hand, including materials, supplies and money, was at the Trust's disposal. The decree provided that the "State treasury is not responsible for liabilities incurred by the Trust," and, on the other hand, that "no State institution or enterprise has the right to take from the Trust its property or articles produced by the Trust except by agreement with the Trust." The higher economic organs were to lay down the general policies for the Trusts to follow, while the Trusts were to act as autonomous economic units. The Trust might obtain short term loans from banks on ordinary commercial lines. Long term loans required the approval of the Supreme Economic Council and the Commissariat for Finance. The profits of each Trust were to be allocated by the Supreme Economic Council. A certain percentage had to be set aside as a sinking fund for renewals. Twenty per cent of the remaining profits were then set aside as a general reserve until the reserve fund amounted to one-half the total capital. From the remaining profits, commissions and bonuses were to be paid to employees, a fund was to be established for improving labor conditions, and the remainder turned over to the state treasury.

In addition, the Trust was subject to all forms of taxation on the same basis as private firms. This provision aimed to increase production by stimulating competition between the Trusts and the industries leased to private persons, and also to ensure that the overhead costs of the state should be as far as possible equally distributed over production. The decree of April 10, 1923 further provided that Trusts could sell their products at prices freely arranged with purchasers, although in special cases the Supreme Economic Council could fix prices for articles of general consumption. In all buying and selling transactions, however, "the Trust must give preference, where terms and conditions are equal, to state departments and coöperative associations."

The Supreme Economic Council was to organize the Trust and select its board of management. The Council was authorized to examine and sanction or modify the production and financial programs of the Trust and to control their fulfillment. The Council was also authorized to remove members from the board of the Trust and to appoint new ones. But, the decree added, "the Supreme Economic Council does not interfere in the current administration and the management work of the Trust."

The functions of the board or manager of the Trust included the organization of production and management of all undertakings forming part of the Trust; the preparation of the annual accounts, balance sheets, estimates and production plans; the engagement and dismissal of employees and the purchase and sale of goods for cash or credit. The decree also established a special Control and Audit Commission for each Trust to consist of three members, two appointed by the Supreme Economic Council and the third by the trade union concerned in the industry. The duties of the Commission were to audit the Trust's accounts and plans, and to report to the Supreme Economic Council regarding them.

Trusts were organized both on the vertical and the horizontal principles, depending on conditions in the industry. At the time of the April 10 decree there were 458 Trusts employing 1,146,000 workers, an average of 1,800 workers per Trust. In addition to the large Trusts, there were many small Trusts consisting of petty amalgamations. Such was the case, for example, in the textile industry, in which there were 55 Trusts of which the twenty-seven smallest employed an average of 700 workers. Similarly, in the metal industry there were sixty-one Trusts of which six employed an average of 24,000 workers and the remaining fifty-six an average of only 1,300 workers.[9]

Following the publication of the decree on Trusts, it became clear that the coördination and planning of national economy required a unification of the smaller Trusts. The so-called "scissors crisis" of 1923 which affected Soviet economy as a whole, and with it the conditions of the workers, also revealed serious defects of the Trust system as it then operated. This crisis requires consideration. By 1923, as a result primarily of the restoration by NEP of the private market for farm products, the sown area throughout the Soviet Union had reached about 80 per cent of the 1916 level, and the gross yield of grain about 70 per cent. On the other hand, industrial production had risen only to about 35 per cent of the prewar level.[10] Accordingly, compared with prewar proportions, the agricultural products on the market were far more plentiful than industrial goods, and the rate of exchange in commodities between industrial centers and the villages was very unfavorable for the latter. This discrepancy between industrial and agricultural prices, known as the "scissors," was further stimulated by the general rise in prices due to the rapid depreciation of the ruble. The peasant replied by restricting his purchases, causing a partial stagnation in industry.

To meet this crisis the government undertook to lower industrial prices and raise agricultural prices. For this purpose, the State Bank rationed its credits to industry, forcing the Trusts to unload goods on the market at lower prices. A Commissariat for Internal Trade was created which fixed maximum selling prices. In order to regulate the commercial activities of the Trusts, Syndicates were established which were joint buying and selling organizations and at the same time functioned as coördinating bodies between the various Trusts. The Syndicates took over all the trading functions of the Trusts, including the purchase of raw materials. Like the Trusts, they were subject to the general supervision of the Supreme Economic Council, but they were directly responsible

[9] Burns, *op. cit.*, p. 45.   [10] Dobb, *op. cit.*, p. 224.

to the Trusts themselves. Steps were also taken to reduce costs in industry. The less productive plants were shut down and resources were concentrated on those which were essential. By 1924 industrial costs had been reduced an average of 20 per cent.[11] The currency was stabilized by abolishing the old ruble and replacing it by notes issued by the State Treasury and convertible into Chervontsi (State Bank notes). These factors contributed to the solution of the "scissors" crisis. By October 1924 the exchange ratio between industrial and agricultural products had declined from three to one to three to two.

The solution of the "scissors" crisis was followed by rapidly increasing production in both agriculture and industry. The gross production of industry during the fiscal year 1924-25 attained 67 per cent of the prewar level, and the gross agricultural output 85.4 per cent. By 1926 the prewar industrial level was almost achieved. Concentration in industry reduced the number of census enterprises from the prewar figure of 8,516 to 5,883 in 1926. The number of plants employing more than 1,000 workers rose to 8.4 per cent of the total number of enterprises, as compared with 5.5 per cent before the war; and the number of workers employed in such enterprises constituted 61 per cent of the total as compared with 47.2 per cent before the war.[12]

But this progress raised new problems. Industry was confronted with the necessity of replacing and renewing its equipment. The great depreciation of plant equipment suffered during the war and civil war could not be offset for a number of years, since the military struggle necessitated the suspension of repair work. Between 1921 and 1924 the expenditures for capital repairs were small partly because the Trusts used their amortization funds to supplement their insufficient working capital and covered only about one-half the current depreciation.[13]

The question was: would the Soviet Union have to obtain the necessary funds from abroad; or could it proceed with its

[11] *Ibid.*, p. 252.   [12] *Ibid.*, p. 292.   [13] *Ibid.*, p. 295.

industrial and social program on the basis of its own resources? In the debates within the Communist Party during this period the question was formulated: could socialism be built in one country? There were groups within the Party which sought to solve this problem by advocating extensive concessions to foreign capitalists in order to raise the funds necessary for the development of Russian industry. Others could not see the possibility of any real progress for Soviet Russia towards socialism until there was a socialist revolution in western Europe. A corollary of the last viewpoint was the proposal that Russian industry should raise the necessary capital by obtaining it from the peasants, however greatly or even excessively such a policy might increase the burdens of the peasantry. The Party ruled out all these suggestions. It decided to develop socialist economy with the internal resources of the country; and this not only without breaking the alliance of the workers and the poor and middle peasants, but even further cementing this alliance.

This was a crucial decision and requires some explanation, since it involves the question of the accumulation of capital for the expansion of national economy. In this connection, Soviet 'economists emphasize that one basic difference between the capitalist and socialist forms of economy lies in the redistribution of capital accumulation. "Surplus value," in the sense in which it exists in capitalist economy, does not exist in Soviet economy, since the latter eliminates private profit. Accordingly, while the individual worker foregoes part of the product of his labor so that basic capital may be accumulated, all such capital is spent in ways which accrue to the benefit of the working class as a whole, and none of it goes in the form of profits to unproductive groups of the population.

On the problem of accumulating basic capital the thirteenth congress of the Communist Party, meeting in April 1923, adopted a resolution which stated that "only that industry can be victorious which gives more than it absorbs. Industry which exists at the expense of the budget, i.e. at the expense of agriculture, cannot create a stable and lasting support for the proletarian dictatorship. The problem of creating in state industry a surplus value is a problem of the fate of the Soviet power, i.e. the fate of the proletariat. . . . An extensive reproduction of state industry is unthinkable without an accumulation of surplus value by the state. . . . Through state industry lies the road to a socialist society." [14] The resolution then went on to say that "the state trusts and combines have as their basic problem the securing of surplus value for the purpose of state accumulation, which alone can guarantee the raising of the material level of the country and a socialist reconstruction of the whole of national economy." [15] The fifteenth party congress, which met in the fall of 1926, declared that the "tempo of the development of basic capital will depend upon (a) the extent of accumulation of socialized industry; (b) the utilization through the government budget of the profits of other branches of national economy; and (c) the utilization of the savings of the population by drawing it into coöperatives, savings accounts, internal loans, credit systems, etc." [16]

While this approach to capital accumulation definitely ruled out suggestions that the peasant be made the chief source of such accumulation, it raised the problem of the relation between basic capital and wages. One Soviet economist [17] has analyzed the question of the accumulation of capital under present Soviet conditions in the following manner:

"It would be thoughtless to suppose that under socialism the worker receives as his individual allotment the full product of his labor for his personal consumption. In his Criticism of the Gotha Program, Marx clearly pointed out the impossibility of the worker receiving the full product. The total product of the labor of all workers constitutes the entire social product of a given society. From this it is necessary to deduct, first, the part needed for restoring the depreciated means of production; an

---

[14] *Directives of the Communist Party Concerning Economic Problems* (Russian), Sotzekgiz, Moscow-Leningrad, 1931, p. 111.
[15] *Ibid.*, p. 115.
[16] *Ibid.*, pp. 337 ff.
[17] See N. Voznesensky, "The Problem of the Economics of Socialism," *Bolshevik*, Nos. 1-2, January 30, 1932, p. 26.

additional part for expanding production; and a reserve fund
as an insurance against accidents and unforeseen natural calamities. The remainder is that part of the total social product
which is to be used for consumption. But before this can be
distributed to individuals, the following must be set aside: the
general expenses for that administration not directly connected
with production; a share for the social satisfaction of needs
such as schools, hospitals, etc.; a fund for the support of those
who are unable to work, etc. Only after this is done do we
finally have that part of the consumption fund which is divided among individual producers. This is the part which is
distributed as the individual allotment. The other parts constitute the social accumulation, reserve, and socialized consumption funds. The problem of what part of the work day should
go for consumption, and what part should be put into the fund
of socialist accumulation is concretely a historical problem,
and will be solved in each case by a planned directive of the
proletarian state.

"There exists a relative contradiction between accumulation
and consumption [in Soviet economy]. But this is only a contradiction between the present and the future. It does not
contain antagonistic class contradictions. Over a long period
of time the problems of accumulation and consumption under
socialist production coincide. It should also be remembered
that since the U.S.S.R. finds itself in capitalist surroundings
and has to struggle for its economic independence, it finds it
necessary to secure an increased and intensive socialist accumulation. During the Second Five-Year Plan, on the basis of the
level attained by the industrialization of the country and its
increased economic independence, it will become possible to
have a further considerable increase in consumption. Throughout the transition stage of economy, especially under socialist
economy, the absolute funds for consumption are constantly
increasing, thus bringing about an improved standard of living
for the workers. This is directly connected with the elimination
of exploitation and the consequent abolition of surplus value."

In connection with the problem of capital accumulation, it

must be remembered that Soviet economy is able to utilize for productive purposes capital funds formerly consumed by the nonproductive classes of the old régime. Under Czarism, very large sums of money were wasted by the nobility, the capitalists, the Czar and his court, and the vast bureaucratic machine. Furthermore, from 1894 to 1913, Russia paid 7.2 billion rubles in interest on foreign loans. During these twenty years, loans from abroad totaled less than four billion rubles. Even if other inflows of capital are added to this sum, it appears that during these twenty years Russia paid to foreign capital two billion rubles more than it received.[18] The Soviet régime is free of such expenditures. The surplus value which formerly went to unproductive groups of the population and was expended by them largely for wasteful luxuries, and the large sums which flowed out to foreign capital, are now available for investment in productive processes within the country. This is one of the factors which has enabled Soviet economy at the same time to accumulate capital and to increase the wages and consumption of the workers.

Following the rejection of proposals that the basic capital necessary for the expansion of industry be squeezed from the peasant, it became necessary to examine the relations between workers' wages and industrial productivity in order to ascertain whether or not there was an uneconomic gap between the two. Because the profits of Soviet industry are not for private owners but for the welfare of the mass of productive citizens, the tendency is to increase wages whenever possible. As a result, it was found that between 1922 and 1924 wages had risen 100 per cent while the output per worker had increased only 45 per cent. Thereafter efforts were concentrated on reducing the percentage of labor costs in the total cost of production by increasing labor productivity and this campaign attained a considerable measure of success. The decline in production costs resulted in profits which the Trusts partly invested in their own enterprises and partly

[18] Stenographic Report of the XV Conference of the Communist Party [Russian], second edition; Gosizdat, Moscow-Leningrad, 1928, p. 1012.

turned over to the government. These additional profits were invested by the government in basic industries like electricity, transportation and the metal trades which also received government grants from the proceeds of taxation. Such measures enabled Soviet economy to spend some two billion rubles during 1925-26 for capital investments. At the same time real wages showed a steady rise.

Another problem confronting national economy arose from the relations between town and village and the urgent necessity of modernizing agriculture. There were economists who proposed that these problems be solved through the "agrarianization" of Russia. They urged that efforts be concentrated on developing agriculture in advance of industry. This was to be done by encouraging the kulaks who leased large pieces of land and exploited hired labor. By exporting large amounts of agricultural produce, these economists argued, Russia could obtain equipment abroad for the development of agriculture by the individual peasant. With the profits obtained from the surplus products of agriculture, Russia could then step by step build up its industry. The government rejected this plan as rendering the country too dependent on foreign powers—making it in effect a "colony"—and endangering the development of socialist economy. It held also that the system of primitive small-scale cultivation would be unable to solve the problem of supplying an adequate quantity of foodstuffs and raw materials even to satisfy domestic requirements, let alone producing a surplus for export, and therefore decided that socialist industry rather than kulak agriculture was to take the lead in developing national economy.

At the same time, socialist industry itself could have a continued and unrestricted growth only on the basis of the reorganization of agriculture in the form of large state and collective machine-operated farms. National economy as a whole, as well as socialist industry, required for its development a much greater supply of foodstuffs and raw materials from agriculture than the atomic, inefficient and unproductive system of petty farming could possibly produce. Before the revolution there were in the territory now included in the Soviet Union about 16,000,000 peasant farms and a number of large estates. The breaking up of the large estates and the parceling out process which took place in the years following the revolution soon increased the number of individual peasant farms to 25,000,000. Their productivity was extremely low; hence the reorganization of agriculture was imperative. The peasants were at first hostile to reorganization; they were illiterate and ignorant of modern agricultural methods. Even the kulaks knew very little about the uses of agricultural machinery. The Bolsheviks, who led the proletarian revolution and directed the seizure of land by the peasants, with the consequent division of land, have always been ardent advocates of large-scale agricultural production. As far back as March 1918, the Soviet government enacted the Land Law, which provided for the creation of state farms, using some of the larger nationalized estates for that purpose. The law also encouraged the joint cultivation of land by villages and groups of peasants. At first the state farms were simply large estates of the former landowners held by the government as the basis for future development in large-scale agriculture. They were administered through the Commissariat of Agriculture, and conducted as model farms to demonstrate to the peasants the superiority of large-scale over individual production. In 1922, when industrial enterprises were organized into Trusts, over 1,100 of the largest and most efficient state farms were combined into the State Agricultural Trust. In this the smaller state farms were not included; they were left to the direct supervision of the provincial offices of the Commissariat of Agriculture. The government never entertained the idea of forcibly converting peasant agriculture into state agriculture. Such a procedure is economically unfeasible and politically inadvisable, since it would rupture the alliance of the workers and peasants (the so-called *smytchka*). The policy pursued was that of removing obstacles in the way of improving peasant farming and at the same time to strengthen agricultural coöperation among the peasants. For this purpose it was necessary to assist the "middle peasant," to give him the means of developing his land, to break his connections with the kulak, and to draw him into a closer alliance with the poor peasants and the industrial workers.

The 25,000,000 peasant farms remained outside the organizations embracing the state farms, but many of them developed various kinds of coöperatives. In the early stages of Soviet economy, coöperative peasant organizations were formed chiefly for the purpose of selling some particular product such as eggs, butter or flax. Later peasant coöperatives were organized for the purpose of obtaining agricultural machinery to be used in common. There were also a few *communes* in which means of production and property, including houses and livestock, were held in common, and the income divided equally among the members. These existed chiefly in places where groups of settlers from industrial areas opened up new land. Another type of producers' peasant coöperative was the simple collective, a joint producing coöperative organization, formed in peasant villages, in which there was no general pooling of property and coöperation took the form of the joint working of the land and other collective work. The third type, the *artel*, was intermediate between the *commune* and the simple collective. It involved the pooling of certain means of production; but there was no common ownership of all property and no equal distribution as in the case of the *commune*. It was, instead, based on the share system, the individuals and households concerned receiving from the aggregate production in proportion to the labor they contributed, some allowance being made for the equipment and livestock contributed by the members to the common stock. This is the basic form of collective farm existing to-day. In all these forms of collective agriculture, management is in the hands of a committee elected by the individuals or households involved. Beginning with 1924 special attention was paid to developing coöperative agriculture. In that year the number of households belonging to producers' coöperatives rose to about two million, an increase of 30 per cent over the previous year; while the financial resources of such coöperatives doubled. However, the mass collectivization movement began to develop only several years later.

The year 1926 marked the end of the period of economic rehabilitation. Soviet Russia had overcome the ruins of war and civil war. In that year industrial production, 40 per cent higher than in 1925, had almost reached the prewar level. The output of the census industries had increased from 1,772,000,000 rubles in 1921 to 9,120,000,000 rubles in 1926, in terms of prices prevailing in the latter year. In agriculture the sown area in 1927 totaled 279,000,000 acres as compared with 281,500,000 acres in 1916. The 1916 figure for large-horned cattle had already been surpassed in 1925. Capital investment in industry had risen from a few tens of millions of rubles in 1921-22, not enough even to cover amortization, to 811 million rubles in 1925-26.[19]

Not only was there an expansion of national economy, but new relations had been established in production. In 1926-27 state industry accounted for 91.3 per cent of the output of census industries; coöperative industry 6 per cent; and private industry only a little over 2 per cent. The railways were completely in the hands of the government, which also maintained the monopoly of banking, credits and foreign trade. By 1926-27 retail trade was largely socialized, 80 per cent of it being carried on by state and coöperative trading organizations. In agriculture the position of the kulak was being weakened by the growing power of the state, while the "middle peasant," who does not exploit hired labor, cultivated 72 per cent of the sown area, owned 81 per cent of the working horses and produced 71 per cent of the agricultural produce sold on the market.

The attainment of the prewar level marked an enormous advance from the low state into which Soviet industry and agriculture had fallen by 1921; but this advance did not involve a high degree of well-being for the country. Industry was as yet unable to meet the rapidly growing demands of the awakened population. Important branches of industry—such

[19] *Social Economic Planning, op. cit.,* p. 71.

as chemical, machine-building and automotive enterprises—
were virtually non-existent. The agricultural system was restoring its production but it was still predominantly small-
scale and primitive; it was therefore unable to keep pace with
the rapidly developing industries. It could not supply them
with a sufficient quantity of raw materials or the cities with an
adequate supply of foodstuffs. Nevertheless, the restoration of
the prewar level meant that the Soviet Union was ready for the
next economic advance. National economy was to go through a
process of intensive industrialization in which socialist forms
of production were to play the leading rôle. Agriculture was to
be mechanized and socialized on a large scale. These aims required an immediate concentration on the rapid development
of the basic industries.

CHAPTER III

PLANNED ECONOMY

IN analyzing the prerequisites of economic planning in the U.S.S.R., Soviet spokesmen point out that the Soviet system is based on the premise that land and all the means of production belong to society as a whole. Private profit is eliminated and production is carried on primarily for the purpose of supplying the needs of society and of its individual members. A fundamental aim of the Soviet system, they say, is to abolish those social-economic factors which give rise to class differences and to create a classless society based on socialist forms of economy. Such far-reaching social results cannot be left to the blind operations of chance. Consequently, planning is an integral part of the Socialist system as such, and the idea of a comprehensive social-economic plan for coördinating the processes of national economy was included in the Soviet program from the very inception of the present régime.

The formulation of such a plan, however, was not possible at once. The economic disorganization inherited from the old régime made comprehensive long-range planning impossible in the first year of the Soviet Republic's existence. During the civil war period conditions were hardly more favorable. The territory of the new state was constantly changing, and for some time important economic regions—such as the Donetz coal and metal areas, the metal districts of the Urals, the Baku oil fields, and the cotton areas of Central Asia—were completely cut off from the center. As a result of the world war and the civil war, industrial production in 1920 was only 18 per cent of the prewar level and grain production only about 50 per cent.[1]

[1] *Social Economic Planning in the U.S.S.R., op. cit.*, p. 69.

These conditions made it extremely difficult to develop national economy in accordance with a comprehensive plan. At best it was possible only to keep industry going. During the civil war period Soviet economy was planned to some extent, but the planning was narrow and limited in scope. It was of necessity concerned chiefly with keeping strict account of the available stocks of articles of consumption and with attempts to distribute them most effectively. The first industrial plan was drawn up by the Supreme Economic Council in 1919 for the metal industry in the Ural region, but the absence of complete control at that time made it difficult to calculate production and distribution in advance with the desirable amount of exactness.

Despite the difficulties of this period, however, an important advance in economic planning was made in 1920 with the drafting of the Goelro (State Electrification) plan for the reconstruction of national economy on the basis of the electrification of the country over a period of fifteen years. Under existing circumstances the Goelro plan was bound to be merely a skeleton plan indicating a general direction. The Soviet planning bodies knew the needs of industry and the extent of the available natural resources, but they could not be certain of other important factors. They could have no assurance on such matters as the distribution of labor power, the output of raw materials in the necessary quantities, or the production of tools, machinery and other equipment. The Goelro plan has already been carried out in regard to the amount of current scheduled for production; but it is significant that the original plan did not provide for the construction of the great Dnieprostroy hydro-electric plant—the largest in the world. It was the product of a period when some of the premises for effective planning existed, but others of fundamental importance had still to be developed. Nevertheless, the Goelro plan already contained in embryo the two types of plan characteristic of Soviet economy: the long-range plan and the annual operating plan, known as the Control Figures.[2]

[2] See Chapter II.

The Goelro plan was a partial plan, Soviet spokesmen explain, because the state at that time had only partial control over the decisive elements of national economy. Only those premises for planning were present which came with the Soviet system itself. The state possessed the economic key positions. It had nationalized the land, the natural resources, large-scale industry, transportation and the banks. It exercised a monopoly of foreign trade which enabled it to regulate exports and imports in full accord with the general program for the development of national economy. Political power was in the hands of the working class represented by the apparatus of the Soviet state which exercises the "dictatorship of the proletariat." These factors constituted the basic premises for planning.

But effective nation-wide planning required additional premises. The nationalized economic key positions had to be brought completely under the guidance and direction of the state; they had to be controlled fully before their activities could be coördinated and planned in advance. For this purpose it was necessary to extend the socialized sectors of industry and agriculture. The development of elements hostile to the Soviet system of economy had to be curtailed and the development of socialist elements had to be stimulated. It was necessary to organize all branches of national economy into a unified system combining raw materials, labor, production, and distribution so that the country's resources could be exploited in the most effective manner in the interests of society and of its individual members. To enable this whole system to work it was necessary to have a stable currency as a medium of exchange. Furthermore, centralized control had to be accompanied by decentralized management so that the various republics, regions, districts, and separate enterprises could participate in the responsibilities involved in nation-wide planning. The Supreme Economic Council had to develop a system of coördinating and directing bodies for each sphere of industry, and these bodies had to be reën-

forced by a network of organizations consisting of those who
participate directly in the industrial process.

These premises for effective nation-wide planning were developed in the years following the civil war. The creation of
Gosplan in 1921 as the central planning authority was in
itself an indication of the enlarged possibilities of planning.
During the first year of its existence Gosplan was able to
verify some partial annual plans which had already been
drawn up by various economic organs, such as the fuel plan
and the outline of a plan for a sowing campaign. It also drew
up an economic plan for 1921-22, which, under the prevailing
circumstances, was chiefly a food plan. By 1922-23 it was
already possible to outline an industrial plan which was
actually carried out 85 to 90 per cent. The plans of the various
economic commissariats and the various budgets were examined; an export and import plan, and plans for the restoration of the famine areas were drawn up, and the outline of a
five-year plan for the development of national economy was
drafted.[3]

Subsequently, the rapid restoration of national economy
made it possible to take another step forward in social-
economic planning. In 1925 all the separate annual economic
plans were brought into a single system known as the Control
Figures for a given year. The first control figures were for the
fiscal year 1925-26. These figures assign annually in advance
to every important branch of socialized economy definite tasks
for its development during the coming year. They calculate the
probable crops of the various agricultural products expected
from the next harvest; they assign specific tasks to state and
coöperative organizations with regard to the collection of grains
and raw materials; they outline plans for extending the areas
under cultivation and for increasing their productivity by supplying agriculture with machinery, chemical fertilizers, etc.;
they determine the policy regarding the level of agricultural
and industrial prices for state and coöperative organizations;
they fix the amount of exports and imports and the minimum

[3] *Social Economic Planning in the U.S.S.R.*, *op. cit.*, pp. 40-41.

balance of foreign trade and international settlements; they estimate the income and expenditures of the state budget, the possible limit of currency issue and the income from state industry as a whole, from transportation and from the banks; they establish the policy regarding the course and rates of foreign exchange; they fix the amounts of capital to be invested in industry, transportation, agriculture, housing, public construction, etc. In this way the Control Figures outline a general economic plan for Soviet economy for a year in advance; they comprise, in rough approximation, the provisional balance sheet of the reproduction of wealth on an increasing scale in the national economy of the country. In the past five years they have developed from estimates and directions along separate lines into an integrated system of directives covering production and distribution for the whole of national economy.[4]

The development of the control figures as a method of prognosis, combined with the expansion of national economy as a whole, and particularly the increasing predominance of the socialized sector of economy, finally made social-economic planning possible on a large scale. By 1926 the state controlled national enconomy to a sufficient extent to warrant the drafting of the Five-Year Plan. In the autumn of that year, Gosplan, as the central planning body, drew up the first draft of the Plan. It was subsequently revised by the introduction of two variants: the "minimum" variant and the "optimum" variant. The latter, originally based on the possibility of exceptionally favorable circumstances for the realization of the Plan, including additional resources from abroad, was the one accepted by the Congress of Soviets as the official plan. At first the Plan was drawn up to cover the period from 1926-27 to 1931-32. In its final form, published in 1929, it covered the period from 1928-29 to 1932-33. Later the fiscal year was made to coincide with the calendar year, and the Plan, as it now stands, is to be completed in its main essentials by the

[4] G. T. Grinko, *The Five-Year Plan of the Soviet Union*, International Publishers, New York, 1930, pp. 22-23.

end of 1932, or in four and a quarter years from the time it
went into operation.

It took about three years to prepare the Five-Year Plan,
which was the work, not of a few individuals, but of a nation
interested in directing and expanding its economy. The Communist Party, the highest political authority of the country,
laid down the basic economic and political principles to be
followed in drafting the Plan, while economic bodies, scientific institutions and organizations of workers and peasants
contributed suggestions which were adopted.[5]

In general it is characteristic of Soviet economic plans that
they are not the product of Gosplan exclusively but are developed through the combined efforts of all the economic organizations. The industries, the coöperatives, the banks, the
trade unions, the economic commissariats, the local soviets,
the scientific institutions, indeed every separate factory and
every state and collective farm in the country, participate
directly in the drafting of the nation-wide social-economic
plan. Gosplan directs and coördinates all planning activities
and works out the final plan; at the same time, the system
of counter-planning, extensively developed in the Soviet enterprises, enables the workers themselves to check and elaborate the control figures of their enterprises and to modify
general plans on the basis of their immediate knowledge and
experience. In this sense, Soviet economic plans, according to
Soviet authorities, are the product of the creative efforts of
the entire people.

This system renders Soviet planning at once integrated
and flexible. It is a dynamic process rather than a rigid system. The extent to which the annual plan is carried out modi-
fies the remainder of the long-range plan of which it is a part.
The formulation of the long-range plan, in turn, is conditioned
by the attainments of the preceding long-range plan and
towards its conclusion becomes the starting point for the
next long-range plan. The successes of the annual Control
Figures thus opened the way for the Five-Year Plan, which

[5] *Ibid.*, p. 29.

was the direct result of the expansion of national economy
and the need to expand it still further. A long-range plan
became necessary because vast projects for power plants, factories, state and collective farms required several years for
their execution and could not be covered by the Control Figures drawn up for one year. The Five-Year Plan signified that
Soviet economy has reached a stage where long-range planning
was both necessary and possible. The Plan, however, did not
set out to achieve all the objectives of the Soviet system in
the space of five years; it was merely, according to Soviet
authorities, the next step in a general and continuous system
of planning and was to be followed by other plans.[6] In addition, the system of annual Control Figures is retained.

Soviet planning is based on strict business accounting and
careful calculation; but its socialist nature precludes certain
features characteristic of various suggested plans in capitalist
economy. Soviet planning cannot be compared with the methods of regulation and control sometimes adopted by the governments of capitalist countries, particularly in war-time. An
analysis of the structure and operation of the two systems
shows that in general it is misleading to compare Soviet economic phenomena with capitalist economic phenomena which
happen to have the same name or similarities in external form.
On the basis of certain external characteristics it might be
said that Soviet banks and credit institutions, trusts and syndicates, state enterprises, corporations and monopolies have been
taken over from the capitalist system; but in Soviet economy
such institutions have other functions, and their essential economic and social nature is markedly different. In capitalist
economy such institutions operate primarily for the profit of
private owners; in the Soviet system they operate primarily
as public utilities aiming to give the population the best possible services at the lowest possible cost, and facilitate the
development of national economy as a whole. There are basic

[6] Peter A. Bogdanov, *The Prerequisites and Aims of Soviet Planning*,
Address before Academy of Political and Social Sciences, Philadelphia, April
15, 1932.

differences in organizational structure and social control, as well as in function, between the Soviet trust and the trust in capitalist countries. The latter represents its shareholders, is controlled by them, and its major function is to obtain the highest possible profits for these shareholders. The Soviet trust, on the other hand, represents the workers and the workers' state, is controlled by them, and its major function is to advance socialist economy so as to assure the highest possible living standards for the population.

The Soviet worker—to take another instance—receives wages, but these wages are not based on the fluctuations of demand and supply, as is the case in capitalist countries, even where wages may be subject to some minor legal regulations or adjustments resulting from actions by organized labor or organized capital. In Soviet economy, labor is not a commodity either in law or in fact. The workers are the collective owners of industry. Wages, therefore, are based on the workers' needs, the requirements of national economy, and the available resources. At the same time, during the transition period of laying the economic foundations of a socialist society, allowances must be made for differences in the skill and labor productivity' of the individual worker. Another example of the differences between the two systems of economy is the rôle of machinery. In Soviet economy machinery is not introduced solely for the sake of reducing production costs even if such a reduction involves the dismissal of workers or the lowering of wages; machinery is introduced primarily in order to accelerate industrial development and expand production, thereby making it possible to increase wages and shorten hours of labor. The reduction in cost secured by the introduction of machinery is used as a major lever for raising living standards. Similarly, the piece-work system was introduced at the time of the inauguration of NEP not for the purpose merely of reducing costs by stimulating competition among the workers. The Soviet piece-work system aims in part to eliminate abuses by workers who may not yet have freed themselves from the acquisitive psychology of the old régime. But its primary aim is to increase personal incentive and the employee's interest in his work. Moreover, it enables Soviet economy to adjust the worker more effectively to his work by giving the less efficient worker more suitable employment. The workers themselves participate in setting the piece-work rates and increased production resulting from the piece-work system does not create unemployment.

These circumstances are due to the fact that Soviet economic planning aims to increase production not as an end in itself but for the purpose of radically and steadily improving the living standards of the mass of the population. In this respect the differences between Soviet planning and the type of government regulation practiced in capitalist countries has been stated as follows by the U.S.S.R. Chamber of Commerce:

"The predominant position of the state and the coöperatives permits the planned regulation of the national economy as a whole, even though not all branches of the latter are in the hands of the state. We consider the unity of the political and economic aims of the ruling class the premise for such planned direction. Here we have the fundamental difference between the economic policy of the Soviet state and the economic measures of the capitalistic countries in which the guiding principle is not concerned with the growth of the productive forces or the improvement of the welfare of the whole population, but merely with the interests of certain groups of the population. The interests of these groups but rarely coincide with the requirements of production and the interests of the entire population, and in fact they are very often in direct opposition to them. The Soviet state is a state of workers, and its policy is based on the interests of the whole working population. This is the source of strength of the Soviet Government, and it enables it to introduce such basic and fundamental measures which are in the interests of the workers and peasants (except the kulaks) ; in other words, in the interests of practically the whole population of the U.S.S.R." [7]

[7] *Economic Conditions in the U.S.S.R.*, issued by the U.S.S.R. Chamber of Commerce, Vneshtorgizdat, Moscow, 1931, pp. 9-10.

As a result of these basic premises of Soviet planning, the expansion of national economy and the expansion in purchasing power are part of a single integrated process. Hence, there is no limit to the consumptive capacities of the population. In Soviet economy demand always tends to exceed supply. Since the workers are the collective owners of industry, there can be no limit to the satisfaction of their demands except the limits imposed by actual production and the necessity of developing industry to higher levels. The expansion of national economy stimulates the demands of the masses of the population; these demands in turn stimulate the still further expansion of national economy. Consequently, overproduction, depression and unemployment are eliminated. Prior to 1931 there was an unemployment situation in the Soviet Union. The number of unemployed was greatest in 1929. This unemployment was due to the unregulated influx of peasants from the villages into the industrial centers, and to the fact that industry had not yet expanded to the point where it could absorb in a planned manner the increasing number of new workers. By 1931, however, the collectivization of agriculture opened new possibilities for the peasant in farming. At the same time, peasants and workers who migrated to industrial centers easily found employment because the steady expansion of national economy on a planned basis increased the demand for workers.

Soviet economists maintain that once the disabilities inherited from the previous economic system have been overcome and industry and agriculture are socialized, unemployment is permanently abolished. It cannot, they say, return in Soviet planned economy, which will always be able to absorb new workers. Similarly there can be no overproduction and no depression, they maintain, because the planned and steady rise in wages and in the income of the peasants which accompanies the expansion of economy, enables the population to buy goods so rapidly that industry must develop at an unusual rate in order to keep pace with the growing demands of the consumer and the increasing requirements of national economy itself. Overproduction, depression, and unemployment, according to Soviet

theory, do not occur in the Soviet economic system where production and purchasing power grow concomitantly and where
every phase of the social-economic process is coördinated and
planned in relation to every other phase with the direct aim or
improving living standards and eliminating the bases of class
differences.[8]

For the planning of the development of national economy,
the Soviet population has at its disposal a country exceptionally
rich in natural resources. Its area occupies about 8,200,000
square miles or about one-sixth of the earth's surface. Of this
area 20 per cent is unusable land, but the rest is arable or
fruit-growing land, meadows, commons for pastures, and
forests. Coal reserves are estimated at 552 billion metric tons
or seven per cent of the world's total; in this respect the Soviet
Union is exceeded only by the United States, Canada and
China. Its oil reserves are estimated at 3 billion tons, or 35 per
cent of the world's total oil deposits; in this respect the Soviet
Union leads the world. Its hydraulic resources are estimated at
64,819,000 horse-power or 19.7 per cent of the world's total resources, almost equaling those of the United States. Iron ore
deposits are estimated at 1.65 billion tons or 4.9 per cent of
the world's resources. Timber resources are estimated at 913,-
040,000 hectares (2,191,296,000 acres), or 27.9 per cent of the
world's resources, the largest in the world. The Soviet Union
leads the world in deposits of potassium, gold, manganese, and
platinum. Of the world's total area of land under wheat about
17.5 per cent is in the Soviet Union; of the area under rye about
60 per cent; barley 20 per cent and oats 20 per cent. Of the
world's total livestock the Soviet Union has: horses, 27 per
cent; cattle, 10.6 per cent; sheep, 12.6 per cent and pigs, 9.5
per cent.[9]

Statistics regarding natural resources in the Soviet Union are
continually revised, because steady exploration and survey
reveal greater and greater resources. Thus in 1913 the total

[8] Bogdanov, loc. cit.
[9] Soviet Union Year Book, compiled and edited by A. A. Santalov and
Louis Segal, Allen & Unwin, Ltd., London, 1930, pp. 89-90.

coal supplies of Russia were estimated at 233 billion tons, while in 1931 they were estimated at 552 billion. Similarly, a statement submitted by the Soviet Union at the London Power Conference in 1924 estimated Soviet oil reserves at 2.88 billion tons, giving the Soviet Union first place among the countries of the world in regard to oil deposits. But subsequent prospecting has revealed unsuspected oil reserves both in old and new regions. The Baku oil fields have been worked for about 60 years; those of Grozny, 40; and those of Maikop and Emba, 20; but it is only recently that steps have been taken to branch out beyond these localities. Prospecting still remains to be done in many regions of the Soviet Union.[10] Similarly, the charting of the Soviet Union's water power is incomplete. It is estimated that the total known water power is about 65 million horse-power; but Soviet scientists believe that still greater resources exist in Siberia, the Ukraine, etc.[11]

The actual extent of all the mineral wealth in the Soviet Union has never been definitely established, but the Soviet planning system does not leave the development of natural resources to accident. It includes, both in regard to industry and agriculture, a broad program of planned economic geography. Prior to the war the territorial division of Russia did not correspond to the economic interests of the country or to the interests of the individual nationalities. In most cases these interests and the territorial divisions were in direct contradiction. In undertaking to industrialize the country, the Soviet planning system had to develop industry on a socialist basis in such a way as to distribute it properly throughout the vast expanse of the Soviet Union. It had to solve the problems presented by the enormous distances of the country. Furthermore, it had to meet the needs of the national minorities whose economic and cultural progress is one of the aims of the Soviet régime. In the Czarist era the bulk of industry was concentrated in the European part of Russia, a relatively small section of

[10] See I. M. Gubkin, "The Natural Wealth of the Soviet Union and Its Exploitation," *Cooperative Publishing Society of Foreign Workers in the U.S.S.R.*, Moscow, 1932, pp. 20-43.

[11] *Ibid.*, p. 49.

the empire. A similar situation prevailed for a number of years under the Soviet régime. The problem of industrializing the country on a planned basis involved the task of industrializing the outlying industrially backward regions. Indeed, the industrialization of the Soviet Union as a whole within the time planned was possible only if the extensive productive forces of the backward regions were opened and included in the planned system of national economy. Regional studies are therefore organized with a view to assisting in the territorial expansion of national economy. Such studies seek to discover the natural productive forces of any given region as well as the valuable deposits which may be hidden in the soil. The development of planned economic geography has made it possible to open entire new economic regions, involving the creation of immense industrial enterprises like Magnitogorsk and Kuznetsk, or the development of specialized agricultural areas like the sugar, rice, and cotton districts of the North Caucasus or those regions of western Siberia which specialize in wheat-growing.

In general, Soviet planning specifies the speed and direction of the entire social-economic process. The concrete aim of Soviet planning is to industrialize national economy, to convert a backward agrarian country into a highly developed industrial country in the shortest possible period of time. All necessary steps were to be taken to expand national economy as a whole. Moreover, the Plan aimed to increase the predominance of the socialized sector of national economy. Accordingly, it was necessary to mechanize and socialize agriculture. The program involved a vast social-economic process in which agriculture is raised from the individual to the collective level and the gulf between town and country is gradually eliminated. The extensive program for the socialization and mechanization of agriculture left its mark on the Five-Year Plan and emphasized its character as a program for laying the economic foundations of socialism.

In inaugurating the Five-Year Plan, Soviet economy set itself the goal of "overtaking and surpassing" the technical and economic levels of the advanced capitalist countries. The Soviet

Union had developed so far beyond the ruins of the World War and the civil war, that it no longer measured its economic progress against the limited achievements of the Czarist régime, but against the advanced achievements of the western countries. By 1927-28 the national income had risen to a level 105 per cent of the prewar income. Since 1922 the national income had been rising at an annual rate of 10 per cent, a rate of advance which had no precedent either in the history of prewar Russia or of the advanced capitalist countries.[12]

Before the Plan was put into operation, the Soviet Union had already exceeded prewar production in most important branches of industry. The coal output of 1927-28 amounted to 122 per cent of the 1913 output; petroleum 126 per cent; electric power 260 per cent and agricultural machinery 187 per cent.[13]

The Plan was to accelerate this process by increasing the production of enterprises essential to the industrialization of the country. On the other hand, it had to overcome certain handicaps, such as the inadequate production of iron ore, which in 1927-28 was only 62 per cent of the prewar level and of pig-iron which was 79 per cent of the prewar level. The Plan also had to overcome the shortage of manufactured goods—the gap between demand and supply. Actually in 1927-28 the output of consumers' goods was in general above the prewar level, cotton fabrics being 22 per cent above, woolens two per cent, and sugar four per cent; but the increased population together with the steadily improving living standards of the workers and peasants made the demand far in excess of the increased output.

In seeking to industrialize and socialize agriculture, the Five-Year Plan had to provide for the solution of certain serious problems. In 1927-28 the gross production of the leading industrial crops, such as cotton, sugar beets, flax, etc., was either at or below the prewar level.[14] A number of factors made it imperative to expand this branch of agriculture in order to meet the growing needs of industry and the increasing demands of the workers and peasants, in order to reconstruct agriculture

[12] Grinko, *op. cit.*, p. 38.   [13] *Ibid.*, p. 35.   [14] *Ibid.*, p. 36.

and in order to diminish the dependence of the Soviet Union on foreign countries for agricultural raw materials. Likewise, the Plan had to meet the deficiency in grain production. In 1927-28 the sown area was 94.8 per cent of the 1913 area. The total grain production during the period of rehabilitation (1921-1927) fluctuated between 90 and 96 per cent of the average production for the five years from 1909 to 1913. In order to increase production, the Plan had to provide for a progressive improvement in farming methods, and it was considered that this must necessarily involve the strengthening of the socialized section of agriculture, i.e., the state and collective farms. Transportation offered similar problems. In 1927-28 the total railway mileage was 30.5 per cent larger than the pre-war mileage. But the rapid expansion of industry and agriculture necessitated the further growth and improvement of the transportation system. The Plan also had to coördinate and direct the financial and credit system.[15]

The program for expanding national economy provided that during the ensuing five years the investment of capital in the whole of national economy should total 64.6 billion rubles, as compared with 26.5 billion invested in the previous five years. As a result of these investments the total basic capital of the country was to rise from 70 billion rubles in 1927-28 to 128 billion rubles in 1932-33, an increase of 82 per cent. The value of industrial production was to increase from 18.3 billion rubles in 1927-28 to 43.2 billion in 1932-33, a gain of 136 per cent. The value of agricultural production was to grow from 16.7 billion rubles to 25.8 billion. Railway traffic was to rise from 88 billion to 163 billion ton-kilometers. As a result of the increases planned in the various branches of the national economy, the national income was to double, going from 24.4 billion rubles to 49.7 billion. In order to lay the foundations for an independent socialist economy, the Five-Year Plan proposed to apply 78 per cent of industrial capital investments to those branches of industry which produce the means of production.

[15] *Ibid.*, p. 38; see also *Economic Handbook of the Soviet Union,* issued by the American-Russian Chamber of Commerce, 1931, p. 68.

The share of the socialized sector was to increase in industry from 80 per cent to 92 per cent; in retail trade from 75 to 91 per cent and in agriculture from 2 to 15 per cent.

The Five-Year Plan was not intended to be a narrow plan of economic growth. It went far beyond the economic plans suggested in other countries which seek no more than the regulation of production and the elimination of fluctuations. Soviet planning seeks to reconstruct the whole of national economy and to change basic social relations. The Five-Year Plan was above everything else a step in the development of socialism. It was also a step in the general process of raising living standards. Accordingly, sections of it were specifically devoted to eliminating unemployment, raising wages, shortening hours, increasing social insurance and labor protection, extending educational and cultural activities, and in general improving working and living conditions.

One of the most important problems which the Five-Year Plan had to solve was that of the labor resources of the country and their utilization. The natural growth of the Soviet population proceeds at a rate greater than that of any other western country. The annual rate of natural increase in the Soviet Union is 23 per 1,000 as compared with 1.3 per 1,000 in France, 7.9 in Germany, 6.4 in England, and 10.3 in Italy. In the Soviet Union with a population of about 160,000,000 the annual increase is at least 3,500,000, as compared with 2,500,000 in all the other countries of Western Europe whose aggregate population is 370,000,000. The Five-Year Plan, therefore, envisaged an increase of 18,000,000 in the population between the fiscal years 1927-28 and 1932-33, and an increase in the working population of about 10,000,000.

The industrial development under the New Economic Policy was accompanied by a tremendous growth in the urban population, at a rate greater than in prewar Russia or in other leading countries. In Germany, England and the United States, in the period from 1900 to 1905, the annual rate of growth of the urban population was approximately 3.3 per cent. The United

States alone maintained that rate from 1900 to 1910. In the
Soviet Union, on the other hand, the urban population increased 5.5 per cent in 1926 and 5 per cent in 1927. It was estimated, therefore, that during the period covered by the Five-
Year Plan from 2,500,000 to 3,000,000 people would migrate
from the villages to the cities to be absorbed in urban economy.
The Plan, accordingly, envisaged an increase in the number
of wage-earners from 11,350,000 in 1927-28 to 15,764,000 in
1932-33, an increase of 39 per cent. An interesting forecast of
the Plan, in view of subsequent developments, referred to unemployment. In 1927-28 there were 1,100,000 unemployed
wage-earners registered at the labor exchanges. This figure, according to the Plan, was to be reduced to 400,000 by 1932-33.

The productivity of labor, according to the Five-Year Plan,
was to increase 110 per cent in industry, 60 per cent in construction, and 75 per cent in transportation. Money wages were
to increase 47 per cent during the five years. Taking into account the reduction in living costs the real wages of industrial
workers were to increase 70.5 per cent by 1932-33 as compared
with 1927-28, and 109 per cent as compared with 1913. The
Plan also provided for the general introduction of the seven-
hour day. The average normal working day was to be reduced
from 7.71 hours in 1927-28 to 6.86 hours in 1932-33, a decrease
of 11 per cent. In 1927-28 the working day in industry was
already 2.18 hours per day shorter than in 1913; by 1932-33
it was planned to be 3.21 hours shorter. The social insurance
budget was to be increased from 969,000,000 rubles to 1,950,-
000,000 rubles, or more than 100 per cent. One of the most
important provisions of the Plan was for old age insurance,
which by 1932-33 was to be extended to all classes of people
working for hire. Living conditions were to be radically improved. The per capita consumption of food products by the
city population and the area of living quarters were to be increased all along the line. The Plan also provided for a marked
rise in the cultural level of the people. Literacy in the cities was
to increase from 78 per cent of persons eight years of age and

over in 1927-28 to 87 per cent in 1932-33, and in the rural districts from 48 to 75 per cent.[16]

The extent to which this program has been carried out is now common knowledge. The rapid extension of Soviet national economy at a time when the rest of the world is passing through a severe economic crisis has been the subject of worldwide comment, particularly since the announcement that the Plan is to be completed in most of its essential provisions by January 1, 1933 instead of October 1, 1933, as originally provided, or in four and a quarter years instead of five. Since the inauguration of the Plan, Soviet industrial production increased by 3,296,000,000 rubles in 1929; 3,635,000,000 rubles in 1930 and 4,800,000,000 rubles in 1931. In a number of industries the Plan was completed as early as 1931, notably in the oil, electrical, tractor, and machine-building industries. On the basis of incomplete data, Premier Molotov of the Soviet Union reported on December 22, 1931, that in 1929 the Plan was fulfilled 106 per cent; in 1930, the second year of the Plan, 107 per cent; and in 1931, the third year, 113.[17]

The Soviet planning system has raised every branch of national economy to unprecedented levels. This becomes clear if achievements under the Five-Year Plan are compared with 1927 when the prewar level of production was reached in most branches of economy. Capital investments rose from 6.53 billion for the whole of national economy in 1927 to 11.36 billion in 1930. Investments in the socialized sectors of national economy rose from 3.13 billion rubles in 1927 to 10.13 billion in 1930 and 16.05 billion in 1931, a gain of almost 400 per cent in four years. Total capital investments in industry and electrification increased from 1.45 billion rubles in 1927 to 3.90 billion in 1930, and in the socialized sector of industry and electrification from 1.39 billion rubles in 1927 to 3.88 billion in 1930 and 7.26 billion in 1931. Capital investments

[16] For details of the Five-Year Plan see G. T. Grinko, *The Five-Year Plan of the Soviet Union*, and *The Soviet Union Looks Ahead*, Horace Liveright, New York, 1930.

[17] *Economic Review of the Soviet Union*, February 15, 1932, p. 77.

in the whole of agriculture rose from 2.30 billion rubles in
1927 to 3.03 billion in 1930, and in the socialized sector of
agriculture from 0.17 billion rubles in 1927 to 2.39 billion in
1930 and 3.46 billion in 1931.

Under the Five-Year Plan, the value of the total output
of census industry (measured in 1926-27 prices) rose to 27.92
billion rubles in 1931, as compared with 2.51 billion in 1922
and 12.05 billion in 1927; the output in 1931 represented a
gain of 132 per cent over the total for 1927. The output of
producers' goods rose from 5.37 billion rubles in 1927 to 14.05
billion in 1931, a tremendous increase over 1922 when the
output was only 1.09 billion rubles. Similarly, the output of
consumers' goods rose from 1.42 billion rubles in 1922 to 6.68
billion in 1927 and 13.87 billion in 1931. The length of railway lines increased from 58,500 kilometers in 1913, the last
prewar year, to 75,700 in 1927 and 80,100 in 1931. Freight
operations increased from 65.7 billion ton-kilometers in 1913
to 81.7 billion in 1927 and 149.4 billion in 1931; while passenger operations, which totaled 25.2 billion passenger-kilometers in 1913 and 22.4 billion in 1927, rose to 61.1 billion in
1931. Both freight and passenger operations are now considerably more than double the prewar figures.

The rapid development of electrification has been one of
the most striking features under the Five-Year Plan. In 1913
all power plants in Russia had a capacity of 1.01 million
kilowatts; by 1927 the total capacity was 1.67 million kilowatts and by 1931 the figure had risen to 3.97 million, or 293
per cent above the prewar level. Between 1927 and 1931 the
total output of electric power rose from 4.17 billion to 10.6
billion kilowatt-hours, as compared with 1.95 billion before the
war, an increase of 444 per cent over the 1913 figure.

In agriculture, the sown area was 116.7 million hectares
in 1913; 115.0 million in 1927; and 136.6 million in 1931.
The gross production of grain crops was 80.1 million tons in
1913; 72.8 million in 1927; and 83.6 million in 1931. The number of state farms increased from 3,000 in 1928 to 5,380 in
1931; their sown area increased during this period from 1.74

million to 10.60 million hectares; and their gross output of
grain from 1.13 million to 3.26 million tons.

In line with the growth of the national economy, the total
number of wage-earners rose from 11,200,000 in 1913 to 10,-
900,000 in 1927 and 18,700,000 in 1931, while trade union
membership increased from 6,700,000 in 1922 to 9,600,000 in
1927 and 16,500,000 in 1931. Average annual wages increased
from 624 rubles in the fiscal year 1927 to 1,096 rubles in 1931,
a gain of over 75 per cent.[18] By the end of 1931, the monthly
income per worker's family had increased 64 per cent as compared with 1929.

The expansion of national economy which marked the first
two years of the Plan, continued during 1931 at so rapid a
pace that in most cases the original schedules of the Plan set
for the third year were greatly exceeded. A report in January
1932 made by G. K. Ordzhonikidze, Commissar of Heavy
Industry, stated that in 1931 the ouput of large-scale state
industry as a whole amounted to 27.1 billion rubles, an increase of 21.7 per cent over 1930 and 38 per cent above the
figure originally set for the third year of the Plan. The output
of heavy industry showed a gain of 28.7 per cent over 1930
and of 68.6 per cent over the original third-year schedule.
Although the main emphasis has been placed on heavy industry, considerable progress has also been made in developing
the supply of consumers' goods. The 1931 output of the large-
scale state food industry totaled 5.2 billion rubles, an increase
of more than 26 per cent over 1930. During the same year
the output of light industry, including textiles, shoes and
leather, rubber and soap, was 13 per cent above the 1930
output. During 1931 the capital investments in large-scale
industry equaled the total investments for the preceding
three years.[19]

A vast construction program is being carried out under the
Five-Year Plan involving the opening of hundreds of large

[18] See *The National Economy of the U.S.S.R.*, statistical handbook issued
by the Central Bureau of National Economic Statistics, State Social-
Economic Publishing House, Moscow-Leningrad, 1932.

[19] *Economic Review of the Soviet Union*, March 15, 1932, p. 123.

new industrial enterprises. During 1929 and 1930, the first
two years of the Plan, the following were some of the enterprises completed and set in operation: The 535-mile pipe-line
from Baku to Batum with an annual capacity of 1,640,000
metric tons of oil; the 390-mile Grozny-Tuapse pipe-line; the
Kerch steel mill in the Crimea with an annual capacity of
350,000 tons of pig iron; the Georgian cement plant with an
annual capacity of 720,000 barrels; the Gusevo glass works,
with an annual capacity of 400,000 cases of glass; the
Bobruisk wood-working combine in White Russia with an
annual capacity of 710,000 cubic meters; the Ivanovo-Voznesensk textile combine with an annual capacity of 80 million
meters; the Konstantinovka superphosphate plant with an
annual capacity of 300,000 tons; the Krasnoural copper smel-
ter in the Urals with an annual capacity of 25,000 tons; the
Konstantinovka zinc works in the Ukraine with an annual
capacity of 14,000 tons; the Belovo zinc plant in Siberia with
an annual capacity of 12,000 tons; the Rostov agricultural
machinery plant with an annual capacity of 25,000 combines
and other machines; the Stalingrad tractor plant with an
annual capacity of 50,000 tractors; the Mariupol pipe rolling
mill with an annual capacity of 100,000 tons of seamless pipes;
the Balakhna (Volga) paper mill with an annual capacity of
110,000 tons of newsprint; the Syas cellulose combine with
an annual capacity of 75,000 tons of cellulose and 40,000
tons of newsprint; the Schachti power plant in the North
Caucasus with a capacity of 92,000 kilowatts; and the
Bobrikov power plant with a capacity of 348,000 kilowatts.

During 1931 new plants with a total value of 3.5 billion
rubles were completed, including the Nizhni Novgorod automobile plant with an annual capacity of 140,000 cars; the
AMO automobile plant in Moscow (30,000 trucks); the
Kharkov tractor works (50,000 tractors); the first section of
the Ural machine-building plant (100,000 to 150,000 tons of
heavy machinery especially for mining and metallurgy); the
Moscow machine-tool plant (6,200 screw machines); the
Nizhni Novgorod machine-tool plant (12,500 milling ma-

chines) ; the Ural copper-smelting plant (20,000 tons of copper) ; and the Moscow bicycle plant (300,000 bicycles).

The year 1931 also witnessed the completion of a number of new electric power plants and new installations in old plants with a combined capacity of over 1,000,000 kilowatts, as much as in the two preceding years and nearly equal to the total capacity of all Russian power plants in 1913. Some of the most important of the new power stations and installations are: Zuevo, 150,000 kilowatts; Kashira, 100,000 kilowatts; Nigres, 94,000 kilowatts; Ivgres, 72,000 kilowatts; Leningrad (second plant), 48,000 kilowatts; Cheliabinsk, 48,-000 kilowatts, and Magnitogorsk, 36,000 kilowatts. On May 1, 1932, the first section of the immense Dnieprostroy power plant, the largest hydro-electric station in Europe, was opened.

The first few months of 1932 witnessed the opening of the huge new combine harvester plant at Saratov; the giant Berezniky chemical combine, which will specialize in the production of chemical fertilizers; the first section of the Magnitogorsk steel mill; the Moscow ball-bearing plant; and the Volkhov aluminum works. Among the projects which were started during the first quarter of 1932 were an electric locomotive plant at Kashira, which will be completed in 1933 and will produce 1,600 locomotives annually; a textile mill in Barnaul, in west Siberia, the weaving department of which will have 4,700 looms; a huge hydro-electric project at Cheboksari in the Chuvash republic, the eventual capacity of which will be 400,000 kilowatts; a clothing factory at Leningrad which will employ 18,000 workers; and a new 500-mile railway trunk line from Moscow to the Donetz Basin.

Many of the gigantic industrial enterprises created and opened under the Five-Year Plan are the largest in Europe, and among the largest in the world. Such are the Nizhni Novgorod automobile plant, the Magnitogorsk steel mill, the Moscow ball-bearing plant, the Gusevo glass works, the Ivanovo-Voznesensk textile combine, the Stalingrad and Kharkov tractoi plants, and the Balakhna paper mill.

One of the most striking achievements under the Five-Year Plan was the extensive collectivization of peasant farms. On October 1, 1927, only 286,000, or a little over one per cent, of the total number of peasant households were organized in collectives. The Five-Year Plan called for the collectivization of 9.6 per cent of the total number of peasant households by 1932-33. But the collectivization movement proceeded so rapidly that by the end of 1930, the percentage of peasant households organized in collectives had reached 24 and by the end of 1931 the percentage was 62. In the 1931 spring sowings the collectives accounted for 61 per cent and the state farms for 9 per cent of the total. This meant that the socialized sector of agriculture accounted for 70 per cent of the total sowings as against 13.3 per cent scheduled by the Five-Year Plan for 1932-33.[20]

This transformation of agriculture from an individual to a collective basis was due in large measure to the mechanization of agriculture, and to the advantages of large-scale farming as demonstrated to the peasantry by the successful operations of such model state farms as Verblyud, in the North Caucasus. Collectivized agriculture based on machinery increased the yield considerably. Preliminary figures for gross production of grain and industrial crops in 1931 showed an increase of 6.5 per cent over the previous year, while the marketable output showed a gain of 9 or 10 per cent.[21]

While collectivization has proceeded at an extraordinary rate and now embraces over 60 per cent of the peasant households, a considerable part of agriculture is still carried on by millions of individual households. However, even this part of national economy is not left to the fluctuations of the market but is influenced by the Soviet planning organizations. The government stimulates the cultivation of certain crops rather than others by preferential taxes imposed in accordance with the general plan for national economy. Tax exemptions are established annually at the commencement of the agricultural

---

[20] *Economic Review,* January 15, 1932, p. 30.
[21] *Ibid.,* January 15, 1932, p. 30.

year in conformity with the annual control figures. The government further influences agricultural production by individual peasant households by fixing procurement prices for that part of the agricultural output which is purchased by the state and coöperative organizations. State and coöperative organizations have practically a monopoly in the agricultural produce market. The state is the largest buyer of agricultural products. State and coöperative organizations which purchase farm products have considerable financial resources of their own in addition to credits which the government grants them, and have special privileges in storage and transportation. Another factor which enables the state planning organizations to influence private agricultural production is the system of contracting in advance for part of the crop or for the whole of the agricultural output. The influence is maintained by fixing prices in advance and granting credits either in the form of cash or in goods, which may be manufactured products or agricultural implements. This contract system has been a powerful factor in regulating the production of the private sector of agriculture and combined with the other measures brings the millions of individual peasant households within the planning system. This is all the more true since the base of agriculture has been transferred under the Five-Year Plan, from individual to collective production.

The rapid development of Soviet economy under the Five-Year Plan combined with the sharp decline in industrial production in other countries has raised the Soviet Union to second place among the countries of the world both as regards national income and the volume of industrial output. In 1931 the net income of all branches of national economy in the Soviet Union totaled 37.8 billion rubles in 1926-27 prices or 25.5 billion rubles in prewar prices. This was nearly double the 1913 figure of 14 billion rubles and exceeded the national incomes of France, Great Britain and Germany prior to the depression. In 1928 the Soviet Union occupied fifth place among the countries of the world in the volume of industrial production, coming after the United States, Germany, Great

Britain and France. By July 1931, according to figures issued by the German Economic Research Institute, the Soviet Union had reached third place, outstripping Britain and France. By August of that year Soviet industrial production exceeded that of Germany and was second only to that of the United States. In 1928 the share of the United States in the world's industrial output was ten times that of the Soviet Union; by October, 1931, it was only about three times as great.[22]

Soviet Industry reached the prewar volume of production in 1926-27. Under the Five-Year Plan the prewar figure was almost doubled by 1930. In the following year the volume of industrial output was two and a half times the prewar volume and eleven times the 1922 output. For many individual industries the ratios were even higher. From 1922 to 1931 the average annual rate of increase was 32.5 per cent. During the three years in which the Five-Year Plan has been in operation (1928-31) the rate of increase in industrial production has ranged from 22 to 25 per cent. This is considerably in excess of the rate of increase in other countries during the years 1924-29, and is even greater than the rate of increase in other countries during their most rapid industrial development. In the United States, for example, the annual rate of increase during the period from 1870 to 1890 was 8.5 per cent. In Czarist Russia the average annual rate of increase for the years 1901-08 was 3.7 per cent and for 1908-13 a little over 10 per cent, or less than half the rate at which Soviet industry has increased its volume of production.

According to statistics published by the League of Nations and the German Economic Research Institute, the volume of industrial production in the Soviet Union increased 86 per cent from 1928 to 1931, while the volume of production in the rest of the world declined 29 per cent in the same period. Accordingly, the Soviet Union was by the end of 1931 first among the countries in the world in the production of timber

[22] *Izvestia*, November 7, 1931; *Za Industrializatsiu*, January 1 and 30, 1932; and *Pravda*, January 31, 1932.

and peat, second in the production of oil and agricultural machinery, third in the output of pig-iron and the machine-building industry as a whole, and fourth in the output of coal, steel, and electrical products. The share of the Soviet Union in the world's total output of some of the chief branches of industry in 1931, as compared with 1925, was as follows: [23]

	(*In per cent*)	
	1925	*1931*
All industry	2.8	11.2
Electric power	2.4	4.5
Electrical industry	1.4	10.0 *
Oil	9.0	14.7
Coal	1.3	5.1
Pig iron	1.7	8.7
Steel	2.4	7.6
Copper	1.25	4.0

* Data for the world as of 1929, for U.S.S.R. as of 1931.

In regard to the production of electric power, the Soviet Union in 1931 ranked seventh among the countries of the world. Although in this respect it is still far behind other industrial countries, its annual rate of increase in recent years has ranged from 25 to 50 per cent as against 4 or 5 per cent in the United States, Germany, England and France. In 1929-30 the Soviet Union increased its output of electrical energy by a total of 2 billion kilowatt-hours, as compared with France's 1.9 billion and Great Britain's 1.3 billion. This increase has enabled the Soviet Union to proceed rapidly with the electrification of industry. By 1931 about 70 per cent of Soviet industry was electrified as compared with 47.7 per cent in 1925-26. In this respect the Soviet Union is second only to the United States, where 75 per cent of industry is run on electric power.[24]

The Soviet Union also ranks high among the countries of the world in regard to agricultural production. It has the largest

[23] *Economic Review of the Soviet Union*, April 1, 1932, pp. 149-150.
[24] *Ibid.*, p. 150.

total agricultural output of any country, and is among the
three leading producers of grain, flax, sugar beets, cotton and
tobacco. In respect to transportation it is second only to the
United States in the length of air and railway lines and railway
freight operations. The share of the Soviet Union of the world's
total freight turnover was 7.4 per cent in 1931 as compared
with 4.4 in 1913. Passenger traffic on Soviet railways in 1930
totaled 52 billion passenger-kilometers. This was more than
double the prewar figure of 25.2 billion and 20 per cent above
the figure for the United States, 43 billion. In this respect the
Soviet Union now leads the world.[25]

Unprecedented in the history of modern economic development is the fact that the Soviet Union expanded its industries
on a planned basis without the aid of foreign capital. It is well
known that all of the advanced countries of the world have
built up their industries with the aid of outside capital. In the
nineteenth century the United States developed various industries, and particularly the railways, with the aid of European capital. The reparation payment of five billion francs
paid by France following the Franco-Prussian war aided Germany considerably in developing its industries during the
eighties. Similarly, the development of French industry was
stimulated by the great wealth which France acquired during
the Napoleonic wars. Furthermore, the world money market
was never closed to these countries. Following the world war,
various European countries rehabilitated their national economy with the aid of foreign, predominantly American, capital.
Prior to the revolution, Russia, too, developed its industries
with loans contracted abroad. After 1917 it was subjected to a
financial blockade. Yet, by coördinating its natural resources
and labor power on a planned basis, it has been able to pass
far beyond the prewar level of its national economy, and to
rise to second place among the countries of the world in industrial production without the aid of foreign loans and only
a moderate amount of commercial credits.

There is one form of foreign aid, however, which the leaders

[25] *Ibid.*, p. 152.

of Soviet economic policy consider vitally important, and that
is the importation of foreign technical skill, knowledge and experience. Under the Five-Year Plan, the importation of technical assistance and the importation of machinery and equipment are closely connected. Soviet organizations, in purchasing
large quantities of machinery abroad, often arrange to secure
technical assistance for that branch of industry for which the
equipment was purchased. The technical assistance has been
obtained either through the medium of contracts with prominent engineering and manufacturing concerns or through the
employment of individual specialists.

Prior to 1927 the number of technical assistance contracts
was quite insignificant. From 1923 to 1926 only 16 such contracts were concluded. In 1927-28 there was a rapid increase,
over 40 new agreements being concluded in this period. By
1931 the Soviet Union had concluded a total of 115 technical
assistance contracts for industry alone with foreign firms.
These contracts involved almost all the basic industries; the
largest number were in the metal, chemical, electro-technical
and mining industries. In addition, a number of technical assistance contracts were concluded for foreign aid in transportation and agriculture. The technical assistance contracts provide
for engineering coöperation in the construction of new industrial enterprises or the rationalization of old ones, in the
designing of new plants, shops, mines and shafts, in consultation on projects worked out by Soviet engineers, in the preparation of drawings and calculations, and in turning over patents,
designs, etc. to Soviet organizations. Most of the contracts have
been and are being successfully carried out.

The number of technical assistance contracts with American
firms in force at the beginning of 1931 was 47, or 40 per cent
of the total number of contracts. One of the most important
contracts with American firms is that with Colonel Hugh L.
Cooper and Company in connection with the building of the
Dnieprostroy hydro-electric power plant and dam. Other outstanding contracts include those with the International General Electric Company, the Ford Motor Company, the Freyn

Engineering Company, in the metallurgical industry; the Radio Corporation of America; Du Pont de Nemours and Company in the chemical industry; Stuart, James & Cooke, Inc., in the coal industry; Arthur G. McKee and Company of Cleveland, assisting in the construction of the Magnitogorsk steel mill; Albert Kahn and Company, Inc., industrial construction, etc. A considerable number of individual foreign specialists have also been engaged, many of them leaders in their respective fields. In 1931 there were several thousand American engineers, technicians and skilled workers employed in Soviet enterprises. In addition, the Soviet Union maintains technical bureaus in foreign countries for the purpose of enabling Soviet engineers to study the latest methods of modern industry and to apply them to Soviet industry, while groups of young Soviet engineers and mechanics have been sent to such enterprises as the Ford plant at Dearborn and the General Electric plant at Schenectady in order to familiarize themselves with the production methods employed in these works.

The expansion of Soviet economy under the Five-Year Plan has profoundly affected the Soviet worker. Unemployment was completely eliminated by the end of 1930. There has been a steady increase in the number of wage-earners in all branches of national economy. From 1930 to 1931 the increase was especially great, the total rising from 14.6 million to 18.7 million, a gain of 28 per cent in one year. At the same time there has been improvement in labor conditions and living standards. By the end of 1931, the third year of the Five-Year Plan, 83 per cent of all workers in large-scale state industry were working on the seven-hour day. In certain industries—such as iron and steel, basic chemicals, and rubber—all workers were on the seven-hour day; while in the oil, paper, textile, electrical and non-ferrous metals industries 90-98 per cent of the workers were on the seven-hour day. The program for wages set for the final year of the Plan were exceeded by the third year, 1931, when the total wage fund rose to 21.1 billion rubles or 34.5 per cent above the schedule originally set for 1932-33. Average annual wages for workers in all branches of national economy amounted to 1,096 rubles in 1931, an increase of 23.5 per cent over 1930 and of 40 per cent over 1929. By the end of 1931 the monthly income per worker's family had increased 64 per cent as compared with 1929. The social insurance fund —which enters into the worker's "socialized wage"—amounted to 2.5 billion rubles in 1931 as compared with 1.5 billion in 1930 and 1.95 billion set by the Plan for 1932-33. Large sums were also spent for labor protection. For this purpose a total of 77 million rubles was allotted to industrial enterprises under the Supreme Economic Council alone. Investments in housing for industrial workers during 1931 amounted to 575 million rubles as compared with 300 million in 1930 and 63 million in 1925.[26]

The achievements of Soviet economy during the first three years of the Five-Year Plan have made the Control Figures for 1932 the program for the final year of the Plan, which will thus be completed in a little over four years. The fulfillment of the 1932 Control Figures will mean that the schedules of the original Five-Year Plan for 1932-33 will be carried out in the main by the end of 1932. The 1932 program provides for extensive construction work, particularly the completion of projects already under way; an even higher rate of increase in industrial production than in the first three years of the Five-Year Plan; special attention to the development of coal, metal, transportation and machine-building; the increasing predominance of the socialized sector of national economy; and considerable improvements in the living standards of the people. Capital investments for 1932 have been set at 21.1 billion rubles as compared with 16.1 billion in 1931, an increase of 31 per cent. Over half of the 1932 capital investments have been allocated to industry. The bulk of it will go for the reconstruction of old plants and mines and the building of new ones. A considerable part of the investments in construction work in 1932 will go toward the completion of plants started in earlier years. Largely on the basis of these capital investments, it is planned that the volume of industrial production in 1932 will

[26] *Ibid.*, April 1, 1932, pp. 154-157.

increase 36 per cent. Capital investments for agriculture are set at 4.36 billion rubles, an increase of 21 per cent over 1931. It is planned to have 75 per cent of the peasant households collectivized by the end of the year.

On the basis of the increased output of heavy industry and agriculture in 1932 light industry will be expanded. Production of consumers' goods in 1932 is scheduled to register an increase of 29 per cent over 1931; cotton is scheduled to increase 24 per cent over 1931; shoes, 19 per cent; and the total output of the food industry, 36.6 per cent. The total wage fund is scheduled to amount to 26.8 billion rubles, an increase of 27 per cent over 1931 and 71 per cent over the figure originally set by the Five-Year Plan for 1932-33. The seven-hour day will be extended to include all industrial workers. Nearly 3 billion rubles is planned to be invested in housing construction and municipal works. The number of workers is expected to increase to 21 million as compared with 18.7 million in 1931 and 15.8 million originally scheduled for the fifth year of the Plan. The Control Figures plan a national income of 49.2 billion rubles for 1932, an increase of 30 per cent over that of the previous year. The socialized sector of national economy is expected to furnish 91 per cent of the national income in 1932 as compared with 81.5 per cent in 1931 and 52.7 per cent in 1928.[27]

The foundation laid during the first three years of the Plan is expected by the Soviet authorities to make it possible to fulfill the ambitious program set for the fourth year. Even if the program is not carried out completely in some details, there is no doubt that the success of the Plan as a whole is already definitely assured. The first Five-Year Plan aimed primarily at preparing the foundations for a socialist economy by developing the heavy industries and socializing agriculture on the basis of mechanization. Its success has created the premises for the Second Five-Year Plan, which aims to use these foundations for the purpose of developing a socialist society. The new plan provides for the expansion and creation

[27] *Ibid.*, January 15, 1932, pp. 30-34.

of those branches of industry which produce the means of production in order further to ensure the technical development of national economy. At the same time, in order to continue the improvement of living standards, it aims to expand the output of consumers' goods. During the period covered by the Second Five-Year Plan continued attention will be given to the development of heavy industry. The attention given during the first Five-Year Plan to heavy industry has already resulted in such achievements in the production of the means of production as to make it possible for the new plan to provide for marked increases in the means of consumption.

Agriculture and light industry—including the food industry—are to be developed so that by 1937 the supply of consumers' goods is expected to be double or triple that of 1932. The new plan aims to increase greatly the available housing accommodations and the network of socialized restaurants, laundries, and day nurseries in order to make further progress in the program, initiated by the Five-Year Plan, of releasing women from domestic drudgery. Old cities, like Moscow and Leningrad, are to be rebuilt and new ones are to be created organized on socialist principles. The principal industrial cities are to be made into cultural as well as economic centers. The network of educational institutions, both elementary and higher, and of workers' clubs, theaters, lecture halls, and stadiums is to be extended and the production of books, motion pictures, radio apparatus, cameras and musical instruments is to be increased. The first Five-Year Plan ushered in universal compulsory elementary education and by the end of 1932 will have abolished adult illiteracy almost entirely. The new Plan aims to extend adult education so that every citizen may acquire at least an elementary knowledge of the social sciences, physics, chemistry, biology and the technical processes of modern production. In this way it is planned to work toward one of the Soviet goals, that of bridging the gulf between physical and mental labor. In order to achieve these aims, a thorough technical reconstruction of industry, transportation and agriculture will be undertaken, involving the extensive use of the most modern machinery. It is planned to double or treble the output of the most important industries, such as the machine-building industry, the coal, iron and steel, and the non-ferrous metals industries. Power production will be expanded to a still greater extent. It is planned to build about 20,000 miles of new railways and to extend greatly water transportation; to increase rapidly the number of automobiles and the network of roads.[28]

These measures are to be taken in order to increase production and consumption, to improve living standards generally, and also as a step toward one of the basic goals of the Soviet system. The second Five-Year Plan, ·in the words of Premier Molotov, aims "to eliminate completely the causes giving rise to class distinctions ... to transform the whole working population into conscious active builders of a classless society."

The nature and achievements of the Soviet planning system have been outlined here in order to give the necessary background for understanding the conditions under which Soviet labor works and lives. The fulfillment of the Five-Year Plan has involved tremendous effort on the part of the workers, who have had to overcome many difficulties and mistakes. The energies of the country are now concentrated upon eliminating those defects which still exist. There continues to be, for instance, a shortage of consumers' goods, due to the necessity in the early stages of Soviet economy of stressing the development of the basic industries and to the rise in demand beyond the development of those branches of industry which produce consumers' goods. At the same time, the quality of manufactured products is still in many cases poor. The burden of backwardness in organization and inefficiency in industrial management which Soviet industry has inherited from the old régime, continues to be an obstacle requiring constant struggle and improvement. While labor discipline grows steadily better, enterprises still face the problem of eliminating its serious imperfections, such as the

[28] *Ibid.*, February 15, 1932, p. 76.

tendency of meetings and committees to interfere with centralized management. Another difficulty which still has to be
abolished is the bureaucratic habit of some executives to evade
direct responsibility by "passing the buck" to various committees or to other officials.

The Soviet authorities ascribe their principal difficulties
not to any inherent defects in the system, but to the lack of
skill and experience, to the low cultural and technical level
of the population inherited from the old régime and to the
fact that they are working along new and unprecedented lines.
It is characteristic of the Soviet system that strict account is
kept of all difficulties and errors. They are openly acknowl-
edged and discussed throughout the country in the press, in
workers' organizations and in political bodies. This nation-
wide system of "self-criticism" which subjects all shortcomings to the light of publicity and discussion, has been one of
the most important factors in helping to eliminate obstacles
to progress. The difficulties confronting Soviet industry, and
the various methods employed in overcoming them have been
described as follows by Mr. Walter Polakov, an American
factory-management engineer who has worked as a consultant
for Soviet enterprises: [29]

"One of the reasons for Russia's difficulties is that her
national plan is administered by a few thoroughly able men,
while the management of her various industries suffers from
a lack of equally competent executives.... The lack of discipline among workers and the avoidance of responsibility often
encountered among engineers diminish the efficiency of the
whole Soviet industrial system. Coupled with a lack of clearly
defined authority throughout the administrative scheme, it
makes quick action on vital policies rather difficult. To correct the situation, every effort is now being exerted to'
strengthen the régime of individual leadership with a strict
personal authority and responsibility. I found that usually the
best way to get results in inaugurating a new factory policy

[29] Walter Polakov, "How Efficient Are the Russians?" *Harper's Monthly
Magazine,* December, 1931, pp. 37-47.

was to take it to the workers themselves. The engineers often would refuse to take any initiative, knowing from experience that any decisions they made might be subject to a lengthy series of controversies among the men in the shop and at the headquarters.

"The lack of discipline which is so noticeable in Russian industry is not due ... to any lack of rules and regulations, or to their non-enforcement; it is an inner self-discipline that is wanting. The average Russian worker's background is agricultural. His habits of work, his attitude of mind have been shaped on the farm and inherited from generations of peasants. Thus he is accustomed to working hard in the summer when the crops must be cared for and of hibernating in the winter. He has no predisposition for the regularity of effort, for the sustained coöperative labor which is a part of an industrial system. Transplanted to a factory community, he must be stimulated by mass-meetings, by bands and speeches and by every device of propaganda. ... Following such a mass-meeting plant production usually shows a great increase. Everybody works with tremendous energy. But then inevitably comes the reaction.

"It is evident now why the lack of skilled workmen is often cited as one of Russia's most serious handicaps. But great as this obstacle is, and long as it may take to develop an industrial-minded army of workers from a predominantly agricultural population, it is not insurmountable. Russia is already aggressively, and with increasing success, finding a remedy for its skilled labor shortage through an intensive and unique system of workers' training."

One factor which aids in overcoming mistakes and difficulties is the ability of the Soviet system to concentrate at any given moment, under the guidance of a unified idea and a unified national will, all the combined resources of the state and of national economy on the most important economic problems. This is readily understood if we examine the relationship of the economic apparatus to the governmental and political structure of the Soviet Union.

The guiding principles of Soviet industry are laid down not by administrators or any purely economic body, but by the central political body of the Soviet Union, the Congress of Soviets. This body is composed of delegates from the local soviets of the cities and provinces which, in turn, are composed of delegates elected in factories, wards, districts and smaller towns. The Congress of Soviets, elected every two years, passes on reports and resolutions outlining the general policy of the country. These reports and resolutions are prepared by various government departments on the basis of general lines of policy outlined by the Council of People's Commissars, corresponding to the cabinet in France or England. The Council, in formulating policies, follows the general lines laid down by the Communist Party which are later elaborated by government departments and adopted or modified by the Congress of Soviets or the All-Union Central Executive Committee which it elects. In all these bodies the workers, through the factory committees, trade unions and local Soviets, play a dominating rôle. They also constitute the bulk of the Party membership which increased from 23,600 in 1917 to 2,457,324 in July 1931, of whom 65.6 per cent were workers, 24.8 per cent peasants, and 9.6 per cent intellectuals, office employees, et cetera. By the end of 1931, Walter Duranty, Moscow correspondent of the New York *Times*, reported that the Party membership had reached 2,750,000 with "a particularly noticeable adherence of 'shock brigade' workers and collectivized peasants." The Communist youth organization now has about 6,000,000 members and the Young Pioneers about 7,000,000, so that "the Soviet state begins the fifteenth year of its existence with the Communists numbering a full ten per cent of the total population, instead of being the 'infinitesimal tyrannical minority' upon which foreign critics laid so much stress in the earlier years." [30]

Party organization is founded on the principle of "democratic centralism." Its basic unit is the factory which consists of the Party members working in a particular factory or plant.

[30] New York *Times*, January 2, 1932.

In the rural regions there are village cells. Each cell sends delegates to city, district and provincial organizations of the Party. These, in turn, send delegates to the Party congress which represents the entire membership of the Party throughout the country and is assembled once every two years. The congress elects a central committee which holds office until the next congress. Prior to each congress the entire Party discusses current problems in local cells and organizations and in the press. Proposed policies for the coming year are outlined and discussed in detail. Statistical and other material is published and debated, and criticism is not only permitted but encouraged up to the time the congress makes its final decisions. Once these decisions are taken, however, Party members are obliged to carry them out. When the Party congress meets, the Central Committee of the Party lays proposals before it which are discussed and amended. The reports and decisions of the congress are published in the press, and discussed and explained in all Party organizations. They are also explained by Party members to non-Party workers and peasants at factory, village, trade union and coöperative meetings.

After the general line has been mapped out by the Party congress and the Congress of Soviets, the government departments, combines, trusts and factories work out the detailed application of these policies. It is then the task of the Party cells in the factories and villages to see that instructions are carried out. They must call attention to defects in production and administration, and make special effort to overcome difficulties. They attempt to accomplish this not by direct interference with the management but by working through the Party members who are in the factory management, the board of the trust or combine, the factory committees and the trade unions. Whenever necessary, the cell can appeal directly through the Party machinery to the higher economic and trade union instances. The Party cell, consisting primarily of workers in industry and agriculture, plays a leading rôle in increasing production, attaining higher labor productivity, improving labor discipline, and obtaining better labor conditions and wages. Among other tasks, it is the duty of the Party cell to counteract bureaucracy and to protect the interests of the workers against any infringement on the part of the administration. The dominating elements in the individual enterprise are the Party cell, the factory committee and the management. This combination is known as the "triangle of factory control."

The administrative structure of Soviet industry has remained, on the whole, as described in the previous chapter; but the expansion of national economy under the Five-Year Plan necessitated some changes which were embodied in a decree issued February 13, 1930. The decree reflected the experience of Soviet industry over a period of twelve years and was designed to fit the socialization and reorganization of economy which had taken place. National economy had traveled a long way since the introduction of NEP. The State and coöperative sections of industry had steadily absorbed what was left of private industry. Practically all of large-scale industry was operated directly by the state, while a number of medium sized enterprises were conducted by producers' coöperatives. By 1928-29 these socialized enterprises, both State and coöperative, produced 89.7 per cent of the total output of the country. By 1929-30 their share of the total output had risen to 94.5 per cent. To meet this situation, industry was reorganized under the decree of February 13 along two main lines: the further coördination and centralization of planning and technical supervision; and the further decentralization of executive functions. There was to be a greater degree of operating independence on the part of individual enterprises and the various departments of the enterprises. Soviet industry is at present organized on the basis of state planning and economic accounting (khozraschiot).

Each unit of the industrial structure is financially independent and individually responsible for its obligations. State planning, as we have seen, is centered in Gosplan. On the other hand, the organizational structure of industry is a series of links leading from the Commissariats in charge of industry to the factory department. All of these links, except the Commissariats, work on the system of "economic accounting." The result has been a division of jurisdiction among the various links in the chain. The rights and duties, the responsibility and authority of each economic unit are definitely fixed. Each unit has at its disposal specified cash funds; it receives and disposes of materials and money on the basis of a strict system of cost accounting. The economic units can receive credits only from the State Bank, which grants them credit facilities within certain definite limits. These are based on the achievements and scope of the enterprise. The system of "economic accounting" makes it possible to check up causes of failure and to make organizational changes when necessary.

The direction of state industry is now in the hands of four government departments. By a decree of January 5, 1932 the Supreme Economic Council was reorganized into a Commissariat for Heavy Industry. At the same time special commissariats were created for light industry and for the lumber and forestry industry.[31] A fourth government department—the Commissariat of Internal Supply—directs all state industries which supply the country with food, such as fishing, sugar, flour-milling, canning and so on.

The central bureaus of the Supreme Economic Council, which formerly supervised the work of various industries, and the syndicates which carried on marketing operations were abolished under the decree of February 13, 1930. The functions of both were concentrated in a system of "united industries" called combines. The combines are organized according to the various main branches of industry. Trusts and enterprises are grouped together according to these main branches and placed under the jurisdiction of a combine. The combines, after a while, became unwieldy, some including as many as 200 industries. On June 23, 1931, in a speech before the Conference of Industrial Managers, Stalin urged that this situation be remedied. On the basis of his recommendations, several of the bigger combines were broken up into smaller combines.

By 1931 each combine was carrying out the planned sched-

[31] *Economic Review*, February 1, 1932, p. 68.

ules of the Supreme Economic Council as a separate economic unit, operating on the basis of "economic accounting." The combine has two kinds of functions. Its administrative function is to regulate the work of the enterprises under its jurisdiction. This includes planning, the assignment of definite schedules of production and finance. It checks the execution of these programs and exercises technical supervision. Administrative functions cover production, new construction, the supplies of raw materials and equipment, marketing, financing, labor regulation, and the training and allocation of workers. In order to facilitate the supervision by combines of technical reconstruction and the training of skilled workers, many scientific and technical institutes and vocational colleges are being reorganized to specialize in definite fields under the jurisdiction of the corresponding combines. The executive functions of the combine are to supply raw materials, fuel, and equipment to the enterprises and trusts under its supervision. It markets their output, supervises their financing, and in some cases directly engages in production and new construction. Combines under the jurisdiction of the Commissariat of Internal Supply include state industries and producing, agricultural and consumers' coöperatives. Such coöperatives contribute to the basic capital of the combine to which they are subordinated.

The combines constitute the basis for the concentration of the technical and economic direction of industry. They do not, however, destroy the existing administrative division of industry into those which cover the entire country and those which cover the autonomous republics and various localities. Industrial enterprises which are republican or local in scope constitute part of an All-Union combine, but remain under the jurisdiction of republican or local economic organs and retain their connection with republican or local budgets. All-Union combines have direct supervision over republican and local enterprises only in executive and economic matters, such as marketing, supplies, technical direction, centralized accounting and financing. Planning is carried out by the economic bodies of the constituent republics and their local organs. As a result of this reorganization, the function of the trusts has changed. When trusts were first organized in 1923 their principal task was to put existing plants in running order, and to organize the marketing of commodities. The trust was then an all-inclusive central organization which directed the entire economic activity of enterprises in a given branch of industry. Later Soviet industry adopted a system of functional specialization. Syndicates were organized to handle the marketing of the industrial output, special organizations were established to control supplies and an industrial credit center was created. The work of the trusts, consequently, became limited to the organization of production and reconstruction and the fulfillment of planned schedules outlined by the Supreme Economic Council.

The Five-Year Plan caused a further transformation of the trust, which is now limited exclusively to production and reconstruction, more specifically, to the rationalization and reconstruction of enterprises subordinated to them. To facilitate this change, the trusts are grouped together according to the main branches of industry in combines which handle the commercial and financial functions formerly exercised by the trust. In some branches of industry, such as the metallurgical, automotive, tractor and electro-technical industries, where production is concentrated in a few large plants, the trusts have been entirely abolished. These enterprises are now part of various combines. In a few other branches of industry, where the producing plants are widely scattered, the trusts still retain their old functions of supply, marketing, and finance.

These aspects of Soviet industry have been mentioned in order to explain the worker's background, the nature of the employer with whom the individual worker and the trade union enter into labor agreements. For this purpose some idea is also necessary of the structure of the individual enterprise. Under the present system of industrial organization, factory management is based on the following principles: In accordance with the requirements of internal economic accounting, each individual enterprise must be self-sustaining within certain defined limits. Its management bears full responsibility for carrying out the schedules assigned to it by the organization of which it forms a part, such as a trust, combine, etc. Furthermore, in accordance with the principle of one-man administration applied in Soviet industry, almost since its inception, the manager of an enterprise, who is appointed by the combine or trust, directs its entire activity. He engages and discharges the members of the administrative and technical staff and bears full responsibility for its successful functioning. In carrying out these duties the manager coöperates with the workers who exercise a considerable degree of initiative. Formerly, the general practice had been for the manager to restrict himself solely to the general supervision of production, leaving technical direction in the hands of technicians and specialists. At present the manager assumes technical as well as general supervision.

The reorganization of industrial management has affected not only the individual enterprises but also its various subordinate departments. The latter are no longer merely mechanical subdivisions of the factory, but separate units, functioning on the basis of internal economic accounting within the limits of the planned schedule of the enterprise. The management of each department remains subordinate to the factory management but bears responsibility for its own work and directs its administrative, technical and economic operations. Its specific tasks are the organization and rationalization of production processes, the distribution of work and tools of production, the instruction of workers in new technical processes, and the fulfillment of the tasks set by the planning organs of the factory. The application of economic accounting, from the combine down to the factory department —and even to each work-bench in the department—tends to stimulate the workers to exert their best efforts to carry out the planned schedule and to apply new methods of shop management. Soviet industry is thus a dynamic system, in which supervision and planning are centralized and administration and responsibility decentralized.

CHAPTER IV

TRADE UNIONS

IN the Soviet industrial structure the worker occupies a unique position, both as an individual guarded by an elaborate system of labor law, and as a member of the trade unions which play an important part in the entire Soviet scheme of things. Under the Czarist régime, trade unions were entirely illegal up to 1905. Such workers' organizations as existed were seldom on a craft or industrial basis. They were chiefly mutual benefit, aid, benevolent, burial and sickness societies. With the development of industry and the growth of the working class the number of such societies increased in the 90's, particularly in Poland and the Baltic provinces. In the latter region there were 98 workmen's benefit societies and 113 burial societies in 1898. Such societies could be organized only with the permission of the Minister of Finance and the Minister of the Interior who strictly limited their forms and functions. They were, furthermore, under the close supervision of the police. Nevertheless, in the absence of other organizations, they became the center for workers dissatisfied with the conditions prevailing in industry.

The societies were channels through which the revolutionary political parties reached masses of workers. These activities, political and economic, were illegal, but the widespread discontent they revealed induced the government to form unions under police control for the purpose of diverting and dissipating this discontent. Such was the police union formed by Zubatov, chief of the Moscow secret police, in 1901. Barred by the law from establishing their own trade unions, the workers entered the police union in great numbers and through it initiated extensive strikes. As a result, the manufacturers persuaded the government to dismiss Zubatov and to curb the union's activities. It was at the head of a similar government-controlled union that the priest Gapon led the workers' procession on "Bloody Sunday," the prelude to the revolution of 1905.

That year was marked by the formation of Russia's first workers' trade unions. These organizations participated in the nation-wide strikes which accompanied the revolution and eventually compelled the Czar to issue the October manifesto establishing the Duma. The first trade union conference, in which 26 unions from Moscow and 10 unions from other cities were represented, met in 1905; a second trade union conference met the following year. It was estimated at that time that there were more than 200,000 organized workers in Russia. Subsequently the government repressed the revolution and exterminated all labor organizations. Trade unions were prohibited by law, their funds confiscated, and their leaders arrested, exiled or killed. During 1907 about 104 trade unions were destroyed. The workers thereupon formed underground unions which conducted their activities in spite of the law. In 1912-13 a series of strikes revived the trade union movement, but under the strain of the world war and government repression they once more practically disappeared.

Following the revolution of March 1917, trade unions entered a new era. The workers organized in large numbers immediately. On March 15 twenty-two trade union met in Moscow and founded a Council of Trade Unions. Similar councils were organized in Petrograd and other cities. These trade union councils played a leading rôle in the soviets and some unions played an important rôle in the revolution which established the Soviet state.

During the early days of the Soviet régime, the trade unions participated in carrying out the policy of having the factory committees control enterprises. Thus the first All-Russian Trade Union Congress, which met in Petrograd in January

1918, demanded the control and regulation of industry by the trade unions. It also urged "the closest coöperation and inseparable connection between the trade unions and the soviets of workers' delegates," and added that "in the process of development the trade unions will inevitably be converted into organs of socialized government, participation in which will be obligatory for all persons engaged in any given industry." Subsequently, in order to regulate the activities of the factory committees, these were merged with the trade unions, being made units of the trade union organization. At the same time trade union representatives sat in the Supreme Economic Council. The trade unions thus acted as a link between the state and the factory committees representing the workers in the individual enterprises.

At the Congress of Trade Unions which met April 20, 1918, the issue was raised of subordinating the trade unions to state control in industrial management. The government proposed the introduction of individual management and responsibility in industry. It also proposed the introduction of piece-rates, premiums, bonuses and scientific management in order to increase productivity. There were some delegates who opposed these measures on the ground that it would revive the relationship between employer and employee which prevails under capitalism, and would destroy the independence of the trade unions. Instead they proposed a system of "collective responsibility" to be shared jointly by the factory committee and the trade union for a minimum program of production to be determined by the Supreme Economic Council and representatives of the trade unions. The majority of the delegates, however, felt that there was a wide gulf between the measures proposed by the government under conditions of capitalism and under a workers' state. They maintained that these methods would not be used to extort larger profits from the workers for the benefit of stockholders; but would be used to increase production and strengthen the construction of socialist industry. The trade union congress approved the proposed methods in principle; but the intervention of civil war postponed their general application in industry until 1920.[1]

During War Communism, when everything was subordinated to military necessity, the influence of the trade unions over factory administration declined. In the early days of the revolution it was the trade unions or the local soviet authorities who took the initiative in controlling or nationalizing enterprises and appointing industrial administrators. The government merely gave formal approval to the acts of the trade unions. After the summer of 1918, however, the appointment of administrators was concentrated in the hands of the Supreme Economic Council. In practice the trade unions were consulted regarding policies and appointments; often they made their own proposals and nominations. But the tendency of the trade union leaders was to subordinate themselves to the requirements of the state at war. This was part of the general policy followed during War Communism of concentrating appointments and administration in the hands of central bodies to a very high degree.

The catastrophic decline in national economy as a result of the world war and the civil war was accompanied by a severe decrease in labor productivity. The government was faced with the problem of raising the level of labor productivity and effectively distributing the available resources of labor power. Some attempts were made to solve this problem by introducing military methods. Red Army units, released from military service by the termination of the civil war, were put to work on the "economic front." This measure resulted in some success in the gathering of wood fuel and the repair of railways; but it failed to solve the labor crisis caused by economic collapse and physical exhaustion. As a result of prevailing conditions, many workers absented themselves from the enterprises.

The introduction of NEP in 1921 effectively met this crisis by the reorganization of industry and the restoration of the market. The entire trade union machinery was reorganized.

[1] Dobb, *op. cit.*, pp. 55-56.

Beginning in February 1922, a campaign was inaugurated for placing trade union membership entirely on a voluntary basis. Trade unionists were given the freedom to decide whether or not they wished to remain members of the trade unions and to pay individual contributions. About 95 per cent of the members voted in favor of rejoining the trade unions on this new basis. Since then the rôle of the trade unions has been based on Lenin's policy that they are to be the connecting link between the state and the working rank and file and a gateway for workers to socialist ideas and principles, a school of communism. This policy was embodied in a number of resolutions adopted by the Communist Party at various times.

At the time of the inauguration of NEP other policies were proposed with regard to the functions of the trade unions which deviated from Lenin's conceptions, but these policies were rejected. Trotzky, for example, favored the use of the unions for furthering labor discipline and increasing labor productivity. He considered that the unions as they then existed were a hindrance to the development of national economy and wanted to convert them into organs of the state. They were to be quasi-military in form, and their main function was to be the maintenance of working discipline. On the other hand, Tomsky, secretary of the All-Union Council of Trade Unions, urged that the unions should have an existence entirely separate and independent from the structure of the state. They were to be a means of protecting the interests of the workers against the state as represented by the administrators of industry. This position, which Tomsky maintained from time to time, will be discussed later.* Trotzky's proposals were rejected as tending to militarize labor and to debase completely the very fundamental concept of the trade union. Tomsky's proposals were rejected on the ground that they failed to give due weight to the fact that the trade unions are an integral part of the Soviet system and of the ruling class of Soviet society. Accordingly, the general line adopted by the Party regarding trade unions was that they were not to become

* See pp. 126-7.

subordinate to the state apparatus, but were to have a large measure of independence. At the same time the interests of the workers are protected by their dominant rôle in the Party, the state apparatus, and the trade unions themselves as well as by an elaborate system of labor laws.

The fundamental law regarding trade unions is embodied in the Soviet Labor Code issued in 1922. According to this Code, trade unions are unions of producers in which citizens employed for remuneration in state, coöperative and private undertakings, institutions and businesses are organized. Such unions may appear before the various authorities in the name of the wage-earners whom they represent as parties to collective contracts, and may represent their members in all matters relating to work and conditions of life.[2]

The trade unions are organized in accordance with the principles drawn up by the competent congresses of these bodies. To facilitate their work the Code grants them special concessions. No clubs, societies, and organizations can have a legal existence in the Soviet Union until they register with the government; but trade unions are exempt from this regulation. Instead, a trade union obtains legal status by registering with the All-Union Council of Trade Unions. Thus a trade union comes into existence with the approval not of the government but of the national body of trade unions.[3] Trade unions are entitled to acquire and manage property, and to conclude contracts and agreements of all kinds under the legislation in force.[4] The Constitution of the Soviet Union provides that all government bodies must in every possible way assist the trade unions, particularly with regard to buildings, transportation, posts and telegraphs, and the like. This means lower rents, lower transportation rates and other concessions, all of which reduce the trade union's overhead costs.[5]

The Code provides that the principal body representing the trade union in all enterprises shall be a committee elected by the wage-earning and salaried employees, the so-called factory

[2] Labor Code, Paragraph 151.   [4] *Ibid.*, Paragraph 154.
[3] *Ibid.*, Paragraph 152.   [5] *Ibid.*, Paragraph 155.

committee. Where the enterprise is too small for a factory committee, there may be instead an authorized delegate of the trade unions. In each industry, the trade union determines the procedure by which such factory committees are elected. The Code charges the factory committees with the following duties:

"It shall safeguard the interests of the wage-earning and salaried employees which it represents in relation to the management of the undertaking, institution or business in respect to matters connected with the employment and conditions of life of employees. It shall represent the employees before the government and other public authorities. It shall see that the legislative provisions concerning the protection of workers, social insurance, the payment of wages, and the regulations for hygiene, and the prevention of accidents, et cetera, are faithfully carried out by the management of the undertaking, institution or business, and shall coöperate with the state authorities concerned with the protection of the workers. It shall take steps to improve the social and material situation of wage-earning and salaried employees. It shall coöperate in the regular carrying on of production in state undertakings, and participate in the regulation and organization of economic activities through the competent trade unions." [6]

The Code makes special provisions for facilitating the work of the factory committee and protects its members in their relations with the management. The factory committee has certain members chosen by the committee itself who devote their full time to carrying out the committee's functions. Their regular wages are paid to them by the factory while they are engaged in this service. In enterprises employing not more than 300 workers, only one member of the factory committee may be released for this service; in enterprises employing between 300 and 1,000, two members may be released; between 1,000 and 5,000, three members; and over 5,000, five members. In no case can the wages paid to a member of a factory committee released for this service be less than the scheduled rate

6 *Ibid.*, Paragraphs 156-158.

of pay in his former occupation. To protect them against managers who disapprove of their activities, such members of a factory commitee are ensured by the Code of further employment on the expiration of their term of office. They return to work on the basis of the labor contract in force immediately before their election to the factory committee and such changes as may have been made in the contract during their service on the committee. The management of a factory, plant, or office cannot discharge a member of the committee. A committee member may be discharged for the infraction of factory rules or discipline only by agreement with the trade union.[7]

According to the Code, managers are not permitted to hinder the activities of the factory or office committees or the trade union meetings which elect them. General meetings of the trade union or meetings of delegates are held as a rule outside working hours.[8]

The management must report to the committee regarding new employees which it plans to engage as well as those whom it has already engaged for work. If the union believes that in hiring new employees the management has violated the labor laws or the collective agreement, the factory or office committee may raise objection within three days after being notified of the disputed engagement. If the employer disagrees with the committee's objection, the committee has the right, no later than three days after the objection is raised, to refer the dispute to the local department of the Commissariat of Labor. In places where there is no local labor department, such disputes may be referred to the local labor inspector. The labor department or inspector must decide the dispute within

[7] *Ibid.*, Paragraphs 159-160.

[8] Under ordinary conditions certain kinds of meetings may be held during working hours; but because of the existing labor ьhortage, a decree issued March 25, 1931, prohibits workers from engaging in organizational activities during working hours. Trade unions, coöperatives and Party units must hold their meetings after working hours. A decree issued October 20, 1930, prohibits for a period of two years the assignment to organizational work of employees in industry or transportation. See *Economic Review*, June 1, 1931, p. 260.

three days after the submission of the employer's statement. Such decisions are final unless revised on appeal by higher labor organs. If it is necessary to reduce the number of employees in any enterprise, the management must submit to the factory or office committee a list of those to be dropped at least two weeks before dismissal.[9]

The expenses of the factory or office committee must be paid by the management of the enterprise on the basis of an estimate approved by the trade union concerned. It must not, however, exceed two per cent of the total wage-fund of the employees in the enterprise. The trade union sees to it that such expenses are paid at the proper time and may supervise the committee's accounts.[10] The management must grant the factory or office committee the use of a room or office free of charge, with the necessary equipment both for the business of the committee itself and for delegate and general meetings. Access to this room must be free to all persons who have business with the committee.[11]

These provisions of the Labor Code not only give the factory committee legal sanction as the basic unit of the trade union and the enterprise, but grant it extensive powers in safeguarding the interests of the workers. The Code goes even further in strengthening the rôle of the trade union in factory administration. It provides that representatives of the trade unions shall have the unrestricted right to enter all workshops, departments, and laboratories of an enterprise.[12] Any violation of the Labor Code's provisions regarding trade unions and factory or office committees is a criminal offense punishable under the penal code.[18]

One of the most important functions of the trade union is to draw up and enter into collective agreements with the management of enterprises and to see to it that these agreements are carried out. The collective agreements cover such

[9] Labor Code, Paragraph 161.
[10] *Ibid.*, Paragraphs 162-164.
[11] *Ibid.*, Paragraph 165.
[12] *Ibid.*, Paragraph 166.
[18] *Ibid.*, Paragraph 167; see also section 134 Penal Code.

matters as wages, hours, working conditions, relations between
the management and the factory committee, and so on. The
conditions set forth in the collective agreements may not be
less favorable than those provided in the Labor Code. A more
extended description of collective agreements is given in the
next chapter.

All Soviet trade unions are organized along industrial lines.
There are no craft unions, this type of union being unsuited
to a planned and coördinated national economy conducted
along socialist lines. There are, however, special craft or departmental groups in some of the unions, associated chiefly
for scientific purposes, such as the engineering and technical
sections of most national unions. Until recently there were
twenty-three national trade unions covering the whole of
Soviet economy. In 1931 this number was increased to 44 following a general reorganization by the All-Union Council of
Trade Unions. A number of large unions, some of which had
more than 1,000,000 members, were broken up into smaller
units corresponding to the different branches of each industry.
The Metal Workers' Union, for instance, which formerly had
1,200,000 workers, has been subdivided into seven independent
unions, for the metallurgical, transport and machine-building,
agricultural machinery, electro-technical and power, automotive (automobile, tractor and aviation), general machine construction, and non-ferrous metal manufacturing industries.
Similarly, the miners' union has been divided into four independent unions for the mining of ores, coal, oil, and peat. The
Agricultural Workers' Union has also been broken up into
four independent unions to cover respectively the state grain
farms, the state stock farms, the machine and tractor stations,
and agricultural and sugar laborers. The former unwieldy
unions for workers in the chemical, textile, construction,
municipal and commercial enterprises have all been reorganized into three separate unions apiece.

This reorganization in no way abandoned the basic principle of industrial unionism. The change into smaller units
was necessitated by the rapid expansion of national economy

under the Five-Year Plan. The success of the Plan resulted in the abolition of unemployment and the addition to industry of 2,000,000 new industrial workers, of whom 800,000 were women. It became necessary to effect a further reorganization of the trade unions as mass organizations of the workers; and to increase their participation in the management of industry, especially in regard to concrete problems and new methods of production. It was also necessary to expand their material and cultural services to the mass of workers. The existing unwieldy trade unions were unable to meet adequately the tasks of industry, which had already been reorganized in 1929 because of the expansion of national economy. The Metal Workers' Union, for instance, with 1,200,000 members had to deal with 28 combines and analyze 28 reports on control figures; the Food Workers' Union with 30 combines. This made it difficult to handle the problems which arose in connection with the daily work of the industries. Consequently, the unions were reorganized to correspond to the changed structure of industry. Under the new system each union has production sections corresponding to the branches of the industry concerned, and production councils for the separate trades. The formation of smaller and more mobile trade union units allows for a greater integration of production and for closer contact with the masses of workers.[14]

All persons working for a wage or salary are entitled to join a trade union. Workers are free to join or not to join a union, and to leave it any time they wish. Persons working for themselves in small production, professional men who practice for themselves without occupying state positions, and others who do not work for a wage or salary cannot join a trade union. However, doctors, dentists and hygiene specialists who work for the state are entitled to membership in the Medical-Sanitary Workers' Union. Similarly, other professional groups, such as teachers, writers, scientists, actors, musicians, etc., are organized in unions. Trade unions are closed to disfranchised

[14] N. M. Shvernik, *Further Improvement in the Work of the Trade Unions*, Moscow, 1931 [Russian]; see also Soviet Union Review, Vol IX, No. 6, 1931.

citizens—such as priests and former agents of the Czarist police—as well as to minors under 16. Apart from such exceptions, any manual, clerical or intellectual worker may join a union irrespective of race, sex, nationality, age, color or political views. There is, however, no "closed shop." Not only do workers join unions voluntarily, but no worker may be excluded from employment anywhere because he is not a member of a trade union. Prior to the disappearance of unemployment under the Five-Year Plan, there existed "preferential shops," in which under collective agreements with the trade unions the management agreed to hire union members first if they could be secured. A trade union may expel a member if he is convicted of violating the criminal code, if his dues are three months in arrears without valid cause, or if he loses his ability to work.

The growth of Soviet economy has been accompanied by a rapid expansion in the number of wage and salary earners, which rose from about 6,500,000 in 1922-23 to 18,700,000 in 1931. Trade union membership rose from 6,700,000 in 1922 to over 16,000,000 in 1931. These members participate actively in trade union affairs through the factory or office committee. The union member pays dues, amounting to two per cent of his earnings, to a voluntary collector approved by the factory committee, which turns over the dues to the next higher union body. The factory or office committee itself is supported by the management of the enterprise, receiving a specified percentage of the payroll. The provincial or regional union organization which receives the dues from the factory committee uses these funds for the work of its various departments engaged in cultural, economic and organizational activities and the protection of labor. Reserves are set aside for cultural work and for aid to needy members. The provincial unit pays to the central administration of the union of which it is a part from 5 to 25 per cent of its income, while 10 per cent of its income goes to various inter-union organizations. The amount of income spent on administration is comparatively slight. Union officials receive salaries which are usually about the same as those of skilled workers, and those who are Party members are limited as a rule to 300 rubles a month. It has been estimated that the provincial bodies spend 50 to 75 per cent of their funds for work among the mass of workers. The central bodies, which are supported by the provincial units, must in turn pay from 10 to 15 per cent of their income to the Central Council of Trade Unions, the highest trade union body in the country. They also set aside funds for cultural work, aid for the unemployed, the training of apprentices and technicians, medical work, rest homes and sanatoria for their members. Small strike funds are also concentrated in their hands, since the law does not restrict the right of workers to strike.

Regarding the finances of Soviet trade unions, an American trade union delegation which visited Russia in 1927 under the chairmanship of James H. Maurer, President of the Pennsylvania State Federation of Labor, and including among its personnel Stuart Chase, Prof. Paul Douglas, Prof. R. G. Tugwell, etc., reported as follows:

"The aim of the unions is summed up in popular posters issued by some of the industrial unions reading: 'less for the union apparatus; more for the service of the union members.' In this connection it may also be noted that the salaries of the highest trade union officials in the areas like Moscow, where the cost of living is highest, is a little over $112 a month. Provincial and lower officials receive less. There seems to be no tendency to develop high paid officials, receiving substantially more than the skilled workers whom they represent."

The trade union is in direct contact with the worker at the bench or desk through the factory or office committee. Members of factory committees hold office for one year. Their work may be reviewed and a new election held at the end of six months if the workers in the enterprise demand it. In most unions, the factory or office committee or individual members of it may be recalled at any time and a new election held on the request of one-third of the trade union members in the enterprise. The factory committee has sub-committees in charge of the protection of labor, cultural work, standardization disputes, and production. A member of the committee usually heads each sub-committee. The other members of the sub-committees are appointed either from the factory committee or are chosen from among the other workers in the enterprises.

The sub-committee for the protection of labor carries on all the work connected with the protection of the workers against industrial accident and ill-health. It sees to it that laws relating to sanitation and the guarding of machines are strictly carried out by the management. It directs the sending of sick or disabled workers to hospitals, rest-homes or sanatoria. It establishes and maintains communal baths, laundries and restaurants, and supervises children's institutions maintained in connection with the factory. It also concerns itself with the establishment and maintenance of coöperative and workers' apartment houses.

The cultural sub-committee carries on a wide variety of activities intended to raise the cultural level of the workers. It helps to improve their skill and to enrich their cultural lives during work and leisure. For this purpose it organizes classes, circles, lectures, concerts, theatrical performances, movies, libraries, schools, clubs, communal dances, sports, physical culture, hikes, excursions, choruses, reading rooms, etc. It takes charge of the expenditure of the money paid by the industry to the trade union for cultural purposes under the collective agreement. The technical staff which accompanied the first American trade union delegation to the U.S.S.R. has described the cultural activities of the Soviet trade unions as follows:

"Lying somewhat outside the system of education, but nevertheless functioning as important educational institutions are the labor unions. These powerful organizations are brought into closest touch with the work of education. Not only do they exert influence in the determination of the policies and programs of schools, particularly the factory schools and schools for workers, but they assume direct responsibility for the promotion of certain types of education among their own membership. Each of the unions is expected to devote a certain portion of its income to the promotion of cultural activities, and each of them has its special educational and cultural section. Many of the clubs for young people are founded, supported and controlled by these unions. They organize the cultural life of the workers in the factories and shops, as well as in the workers' rest homes during vacation periods. They also promote plays, excursions to museums and many other types of interest which might be classified as educational. Thus the union is a cultural agency as well as an agency of industry." [15]

The trade union plays an important rôle in determining wage-rates. The valuation-conflict committee which exists in every enterprise is usually represented on the workers' side by two or three of the most intelligent workers in the factory. It bears the burden of responsibility of settling both individual and collective disputes between employees and the management and of settling wage-rates for piece work. The basic wage-rates are laid down in the collective agreement entered into between the union and the management of the trust.

Production committees are now at work in almost all Soviet enterprises. Such committees are composed of representatives of the factory committee and representatives of the management and technical personnel. Through these committees the workers participate in the supervision of production. Its members, representing all the groups working in the enterprise, take up and attempt to solve current problems in production, including labor productivity, conveyor systems, mechanical operations, specialization, standardization and rationalization of processes. The fact that these committees consist of representatives of the management and technical personnel as well as the workers has enabled them to assist in eliminating the

---

[15] *Soviet Russia in the Second Decade,* A Joint Survey by the Technical Staff of the First American Trade Union Delegation. Edited by Stuart Chase, Robert Dunn, and Rexford Guy Tugwell. John Day Company, New York, 1928, p. 284.

conflicts which formerly existed among the three factors of the enterprise. The production committees have increased individual and collective production, facilitated workers' inventions and suggestions, helped in the rationalization of industry and the organization of work on the basis of scientific methods. These committees, however, do not relieve the management of sole responsibility for the operation of the enterprise. They can act only in an advisory and not in an executive capacity.

The factory committee, as the basic unit of the trade union, plays an important rôle in the control and supervision of production through the production conferences which are held in every enterprise periodically. It is the duty of the factory committee to keep the workers informed regarding the economic situation of the enterprise. It reports on this subject to the general or shop meetings of the workers and to the production conferences. The committee seeks to draw the workers into participation in the management of the enterprise by keeping them informed about the operations and plans of the enterprise as a whole. It stimulates the workers to offer suggestions and proposals on the organization of the work, methods of production, and other matters relating to production. For this purpose the enterprises have so-called "suggestion bureaus" for the consideration of workers' suggestions of new working methods, better departmental organization and so on. In a large enterprise this is usually a permanent department of the factory committee. Such a department receives suggestions from the workers and passes them on to the management. There are also special commissions nominated by the factory committee which investigates particular problems. Another link in this system of workers' participation in the control of production is the conference of workers from several factories in the same industry or in the same area which meets to discuss questions of general interest to the workers and enterprises involved.

The production conferences are not limited to a few workers, but are meetings of all the workers in an enterprise or in a department of a large enterprise. The manager of the enterprise is obliged to attend the production conference and to report on its activities to the workers. At the same time, the factory committee submits a report and indicates its attitude toward the important issues contained in the manager's report. In large enterprises it is customary for the production conference to appoint a special commission composed of members of the factory committee and other workers to make a detailed investigation of all the problems raised. They see to it that the management considers the suggestions brought up by the workers at the production conference. This prevents the conference from becoming a mere formality. However, the production conference has no administrative powers. The management is not formally bound by the resolutions and proposals adopted by the conference. Nevertheless, no manager can afford to ignore such proposals. If he considers them impracticable he must so report to the special commission or the next production conference, giving his reasons.[16]

While the factory committee is subordinate to the trade union of which it is a constituent part, within its own sphere of activity—the individual enterprise—it is the autonomous agent of the workers. It defends their rights and represents their daily interests. It is through the trade union and the factory committee that the workers make their views effective. Moreover, the workers are directly represented in the management of the enterprise by the chairman of the production conference who ex-officio becomes an associate director of the plant. This co-director represents the views of the workers directly in the management, supervises the applications of workers' inventions and suggestions, and plays a leading rôle in the organization of "socialist competition" and "shock brigades."

Such is the machinery by which the basic trade union unit maintains contact with the management. Its contact with the worker at the bench is maintained through the system of factory delegates. Every enterprise employing more than 200 workers has factory delegates. These are chosen every six

[16] Burns, *op. cit.*, pp. 107-108.

months by the workers, one delegate to every 10 workers. The
delegates keep the rank and file in close touch with the
factory committee. Each delegate makes formal written reports to the workers whom he represents regarding the activities of the factory committee, and the enterprise in general.
Twice a month these workers' delegates meet to discuss general problems. The main function of the delegate is to speak
for the group of workers he represents, and to make the
influence of his group felt in the factory committee. Con-
versely, he interprets the acts and decisions of the committee
to the rank and file of his group.

The backbone of the trade union is the so-called "activist,"
i.e., the active worker who holds some position of responsibility or performs some union function no matter how modest
in the trade union system. "Activists" are not hired employees
or officials of the trade union. They are workers at the bench
who do full time work at their regular job in the plant or
factory and give their spare hours to union activity. A large
percentage of trade union members are "activists" who are
members of factory committees or sub-committees, dues col-
lectors, delegates, etc. The existence of large numbers of
"activists" illustrates the extent to which real industrial democracy permeates both the trade union system and Soviet
industry.

Starting with the factory committee as the atomic unit, the
trade union system proceeds through to the district (county)
congress of the trade union in a given industry, its regional
(provincial) congress, and finally the federal congress of the
industrial union. Each factory at its general meeting of workers elects delegates to a district conference of the union,
which in turn elects the district administration of the union.
The regional administrations are organized at annual congresses by delegates elected directly by the general meetings
of the workers in the enterprise. These congresses elect delegates to the biennial congress of the federal industrial union
which chooses a central committee to act as the supreme
authority between congressional sessions. A full meeting of the

central committee elects a presidium, a group of officers which directs the work of the national union between sessions of the central committee.

The regional departments of the industrial union not only receive dues from the factory committees, but direct all the work of the district trade union subordinate to it, as well as the work of the factory committees which are constituent parts of it. The regional department and central committee of the union have the right to change or annul the work of their subordinate organs if these run counter to the federal union's general policy as laid down by the congress. Only the central committee can expel or discipline regional or other subordinate unions, a power which is seldom exercised. However, the power of the federal central committee is limited; it cannot simply discharge local administrative officials and appoint its own candidates. To fill vacancies which arise in this manner, it is obliged to call a new congress of delegates, elected directly by the workers in the enterprise, which selects new officials.[17]

The regional trade union offices create their own cultural, wage, economic and organizational departments. They also set up special unemployment and information bureaus, and bureaus for the distribution of books, statistics, legal aid and technical advice. The federal unions have analogous departments which operate for the Soviet Union as a whole. All the federal unions have their headquarters in the Palace of Labor in Moscow along with the offices of the All-Union Central Council of Trade Unions, the highest organ of the trade unions. This body is elected by the All-Union Congress of Trade Unions which meets every two years to decide general policy. The All-Union Central Council of Trade Unions consists of 170 members who choose a presidium to carry on work between sessions of the Council. The Council coördinates and directs in a general way the work of the 44 industrial unions throughout the country. It represents the joint interests of the unions on various government and economic bodies. The All-Union Con-

[17] *Russia After Ten Years,* Report of the American Trade Union Delegation to the Soviet Union, New York, 1928, pp. 17-28.

gress of Trade Unions, which chooses the Council, consists of
delegates elected by the provincial congresses of the various
industrial unions. The provincial trade union is entitled to one
delegate for each 10,000 members. This trade union system is
based on a principle which the Russians call "democratic centralism."

The trade unions have a decisive voice in many branches of
the government. The All-Union Congress of Trade Unions, for
example, has the privilege of selecting the People's Commissar
of Labor at its biennial meeting. The decision of this congress
is obligatory on the government.[18] The Commissar of Labor
reports regularly to the All-Union Congress of Trade Unions,
which discusses his report in detail. In similar fashion, the
trade union councils of the various republics select the labor
commissar for their area at their respective congresses. All
lower officials of the labor commissariat are likewise selected
by the corresponding subordinate trade union body. The local
trade union council selects the labor inspectors who must be
trade union members, and the sanitary and technical inspectors employed by the Commissariat of Labor. These inspectors
work in close coöperation with the trade unions and report to
their congresses. The unions are well represented in the social
insurance departments throughout the country. All labor legislation, including all laws which affect labor in any way, is
drawn up in consultation with the trade unions.

Although the law does not require it, the influence of the
unions is so great that an "unwritten law" obliges all government bodies to consult with the unions before passing any labor
law. Similarly, any revision of the Labor Code requires the
participation of the trade unions. Special commissions formed
for the purpose of drafting labor legislation contain a majority
of trade unionists. If the Council of People's Commissars
should issue a labor law which the trade unions considered unfavorable to the workers, the unions could urge its revision or
repeal through the Central Executive Committee of the Soviet

[18] Robert W. Dunn, *Soviet Trade Unions*, Vanguard Press, New York,
1928, p. 121.

Union or through its presidium, in both of which the trade unions are well represented.

Of the nine members of the Council of Labor and Defense, two must be representatives of the Central Council of Trade Unions. The various commissariats which have supervision over industry include representatives of the trade unions; as do also all regional and local economic bodies. The State Planning Commission (Gosplan) consults trade union representatives on all matters affecting their interests. A representative of the All-Union Council of Trade Unions sits in at meetings of the Gosplan presidium; and trade union representatives work in all Gosplan departments. There are trade union representatives in the following state and economic organs:

The Committee on Transport, the Committee on Standardization and other committees under the Council of Labor and Defense; the Industrial Plan Bureau of the Soviet Union; the Chief Economic Department of the Supreme Economic Council; the Budget Department of the Soviet Union; the Insurance Council; the Committee for Fixing Personal Pensions; the Insurance Conflict Committee; the Committee on Fixing Compensation for Dangerous Work; the Committee for Fixing the Personal Pensions for Scientists; the Budget Committee of the Commissariat of Agriculture; the Workers' and Peasants' Inspection; the Committee for the Struggle Against Accidents; the Auditing Committee of the Coöperatives; the Central Workers' Section of the Coöperatives; the All-Union Coöperative Bank; the Central Municipal Bank; the Council of Housing Coöperatives; the Committee for Lowering Retail Prices; the Council on Technical Standardization; and numerous other public bodies. The trade unions are also represented in the Commissariat of Health and the Commissariat of Education.[19]

The main strength of the trade unions lies in the cities. In the early stages of the Soviet régime, various industrial unions

[19] *Ibid.*, pp. 123-125. Since this list was compiled there have been certain changes; some committees have been abolished, others created, etc. However, in general, it may be said that the trade unions are represented in virtually all state and economic organs.

and workers in particular enterprises "adopted" villages, thus strengthening the link or *smytchka* between the workers and the peasants. The introduction of the New Economic Policy was followed by an increase in the number of wage-workers in the villages. Toward the end of 1923 the trade unions in industries which employ a considerable number of wage-earners in the villages began to organize a large number of village workers into trade unions. The Agricultural Workers' Union is now one of the largest in the Soviet Union, having a membership of nearly 2,000,000 in 1930.[20] Of these more than 400,000 were employed on the state farms. The industrial unions assist and coöperate with the Agricultural Workers' Union. The trade unions of educational workers, employees in coöperatives and state institutions, medical workers and others, participate actively in building up collective and state farms and raising the cultural level of the farm workers. The Agricultural Workers' Union itself conducts during the five winter months courses in agriculture, forestry, politics and economics for farm workers. One of its most important cultural functions is the abolition of illiteracy among village laborers.

At the same time the industrial trade unions have taken an active part in the socialist reconstruction of agriculture. In 1930 more than 25,000 of the best trade union workers, the pick of the working class, were sent to help organize collective farms. All of these had worked ten years or more in industry; in 1931 over 70 per cent of them were still working as organizers on collective farms. The trade unions are training many more such workers for administrative work on collective farms, so that their organizational experience may be at the service of peasants inexperienced in organization. In many cases "shock brigades" of workers go to villages to help in the sowing, harvesting and grain procurement campaigns, and in the repairing of implements. In 1930 a total of 75,000 industrial workers participated in such agricultural campaigns. The trade unions also help to attract workers who are still con-

[20] Shvernik, *Trade Union Problems in the Reconstruction Period* (Russian), p. 35.

nected with the village into the collective farm movement.[21]
The alliance of the workers and peasants is further cemented
by the patronage system whereby a trade union becomes the
"patron" of various regions producing the agricultural raw
material required by the industry in which the union is concerned. Workers of a textile factory, for example, may assume
the "patronage" over a cotton region, sending their best workers to help organize the sowing and harvesting campaigns. This
serves also as an additional assurance to the factory of an
adequate supply of the necessary raw materials.

The trade unions also work very closely with the coöperatives, fostering all kinds of coöperative activities and playing
a leading rôle in the organization of coöperative dining rooms.
They also stimulate coöperative activity by investing funds in
coöperative banks. The boards of these banks include representatives of the trade unions, as do also the boards of other
coöperative enterprises.[22] The trade unions not only assist the
coöperatives, but check up on their activities for the purpose
of safeguarding the workers' interests. Thus in 1930, about
50,000 rank and file trade unionists investigated the work of
the coöperative warehouses and retail stores. Wherever they
discovered that the coöperatives were not keeping up with the
growing demands of the workers, steps were taken to remedy
the defects.

The activities of the trade unions embrace so many phases
of life, that trade union membership brings with it many advantages. Union members pay less for all sorts of services.
There are from 25 to 60 per cent reductions in payments for
public bath houses, moving pictures, theaters, railway and
steamship excursions, museums, radio, sports, etc. The trade
union book is a kind of passport which gives the bearer either
free entrance or reduced prices to many kinds of activities.
Members of trade unions have better chances of getting to
rest homes or health resorts. Union members receive strike
benefits in case of strikes, and are given credit at consumers'
coöperatives. There are also reductions in certain taxes for

[21] *Ibid.,* pp. 33-34.   [22] Dunn, *op cit.,* pp. 132-133.

union members. Clubs conducted by trade unions provide the members with libraries, moving pictures, radio, study courses, theatrical entertainment, and general social fellowship. Members also receive free legal advice from the union's legal staff concerning wages, property, working rights and various personal problems.[23] About 90 per cent of all wage-earners are members of trade unions; but non-union members are equally entitled to the rights and privileges guaranteed to labor under Soviet law and no discrimination can be made in this respect.

The problems of Soviet trade unions are different in principle from the problems of trade unions in other countries. Indeed, the fundamental Soviet conception of what a trade union is and what it should do is so radically different from anything prevailing in capitalist society, that new standards of evaluation are required for gauging the work of the Soviet labor organizations. These organizations have two main tasks: first, to intensify the active participation of the workers in the process of production, and in the solution of economic problems, and to educate the mass of wage-earners to become leaders of national economy; and, second, to defend the workers' interests against possible bureaucratic misconstruction of policies.

The Soviet authorities emphasize the productive functions of the trade unions, without diminishing the importance of their rôle in protecting the workers' interests. Production and protection, they hold, cannot be disassociated. In planned socialist economy, where the workers are the collective owners of industry, their welfare depends upon the growth and prosperity of the enterprise; accordingly, the two main functions of the trade unions must be integrated into a unified activity which simultaneously strives for increased production and increased welfare.

This policy is based on Lenin's concept of the trade union as an integral part of a coördinated socialist society. "With the great revolution which occurs in history when the proletariat takes over the state power," he said on one occasion, "the

23 *Ibid.*, pp. 8-9.

trade unions experience the most profound change in their activities. They become major creators of the new society, because only the broad masses, the millions, can become the creators of this society." On another occasion Lenin urged that "the trade unions must constantly widen the ranks of the builders of socialism ... the tasks of the trade unions are to be the builders of a new life, to be the educators of new millions and tens of millions who will learn by experience not to make mistakes, to discard old prejudices, and to learn by experience to administer the state and industry. Only in this is there an unmistakable guarantee that the cause of socialism will be completely victorious, that there will be no possibility of a return to the past." Lenin also urged that "the trade unions must become the closest and the indispensable collaborators of the state, at the head of which is the Communist Party which guides the entire political and economic work of the conscious vanguard of the working class. Being a school for communism in general, the trade unions must become in particular a school for managing socialist industry and gradually also of agriculture."

In general trade union policy has been based on Lenin's theories. For a short period, however, certain trade union leaders headed by Tomsky tended to stress the worker's position as a seller of labor power rather than as an active leader in the organization of production. As a result of this "defensive" orientation, there developed elements of craft unionism and of departmental narrowness in the leadership of the Soviet trade unions. The inauguration of the Five-Year Plan for the expansion of national economy on a firm socialist basis called particularly for a change of emphasis in the functions of the trade unions and the exclusion of every trace of craft narrowness from their ideology. Accordingly, the Central Council of Trade Unions issued in the fall of 1929 such slogans as "face the factory" and "face production." The new line was amplified at the sixteenth congress of the Communist Party, held in June, 1930, which condemned the narrow trade union policy advocated by Tomsky, who had urged that the sole task of the trade unions is merely to defend the interests of the workers against the management. Rejecting this viewpoint as harmful, the Congress declared that the basic task of the trade unions during the present period of economic expansion is to lead and develop the movement of the workers in the socialist reconstruction of industry and agriculture. The trade unions, the Congress decided, must continue to take the lead in the movement of "socialist competition" and the "shock brigades." They must place "socialist competition" on a higher plane based upon the experience of the participants in the movement. As the leading mass organizations of the proletariat, the trade unions must mobilize tens of millions of workers for the construction of the new socialist society. By such decisions the Party, the government, and the trade unions themselves confirmed Lenin's concept that the rôle of the trade unions is much wider than that of defending the workers' interests in the narrowest sense of the term. They emphasized the idea that in their very essence these interests require the trade unions to be active leaders in the socialist organization and management of industry by the workers since the immediate needs of the workers and their interests as the collective owners of industry are mutually dependent parts of an integrated whole.

In order for the workers to carry out so great a task, a profound change was necessary in their concepts and habits, particularly in regard to labor discipline. Here again it was Lenin who clarified the essential problem involved. Commenting during the period of militant communism on the work of volunteer groups known as "subbotniki" (those who did extra unpaid labor during free hours and holidays), he said: "This is the beginning of a revolution which is more difficult, more essential, more radical and more decisive than the overthrow of the bourgeoisie, because this will mean a victory over our own mediocrity, lack of discipline, petit-bourgeois egoism, over those habits which accursed capitalism has left as a heritage to the worker and the peasant. When this victory will be fortified, then, and only then, will a new social discipline, socialist discipline, be created. Then and only then will a return to capitalism become impossible and communism will become really invincible."

The trade unions, comprising nearly all the workers in the Soviet Union, were bound to take the leading rôle in developing new forms of labor discipline. This became all the more necessary with the inauguration of the Five-Year Plan, involving a tremendous program of construction in all branches of national economy. It was necessary to improve the organization of labor processes in industry, to increase the rate of progress, and to raise labor productivity. Here the workers in the trade unions took the initiative. They developed new forms of organization and new methods of work based on Lenin's concept of competition in socialist economy. "Socialism," Lenin said, "not only does not extinguish competition, but, on the contrary, for the first time creates the possibility of applying competition actually on a wide mass scale, actually drawing most of the toilers into the arena of such work, where their individuality can unfold, where they can develop their abilities, discover their talents, of which there is an inexhaustible reservoir among the people, and which capitalism crushes, suppresses and annihilates. Our task at present, when the socialist government is in power, is to *organize* competition."

This was the general concept behind the various forms of voluntary activity organized by the workers themselves at the outset of the Five-Year Plan. A basic labor method in Soviet economy is now "socialist competition" which involves a contest between groups of workers in an enterprise, or departments in an enterprise, or between factories or groups of factories within an industry, or between two industries, or between "shock brigades." The object of this contest is to see which group can raise most the quantity and quality of production, the standard of measurement being the schedule set by the industrial-financial plan. Under the system of "socialist competition" the various units involved voluntarily oblige themselves to increase labor productivity, lower the number of absences from work, fulfill and exceed the plan for the factory, improve living conditions, raise cultural standards, etc. Similarly, "shock brigades" are voluntary groups of workers who undertake to increase production in their enterprise, improve the quality of their products, lower the costs of production, eliminate waste and inefficiency, and in other ways improve the standards and results of their work. Every member of the shock brigade takes upon himself a number of obligations in regard to these matters. At first, the "shock" method of work was confined to individual workers, but later it became apparent that the successful accomplishment of any one worker depends upon other workers in the same enterprise. Accordingly, "shock brigades," "shock departments" and even "shock enterprises" were organized. By the end of 1931 there were 200,000 "shock brigades" throughout the country with a membership of 3,500,000. The rapid growth of this movement may be gauged from the fact that on January 1, 1930 about 29 per cent of all industrial workers belonged to shock brigades and by January 1, 1932 the percentage had risen to 64.2.

In the past few years various forms of the shock brigade have been developed. Thus, the workers and technicians of a successful enterprise or department may form a shock brigade to aid an enterprise or department whose work is not going so well. This is known as "towing in" a backward enterprise. Another form of voluntary organization is the so-called "through brigade," first started in the Rostov agricultural machinery plant, Selmashstroy, in 1930. This factory received an order on short notice to produce a Soviet planter to be attached to the first Soviet tractor. Thereupon all the departments of the factory were organized into one through brigade which took in the entire process. The brigade knew all the weak spots of every department and took the steps necessary to eliminate these weaknesses. It so organized the work that the planter was turned out on time. The through brigade, comprising all the departments of an enterprise which are engaged in the production of a given commodity, has now become widespread through Soviet industry.

In 1931 the workers in the Leningrad machine-building plant developed another form of voluntary intensive effort for the fulfillment of the Five-Year Plan, the so-called "economic accounting brigade." The aim of this type of brigade is to abide strictly by the economic accounting schedule set by the production plan. For this purpose the brigade sets for its members strict norms with regard to the amount of raw materials to be used. Extreme care is exercised in the maximum utilization of the internal resources of the enterprise. The brigade also conducts a campaign for the best possible care and use of tools, machinery, fuel, etc. By April 1, 1932 figures obtained from 22 regions of the Soviet Union showed that 155,000 economic accounting brigades had been formed embracing 1,500,000 members.[24]

One of the most effective methods developed by the workers for utilizing the internal resources of the enterprise, for discovering hidden possibilities in the plant, and for expanding the schedule set by the production plan is the system of "counter-planning." "The drawing up of plans by the planning bodies of the Soviet Union," Stalin once said, "is only the beginning of planning; the real leadership of planning develops only after the plan has been drawn up, after it has been checked in the place where it is being carried out, and extended, corrected and perfected by those who carry it out." Under the system of "counter-planning," the control figures of a given enterprise are checked and elaborated by the workers themselves. "Planning brigades" and "planning operative brigades" divide the general plan for the enterprise into assignments for the various departments and the individual workers. This has led to the system of "shift counter-planning" whereby each shift takes a few minutes before work to discuss the job ahead of it and the best means of carrying it out. Before work begins the shift assigns to each individual worker the specific task that is required of him. An extension of this system, first

[24] Report of the All-Union Central Council of Trade Unions, *Pravda*, April 12, 1932.

developed by the workers of Dnepropetrovsk, is known as the
"shift calculation method," whereby each worker is kept informed as to the cost of the product made by him during the
shift, the amount of raw material and fuel used, etc. This gives
every worker an opportunity for finding ways of reducing production costs.[25]

The experience gained in "socialist competition" and the
"shock brigade" movement in its various forms, is utilized by
the trade unions when they participate in the planning of
national economy. In the execution of the industrial-financial
plan it has been found that the workers themselves are the
best judges of production quotas, and their suggestions are
used by the trade unions in all planning work. In all these
activities the trade union finds an effective instrument in the
production conference, which has become the basic method
for drawing the workers into the management of industry. The
production conference is also the organizing center for "socialist competition" and the various types of "shock brigades." It
reaches every department and every individual worker at his
bench. The members of the "shock brigade," the *udarniki*, are
the backbone of the production conference. Since they are the
most advanced workers, they set an example to the others, and
draw them into more active participation in production. More
and more workers are participating in the conferences. Thus,
at the beginning of 1932 about 75 per cent of the industrial
workers in Moscow were participating in production conferences as against 35 per cent in 1931. During the same period
the percentage in Leningrad rose from 45 to 75.[26]

"Socialist competition," "shock brigade" work and other
methods of developing "socialist discipline" are among the
main tasks of the Soviet trade unions in carrying out their
slogan of "face production." This was clearly brought out in
the trade union discussions preceding the Ninth Congress of
Trade Unions held in April 1932. In all regional, district and

[25] *Information Bulletin of the Commissariat for Foreign Affairs* (Russian), Moscow, March 5, 1932.

[26] Report of All-Union Central Council of Trade Unions, *Pravda*, April
12, 1932.

republican trade union conferences prior to the all-union congress the central problem discussed was that of raising "socialist competition" to a higher level. All the conferences commented on the great success of the "shock brigade" movement and its penetration into all branches of production, but the necessity of further extending and improving such work was emphasized. The conferences concluded that the continued improvement in the production work of the trade unions calls for the realization throughout industry of the "six conditions" outlined in Stalin's speech of June 23, 1931. These "conditions" stipulated that Soviet organizations must (1) fight against "irresponsibility" in regard to machinery; (2) fight against the misconception of "equalizing" wages; (3) train new skilled workers; (4) change their attitude toward old specialists; (5) conquer technique; (6) improve cost accounting. The trade union conferences also took up the question of further improvements in the living standards of the workers. Commenting editorially on these discussions, *Pravda* urged that a "determined struggle to improve the work of the coöperative store or dining room, a fight against dirt, against queues, against chaos, disorder, against all evil influences interfering with the proper supply of goods for the workers—all these must not be neglected. No aspect of the worker's life is too 'trivial' to be neglected by the trade unions, especially the problem of the workers' living conditions in the new industrial centers." [27]

Prior to the opening of the Ninth Congress of Trade Unions, the Central Council published a report which throws considerable light on the present functions and problems of the Soviet labor organizations. The report opens with a criticism of the old trade union leadership headed by Tomsky which reads in part as follows:

"Instead of mobilizing all the forces of the working class for the development of an increased tempo in socialist construction, for the fulfillment of the Five-Year Plan, and for leadership in the growing productive activity of the wide masses

[27] *Pravda* (Organ of the Central Committee of the Communist Party), Moscow, April 20, 1932.

of proletarians directed toward an increase in the productivity
of labor and toward overcoming the difficulties involved in
the socialist reconstruction of national economy, the old leadership of the trade unions gave precedence to the 'defensive'
work of the trade unions as against the problems of their
participation in socialist construction. Through Tomsky, the
old leadership urged that 'it is impossible at the same time
to manage an enterprise on the basis of commercial cost accounting and yet be the exponent and defender of the workers'
interests.' Actually, this meant leading in the direction of
isolating the trade unions from the struggle for the building
of socialism in our country. This was an expression of narrow
'trade unionism,' departmental and other petit-bourgeois moods
in the trade unions alien to the proletarian. At the same time
it meant a refusal to struggle for the radical improvement of
the material conditions of the workers on the basis of
developing socialist economy and increasing labor productivity. . . . The slogan 'face production' signifies a new stage
in the development of the work of the trade unions, and their
turning to the problem of a wide development of socialist competition. The problem was to make socialist competition the
basis of all productive work of the trade unions, to make it
the decisive method in the daily struggle of the trade unions
for fulfilling and exceeding the industrial-financial plan." [28]
    In this connection it is interesting to note the definition of
the essential nature of "socialist competition" which Stalin
has formulated:
    " 'Socialist competition' and 'competition' are two distinct
principles. The principle of commercial competition involves
the defeat, the death of some and the victory and domination
of others. The principle of socialist competition is one of
comradely help from the advanced ranks to those who are
lagging behind for the purpose of achieving a general raising in the level of production or achievements. Commercial
competition says—'do away with the backward so as to estab-

[28] Report of the All-Union Central Council of Trade Unions for the
Ninth Congress, *Pravda*, April 12, 1932, No. 102.

lish your own domination!' Socialist competition says—'Some
work badly, others well, still others even better. Catch up with
the best, and reach a generally higher level.' "

The Central Council's report devoted considerable space to
such problems as training skilled workers and the general
cultural work which the trade unions carry on. One of the
most important functions of the trade unions is the training
of workers in factory schools and similar institutions, such as
the Central Institute of Labor. Technical courses conducted by
the trade unions increase the skill of old and new workers.
Thus, in the Makeyevka metallurgical plant in the Ukraine
in 1930, some 5,000 out of a total of 13,000 workers were
enrolled in the various technical courses conducted by the
trade union. At the same time, over 50 per cent of the workers in Leningrad, Moscow and the Urals were taking various
study courses. In 1930 a total of 30,000 workers were being
trained at the expense of their trade unions to enter universities and other higher institutions. This is part of the general
policy of training workers to become specialists. In 1930 the
trade unions spent 26,000,000 rubles in preparing workers to
enter higher institutions of learning.

This educational work of the trade unions has enabled
many workers to rise to positions of importance in state and
coöperative institutions. In recent years some 25,000 workers
have been promoted to such positions. In addition to this and
other links with the state and economic apparatus, the trade
unions exercise control through the "patronage" system
whereby a factory may become the "patron" of a government
department or institution. The trade unions also actively participate in the cleansing of the state apparatus when it becomes necessary to remove bureaucrats and inefficient elements.

In reporting on the cultural work of the trade unions, the
Central Council pointed out that from 1929 to 1932 about 500
new workers' clubs were organized by the unions, raising the
total throughout the country to 4,200. The number of trade
union libraries has increased to 25,000; the number of "red
corners" (the part of the clubs devoted to the political educa-

tion of the workers) to 91,000; and the number of trade union cinema theaters to 5,500. At present about 75 per cent of the motion picture theaters in the urban centers are owned and operated by the trade unions. For 1932 the trade unions appropriated 683 million rubles for cultural work as against 160 million rubles in 1928.

While emphasizing the enormous achievements of the trade unions in the cultural field, the Central Council's report also pointed out that at present the chief weakness of this work lies in its insufficient connection with the masses of workers and with production work in the enterprises. There are also shortcomings in the distribution of reading matter. Thus, while the number of trade union libraries has increased, the number of books in them has not kept up with the demands of the workers whose cultural interests are rapidly growing. These aspects of trade union work are considered exceedingly important in the Soviet Union where the trade union is considered a school of socialist education for the workers. This is especially the case now, on the eve of the second Five-Year Plan, the basic political aim of which is "the complete liquidation of capitalist elements and classes in general, the complete elimination of causes which give rise to class distinctions and exploitation, and the overcoming of the remnants of capitalism both in economy and in the consciousness of the people, the transformation of the entire working population of the country into active builders of a classless socialist society." [29]

[29] *Pravda*, April 20, 1932.

CHAPTER V

SOVIET LABOR LAWS

THE main government department for regulating labor questions is the Commissariat of Labor. In addition to general supervision over the execution of labor legislation, this department has a number of other functions, including the regulation of collective agreements concluded between the trade unions and the management of the various enterprises; the adjustment of labor disputes between employers and employees; the regulation of social insurance against unemployment, sickness, disability, pregnancy, childbirth, death, etc.; and the regulation of the training of workers. These and numerous other functions, the Commissariat of Labor exercises either by means of legislation or by direct supervision.

The aim of all Soviet labor legislation is to raise the living standards of the workers to the highest possible level compatible with the general interests of national economy, which, in the long run, means the general interests of the working class. The legislative basis for regulating labor is the Labor Code, which went into effect November 15, 1922. The Code establishes the legal status of labor and is of decisive importance in determining labor conditions. All forms of labor without exception, including domestic labor, are subject to the provisions of the Labor Code, which is binding on all institutions and persons, whether state, social or private. One of the Code's fundamental requirements is that all labor agreements and contracts must provide for conditions at least as good as those called for by the Code itself; otherwise they are void.[1]

[1] Labor Code, Articles 1-4.

The Code further provides that all relations between employers and employees must be specifically defined in all collective and individual labor agreements.

A collective contract under the Code is an agreement between the employer and the trade union, which represents the interests of labor. The Code provides that "the terms of the collective agreement shall apply to all persons employed in a specified undertaking or institution, irrespective of whether they are members of the trade union which has concluded the agreement or not." This provision aims to protect the interests of the unorganized employees, and to eliminate all possibility of less favorable conditions for those employees who are not trade union members; it establishes equal rights and equal labor conditions for trade union members and for those who, for one reason or another, do not belong to trade unions. Collective agreements may be either general, covering a whole branch of production, business or administration within the republic; or local. Wherever a general collective agreement exists, the conclusion of local collective agreements is permitted only in the cases and in the manner specified in the general collective agreement. The time limit for collective agreements is determined by the Commissariat of Labor with the consent of the All-Union Council of Trade Unions. On October 17, 1923 these two bodies ruled that no collective agreement may run for more than one year. One of the Code's provisions is that "assets of trade unions shall not be liable for the fulfillment of collective agreements." Every collective agreement must be executed in writing and registered with the Commissariat of Labor. The Commissariat has the right to modify the agreement if its provisions make conditions for the employees less favorable than those provided by existing labor laws.[2]

A collective agreement may regulate all conditions of labor as well as the procedure of hiring workers; but it concerns itself mainly with conditions of work. As a rule it also covers the obligations of the employer in respect to the trade union,

[2] *Ibid.*, Articles 15-26.

such as subsidies for maintaining the factory committee and for the cultural activities of the trade union. The collective agreement also covers such questions as the naming of the enterprises and individuals affected by the agreement; the method of concluding detailed local agreements if they are anticipated in the general agreement; the period for which the agreement is in force and manner of renewing the agreement upon its termination; and the application of laws which may be passed during the existence of the agreement should any of these laws affect the agreement at any point.

The collective agreement also sets forth the procedure for trial periods for newly hired workers. It covers questions affecting the dismissal of workers, specifying the allowances to which such workers are entitled. The agreement further outlines complete wage-scales for all categories of workers; the system and manner of paying wages; the methods of establishing and revising production standards and payment for piece-work; the conditions of payment for damaged items, lost time, and unfinished piece-work lots. It sets the length of working time, particularly covering types of work in which the length of the working day is not definitely established. It contains specific provisions for labor protection and the improvement of working conditions; it lists the categories of workers entitled to free working clothes and the manner and frequency with which these are to be supplied; it specifies details regarding sanitation and hygiene on the job, including steam-baths, laundries, nurseries, dining rooms, and living quarters.

The collective agreement also lists the categories of apprentices, their pay and their distribution through the enterprise. It stipulates the working conditions for engineers and technicians; the method of hiring, transferring and discharging them; their duties, privileges and rules affecting promotion; and the supply of technical literature, instruments and materials. Finally, the agreement defines the employer's obligations toward the trade union regarding such matters as the schedule of allowances for the factory committee, for the equipment and the facilities at the disposal of the trade union for its work at the enterprise, and for supplying workers with copies of the collective agreement.[3]

A general collective agreement covers a trust or a combine. A government department may conclude a collective agreement with an industrial union only if it operates enterprises or institutions. Thus the Commissariat for Transportation, which operates the whole of the Soviet Union's railway system, has a general collective agreement with the Central Committee of the Railway Workers' Union which covers all railways. General collective agreements cover the entire country or an autonomous republic, as a rule. However, they sometimes provide for the drawing up of local agreements when this is considered desirable. The Commissariat for Transportation, for instance, has found it impractical to conclude a general nationwide agreement with the central committee of the Building Workers' Union because of the great variation in local conditions. These two bodies have therefore agreed to have their subordinate organs draw up local collective agreements. Where the general agreement permits the conclusion of local agreements to cover one or several local enterprises, such local agreements must provide for conditions at least as good as those called for by the general agreement.

The collective agreement is a reciprocal instrument which imposes obligations both upon the employer and upon the trade union. Both sides must bear in mind its effects upon production, since in the long run production determines the workers' living standards. The trade unions have the twofold duty of making the collective agreement effective and of assisting in rasing production and lowering costs. In settling disputes involving collective agreements they take into consideration the necessity of fulfilling the industrial-financial plan. They consider it an important part of their work to assist in strengthening labor discipline and in educating the workers to realize that such discipline leads to improved living standards. Upon the workers at the bench the collective

[3] *Principles of Labor Legislation in the Soviet Union,* State Publishing House, Moscow, 1931.

agreement imposes the obligation of observing factory rules and regulations, performing their tasks in a disciplined manner, taking care of equipment and tools, improving the quality of the product, economizing in the use of raw materials, and reducing the amount of damage to machinery and other equipment.

Employers who violate their obligations under the collective agreement are subject to fines involving in some cases even forfeiture of their property. In serious cases they are held criminally liable and disciplined under the penal code. Individual workers who violate the collective agreement are subject to various disciplinary measures, including dismissal at the discretion of the management and penalties on the part of the trade union. The trade union itself is responsible to its superior trade union organs for observing the collective agreement. The property of trade unions cannot be attached or forfeited for failure to observe the collective agreement. An enterprise has no right to sue a trade union on any ground for failing to carry out the agreement, and the property of the trade union cannot be touched even if individual trade union members commit criminal acts involving the agreement. In this case, responsibility is fixed within the trade union system; the individual worker is responsible to his trade union which, in turn, may be disciplined by the higher trade union organs.[4]

The Labor Code provides that in addition to the collective agreement between the trade union and the enterprise, each employer must also enter into an individual contract with every worker defining their relations. An individual labor contract must be concluded whether a collective agreement exists or not. The collective agreement determines the general conditions of labor; the individual labor contract determines the actual hiring of the individual worker and fixes the specific task for which he is hired. Individual contracts may be concluded either for a definite period not exceeding three years; or for an indefinite period, with no time limit specified in the

[4] *Ibid.*

contract; or for the period required to carry out a specific task. Under the Labor Code, individual contracts "for a definite period" based on the calendar and those which cover "the time required to carry out specific work" are considered contracts for a definite period. The conditions stipulated in the individual agreement must in every case be at least as good as those specified by the collective agreement. Furthermore, the Code prohibits individual agreements from containing any provision limiting the political or civil rights of the employee in any way. The individual agreement must be accompanied by a pay-book which every employee must receive. This book, in which the account of the workers' wages are kept, must state the exact conditions of the workers' employment. Before being hired permanently, a worker may be taken on for trial, but this trial period may not in most cases exceed six days.

An employee may not, without the employer's consent, entrust to another person the performance of the work for which he was hired; on the other hand, the employer may not require the employee to perform any work not connected with the kind of activities for which he was hired, nor any work involving manifest risk of life or not in accord with the labor laws. In exceptional cases, when it is necessary to avert impending danger, an employee may be assigned to any other kind of work. In such cases, the employee's wages cannot be reduced, but if the temporary work is paid at a higher rate than that for which the employee was hired, he must be paid the higher rate of wages. The management of the enterprise or the employer is not permitted to impose fines upon employees arbitrarily; he may impose fines only in cases provided for by the law or in the rules of employment which the trade unions help to formulate.[5]

The termination of an individual labor contract is settled on the basis of Article 44 of the Labor Code which provides that "a labor contract shall expire (a) by agreement between

[5] Labor Code, *op. cit.*, Articles 27-43.

the parties; (b) on the expiration of the term for which it was concluded; (c) on the completion of the work agreed upon; and (d) on the giving of notice by either party under sections 46 and 47. The transfer of the institution, undertaking or business from one authority or owner to another shall not entail the termination of the labor contract." The law in principle differentiates between the breaking of a labor contract by the employer and its breaking by the employee. An employer may terminate an unexpired labor contract only on certain valid grounds enumerated by the law, whether such a contract has been drawn up for a definite or indefinite period. He may terminate an individual agreement under the following circumstances, according to the Labor Code:

"If there is a temporary lack in the enterprise of the kind of work for which the employee was engaged, the employer shall be entitled to assign him to other work suitable to his abilities. If the employee refuses to carry out such work, the employer shall be entitled to dismiss him on payment of a dismissal grant." [6]

A wage-earning or salaried employee may not be transferred from one enterprise to another or removed from one locality to another without his consent, even if such transfer or removal takes place in connection with that of the enterprise or institution; in default of his consent, the labor contract may be rescinded by either party, and in that case the employee shall be paid a leaving grant (amounting to at least two weeks' wages).[7]

An employer may also declare terminated a definite or indefinite labor contract under the following circumstances:

"(a) in case of entire or partial winding up of the enterprise, institution, or farm, and likewise in case of a curtailment of operations;

"(b) in consequence of the closing down of the enterprise for a period of over one month for reasons connected with production;

[6] *Ibid.*, Article 36.   [7] *Ibid.*, Article 37.

"(c) in case of the employee's obvious unfitness for work;

"(d) in case of persistent failure on the part of the employee to fulfill the duties incumbent upon him under the agreement or the rules of shop discipline without sufficient reason for the same;

"(e) if the employee commits a criminal offense which is directly connected with his work and which is established by an enforceable verdict, and likewise if the employee has been sentenced to imprisonment for more than two months;

"(f) if the employee is absent from work without valid reason for more than three days in the course of one month;

"(g) if the employee is absent from work on account of temporary loss of working capacity for more than two months reckoned from the date of such loss; and also in case of temporary loss of working capacity in consequence of pregnancy or confinement lasting more than two months beyond the period of four months specified in Article 92 of the Labor Code;

"(h) in cases where a worker is engaged in work formerly done by another worker and the latter is reinstated by a ruling of a court or of a Conflict Commission.[8]

In case of the employee's obvious unfitness to work, the labor contract may be terminated only by a decision of the Conflict Commission, consisting of representatives of the trade union and an equal number of representatives of the management. In case of persistent failure on the part of the employee to fulfill the contract or live up to shop rules without valid cause, the employer may terminate the agreement as follows: In state institutions and enterprises, and in coöperative and other organizations, the contract may be terminated by order of the employer; but the discharged employee has the right to appeal against his dismissal to the Conflict Commission. In all other enterprises and institutions, the contract in such

[8] See *Ibid.*, Article 47; Decree of the All-Russian Central Executive Committee and the Council of People's Commissars of the RSFSR, August 22, 1927; Collection of Laws of the RSFSR, No. 87, Section 577; and decree of March 25, 1929, Collection of Laws of the RSFSR, No. 26, Section 274.

cases can be terminated only by decision of the Conflict Commission.[9]

In case the employer terminates the agreement because the establishment is closing down or because the employee is unfit to work, as provided for in clauses (a), (b) and (c), the employer must notify the employee of his dismissal two weeks in advance and must pay him two weeks' extra wages. The Labor Code in Article 47 thus recognizes that only serious violations by the employee of the duties incumbent upon him or of labor discipline established by law are sufficient ground for the termination of a labor contract by the employer. Such termination is a form of disciplinary penalty and is one of the means of maintaining labor discipline in the enterprise. In all cases the dismissal must be concurred in by the trade union.

The expansion of national economy and the urgent need for workers has resulted in some changes in that section of Article 36 of the Labor Code which emphasizes the right of the employee to refuse to accept a transfer to another enterprise or another locality. A decree issued on June 3, 1931, provides that within the limits of the locality the management has the right to transfer the worker temporarily to another enterprise for a period of not more than one month. If the employee refuses to accede to the transfer, the management may discharge him. But under no circumstances may the employee be compelled to work where he does not want to. If the management seeks to transfer an employee to an enterprise in another locality, the employee may refuse to go and the management cannot discharge him. The employee who voluntarily agrees to accept a transfer to another locality is granted a number of special privileges under a decree issued on June 18, 1931. These privileges include the right to bonuses amounting to a month's wages; reimbursement for traveling expenses incurred by himself and family; full wages while en route; the right to retain living quarters in the old place of

[9] Labor Code, *op. cit.*, Article 47; decree of January 30, 1930, Collection of Laws of the RSFSR, 1930, No. 7, Section 83.

work and to obtain living quarters for himself and family in
the new place of work; a guarantee that the wages in the
new place of work shall not be lower than in the old place;
preference for his children in schools and playgrounds and
so on.[10]

Except in the cases specified by the laws referred to, the
employer has no right to terminate a labor contract, whether
it be definite or indefinite in form. Article 47 of the Labor
Code assures the worker of stable labor relations and gives
him legal protection against unjust dismissal. In this respect
the worker receives further protection under the Criminal
Code which makes the employer criminally liable for violations of the labor law as well as for unlawful practices in engaging or dismissing workers.[11]

The conditions under which an employee may terminate a
labor contract depend on whether such a contract has been
concluded for an indefinite period, a definite calendar period
or for the time required to carry out a specified task. If the
contract is concluded for an indefinite period, the employee
may terminate it at any time; but he must notify the employer
at least one day in advance if wages are paid weekly, and at
least seven days in advance if wages are paid fortnightly or
monthly. Thus, while the right of the employer to terminate
a labor contract is limited to strictly defined cases, the
worker has the right to terminate an agreement for an indefinite period at any time, regardless of whether he has valid
reasons or not. Furthermore, "a contract of work concluded
for a specified period may be terminated by the employee
before the expiration of such period in the following cases:
(a) if the agreed remuneration is not paid to him when due;
(b) if the employer fails to fulfill his duties under the contract or the labor laws; (c) if the employee is badly treated
by the employer, the representatives of the management or
members of their families; (d) in the event of the deteriora-

---

[10] *Izvestia,* June 22, 1931, No. 170.
[11] Criminal Code, Articles 133-134; also Interpretations of the Supreme
Court of the USSR, 2nd ed., Moscow, 1931, p. 438.

tion of the sanitary and hygienic conditions of work; (e) in all other cases specially provided for by law." [12] Every labor contract may also be terminated at the demand of the trade union. If the employer disagrees with the stand taken by the union, he may appeal to the bodies which settle labor disputes.[13]

While the employer who violates a labor contract is criminally liable under the penal code, no such responsibility is put upon the worker. Indeed, Soviet law contains no provisions even for the civil liability of a worker who has caused his employer damages by terminating a labor contract for a definite period before its normal expiration, or for unlawfully terminating a contract for an indefinite period by failing to give due notice.

The conditions for terminating labor contracts as established by the Labor Code may be summarized as follows: (1) the worker is protected against dismissal without valid cause; (2) the worker is guaranteed the right to terminate a labor contract concluded for an indefinite period regardless of whether he has valid cause or not; and (3) the worker is guaranteed the right to terminate a labor contract concluded for a definite period without notice in case the employer violates the conditions of the contract or the labor laws.

Shop and factory rules, the Labor Code provides, must contain clear, precise and, whenever possible, exhaustive information regarding the general and special duties of both the employees and the management. The extent and nature of liability for their violation must be explicitly defined. The purpose of such rules of employment is to regulate work in enterprises where five or more persons are employed. Such rules are valid only if they are issued in the prescribed manner and brought to the knowledge of all the workers concerned. The rules must not violate the labor laws and regulations or the collective contract in force in the given enterprise. Model rules of employment are issued by the Commissariat of Labor

[12] Labor Code, *op. cit.*, Articles 46 and 48.
[13] *Ibid.*, Article 48.

in agreement with the All-Union Council of Trade Unions and the industrial commissariats. The rules of employment for individual enterprises, whether state, public or private, are drawn up by agreement between the management and the local branches of the trade unions concerned and approved by the labor inspector. An appeal against the decision of the labor inspector may be taken to the local section of the labor commissariat whose decision is final.[14]

The section of the Labor Code dealing with standards of output [15] provides that such standards shall be fixed by the management of the enterprise in agreement with the trade union or the competent trade union officials. An employee who through his own fault fails to attain the prescribed standard of output under normal working conditions is to receive wages proportionate to the work done, but in no case less than two-thirds of the base rate due him. In cases of persistent failure to attain the standard, he may be dismissed as unfit for work, a contingency already provided for in the Code. However, the enormous growth of productivity under the Five-Year Plan and the need for even greater advances in this regard have resulted in additional regulations governing standards of output.

These regulations have been not in the direction of penalizing failure to attain the standard, but of rewarding successful effort to exceed it. In considering collective and labor agreements, standards of output and other factors in Soviet economy, it is necessary to keep in mind that the individual workers not only place their labor at the disposal of the enterprise but are themselves active participants in the organization of production and factory management. They fulfill this function through the trade union, the factory committee, the production conference, and to a great extent through "socialist competition" and the "shock brigades," both of which have exerted a profound influence upon the whole of factory organization.

"Socialist competition" and the "shock brigade" movement

---

[14] *Ibid.*, Articles 50-55.   [15] *Ibid.*, Articles 56-57.

are based on the voluntary activity of the workers who of their own free will assume a number of duties based upon the general interest of the workers in the development of production. But while this activity is voluntary, the government has taken a number of steps to further this method of raising standards of output; it encourages workers who fulfill or exceed their production quotas, or assist backward comrades who are lagging behind in the fulfillment of the industrial-financial plan, or have achieved useful results through "socialist competition," or have improved the efficiency of production processes. An example of government encouragement in this respect may be found in the decree of September 11, 1913, affecting the so-called "brigades for economic accounting." [16]

Such a "brigade" consists of workers who undertake to carry out a definite task in production on a voluntary basis. It concludes an agreement with the management of the enterprise setting forth the conditions for the fulfillment of the task undertaken. The brigade carries out its task on the principle of "economic accounting." Its agreement with the management specifies the limits for overhead costs, the limits for imperfect production, the standard of output, the standards of economy in the use of raw materials and supplies, the time required for preparatory work, the quality and quantity of production and the standards of production costs. The management, in turn, undertakes to provide the "brigade" with raw materials, supplies and tools on time. It also undertakes to carry out on time all the necessary repair work, to organize cost accounting, and to award prizes for the achievements of the "brigade." The decree of September 11 referred to gives this arrangement legal standing. It provides that for all economies in raw materials, equipment, machinery and labor power affected by workers who have exceeded their quota of an assigned task, they shall receive from 20 to 60 per cent of the total savings. This obliges the management to fulfill its promise of rewarding extra achievement; but the decree at the same time specifically absolves the "brigade"

[16] *Pravda*, Sept. 12, 1931.

members of all financial responsibility for their failure to fulfill their agreement with the management. The law guarantees in this way that all forms of "socialist competition" or "shock brigade" activity shall be voluntary.

Incentives to fulfilling and exceeding production quotas are also provided for in new regulations issued on August 13, 1931.[17] These regulations establish special funds for rewarding achievements which result from "socialist competition" and the "shock brigade" movement; as well as special funds for promoting inventions and proposals for improving production. The funds cover all enterprises of state industry, transportation, communications, municipal economy, state farms, tractor stations, construction projects and producers' and consumers' coöperatives. The decree permits the management of each enterprise to determine the extent and form of the awards.

These methods of encouraging voluntary movements to increase production have been accompanied by a strict enforcement of the labor laws, including those affecting the length of the working day. Thus on September 22, 1930 a circular issued jointly by the Commissariat of Labor and the All-Union Council of Trade Unions contained instructions to the effect that any slowness in fulfilling production quotas must be overcome by the better organization of labor, the efficient utilization of equipment, the full use of the legal working day, the elimination of delays in supplying enterprises and workers with raw materials, equipment and tools; the improvement of workers' living conditions and food supply; but there must be no sacrifice of the workers' rest days or any increase in the length of the working day established by law.[18]

The Soviet authorities consider labor protection and the strict enforcement of labor laws inseparable from the expansion of national economy. On the one hand, as they put it, "production is made for man, and not man for production," so that every advance in national economy is followed by corre-

---

[17] *Izvestia,* Aug 20, 1931, No. 229.
[18] See *Izvestia* of the Commissariat of Labor of the USSR., 1930, Nos. 29-30.

sponding improvements in the workers' living standards. On the other hand, labor protection and improved living conditions stimulate "labor enthusiasm" which results in further increases of production.

The Labor Code provides extensive guarantees for protecting the workers' earnings. Wages are fixed by collective and individual labor agreements, but they cannot be fixed below the minimum established by the government at a given time for the category of work involved. Wages may be paid on a time basis or by piece-work. Labor contracts must specifically state the rates to be paid for overtime, but in no case may these rates be less than one and one-half times the normal wage for the first two hours, and twice the normal wage for subsequent hours. Young workers must be paid wages at the same rate as adults doing the same work. An employee who performs various kinds of work which are paid at different rates must be paid at the rate required for the higher paid work. An employee who performs work for which special knowledge or training is necessary must be paid at the rates required for this kind of work whether or not he has a diploma or certificate of technical training. An employee who is transferred to lower paid work must receive his former wages for a fortnight after the transfer.[19]

Wages must be paid at regular intervals, but not less frequently than once a fortnight, and must be handed to the worker during working hours and in the enterprise. An employee who fails to perform his work for reasons outside his control must be paid his average daily earnings. An employee must receive his full wages when he is on leave attending to social work, military service, et cetera. If the base (time) rate is not attained in carrying out piece-work, the work must be paid for according to the actual output, but never less than two-thirds of the base rate. Young persons between 16 and 18, who are permitted a maximum working day of six hours, must be paid at the same piece rates as adult employees; and in addition must be paid wages for two hours at the scheduled

[19] Labor Code, *op. cit.*, Articles 58-64.

time rate applying to them, or for one hour if they work in enterprises on the seven-hour day. Piece-work rates must be changed in proportion to changes made in time work rates. The law also provides for special compensation when a worker is sent on a special mission, or transferred to other work or another locality. The possibilities of attaching a worker's wages on the basis of legal claims made by the employer or other persons are limited. Preference is given to claims made by workers against employers involving wages or compensation.[20]

In state enterprises the rates of pay are now regulated by law. For the purpose of regulating the revision of wages when a collective agreement is being renewed, a special government commission was created in 1926. This commission defines the general limits of increasing wage funds in industry. It also distributes the fund established for increasing wage scales in certain branches of industry and individual enterprises where wage scales cannot be based on productivity. The commissariats for industry and the All-Union Central Council of Trade Unions jointly effect these wage increases in specific industries; they issue special instructions which point out, as the case may be, that the increase aims to raise living standards in backward sections; or to attract workers to important industrial enterprises unable to obtain the necessary labor supply; or to equalize the pay of various groups of workers in a given locality who are equally skilled; or to effect a general increase in the wages of the lower paid groups of workers. In those branches of industry where such special wage increases have not been provided for, increases in pay must depend on increases in production, within limits set by the Control Figures. The ratio of wage increases to increases in production must be in accord with the industrial-financial plan of the individual enterprise.[21]

A recent decree revising wage scales illustrates one method by which Soviet law raises wages. During the first seven

[20] *Ibid.*, Articles 68-76, 77-93.
[21] *Principles of Labor Legislation in the USSR, op. cit.*

months of 1931, the average monthly wages of workers in
industry increased 11.8 per cent compared with 1930. In order
to stimulate production in the most vital industries during
the fourth quarter of 1931 the Supreme Economic Council and
the All-Union Council of Trade Unions issued a joint decree
considerably increasing average wages in the metallurgical and
mining industries as follows: iron and steel, an increase of
23.5 per cent; coal, 12 per cent; other mining industries, 20
per cent; coke and chemicals, 20 per cent. This decree, of
September 20, 1931, on the "revision of the system of wages
in the metallurgical and coal industries" provided that beginning with October 1, 1931, all workers engaged in actual
production in metallurgical departments be placed on a progressive piece-work scale and that no less than 70 per cent of
the workers in subsidiary and auxiliary departments be placed
on a direct, unlimited piece-work scale.[22]

Progressive piece-work is based on the principle of progressively increasing rates. In this case the rate for the
second third of the assigned task is 20 per cent higher than
for the first third; and the rate for the final third is 50 per
cent higher than for the first third. Each unit of output above
the quota is paid at double rates. Time workers employed as
assistants to piece-workers receive wages on a time-bonus
system. In addition to fixed daily wages, they receive special
bonuses depending upon the quality of the work. In the metallurgical industry, for instance, special bonuses are awarded
for good care of equipment, a steady supply of gas, good
care of the blast-furnace notch, prolonging the period between
shutting down the open-hearth furnaces for repairs, reduction
in the breaking of cylinders, etc. Standards of output are
established for a period of one year. Changes in the standard
before the end of that period are permitted only when technological improvements have been introduced which increase
the productivity of labor to a considerable extent.

In order to effect a greater rate of increase in the earnings
of highly skilled workers engaged in arduous or injurious occu-

[22] *Trud*, Moscow, September 23, 1931.

pátions, the decree of September 20 set the ratio between the lowest and highest paid categories at 1: 3.7 instead of 1: 2.8, as was formerly the case. The decree further provided for an increase in the pay of all piece-workers in metallurgical departments. The increase affected both skilled and unskilled workers, although the extent of the increase is higher for skilled workers. The decree also calls for increasing the pay of engineers and technicians who, in addition to their regular salaries, are to receive bonuses depending upon the degree to which they carry out the production plan. Similar provisions were made for the coal industry.

The Labor Code guarantees an eight-hour working day as the norm for workers as well as for persons engaged in intellectual or office work connected with industry. In those enterprises which have adopted the seven-hour day, seven hours is the norm guaranteed by the Code. Persons employed in intellectual or office work not directly connected with industry are guaranteed a normal working day of six hours. Subsequent to the adoption of the Code in 1922, the number of rest days was increased; hence the working day of such employees was increased to 6.5 hours, so as to retain the same amount of working time during the year. The Code also provides a six-hour working day for employees between 16 and 18 years of age, for underground workers and other workers in arduous and dangerous occupations. The working time is reduced by one hour in case of night work; but where work goes on continuously day and night, overtime rates are paid for the extra hour instead of reducing the hours.[23]

The Code provides that employees must be granted a rest and luncheon period during the normal hours of work which must not be counted in the working hours. Employees may use this period in any way they choose, being permitted to leave the place of work if they so desire. As a rule overtime is prohibited. It is permitted only in the following circumstances: for the performance of work absolutely necessary for the protection of the Republic and the prevention of crises and dan-

[23] Labor Code, *op. cit.*, Articles 94-97.

gers threatening the commonwealth; for the performance of work absolutely necessary in the public interest in connection with the water supply, lighting, drainage, communications, and the postal, telegraph and telephone services; in case it is essential to complete work begun during the normal working time, if leaving such work unfinished would entail damage to machinery or raw materials; in case it is necessary to make temporary repairs and adjustments of machinery or equipment, if leaving it unrepaired would interrupt the work of a considerable number of employees. Even in these special cases overtime is permitted only by agreement with the wage-scale and disputes committee or with the competent trade union and the labor inspector. Persons under 18 may not work overtime under any circumstances. No employee may work overtime more than 120 hours a year; or more than four hours within two consecutive days. No employee may work overtime in order to make up for time lost in coming late to work.[24]

The Code further guarantees employees an uninterrupted rest period of not less than 42 hours a week. Every person who has worked uninterruptedly for not less than five and a half months is entitled to at least two weeks' vacation with full pay every year. The minimum vacation with full pay for employees under 18 and for persons engaged in arduous or dangerous work is one month. The time, procedure and order of vacations are settled by committees representing both the employers and the employees.[25]

The rapid expansion of national economy under the Five-Year Plan has resulted in new labor legislation which has improved these provisions of the Labor Code. Many enterprises have adopted the seven-hour day and the continuous working week. In these enterprises the workers do not have the same weekly rest day; instead, rest days, distributed equally over the week, are assigned to various groups of workers. The continuous working week has also been adopted by institutions directly serving the workers. There has been a consequent improvement in the social, communal and cultural

[24] *Ibid.*, Articles 103-108.   [25] *Ibid.*, Articles 109-120.

services at the workers' disposal. The continuous working week has meant an increase in the number of weekly rest days. To balance this the number of national holidays has been reduced to five. The result has been a more even distribution of working and rest days throughout the year. In industrial enterprises working on the basis of three shifts a day, the continuous working week is divided as follows: Each working week consists of four days followed by an uninterrupted rest of 48 hours, after which the worker begins the next week with a new shift. Thus each employee works 12 shifts during a period of 16 calendar days. The standard set under this system is 168 hours of work per month.

In certain enterprises experience has shown that the uninterrupted work-week was not adapted to local conditions. This has been the case in enterprises like the Stalingrad plant, for example, where the necessity of supervision and of responsibility for machines was especially great because of the newness of the plant and the complexity of the operations. In such plants the change of shifts under the stagger system involved in the five-day week tended to accentuate the effects of the shortage of skilled and technical personnel. Accordingly, these plants have been placed on a six-day week in which all employees work five days and take their rest simultaneously on the sixth. Soviet enterprises now operate on both systems, some on the five-day and others on the six-day week. In either case the number of hours per month remains approximately the same for each worker.

The Labor Code prohibits the employment of minors under 16. Minors between 14 and 16 may be employed four hours a day in certain exceptional cases where it is required in connection with their training. At present, with the adoption of universal elementary education, 15 is considered the normal age for entering training in industry. The work of minors between 15 and 18 years of age who have an elementary education may be used as unskilled labor only where there is no factory trade school in the vicinity. The Code prohibits the employment of women and minors under 18 in work which is particularly arduous or injurious to health. Night work is forbidden for persons under 18, for pregnant women beginning with the sixth month, and for nursing mothers during the first six months of the nursing period. Exemption from work is provided for a period of eight weeks before confinement and eight weeks after confinement for women employed in manual labor and those employed in intellectual or office work who have been placed in the same category as manual workers. Other women employed at intellectual or office work are exempt for six weeks before and six weeks after confinement. During the entire period of exemption, the mothers are paid their full salaries by the social insurance fund. Beginning with the fifth month of pregnancy, a woman may refuse to work in any locality except where she is permanently employed. In addition to the rest periods to which all workers are entitled, nursing mothers must be given special rest periods for the purpose of attending to their children. These periods must last not less than half an hour and must be granted at intervals of not more than three and a half hours. The women workers receive full pay for these periods.

While the Code does not explicitly state that men and women must receive equal pay for equal work, this principle is implied in various provisions of the Code and is followed in all labor regulations and in practice. Minors are paid the same wages for a short working day as adults for a full working day if wages are paid on a time basis. In this piece-work system, the scale of minors between 16 and 18 must be the same as that of adults and in addition they must be paid regular wages for as many hours as the adult working day exceeds that of the minor's. The management of the enterprise must provide organized industrial training for a definite contingent of apprentices. The Code establishes a number of legal guarantees safeguarding the interests of the apprentices.[26]

In January 1931, the Central Executive Committee of the Soviet Union set the number of apprentices to be trained in schools connected with factories, construction projects and

[26] *Ibid.*, Articles 121-137.

agricultural enterprises at 1,200,000. It was planned that about 50 per cent of the apprentices in the factory training schools should be girls. In general, the number of women in industry has increased greatly as a result of profound changes in the living conditions of the workers. The prevalence of such institutions as the socialized restaurant, the day nursery, the kindergarten, the communal laundry, and the coöperative store attached to the enterprise has liberated the wives of many workers from household drudgery and enabled them to enter the enterprises on equal terms with men workers. By October 1930 there were about 3,690,000 women in industry. By October 1931 this figure had risen to 5,859,000 and by March 8, 1932 to over 6,000,000.[27]

The strict enforcement of the Labor Code and all labor laws, decrees, instructions and agreements affecting the life and health of employees is entrusted to the labor inspection service and the health inspection service. Both these services are under the jurisdiction of the Commissariat of Labor. Labor inspectors are appointed by the trade union councils with the approval of the provincial labor departments or the Commissariat of Labor. The inspectors exercise wide powers under the Code. They have the right to enter any enterprise at any time of the day or night. They may also inspect all institutions connected with enterprises, such as workers' dwellings, hospitals, *crêches*, baths, etc. They have the right to require the management of the enterprise to submit all necessary information, including books, accounts, and other documents. No enterprise may be opened or started or transferred to another building without the approval of the labor inspection or health inspection. The labor inspection issues instructions for the removal of abuses and defects in connection with the protection of workers; and these instructions are binding on all state, public and private enterprises. The labor inspection also calls to account by administrative or judicial procedure all who violate the Labor Code or other labor legislation. Similarly, the sanitary and technical inspectors of the Commissariat of

[27] *Izvestia,* March 8, 1932.

Labor supervise the detailed application of all regulations regarding industrial hygiene and precaution against accidents. These regulations include a provision of the Code that every enterprise must take the necessary steps to remedy injurious working conditions, to prevent accidents, and to maintain the workshops in a proper sanitary and hygienic condition. The enterprise is obliged to supply special work clothes and protective devices to all workers engaged in injurious occupations or working in abnormal temperatures, dampness or dirt. Where there is risk of industrial poisoning, the enterprise must supply the workers with the necessary antidotes or neutralizing substances.[28]

The Code, as has already been pointed out in the previous chapter, guarantees extensive rights to the trade unions, based upon the general position of the trade unions in the Soviet system. In addition, it establishes extensive rights for parity organs, consisting of representatives of the trade union and the management, both in regard to regulating work in general, and in regard to settling labor disputes and conflicts.

Labor disputes involving the application of working conditions prescribed by law, by collective or individual agreements or by shop rules are settled in two ways: either by conciliation or arbitration via the wage-scale and disputes committees, the conciliation boards, or the arbitration courts; or by decision of the People's Court. Wage-scale and disputes committees deal with questions placed within their jurisdiction by the law or with questions submitted to them by the employee. Conciliation boards and arbitration courts deal with all disputes involving the conclusion, amendment, amplification or interpretation of collective contracts; and disputes arising in connection with the establishment of new labor conditions regarding which the wage-scale and disputes committee has made no decision. Labor sessions of the People's Court deal with disputes arising in connection with the application of labor laws, collective and individual agreements, shop rules and schedules of fines, and decisions of the wage-scale and

[28] Labor Code, *op. cit.*, Articles 138-150.

disputes committees brought up on appeal. The People's Court also deals with infringements of the labor laws or collective agreements which violate the penal code. The trade unions and economic organizations participate in the People's Court.[29]

The wage-scale and disputes committee is composed of representatives of the employer and an equal number of representatives of the factory committee. It may settle disputes only by agreement between both groups of representatives. The committee, however, cannot render decisions which amend, amplify or repeal provision of a collective agreement unless the collective agreement specifically grants it that right. If the representatives of the management and the workers on the committee are unable to reach an agreement, the dispute is taken to the Commissariat of Labor and a conciliation commission is chosen. The latter consists of one or more representatives of the employees and an equal number of representatives of the employers. In addition, the Commissariat of Labor appoints an adviser. This adviser has no legal power to enforce any decision. He sits on the conciliation commission only as a conciliator, a disinterested third party who may advise both sides in the dispute and assist them to come to an agreement. But the decision of the conciliation commission —as in the case of the disputes committee—can be reached only by agreement of the representatives of the employers and employees.

In case the conciliation commission fails to come to an agreement, an arbitration court is chosen which finally settles the dispute. This court consists of representatives of the employees, an equal number of representatives of the employers, and a chairman chosen by both sides. In case the parties to the dispute cannot agree on a chairman, he may at their request be appointed by the Commissariat of Labor. Again an attempt is made to reach a solution by agreement of the disputing parties. It is only when all such attempts fail, that the chairman casts the deciding vote and the decision of the arbitration court becomes final. This method of settling dis-

29 *Ibid.,* Articles 168-169.

putes accounts for the practical absence of strikes in the Soviet Union, despite the fact that the law in no way limits the right to strike. In such few cases as there have been strikes, they have been settled by the methods here outlined which are employed in all disputes between employees and employers. The government enforces all decisions agreed upon by the disputes committees, conciliation commissions and arbitration courts through the machinery of the Commissariats of Labor and Justice.[30]

Compulsory state social insurance for all employees is established by the Code. The social insurance system covers all employees throughout the country regardless of where they work, the nature of their employment or their remuneration. It guarantees employees sick benefits; benefits in case of temporary loss of working ability due to illness, injury, quarantine, pregnancy, confinement, or the necessity of taking care of a sick member of the family; supplementary benefits for the nursing of children, medical supplies, and funerals; unemployment benefits; pensions for permanent disability; old age pensions, and pensions for families whose breadwinner has died or disappeared.

Funds for social insurance must be contributed entirely by the employers; they must not be imposed upon the insured persons nor be deducted from their wages. The social insurance funds contributed by each enterprise are fixed in proportion to the total wage fund. Insurance funds are reserved exclusively for ensuring benefits to employees and must not be used for any other purpose whatever. Social insurance is handled by special bureaus, the personnel of which is selected by the trade unions.[31]

The extensive system of unemployment benefits, established on the basis of the Labor Code, was abandoned in the autumn of 1930 because of the complete elimination of unemployment in the Soviet Union. A person who becomes ill in the interval of leaving one job and finding another receives social insurance benefits for temporary disability. Under the social

[30] *Ibid.*, Articles 170-174.   [31] *Ibid.*, Articles 175-192.

insurance system as it exists at present, all workers are entitled to a pension for permanent disability. If the worker is disabled as a result of an accident connected with his work, or incapacitated by vocational illness, he is entitled to a pension regardless of how long he has worked. If the disability results from other causes, the pension is awarded to manual workers provided they have worked for hire not less than eight years. For other employees the minimum is twelve years. In either case due regard is given to the age of the worker. Persons under 20 who are permanently disabled are entitled to a pension regardless of how long they have worked.

Old age pensions are guaranteed to workers in the mining, metallurgical, electrical, chemical, textile, printing, glass and china, and tobacco industries and in railway and water transportation; but the Allied Council of Social Insurance, in which the trade unions play an important rôle, has the right to extend and is gradually extending old age pensions to employees in other enterprises. Old age pensions are awarded to men who were 60 years of age before ceasing to work and who have worked for hire not less than 25 years, and to women over 55 who have worked not less than 20 years. Miners engaged in underground work are entitled to a pension after they have reached 50.[32]

Social insurance in the Soviet Union is not limited to providing workers with relief and pensions; it is also concerned with increasing production by improving the social and cultural standards of the workers. Of the social insurance budget for 1931, which totaled 2,500,000,000 rubles, about one billion rubles was set aside for such activities as the training of disabled workers in new occupations, the organization of day nurseries, scientific dietetics, sanatoria and rest homes; the training of new contingents of workers; and the building of hospitals.

The basic labor law outlined here is supplemented by nu-

[32] Decree of the Central Executive Committee of the Council of People's Commissars of the USSR, February 13, 1930; Collection of Laws of the USSR, 1930, No. 11, Section 132.

merous decrees, resolutions and instructions. The workers' rights and interests are safeguarded not only in the statutes but are guaranteed by an elaborate machinery for enforcement which includes the government, the trade unions, the Party and various other workers' organizations. Furthermore, Soviet labor law is not formulated from above by a "benevolent" state, but is in effect legislated by the workers themselves through the entire state and trade union apparatus. Through their dominance in the Communist Party, which lays down general policies; and through the trade unions, which are represented in all government and legislative bodies and whose consent is, in practice, necessary for all new labor legislation, the workers effectively embody their interests in the law.

This fact is recognized in Soviet legal theory which looks upon the law not as a system of norms or a summation of psychological theories but as the statutory expression of the material conditions of social life. The law expresses the existing system of social relations which arises from specific conditions of production and exchange. For this reason, whenever a conflict arises between the law and the needs of national economy, in the Soviet Union, preference is given not to legal but to economic considerations. Soviet theoreticians hold that as planned economy progresses, legal regulations will more and more give way to the purely technical regulation of production and distribution; while disputes between individuals will be left to settlement by their own group.

Such modes of settlement in the case of minor disputes already exist and are recognized by the law. Various enterprises have so-called "comrades' courts" composed of three judges elected at the general meetings of the employees. These judges are elected for a period of six months, but may be recalled before their period of office has expired at a general meeting or conference of the employees. These courts within the enterprise handle cases involving insults, whether oral, written or physical; the spreading of false and slanderous statements; assault without injury; petty thefts involving less than 25 rubles from fellow employees, or thefts from the enterprise involving not more than 15 rubles. Bigger thefts go to the regular People's Courts, the judges of which are workers assisted by technical advisers. The comrades' courts also handle breaches of labor discipline, civil suits for sums not exceeding 25 rubles, except suits involving alimony and labor relations which are handled by other juridical bodies. Misdemeanors such as drunkenness are handled by the comrades' courts. Cases may be brought before such workers' courts, either on complaint of the aggrieved party or of a group of the employees in the enterprise where the defendant is employed or by outside workers and public organizations. The court may punish guilty employees by "comradely admonition," public censure, a fine not exceeding 10 rubles for the benefit of some social organization, or a fine not exceeding 25 rubles to repair the damage done. Decisions of this court are final and not subject to appeal.[33]

As a result of the rôle played by the workers in the Soviet Union, all laws regarding the regulation of labor begin with an explanation of the purpose of the law, namely, the needs and requirements of national economy and the welfare of the working class.

[33] Collection of Laws of the RSFSR, 1930, No. 4, Section 52.

CHAPTER VI

WAGES, HOURS AND LABOR PRODUCTIVITY

A CONSIDERATION of wages in the Soviet Union must take into account that they are determined by different factors than wages in other countries. Since most enterprises belong to the workers' state, Soviet economists say that employees of these enterprises cannot be considered wage-workers in the usual sense of the term. They maintain that under capitalism a wage-worker is one who does not possess the means of production and is therefore compelled to sell his labor power to someone who does possess them; but that in the Soviet Union one can hardly set the individual worker in sharp opposition to the state which represents the organization of the working class as a whole. The state, i.e., the organized working class, owns the machines; hence there is not that severance between labor power and the machine which characterizes capitalist economy. As a result, they argue, labor is not a commodity in the Soviet Union and the wage which the worker receives has a different "social content" from the wage in other countries.[1]

In many respects the external form of Soviet wages resembles wages under capitalism. The Soviet worker receives a definite sum of money in exchange for the time he has worked or for the output he has accomplished. In thus being paid money wages the individual Soviet worker does not receive the full product of his labor but only part of it as is the case in other countries. But the similarity, according to Soviet econo-

---

[1] L. Lapidus and K. Ostrovityanov, *An Outline of Political Economy,* International Publishers, New York, 1930, p. 120.

mists, is restricted to this external form. In the Soviet Union the "unpaid" part of the worker's labor does not fall into the hands of another class, but is spent entirely by the workers' state on expanding industry, building schools, aiding the peasantry, and satisfying other requirements of socialist economy which benefits the working class as a whole, both as regards its immediate interests and its future needs. What in other countries would go to private owners in the form of profits and dividends, goes to satisfy the needs of the working class as a whole, and this, in turn, results in benefits to the individual worker.[2] In addition to a direct money wage the Soviet worker receives supplementary payments, either in money or in kind, in the form of social insurance benefits, free medical and dental service, free working clothes; rent, light and heat free or at a nominal cost, etc. All of these add considerably to his direct money wage. The wage of the Soviet worker, therefore, is that part of the product of his labor which is paid directly to him in the form of a definite sum of money or in indirect payments in money or in kind for the satisfaction of his individual needs, as distinguished from the surplus product which goes to meet the social needs of the working class. Theoretically, a developed socialist system would have no markets and no money, hence wages as a special form of distribution would not exist. Each worker would receive the products and services he needed directly from the distribution centers. But at present such an arrangement is impossible, Soviet economists explain, because Russia is passing through a transition period between capitalism and communism. The market exists; and the workers can receive the goods which they produce only in exchange for money, by means of purchase. Consequently, one form—but only one, they emphasize —in which the worker receives part of his product for the satisfaction of his immediate needs is the money wage.[3]

On the basis of this conception Soviet economists maintain that the laws which determine the amount of wages a worker shall receive are different in the Soviet Union than in other

[2] See Chapter II, pp. 52-55. [3] *Ibid.*, pp. 120-126.

countries. In capitalist society, they say, the wage level is regulated by value; the capitalist pays the worker the minimum required for the uninterrupted functioning of the worker's labor power and uninterrupted creation of "surplus value." But since the capitalist's main purpose is the extraction of "surplus value," he does not trouble to safeguard the minimum required for the worker's subsistence if there is a reserve supply of labor in existence. In the Soviet Union, on the other hand, the working class, which owns and controls industry, cannot restrict itself merely to maintaining the minimum required to reproduce the worker's labor power. Accordingly, there is a constant effort to increase wages so that the growing needs of the workers may be satisfied and their cultural growth guaranteed. This steady increase is achieved by the planned regulation of wages on the part of organizations representing the working class, including the government departments and the trade unions.

Soviet economists admit that this regulation is to some extent limited by the influence of blind factors, which, because of the existence of the market, cannot be entirely eliminated. Nevertheless, they maintain that certain factors which determine wages in other countries do not exist in the Soviet Union. For example, wages are paid on the basis of work, regardless of the worker's age, sex, nationality or cultural level. Men and women receive equal pay for equal work. All workers, irrespective of their race or nationality, who perform the same work receive the same pay. Before the war, for instance, the Baku oil industry paid Russian workers higher wages than the Tiurk workers. The Soviet régime has abolished all such distinctions. Furthermore, child labor as a competitive factor to adult labor does not exist. Minors under 16 are forbidden to work except in certain cases where it is necessary for their training; and in such cases minors between the ages of 14 and 16 may work four hours a day. Between 16 and 18 they receive lower pay than adults doing the same work only if their skill is actually lower. When their skill is equal to an adult's they actually receive higher pay, since they get for a

a six-hour day as much as an adult engaged on the same work
in a seven or eight-hour day. In contradistinction to other countries, the influx of workers from rural districts does not result
in wage decreases nor does the existence of a reserve army
of unemployed workers lower wages. Thus between October
1, 1926, and October 1, 1929, the number of unemployed increased from 1,070,000 to 1,241,000, yet average wages during
the same period increased 10.5 per cent in 1927; 12.5 per
cent in 1928; and 9.5 per cent in 1929.[4]

A differential wage-scale, based on differences in skill, training and responsibility of the position held, has been an integral
and basic part of the scheme of Soviet economic organization
since the establishment of the New Economic Policy in 1921.
It was only during the period of War Communism, when
money and the market were abolished, that the extreme shortage of food and other commodities and the exigencies of the
military situation made it necessary to resort entirely to rationing as a method of compensating labor. During this period
there was approximate equality of income, as the only difference was in the size of the ration, which was greatest for
workers engaged in the heaviest work and smaller for workers
engaged in light work, for office workers, etc. But aside from
this period, financial incentives in the form of higher wages
for work requiring higher skill and training have always been
provided.

Soviet economists maintain that in the period of transition
to fully developed socialism and even under socialism itself
differences in wages and salaries will exist. Only under communism will they disappear. They play a particularly important rôle under conditions existing in the Soviet Union
which has been until recently a very backward country industrially and has suffered from a shortage of skilled workers
and technicians. Soviet economy inherited from the old régime
a working class limited in numbers, and an inadequate number of trained engineers. Millions of workers in Soviet industry
to-day were peasants only yesterday. Many of them are still

[4] A. Nelepin, *Wages in the U.S.S.R.* [Russian], Moscow, 1931, pp. 1-6.

half-peasants. Yet the more industry expands the more it needs skilled workers and trained technicians. The acute shortage in this respect is one of the most serious problems confronting Soviet industry. Under these circumstances every available skilled worker and technician must be properly taken care of, new groups must be continuously trained and incentives provided to draw forth the best efforts of workers and specialists. The rapid labor turnover from which Soviet industry has been suffering has been attributed partly to insufficient differentiation in wages between skilled and unskilled workers. In a speech delivered at the Conference of Industrial Managers in Moscow, June 23, 1931, Stalin stated the problem as follows:

"It is not enough to hire workers. To provide our enterprises with labor it is necessary to achieve the attachment of the workers to the enterprises, to make their staffs more or less permanent. Otherwise it would be necessary to begin anew the training of workers, who would have to spend half of their time in learning instead of producing. Can it be said that the personnel of industrial enterprises is more or less permanent? Unfortunately, we cannot say that. On the contrary, we still have a turnover which in a number of plants is not only not disappearing but, on the contrary, is growing. At any rate, you will find very few enterprises where the turnover has not been at least 30-40 per cent during the half or even quarter of the year. Formerly, during the period of reconstruction of industry, when technical equipment was not complicated and the scale of production not great, it was possible somehow to tolerate this turnover. Now the situation is altogether different. In this period of extensive construction, when the scale of production has become gigantic and the technical equipment extremely complicated, the labor turnover has become the foe of production, disorganizing our enterprises.

"Wherein lies the cause of this turnover? In the wrong wage-scale system, in the 'leftist' equalization of wages. In a number of enterprises our scales are so determined that the difference between skilled and unskilled labor, between hard and easy work, has almost completely disappeared. This equalization leads to a situation where the unskilled laborer is not interested in becoming skilled, having no prospect of advancement. Hence, he considers himself a 'visitor' on the job, working only temporarily in order to save a bit and then go elsewhere in 'search of luck.' To do away with this it is necessary to eliminate the equalization of wages and the old wage-scale. We must not tolerate a situation where a steel worker receives the same wage as a sweeper, or a locomotive engineer the same as an office clerk.

"Marx and Lenin said that the difference between skilled and unskilled labor would exist even under socialism, after the abolition of classes, and that only under communism would it disappear. In every industry and enterprise there are leading groups of more or less skilled workers who must be attached to the enterprise if we really want to insure a permanent personnel. They constitute the basic personnel of industry. To attach them to the enterprise means to stabilize the entire staff of workers; it means to undermine basically the labor turnover. They can be attached to the enterprise only by promotions, by wage increases, by establishing wage-scales which would be an incentive to acquiring greater skill." [5]

Stalin's remarks were interpreted abroad as signifying the introduction for the first time in the Soviet Union of differential wage-scales, piece-work rates, and so on, and to this extent indicating a "return to capitalism." This interpretation is erroneous. What Stalin criticized in this speech was the so-called "leftist" tendency in certain enterprises and localities to equalize wages in violation of the government's present policy which seeks to provide further incentives for increasing the quantity and improving the quality of output by paying wages and premiums in accordance with results produced.

A wage-scale system dividing workers into seventeen categories was adopted in 1922. Later in most of the industries the workers were divided into eight categories, the ratio be-

[5] *Economic Review of the Soviet Union,* August 1, 1931, pp. 339-343.

tween the basic wage rates in the lowest and highest paid
categorics being 1:2.8, as indicated in the following table:

Category	Coefficient
1	1
2	1.20
3	1.47
4	1.67
5	1.87
6	2.07
7	2.33
8	2.80

Wage-scales are worked out for extensive periods (usually
one year) by special agreement between the trade unions and
the industrial organizations. Such agreements eliminate the
element of chance and uncertainty in the matter of wages.
Workers in industry are classified into four main divisions:
workers, engineers and technicians, administrative employees
and managers, and apprentices. The number of categories in
each division and the ratio between the lowest and highest
categories differs in the various industries. In the metal industry the division comprising technicians and engineers is
subdivided into sixteen categories with a ratio of 1:4 between
the salaries of the lowest and highest categories. Administrative employees are subdivided into eighteen categories with
a ratio of 1:8 between the wages of the lowest and the highest. This wage-scale system, which was developed in 1927-28
and is being continuously adapted to the growing needs of
industry, is often considerably modified by means of individual contracts between engineers and executives and the
management. Such individual contracts provide for higher
salaries than those specified in the collective agreements. The
great shortage of trained technicians and administrators enables these employees to conclude especially favorable agreements.

The general tendency now is to encourage the worker to
improve his skill by paying proportionately higher wages to

skilled workers. Piece-work is applied wherever possible and as a rule piece-workers earn more than time workers. An extensive system of bonus payments has been established both for time and piece-workers as well as for engineers and executives. In the rubber industry bonuses for time workers have amounted to as much as 139 per cent of the wage-scale. In the machine construction industry bonuses for piece-workers have reached as high as 64 per cent of the normal wages.[6] In the summer of 1931 the coal combine adopted a new system whereby bonuses of five to ten per cent of the basic monthly wage are awarded to "shock brigades" and individuals who fulfill their quota. Where the quota is exceeded, an additional one per cent is awarded for each per cent of overfulfillment. The bonuses are paid each month and are given only to those who have not been absent during the month.[7] Various bonus arrangements are also in force in other industries.

In determining wages, planned Soviet economy takes into consideration the needs of the national economy as a whole, for it is upon the expansion of national economy that the welfare of the worker depends. An increase in wages, generally speaking, is possible only if there is an increase in the productivity of labor. If wages increased while productivity remained unchanged, the growth of national economy would be endangered. In case of stagnant productivity, every increase in the individual consumption of the workers would be a deduction from the resources and funds at the disposal of the working class as a whole for the expansion of national economy. Furthermore, when wages increase out of proportion to the productivity of labor, production costs and therefore the price of the commodities produced rise. In the regulation of prices by the state price-setting bureaus, the basic factor is the cost of production. As a rule, every trust must show a profit on its operations. Consequently, if costs go up the worker himself must pay more for the goods he buys, thereby nullifying the increase in money wages. At the same time, a rising level

[6] Nelepin, *op. cit.*, pp. 6-16.
[7] *Economic Review*, Sept. 1, 1931, Vol. VI, No. 17, p. 405.

of industrial prices compels the peasant to pay more for the goods which he buys. The dissatisfaction which this causes among the peasants may present grave dangers for the alliance of the workers and peasants, which is indispensable to Soviet economy. Such a situation, as has already been pointed out, was the cause of the "scissors" crisis in 1922-24.

For this reason, one of the main problems of Soviet economy from the beginning has been to increase the productivity of labor. Lenin believed that the economic foundation of the revolution, "the guarantee of its vitality and success, lies in the fact that the proletariat pursues and carries to completion higher tempos in the social organization of labor than is the case with capitalism." [8] But in this respect Soviet economy started with serious handicaps. Under the Czarist régime the productivity of labor was extremely low, being about 25 per cent of the productivity of workers in western Europe and the United States. In 1913 the average annual output per worker was estimated at only 2,231 rubles ($1,149). As a result of the economic disorganization which accompanied the world war and the civil war, labor productivity declined still further so that by 1923-24 it had dropped to about 73 per cent of the prewar level.[9]

The problem of increasing productivity had two aspects: it was necessary to increase the productivity of labor, in the narrow sense of the term, that is, in so far as the worker's productivity depends on the conditions of his labor, the quality of the raw materials and the machinery, and so on; and it was also necessary to bring about a more complete and rational utilization of labor time. In order to develop labor productivity in the first sense, it was necessary to develop the technical equipment of industry. This involved the introduction of new machinery, the discovery of new sources of energy and raw materials, and better methods of obtaining and

[8] Lenin, *The Great Beginning* (pamphlet).
[9] *Employment and Unemployment in Pre-War and Soviet Russia*, by Susan M. Kingsbury and Mildred Fairchild. Report submitted to the World Social Economic Congress, Amsterdam, August 23-29, 1931, p. 69.

working up those raw materials. Hence, for Soviet economy, which started with the limited industrial equipment of the Czarist régime, the improvement of technology was of prime importance. The backwardness of technology was one of the chief factors in the low productivity of the Russian worker. The situation was aggravated during the civil war when the machines inherited from the old régime deteriorated and repairs were impossible. It was for this reason that so much stress was laid in the Five-Year Plan on increasing labor productivity by providing new equipment and new plants. It was also necessary to provide for a better organization of the individual enterprise, including better methods of management, better lighting, better ventilation, and a better arrangement of machinery.

From the beginning, Soviet economy aimed both for the technical reconstruction of the productive apparatus of industry and for the better organization of the processes of production and labor. There were nation-wide campaigns to overcome such difficulties as delay in supplying raw materials to enterprises, lack of coördination between various departments of an enterprise, wasteful and inefficient operations which fatigue the worker and dissipate his labor power, and failure to supply the worker at the bench with materials and tools on scheduled time. Attempts were made to introduce a proper divisional specialization of functions, so that no time should be lost in wasteful disputes and explanations.

In spite of the present comparatively low technical level of Soviet industry, where the development of scientific management is still in its early stages, Soviet economists believe that in solving the problem of labor productivity their system of economy has certain advantages. It is nationalized, centralized and coördinated; and the workers themselves, through the trade unions, factory committees and production conferences, actively participate in the campaigns to increase productivity. "Socialist competition," the "shock brigades" and workers' inventions are important factors in raising the level of productivity by the voluntary efforts of the workers themselves. On the other hand, the state stimulates productivity by establishing standards of output, piece-work rates and the bonus system. Soviet economists explain the existence of piece-rates, bonuses and standards of output by the fact that it is difficult for people to free themselves from the concepts and habits developed by centuries of capitalism. There are many workers still so undeveloped, and many so fresh from the traditions of the village, that they cannot grasp the notion that they have a direct interest in the expansion of industry and should therefore exert their best efforts. Having been accustomed to a low standard of living, they are easily satisfied with the regular wage increases which come in the ordinary course of events and make no special effort to improve their skill or increase the intensity of their work. It is in order to stimulate such workers to do their best, Soviet economists state, that standards of output, piece-rates and bonuses have been introduced to bridge the transition between the old psychology and the new. Furthermore, they say, these forms of awarding effort have important differences from similar forms under a capitalist economy. They are not aimed at goading workers into increasing profits for private capitalists with little or no gain to themselves but at raising the output of state industry, thereby laying the economic basis for the eventual abolition of economic inequality.[10] The Labor Code protects the workers in regard to hours, working conditions, overtime, and so on. The piece-work rates are not imposed from above but are established by agreement between the workers and the management. Finally, the expansion of output which results does not lead to unemployment as is often the case in other countries.

The science of industrial management is new in the Soviet Union, but already considerable progress has been made in rationalizing and standardizing production. Thus the number of varieties of finished cotton cloth was reduced from about 4,000 before the war to about 200 in 1928. The number of assortments of woolen cloth was reduced from 4,000 to 60; the

[10] Lapidus and Ostrovityanov, *op. cit.*, p. 132.

number of types of agricultural implements from 950 to 250; and the varieties and dimensions of glass for buildings from 30 to 9. There have also been marked advances in the process of concentrating production in the more modern and efficient plants and closing down obsolete and inefficient plants. Before the war, for instance, there were about 900 factories producing agricultural machinery, most of them very small; by 1929 this number had been reduced to 44. The recently completed Rostov plant for the production of agricultural machinery is designed for an annual output valued at 115,000,000 rubles, which is above the total output of the 900 prewar factories. Similarly, the Donetz Basin contained 1,200 coal mines in 1913; this number was reduced to 340 by 1929. Yet in 1929 the output per mine was 87,000 tons as compared with 21,000 in 1913, while the total output of the Donetz Basin was 30,-000,000 tons in 1929 as compared with 25,000,000 in 1913; so that 29 per cent of the prewar number of mines produced 18 per cent more coal.

The technical growth of Soviet industry and the increased intensity of labor resulted in a steady increase in individual labor productivity, so that by 1928-29 it exceeded the 1913 level by 38 per cent. During that year the output per worker in anthracite mining rose 20.5 per cent over the previous year. This rise was due primarily to an increase in the mechanical processes of mining and delivering coal, and to various improvements in the organization of labor. In the same year labor productivity in machine construction increased 21.9 per cent due to an increase in the supply of raw materials to the factories, the specialization of production, the introduction of new equipment and conveyor systems and improvements in planning work. In textiles labor productivity increased 19.7 per cent due to the concentration of work, the better utilization of machines, and better organization. The basic chemical industries showed an increase of 28.5 per cent due to a better application of new equipment and an increase in the supply of raw materials. The rubber industry showed an increase of 37.6 per cent which was attributed to a shortening of the working day, a change of assortments and the introduction of new equipment. In the match industry there was an increase of 31.9 per cent due to the starting of operation in new factories with modern equipment. The electrotechnical industry showed an increase of 33.4 per cent, brought about by an increase in the supply of raw materials, an improvement in the skill of the workers, and the introduction of new equipment.* As a result largely of these various factors, the total industrial production of 1928-29 increased to 39 per cent above the 1913 level and the output per worker 38 per cent despite the shorter working day. From 1927 to 1930, the output per worker in census industries increased 45.8 per cent. The largest gain, 97 per cent, was recorded in the oil industry. The iron and steel industry showed an increase of 76.7 per cent, and the coal and coke industry a gain of 17.6 per cent. The following table indicates the increase in labor productivity between 1921 and 1930:

GROSS PRODUCTION PER WORKER PER WORKING DAY [11]
(In Rubles, 1926-27 Prices)

	1921	1927	1928	1929	1930	Increase 1930 over 1927 (in per cent)
Census industry as a whole..	5.7	17.9	21.7	23.9	26.1	45.8
Power plants	..	37.2	42.1	45.6	48.1	29.3
Coal and coke	2.3	6.8	7.0	7.4	8.0	17.6
Oil	23.4	50.8	64.9	83.8	100.1	97.0
Iron ore	1.7	4.5	6.3	6.6	6.9	53.3
Metallurgy—iron and steel	1.3	10.3	14.3	16.1	18.2	76.7
Metallurgy—non-ferrous metals	3.6	37.5	30.6	38.9	46.7	27.2
Machine-building	2.7	13.4	15.1	18.3	20.9	56.0
Basic chemical	..	29.4	23.4	26.7	32.9	11.9
Rubber	10.5	31.5	32.7	37.7	45.8	45.4
Woodworking	6.3	14.0	14.2	14.5	19.1	36.4
Paper	3.8	18.4	19.7	24.9	29.0	57.6
Tanning and fur	8.4	45.7	41.2	45.5	45.7	1.0
Textile	5.9	16.7	20.6	24.2	26.2	62.9
Flour milling	53.0	107.1	120.9	125.8	135.2	26.2
Leather shoe	9.1	20.2	20.1	21.3	24.3	20.3
Printing	1.4	11.7	14.6	17.6	19.7	68.4

[11] *The National Economy of the U.S.S.R.*, op. cit., p. 15.
* Control Figures, 1929-30, Moscow, pp. 238-39.

During 1931 labor productivity rose 4.1 per cent. In the first quarter of 1932, labor productivity in heavy industry increased 13.4 per cent over the corresponding period of 1931.[12]

The planning of labor productivity as part of the industrial-financial plan for the whole of national economy is based, to a great extent, on the amount of electrical energy and capital investments available. In addition, such factors as the improvement of living standards, educational and cultural activities, and shorter hours have contributed greatly to raising productivity. The quantity of energy consumed in industry per worker in thousands of kilowatt-hours has been as follows:

1926-27	*1928*	*1929*	*1930*	*1931*
1.12	1.22	1.42	1.78	2.40 [13]

As a result of capital outlays, various industries have shown marked advances in mechanical operations. Thus, in 1913 there were only four coal-cutting machines in the Donetz Basin and only 0.5 per cent of the coal was obtained mechanically. By 1930, however, 56.3 per cent was produced mechanically. In 1932 the number of coal-cutting machines was increased to 1,421 and it was planned to increase the percentage of the coal mined mechanically to 78. The oil industry also has shown marked advances in the productivity of labor due to the application of modern technique and improvements in the organization of production. In 1913 about 98.8 per cent of the entire oil output was produced by bailing and similar primitive methods; in 1929-30 only 3.1 per cent was produced by such methods, and the remaining 96.9 by deep pumping, compressors and other mechanical means. In the steel and iron industry labor productivity has increased primarily because of the installation of twenty-four new blast furnaces and sixty-one open-hearth furnaces between 1928 and 1931.[14]

[12] *Pravda,* April 28, 1932.
[13] *Social Economic Planning in the U.S.S.R., op. cit.,* p. 146,
[14] *Ibid.,* p. 147.

Labor productivity is closely bound up with the worker's training and efficiency. Students of Soviet economy often point out the backwardness of the Russian worker in this respect. It is, of course, true that Soviet industry is technically behind that of the United States, for example, with decades of experience behind it. But a proper estimation of the achievements and potentialities of Soviet economy must take into consideration the negative and positive factors involved. On the one hand, Soviet industry has suffered from the fact that the Russian worker, only recently a peasant, has had little industrial experience, particularly with large-scale machinery which is comparatively new to Russia, as well as from the lack of experience on the part of Russian executives and managers in industry. On the other hand, sufficient consideration must be given to the enthusiasm and speed with which Russian labor and management has been mastering modern industrial technique, a process which has been of prime importance in raising labor productivity.

Col. Hugh L. Cooper, American consulting engineer for the 800,000 horse-power hydroelectric and navigation project under construction on the Dnieper River in the Soviet Union, has described this mastering of machinery as follows: "Our job is the first construction job in the history of all Russia where large-scale mechanization was ever tried; and if you ever have a similar experience trying to teach people to use 40-ton locomotive cranes, air compressors, air drills, and all the other apparatus, such as we sent over there, don't get discouraged, because you eventually can win. The first year we had 48 locomotive cranes over there, and for the first year about half of these cranes were picking the other half out of the ditch. I never saw so many cranes go over so fast as they did that first year, and the astonishing thing to me was that in all that devastating, horrible experience, there never was a single Russian killed.... To teach these people not merely how to do this work but to do it with the heavy apparatus it was necessary to ship over there in order ever to accomplish the job, was a heartbreaking undertaking; but thanks to the

excellent men I have over there, we have won out. I believe
you will agree with me in this statement: that if we have been
the pioneers in teaching these people how to use great, heavy,
labor-saving machinery for the first time, the experience of
teaching them and their experience in learning will go down
in history as of greater value to the whole nation than the
power plant itself." [15] Similar testimony has been given by
many other prominent American engineers who have been
employed in Soviet industry. In describing their experiences
they almost invariably emphasize the enthusiasm for learning
among the Russian workers and their rapidly increasing skill.

Another aspect of this problem is described in an open letter
addressed early in 1932 by the workers of the Stalingrad tractor
factory to Stalin. This factory was the first modern mass-
production plant built in the Soviet Union. Both in regard to
the errors committed and the remarkable results finally
achieved, it is typical of the problems faced by the young
industry and the rapidity with which Russian labor is mastering modern technique. Part of this letter follows:

"The enemies of the Soviet Union made much of and exaggerated our mistakes and failures. Even friendly foreign
specialists said to us: 'You have built an immense plant. But
—you can't run it yourselves.'

"The problem before us was to become experts ourselves.
We had to master the technique of production, of the utilization of up-to-date equipment. We had to master in a few
months the experience which the United States had accumulated in decades. As a result of eighteen months of persistent effort we have succeeded in solving this problem, as
the following production figures show: July, 1930—5 tractors,
January, 1931—602, December, 1931—2,725. (In April 1932
the plant turned out 2,991 machines.)

"Already the Stalingrad tractor works has made over 20,000
tractors. We have learned how to make three-fourths of the

[15] Hugh L. Cooper, Address before Society of American Military Engineers at the Engineers' Club, Philadelphia, February 25, 1931. *Engineers
and Engineering*, April, 1931, Vol. XLVIII, No. 4, p. 76.

complicated imported tools and machines. Our neighbors, the workers of the 'Red October' steel works, have learned to make high-quality steel. The Stalingrad tractor is now made entirely of Soviet materials. The Diesel tractor will mark a great advance over the most modern designs used abroad, saving the U.S.S.R. 100 million rubles a year in the use of fuel alone.

"The lessons of Stalingrad have been of tremendous value in teaching the Soviet Union how to master new industries and how to construct and put into operation far more swiftly the new giant construction projects of the Five-Year Plan. In particular, the Kharkov tractor factory was set in proper working order and started producing tractors far more quickly than we did.[16]

"How did we do this? How was it that in the first half of 1931 the works produced, with many breaks, only 5,722 tractors, but in the last half 12,686? In February, 1931, the most difficult moment in the life of the factory, our want of technical skill and out-of-date methods of work came up sharply against American technique. The machines produced far less than they should have done, the factory did not obey our resolutions.

"What were the mistakes we made? We had the worker's ardent desire to achieve. We had the best machines. All the same our program was not being accomplished. The will was not enough. We had to add skill, efficiency, new methods of work. Our lathes had no regular masters. Dozens of them got out of order and it was nobody's business. The forge hammers passed from hand to hand; the castings, the dies became useless. In the foundry, scrap reached 90 per cent of the castings.

"We had on paper a continuous working week, resulting in sheer irresponsibility. In February alone there were 900 cases of breakage in machines. The levelling tendency in wages brought about actually lower wages in the forge and foundry, where the heaviest work was done. So men drifted away from

[16] The Kharkov tractor plant started production in October, 1931; in November it produced 391 tractors and in April 1932, 1,950 machines.

these jobs. There were no standards set for any of our machines. We underestimated the need to look after the living conditions of and cultural services for the workers. We were content with the fact that when the works were opened there had also been constructed a new workers' settlement, with a water supply, drainage and central heating system installed; that gardens had been laid out and a school and large factory training school built and opened. But we failed to note that all this was wholly insufficient in comparison with the demands made by the workers. We had to reconstruct fundamentally our methods and organization of work and we started to do this on the basis of your six points of efficiency.

"We had to organize a regular labor supply by contracts with the collective farms and by mechanizing the work. We helped the collective farms which we adopted to mechanize their labor and thus release workers for our plant. We taught them in the factory schools.

"For construction work we had 2,000 workers and needed 9,000. Nevertheless, by rationalizing the work we exceeded the plan by 1 per cent. We are working out a conveyor system for transporting parts from the foundry and forge, releasing hundreds of hands from this heavy work. By improvements in cultural and household facilities, we released 350 workers' wives from household duties and got them into production. By building day nurseries and kindergartens we are getting a further supply of women workers.

"We had to get rid of the excessive labor turnover and of wage-scales which did not correspond with work done, organize proper wage-scales, and raise the standards of living. The heavy and poorly-paid foundry and forge work was put on the progressive piece-work system with a resultant rapid rise in wages. In the forge the average wage was 112 rubles in March, 1931, but 250 in December. In April the foundrymen got 98 rubles, but in December 177. Skilled toolmakers are getting 350-400 rubles a month. As a result these feeder departments now keep the conveyor supplied with parts.

"We now have a model kitchen factory which supplies 37,000

dinners daily; special food is given those working under great heat. Our coöperatives have begun to be reorganized, with a special store for the 'shock' workers and two for the technical personnel. A short time ago we opened the best dispensary in the Lower Volga Region, employing 100 doctors. We built a factory training school for 2,500 workers' children. We can see the new sound films in our Udarnik Theater (which has an attendance of 6,000 a day) as quickly as they get them in Moscow. Soon we shall complete a club building for 3,000 workers and a circus to seat 4,000. Our physical culture circles have grown from 150 members in December, 1930, to 6,000 to-day. Though municipal construction is far from completed, we have already planted thousands of trees, built squares and boulevards, and asphalted some of the streets. Our transport connections with the town have been improved considerably. All these measures have led to the practical cessation of labor turnover. The workers now stick to our plant.

"We had to get rid of irresponsibility, organize work properly, assign duties correctly. We changed our uninterrupted working week to a six-day week, assigning each machine and combination of machines to definite workers and foremen who were held responsible. This cut down breakages at once, and productivity more than doubled in some departments, not only on account of piece-work, but because each worker knew what his job was, and studied his machine.

"We had to create from our working class our own technical specialists. To-day 68 per cent of our engineers and technical personnel are graduates of Soviet institutions. Workers and their children who have passed through the technical schools direct various departments of the works. The young specialists are becoming good organizers and directors of production, but even now we are far from satisfied. We need more and more specialists not only for Stalingrad but for scores of other works. We have a higher technical institute in which 75 per cent of the students are workers. We have a factory training school for 2,500 pupils; our workers' evening university, has 2,400 students.

"We had to change our relations with the old-school engineers and encourage them to take part in our tasks. Many of these specialists, fired by the enthusiasm and self-sacrifice of the workers, have become examples of devoted labor. We give special attention to their living conditions and food supplies, and don't suspect them for every mistake they make, but allow for a certain amount of professional chance-taking.

"We had to strengthen internal accounting and build up reserves within the industry. The first to fulfill your instructions were the smelters. They put all the cupolas on a cost-accounting basis, saving in the first month 30,000 rubles. To-day our plant is run in the main on a strict accounting basis. We have 326 workers' accounting brigades and 7,000 shock workers; each brigade has its agreement with the management and carries it through. The chief result has been to lower costs. Our tractor cost has been cut 50 per cent in a single year. The foundry made a specially good record in ten months, cutting to a third the cost per ton of malleable castings and reducing by half that of the solid castings.

"We pledge ourselves to reach by May 1 an output of 144 tractors daily [this program was carried out] to make in 1932 a total of 40,000 tractors. This year must see the production of a tractor which will be a model for quality. We pledge ourselves to build in 1932 a second factory training school, model houses for all our workers, a House of Technique, and to make our factory a model one in all respects." [17]

The statement is sometimes made that it is the inefficiency of the Russian worker which is responsible for the absence of unemployment in the Soviet Union, since, it is said, it takes three or four Russian workers to perform a job which one American worker could do. A closer analysis of Soviet economy would reveal that the absence of unemployment is due to

[17] *Economic Review of the Soviet Union*, March 15, 1932; Vol. VII, No. 6, p. 129 ff.

other factors. The basic reason is, as Professor Calvin B. Hoover has pointed out, that there is no limit to the purchasing power of the Russian people. The social-economic structure of the Soviet Union permits the unlimited growth of the effective demands of the consumers, and consequently the increase in the demands of industry, which, in its development to meet the needs of the consumer, itself becomes an important consumer of goods. Any increase in the efficiency and labor productivity of the Soviet workers results in increased goods and services which can be indefinitely absorbed by the population directly, and also indirectly, through industry, which, in the final accounting, increases goods and services for the population.

Soviet economists, on the other hand, point out that in capitalist countries increased productivity due to rapid mechanization and more efficient technique results in so-called "technological" unemployment; whereas in the Soviet Union it has resulted in increased wages, improved living standards, and the elimination of unemployment. Furthermore the rise in the productivity of Soviet labor has been achieved without extending the length of the work-day. On the contrary, the work-day has been progressively reduced until it has become the shortest in the world. Compared with 1913 the work-day has been cut by one-third. Often the length of the work-day in prewar industry was 11-12 hours. In some industries it was as high as 16-18 hours.[18] Immediately upon taking power, the Soviet government established an eight-hour day, with a six-hour day for underground miners. Subsequently the seven-hour day was introduced. Since 1903 the average working day for all factory and mine workers has changed as follows:

Year	No. of hours
1904	10.7
1913	9.87
1918	7.69
1931	7.02 [19]

[18] Nelepin, *op. cit.*, p. 52.   [19] *Ibid.*, p. 52.

In the coal industry the average length of the work-day has been reduced from 10.6 hours in 1913 to 7.0 hours in 1931; in the metallurgical industry from 10.7 hours to 7.1; in the machine-construction industry from 9.73 to 6.25; in the chemical industry from 10.01 to 7.0; and in the textile industry from 10.11 to 7.02 hours.

LENGTH OF WORK-DAY FOR WORKERS IN CENSUS INDUSTRY
IN U.S.S.R.

(including overtime work)

Year	Hours	Percentage
1913	10.0	100.0
1921	8.5	85.0
1925	7.6	76.0
1927-28	7.45	74.5
1928-29	7.37	73.7
1929-30	7.15	71.5 [20]

Soviet law, as has been pointed out, prescribes a shorter work-day for harmful or dangerous industries. In 1928, even before certain industries were put on the seven-hour day, 14.4 per cent of all the adult male workers in the country, 4.7 per cent of the adult women workers and practically all of the minors were on a work-day of six hours or less. In order to obtain the greatest possible use from the machinery and equipment, in certain types of enterprises which operate on the multiple-shift system, the seven-hour day has been increased to 7.5 hours. The law, however, requires that the total number of hours which the worker puts in per month does not exceed the seven-hour limit, namely, 168 hours per month. This system is in force in factories which have introduced the five-day working week, in which the equipment works uninterruptedly, while each individual employee works only four days out of the five-day week. Under this system the worker usually gets 48 hours' rest after every four days of

[20] *Ibid.*, p. 52.

work. This is accomplished by alternating the shifts each week. For instance, a worker who finishes his four days of work at 4 o'clock Thursday afternoon does not report for work again until four o'clock Saturday afternoon; then for four days he works on the second shift instead of on the first shift as in the previous week. In some factories it has been found unsatisfactory to keep the plant running continuously without any shutdown for repairs. In such cases a six-day week in which each worker is on the job five days out of six has been established, and the entire plant is closed down on the sixth day. However, the five-day uninterrupted work week is still the basic form of the organization of work, and the majority of workers in industry work on this system.

Other factors which enter into shortening the work-day are the right of the worker to take time off for meals, the time allowed off for nursing mothers, and the practice now being adopted of allowing free periods of rest and physical exercise. During 1931 about 70 per cent of the workers were on the seven-hour day. During 1932 it is planned to have 92 per cent on the seven-hour day and under the Second Five-Year Plan it is intended to establish an average work-day of six hours for all workers.

Soviet economists contrast the steady reduction in hours with the long work-day prevailing in other countries. In Germany, for instance, over 54 per cent of the workers worked more than 48 hours a week in 1930, and over 13 per cent more than 54 hours per week. An investigation conducted by the German Association of Trade Unions in February 1930 revealed that as high as 75.6 per cent of the workers were working more than 48 hours per week. In Great Britain there is an attempt under way to abolish the eight-hour day for miners which was established in 1926. According to official statistics, over 100,000 miners worked more than the legal working time in 1930. In the United States, the average length of the work-week in 25 leading branches of industry, not including mining, was 49.6 hours at the beginning of 1927. During 1928 the average work-week in the textile industry was 53.4 hours and in the steel industry 54.4 hours.[21] In contrast to the six-hour day prevailing in Soviet mines (from bank to bank, which actually means a considerably shorter time spent at work), the International Labor Office in Geneva proposed in June, 1931 to limit the working time of underground workers in the coal mines to 7.75 hours a day. But by permitting various forms of "normal and extra overtime," these proposals in effect established a work-day for coal miners which ranges from 8.5 to 9 hours.

The steady reduction in the length of the working day has in the Soviet Union been accompanied by progressive gains in both nominal and real wages. As a result of the disorganization of economy during the world war and the civil war, real wages declined from an average of 25 rubles a month in 1913 to less than seven rubles a month in 1920; [22] but with the development of national economy since 1922 there has been a steady increase in real wages by from four to twenty per cent a year.

In the fiscal year 1928-29 nominal wages were 190 per cent and real wages 43 per cent higher than in 1913. Real wages of metal workers were 36 per cent above the prewar figure, of textile workers 69 per cent, and food workers 154 per cent.[23] In 1930 the annual wages of all persons working for hire showed a gain of 12.6 per cent over the preceding year, and in 1931 there was a further gain of 23.5 per cent.

These figures refer only to direct money wages and do not take into account indirect payments which the Soviet worker receives through social insurance benefits, free medical aid, vacations with pay, low or free rent, educational facilities, free working clothes, and so on, which increase the wage by an average of from 20 to 35 per cent. If these indirect payments, which were almost non-existent before the war, are included, real wages in 1929 were 69 per cent above the prewar average

[21] *Monthly Labor Review*, 1928, p. 8.
[22] Kingsbury and Fairchild, *op. cit.*, p. 72.
[23] *Ibid.*, p. 72.

and at the end of 1931 they were estimated at about double the prewar figure.[24]

Industries such as metal, wood, leather and the printing trades, which paid the highest wages in 1913 also pay the highest wages at present, while those which paid the lowest wages in 1913 do so at present; but it is worth noting that the rate of increase in the lower paid industries has been from two to four times as great as in the higher paid industries. In 1913, for instance, the average wages of the cotton textile worker were 45 per cent of the wages of the metal worker; while in 1931 the cotton textile worker's wages were 70 per cent of the metal worker's.

For a few years prior to 1931 average wages increased at the rate of about 10 per cent a year. However, in 1931, due to large blanket increases in wages in coal, steel and transportation, the gain was over twice as great. The average wages for all wage-earners, including agricultural labor, increased from 702 rubles a year in 1928 to 887 rubles in 1930, a gain of 26 per cent in two years. In 1931 average wages of all wage-earners showed a gain of 23.5 per cent, rising to 1,096 rubles. The average annual wages of workers in census industry increased from 778 rubles in the fiscal year 1926-27 to 1,167 rubles in 1931, a gain of 50 per cent in a period of 4¼ years. The yearly wages of railroad workers during the same period increased 48 per cent (from 770 to 1,142 rubles). Between 1928 and 1931, the average monthly wages of workers in census industry increased from 70.94 rubles to 96.01 rubles, a gain of 35.3 per cent. The greatest gains were in heavy industry. The wages of coal miners rose 48.5 per cent during this period; in oil extraction the increase was 36.1 per cent; iron and steel—36 per cent; machine construction—30.1 per cent; and woodworking—39.5 per cent. In light industry, paper showed the greatest rate of increase, 35.9 per cent. Wages in the coal and metallurgical industries were further increased by a joint decree of the Supreme Economic Council and the All-Union Central Council of Trade Unions issued on September

[24] Nelepin, *op. cit.*, p. 49.

I

NUMBER AND WAGES OF PERSONS WORKING FOR HIRE IN THE U.S.S.R., 1926-27—1930

	Number of Workers (in thousands)				Average Annual Wages (in rubles)			
	1926-27	1928	1929	1930	1926-27	1928	1929	1930
I. Industry	3,261	3,495	3,761	4,636	750	843	929	1,013
1. Census industry	2,838	3,087	3,353	4,235	778	870	958	1,033
a. Workers (including apprentices)	....	2,690	2,921	3,642	....	823	905	958
b. Employees	....	269	299	426	....	1,478	1,606	1,818
c. Miscellaneous (janitors, errand boys, etc.)	....	128	133	167	....	566	614	677
2. Non-census industry	423	408	408	401	561	639	692	795
II. Construction	547	723	923	1,598	911	996	1,063	1,100
III. Transportation and posts and telegraphs	1,352	1,365	1,422	1,668	770	855	911	1,022
1. Railroads (including repair shops)	961	971	984	1,084	770	859	908	1,033
2. Water transport	111	104	111	132	799	899	1,021	1,151
3. Local transport	185	195	219	310	782	846	962	1,034
4. Posts and telegraphs (including village mail carriers)	95	95*	108	142	712	776	719	799
IV. Trade	583	601	704	848	739	768	795	884
V. Finance	86	95	114	122	920	981	997	1,085
VI. State institutions	2,245	2,362	2,499	2,609	697	781	859	967
1. Educational	715	789	844	915	544	678	758	887

2. Health and veterinary.....	365	414	442	470	569	638	694	748
3. Others.....	1,165	1,159	1,213	1,224	830	903	990	1,111
VII. Miscellaneous **	792	904	982	948	290	296	303	330
TOTAL (I.-VII.)	8,866	9,545	10,405	12,429	709	786	854	956
VIII. Agriculture	2,124	2,007	1,989	2,158	274	305	385	495
State Farms	....	345	399	694	....	327	380	543
GRAND TOTAL	10,990	11,552	12,394	14,587	....	702	779	887

* Not including village mail carriers. ** Made up chiefly of part time day workers and domestic help.

II

AVERAGE MONTHLY WAGES OF WORKERS IN CENSUS INDUSTRY (Excluding Apprentices), 1927-1931

(in rubles)

	1927	1928	1929	1930	1st Quarter 1931	Ratio, 1931 to 1927 (in per cent)
All census industry *	64.64	70.94	77.65	83.30	87.93	136.0
Coal	59.34	63.27	68.81	76.47	83.97	141.5
Oil (extracting)	70.60	77.95	85.50	90.15	99.05	140.4
Iron and steel	68.79	75.61	83.82	88.30	90.05	130.9
Machine-building	82.37	92.94	103.29	108.36	109.63	133.1
Wood-working	55.72	69.98	65.60	72.90	72.58	130.3
Chemical	74.87	82.09	85.85	88.06	91.28	121.9
Food	65.96	73.37	79.06	79.93	81.37	123.4
Cotton textile	55.87	59.89	65.00	64.29	68.29	122.2
Leather and shoe	80.33	86.72	86.49	88.78	91.56	114.0
Paper	60.23	67.04	75.53	82.50	85.70	142.3

* Except peat and sugar industries.

20, 1931, which reorganized wage-scales in these industries, involving increases for all categories of workers but relatively larger ones for the more highly skilled workers. On October 1, 1931, a new wage-scale went into effect by order of the Supreme Economic Council and the Cen†ral Council of Trade Unions providing for a general increase in the wage-fund of 30 per cent. The new scale raised wages for various groups of workers and provided for large bonuses for those who fulfill the production quotas.[25]

The steady increase in money wages has affected not only the workers in industry and transportation but in other branches of the national economy as well, and in the government, health and educational services. From 1927-28 to 1930 the annual wage of employees in commercial and credit institutions increased 19.6 per cent and the wages of administrative and municipal employees 28.5 per cent. The wages of lower paid officials increased 91 per cent. During the same period the wages of employees in the health and sanitation services rose 28.5 per cent, and the wages of educational workers, including teachers, 49.4 per cent. In 1931 the annual wages of these two groups were increased another 10 per cent. The number of employees in education, health and sanitation increased from 1,080,000 in 1926-27 to 1,365,000 in 1930.[26]

In 1931—the third year of the Five-Year Plan—the total wage fund of the Soviet Union rose to 21,100,000,000, as compared with 12,500,000,000 rubles in 1930, and was 34.5 per cent above the original schedule set for the fifth year of the Plan. The program for 1932 was set at 26,800,000,000 rubles or 71 per cent above. Workers in the coke, ore, coal and metallurgical industries received wage increases during 1931 ranging from 20 to 36 per cent, while the more highly skilled transportation workers received increases ranging from 35 to 50 per cent. The 1932 program calls for further wage increases averaging 10 per cent for all workers, for industrial workers 11 per cent, for those employed in heavy industry from 16 to 20 per

[25] *Economic Review of the Soviet Union,* Vol. VI, No. 20, p. 464.
[26] Nelepin, *op. cit.,* pp. 17-22.

cent, for railroad workers 13 per cent, and for teachers and medical workers from 21 to 30 per cent. The progressive piece-work system is being extended in those branches of industry where it is already in operation and has been introduced in a number of other industries, such as the chemical, cement and machine-construction industries.[27]

There have been steady wage increases also for workers on state farms, amounting to 150 per cent in the three years from 1928 to 1931. The number of such agricultural workers increased from 345,000 in 1929 to 1,289,000 in 1931, an increase of more than 270 per cent.[28] The following table indicates the increase in the wages of state farm employees:

Average Monthly Wages of State Farm Employees (in rubles)

	1928	*1929*	*1930*	*1931*
All workers	22.40	26.33	40.00	55.35
Permanent	34.00	38.50	53.58	60.66
Seasonal	28.16	35.00	40.66	48.72
Casual	17.08	19.16	30.83	50.16 [29]

Again, these wages do not include the so-called "socialized wages," such as social insurance, free municipal services, and so on. According to a study made by the Workers' and Peasants' Inspection, these "socialized wages" amount for most state farms to 23-25 per cent of the money wages and for some farms to as high as 48 per cent. In addition, it should be noted that the wage level of the agricultural worker is approaching that of the industrial worker. Thus, in 1928 the average wage of the agricultural worker was only 30 per cent of the industrial worker's average wage; in 1931 it was 60 per cent. At the "Giant" state farm in the North Caucasus the average annual income of a tractor operator's family in 1931 was 1,314 rubles as compared with 1,374 rubles for an industrial worker's family in the North Caucasus. This con-

[27] *Economic Review of the Soviet Union*, Vol. VII, No. 7, p. 155.
[28] Nelepin, *op. cit.*, pp. 25-27.
[29] *Social Economic Planning, op. cit.*, p. 139.

trasts with the United States where the agricultural worker's wages is about 43 per cent of the industrial worker's; Germany, where it is 35; and Denmark, where it is only 25 per cent. In Germany the industrial worker spends for his cultural needs three times as much as an agricultural worker. In this respect, a tractor operator on the "Giant" state farm is on the same level as the industrial worker in the same region. This is especially significant in view of the fact that tractor operators were until recently, for the most part, illiterate peasants working for kulaks.[30]

In industry as in agriculture, the number of workers receiving low wages is steadily decreasing, while the number of workers receiving high wages shows a continued growth. In 1923 about 63.8 per cent of all workers were earning not more than 40 rubles a month; in 1930 such workers constituted only 8 per cent of the total number of workers. At the same time, the group of workers receiving more than 100 rubles a month rose from 1.5 per cent of the total number of workers in 1923 to 29.5 per cent in 1930,[31] as indicated in the following table:

PERCENTAGE OF WORKERS RECEIVING MONTHLY WAGES OF:

Year	Less than 40 rubles	40-60 rubles	60-80 rubles	80-100 rubles	100-150 rubles	Over 150 rubles
1923	63.8	22.8	8.7	3.2	1.4	0.1
1924	52.4	28.3	11.4	4.6	2.9	0.4
1925	31.4	31.2	18.2	9.8	8.0	1.4
1926	21.3	31.4	22.2	12.7	10.6	1.8
1927	13.7	27.2	24.7	15.0	15.4	4.0
1928	11.1	25.6	24.8	16.8	17.2	4.5
1929	9.8	25.4	25.0	17.2	17.9	4.7
1930	8.0	20.9	23.4	18.2	21.9	7.6 [32]

An important factor in increasing real wages has been the decline in the number of dependents and the increase in the number of wage-earners per family, due largely to the entrance into industry of many women workers. Thus, between

[30] Ibid., pp. 17-22.
[31] Ibid., op. cit., pp. 17-22.
[32] Ibid., p. 138.

November, 1929 and February, 1931 the average number of dependents per worker decreased from 2.25 to 1.7, while the number of wage-earners per family went from 1.28 to 1.46. Whereas the wage increase per worker during this period was 10.4 per cent, the total income per worker's family increased about 25 per cent. The following table indicates the average number of workers per family, the average monthly wages per worker and the average income per family in the Soviet Union: [33]

Date	Average No. of Wage-Earners per Family	Average Monthly Earnings per Worker (in rubles)	Average Monthly Income per Family (in rubles)
Oct.-Dec., 1929..	1.28	79.43	101.67
Oct.-Dec., 1930..	1.43	83.29	119.10
Jan.-Feb., 1931.	1.46	87.72	128.07 [34]

During 1931 the average annual wages for workers in all branches of national economy amounted to 1,096 rubles, an increase of 23.5 per cent over 1930, and 40 per cent over 1929. By the end of the year, the monthly income per worker's family had increased 64 per cent over the 1929 figure.[35] This was in part due to the elimination of unemployment and the consequent increase in the number of members per family gainfully employed.

As has already been pointed out, the Soviet wage system is based on the principle of equal pay for equal work irrespective of age, sex or race. Gosplan figures for 1929-30 showed that the wages of Soviet women workers as compared with men in the machine construction industry were almost equal; in the textile industry, 85.2 per cent to 102.3 per cent; in the printing industry from 81.8 to 94.5 per cent and in the rubber industry, 86.6 per cent. From 1927 to 1930 the increase in wages of women workers fluctuated in various branches of industry from 28 per cent (cotton textile industry) to 40 per cent (in iron and steel industry).

[33] *Ibid.*, p. 51.
[34] *Ibid.*, p. 50.
[35] *Economic Review*, April 1, 1932, p. 155.

WAGES OF WOMEN WORKERS IN INDUSTRY IN THE U.S.S.R.[36]

Average Daily Wage of Women Workers
(in kopeks)

Branch of Industry	March 1927	March 1928	March 1929	March 1930
Special machine-building	243.3	301.1	347.3	367.9
Transport machine-building ...	187.8	214.2	274.7	293.3
Iron and steel	158.5	181.3	211.7	222.0
Cotton textile	205.1	223.4	248.1	262.6
Flax and linen	145.0	164.3	174.9	188.8
Rubber	345.2	374.7	412.7	417.9

The wages of apprentices in the factory trade schools during the period from 1926 to March, 1930, increased 34 per cent in the textile industry; 53 per cent in the metallurgical industry; 69 per cent in transportation and machine construction; and 54 per cent in the printing trades. By the end of 1929 two-thirds of all minors in heavy industry were working six hours a day and one-third only four hours. In computing real wages for women and minors account must be taken of the fact that all workers under 18 receive one month's vacation a year with full pay; and that women manual workers receive eight weeks vacation before and eight weeks after childbirth with full pay, and office workers a total of twelve weeks.[37]

The table on the following page indicates the improvements made in the material and cultural life of the Soviet wage-earners. It will be noted that in this table the figures for 1931 represent the program. This program was considerably exceeded; the wage fund in 1931 was 37 per cent above the expected total, amounting to 21,100,000,000 rubles. Likewise, the social insurance fund, which was scheduled to total 2,173,000,000 rubles, actually totaled 2,500,000,000 rubles in 1931 as compared with 1,514,000,000 rubles in 1930. The items shown in the table do not complete the list of factors which enter into the so-called "socialized wage" which is discussed in further detail in the next chapter. Millions of rubles are spent on vacations with full pay, as provided for by the Labor

[36] Nelepin, op. cit., pp. 30-31.
[37] Ibid., pp. 29-32.

Code. Thus a total of 107,000,000 rubles was spent on such vacations, in 1927-28, and 364,000,000 rubles in 1931. Another item is the maintenance of students in the factory training schools, which in 1927-28 involved an expenditure of 19,-000,000 rubles. This sum was increased to 154,000,000 rubles in 1931, an increase of over 700 per cent in three years. Among other items which make up the "socialized wage" are the short-term training courses for workers, now embracing over 1,000,000 workers and involving an expenditure of more than 235,000,000 rubles. The actual increases in all these fields exceeded the schedules originally set by the Five-Year Plan.[38]

Wage Funds	1927-28	1928-29	1929-30	1931	Per cent Increase 1931 over 1927-28
	(in mill. of rubles)			(program)	
Individual wage fund.....	7,801.0	9,640.0	12,508.0	15,368.0	97.0
Ratio to 1927-28..........	100	123	160.3	197.0	....
Socialized Wage Funds:					
(1) Social Insurance......	980.1	1,176.0	1,514.0	2,173.0	118.1
(2) Industrial workers' welfare	60.0	88.0	125.0	285.0	375.0
(3) Additional expenditures by the enterprise (free municipal services, cultural activities) *	355.8	440.2	574.6	679.6	91.0
(4) Housing construction..	419.7	510.9	595.0	1,117.0	166.1
(5) Educational fund.....	994.0	1,448.0	2,700.0	4,088.0	311.3
(6) Health services.......	552.0	670.0	997.5	1,271.0	130.2
(7) Socialized restaurants..	10.0	25.0	65.0	120.0	1,100.0
Total socialized wage funds	3,371.6	4,358.1	6,571.1	9,733.6	......
Ratio to 1927-28..........	100	129.3	194.7	287.6	
Ratio to individual wage fund	43.2	45.2	52.5	63.1 [39]	

* The amounts given under items 2 and 3 are smaller than in actuality since they include only expenditures for workers in industry and do not include workers in transportation, etc.

The progressive rise in the wages of all Soviet workers has proceeded at such a rate that the program set for wages by

[38] *Social Economic Planning in the U.S.S.R.,* op. cit., p. 137.
[39] *Ibid.,* p. 137, and *Economic Review,* April 1, 1932, p. 155.

the Five-Year Plan for the final or fifth year, was exceeded in 1931, the third year of the Plan. Recent increases in the total payroll, in average annual wages, and in social insurance funds are indicated in the following table:

	1930	1931	1932 (program)	1932-33 *	Increase 1931 over 1930 (in per cent)	1932-33 *
Total wage fund (bill. rubles)	12.5	21.1	26.8	15.7	68.8	34.5
Average annual wages (rubles)	887	1,096	1,208	994	23.5	10.2
Social insurance fund (bill. rubles)	1.5 †	2.5	3.49	1.95	66.7	28.2 [40]

* Original schedules for final year of the Five-Year Plan.
† 1929-30.

Wages of Russian workers, both nominal and real, have shown striking gains in comparison with wages in the advanced capitalist countries. According to a study made by the International Labor Office, if the real wages of English workers in 1905-09 be taken as 100, then real wages in Germany during this period were 63.5, in France—55.5 and in Czarist Russia only 34. But in the spring of 1928 the real wages for the various capitals were as follows: London, 100; Berlin, 71; Paris, 56; Moscow, 52; Prague, 47; Vienna, 45; Rome, 43; and Warsaw, 40.[41] Since 1928 there have been further gains in Soviet wages and declines in most of the other countries. The following table indicates the movement of wages in Germany:

Year	Employment Index	Cost of Living Index	Nominal Wages (total fund Index)	Real Wages (total fund Index)	Ratio of Wages to Minimum Budget	Ratio of taxes and other payments to wages
1913-14	100	100	100	100	87.1	....
1925	96	140	121	86	77.8	7.0
1926	85	141	115	81	74.4	9.0
1927	94	148	133	90	85.1	10.0
1928	94	122	143	90	87.1	11.0
1929	90	154	143	93	85.0	11.0
1930	79	147	126	86	77.7	13.0 [42]

[40] *Economic Review*, April 1, 1932, p. 155.
[41] Grinko, *op. cit.*, p. 129.
[42] J. and M. Kuczynski, *Die Lage des Deutschen Industriearbeiters.*

In the United States it has been estimated that in the years preceding the depression a minimum of $2,100 a year was necessary to maintain a decent standard of living for a family of five. Figures for 1929, which take no account of unemployment, show that the majority of skilled workers received wages which covered only 74 per cent of the minimum budget; while the wages of unskilled workers covered only 54 per cent. In 1930 the payroll of manufacturing industries in the United States showed a drop of 20 per cent as compared with 1929, while the number of workers employed was 14 per cent lower. During the first quarter of 1931 the total payroll as compared with 1926 showed a drop of 39 per cent in the steel, iron and machine-construction industries; 46 per cent in automobiles; 38 per cent in textiles and 50 per cent in clothing. The *Monthly Labor Review* for March, 1932,[43] gives the following average index for the total payroll in 54 industries of the United States from 1926 to 1931:

Year	Index
1926	100
1927	96.5
1928	94.5
1929	100.4
1930	80.3
1931	60.2

A survey of 89 industries showed that by January, 1932, the index for the total payroll was down to 48.6 as compared with 63.7 in January, 1931. The same issue of the *Monthly Labor Review* gives the following average indices for employment in 54 American industries:

Year	Index
1926	100
1927	96.4
1928	93.8
1929	97.5
1930	83.7
1931	70.9

[43] *Monthly Labor Review*, Vol. 34, No. 3, p. 705.

To Soviet economists, a steady rise in wages seems a logical consequence of their system. In Soviet economy, they say, where all the means of production belong to society as a whole, the available natural resources and productive forces of the country are used to the fullest possible extent to improve the living standards of the population; it follows as a matter of course that the expansion of national economy and the rise of labor productivity should always be accompanied by the reduction of hours and the increase of both direct and socialized wages.

CHAPTER VII

SOCIALIZED WAGES

THE Soviet worker's real wage consists not only of direct money wages, but also of "socialized wages" which include such factors as social insurance for illness, accident, maternity, industrial and occupational diseases, old age pensions; sums spent for the prevention of accidents and prophylactic measures; socialized medicine; socialized housing and tenancy; municipal services; and the construction of socialist cities. As a separate factor, quite peculiar in its character and of major importance, is the fact that the workers have at their service the socialized distribution of commodities and services, and the increased consumption of food, clothing and other articles at low prices.

Among the most important factors in the Soviet worker's "socialized wage" is social insurance. The Labor Code provides for social insurance to cover free medical aid; payment during temporary incapacity to work due to illness, accident, quarantine, pregnancy, childbirth, or the necessity of caring for a sick member of the family; supplementary benefits for retirement, the care of infants, and death; unemployment relief; the payment of invalid insurance; and payment to persons whose breadwinner has died or disappeared. In addition to these insurance services, an old age pension system was established on May 15, 1929. None of the persons receiving the benefits of social insurance contribute to the insurance funds.

These funds are administered by a system which differs from the administration of such funds in all other countries. Invalid insurance organizations in Germany and other countries are administered either by the employers alone, or by representatives of the employers and the workers, or by representatives of both with the participation of public officials. In the Soviet Union social insurance bodies are administered ex-exclusively by representatives of the insured employees. Administration is in the hands of general insurance organizations established on a geographical basis covering various regions and districts. These societies assist all employees within the district. In the case of the railway and water transportation systems, special insurance organizations have been formed to include all the employees on a railway or water transport system within a given district.

Each of the insurance organizations is headed by a committee elected by the district or regional trade union conventions. The trade unions also choose the auditing commissions which supervise the committees at the head of the insurance organizations. To facilitate contact with the rank and file of workers, there are branch insurance offices in the individual enterprises. Branch offices also exist in the various sections of the city and the various neighborhoods. The administrators of these branch offices are appointed by the committee in charge of the insurance organization in agreement with the competent trade union. The administrators of the insurance organizations and of the local branches must make regular reports to the trade unions. They must also carry out all instructions of the latter provided these do not contradict the law. The local insurance bodies must also report to the higher insurance bodies. Territorial insurance bodies administer the regional and district bodies. The administrative and auditing committees of the territorial organizations are also chosen by the corresponding trade union convention. As a rule, the territorial bodies do not handle the direct care of insured employees, but confine themselves to administrative functions. They also set up health and medical stations, rest homes, sanatoria, and invalid homes for the entire territory under their jurisdiction.

The entire social insurance system in each of the seven federated republics comprising the Soviet Union—the R.S.F.S.R., the Ukraine, White Russia, Turkmenistan, Uzbekistan, Tajikistan and the Transcaucasian Republic—is administered by the Commissariat of Labor in that republic through its national insurance office. Social insurance for the whole of the U.S.S.R. is administered by the All-Union Commissariat of Labor through the All-Union Insurance Office. The heads of these national offices are appointed by the corresponding commissariat of labor in agreement with the competent trade union federation. These officials, like the administrators of the subordinate insurance offices, report to the trade union federations and consult them on all important measures.

In addition to these bodies there is an All-Union Council of Social Insurance. The purpose of the council is to regulate the entire insurance system through the Commissariat of Labor. It consists of representatives of the Central Council of Trade Unions and representatives of the economic commissariats—the commissariats of industry, trade and finance. The chairman of the insurance council is the head of the All-Union Insurance Office of the Commissariat of Labor. There are also in the council, with the right of a consultative vote, representatives of each of the health departments of the seven republics. The chairman of the council is ex-officio a representative of the trade unions, thus giving the workers' organizations the leading rôle in the council. The All-Union Council of Social Insurance directs the general policy of the All-Union Insurance Office; approves its plans, proposals and reports; and settles the rates and conditions of benefits for the country. Similar councils exist in connection with the labor commissariats of the seven republics.

The entire social insurance system is thus coördinated. There are no special or independent societies for various forms of insurance to cover illness or unemployment or permanent disability as there are in other countries. The Soviet insurance system cares for all employees in all cases where they have lost their earnings. The centralization and integration are convenient for the insured and save a great deal of overhead cost, leaving more of the insurance funds for actual benefits to the workers. Thus, while insurance organizations in other countries commonly devote six or seven per cent of their expenditures to overhead, the Soviet insurance bodies pay out for this purpose only about two per cent of their outlays.

Article 175 of the insurance law provides that social insurance must be extended to "all employed persons" regardless of whether "they are employed by state, community, coöperative, concession, rented, mixed or private" enterprises, and regardless also "of the nature and length of time of their work and the method of their remuneration." The only exception to this comprehensive law are persons employed at short time seasonal work who are entitled only to a part of the social insurance services. The reason for this limitation is that the majority of short-time seasonal workers are peasants whose chief source of income is agriculture and who engage in wage-labor merely as a means of supplementing their incomes. If their work lasts more than six months seasonal workers are entitled to the full benefits of social insurance. If the work lasts for a shorter period the worker is entitled to partial benefits. Seasonal workers who are partially insured are not entitled to unemployment benefits or sick benefits nor to relief for their dependents in case they die of causes unconnected with their work. This limitation is intended to cover peasants who leave their seasonal work to return to the village. Such seasonal workers, however, are entitled to relief in cases of temporary illness, or, in the case of women, to benefits for pregnancy and childbirth. They are also entitled to benefits in cases of industrial accident or the death of the breadwinner through such an accident.

Insurance funds are supplied entirely by the "factories, administrative bodies, businesses or persons using wage-labor." These bodies have no right to compel the insured to contribute to the insurance funds or to make deductions from wages for that purpose. Employers making such illegal deductions violate the penal code.

The funds of all the insurance bodies constitute a single all-union fund. The funds of each local or district insurance office are not its property; they belong to the All-Union Fund for

Social Insurance. The law determines the amount to be paid by each enterprise to the social insurance fund on the basis of three scales. These include a normal scale, a supplementary scale and a scale for partial insurance. The normal scale is divided into several categories depending upon the danger involved in the various industries. On this basis, enterprises in the first category, covering the least dangerous trades, pay into the social insurance fund an amount corresponding to 16 per cent of their total payroll; enterprises in the second category pay 18 per cent; in the third 20 per cent and in the fourth 22 per cent. In addition, enterprises in heavy industry, such as metal and mining, pay the supplementary scale, corresponding to 10 per cent of the insurance fund; in transport 12 per cent; and in timber 14 per cent. The scales for partial insurance range from 0.5 per cent of the payroll for seasonal work lasting less than a month during the year to 8 per cent for seasonal work lasting more than a month.

Insured employees are entitled to free medical and prophylactic treatment at clinics, first-aid stations, hospitals, sanatoria, and at home, and to free dental and orthopedic treatment. These services include free medicine, artificial teeth, eyeglasses, bandages, artificial limbs and anything else which the patient may require. Such privileges are extended not only to insured employees and recipients of relief but also to all members of their families. The insurance bodies and trade unions take an active part in the organization of the health service. They participate in the budget commissions of the health offices which supervise the plans for the organization of the health services and handle the money assigned for this purpose. Employees are also entitled to free treatment in sanatoria, health resorts and rest homes where many workers spend their annual vacations.

Insurance benefits for temporary incapacity to work cover not only all kinds of illnesses, but also all other cases of temporary incapacity, such as subjection to quarantine in case of infection in the neighborhood in which the employee lives, the pregnancy or confinement of a woman employee, or the need of taking care of a sick member of the family. In all these cases, workers draw benefits from the insurance fund from the first day of their incapacity until the restoration of their working capacity. Relief in such cases depends upon the length of service of the insured. The period of relief for temporary incapacity to work as a result of illness, quarantine or the care of a sick member of the family is not limited to any length of time with the exception of seasonal workers. These workers receive insurance benefits only until the end of the working season, after which they draw unemployment benefits.

Relief in case of temporary incapacity is paid to all insured persons without exception to the full amount of wages. This includes married and unmarried persons alike, as well as patients in clinics and hospitals. A limitation exists only in regard to the first five days of illness in case the illness lasts less than fifteen days. In such cases full wages are paid for the first five days only to industrial workers who have worked for three years or more. Other employees draw in such cases 75 per cent of their wages for the first five days and their full wages for the remaining ten days. However, if the illness lasts more than 15 days, all employees are entitled to full wages for the first five days.

About 50 per cent of the insured employees in the Soviet Union apply to the insurance treasuries for relief for temporary incapacity. This percentage includes only one application for each applicant and does not take into account additional applications. The system of paying full wages for temporary incapacity and granting relief from the first day of illness permits the worker to leave his job as soon as he feels ill. He is not compelled, through fear of losing all or part of his wages, to continue working until his illness becomes serious.

Maternity relief for women employees includes a regular insurance payment to the woman and a supplementary payment for the care and nursing of the child. Relief in cases of pregnancy and childbirth is paid to all insured women employees regardless of length of service. An exception to this rule are seasonal women workers and agricultural workers who are covered by partial insurance. However, maternity relief is paid to partially insured women employees and domestic workers if they have been engaged in wage-labor for one year altogether, and to agricultural workers, if in the course of the two years preceding pregnancy they had worked for wages at least six months. This exception was made to counteract the tendency of peasant women to leave their villages after they had already become pregnant and obtain temporary work with the sole aim of drawing maternity insurance. But even this exception is losing its importance as a result of the growth of state farms which employ more and more workers as regular wage-earners.

Insurance for pregnancy and childbirth covers eight weeks before and eight weeks after confinement. For women engaged in mental work the insurance period is six weeks before and six weeks after confinement, although in types of mental work involving special strain the period is the same as for industrial workers. The payment is equivalent to the woman worker's full wages beginning with the first day of the twelve or sixteen-week period. In addition, maternity benefits include a lump sum for the layette, free medical attention, and supplementary sums for feeding the child for nine months after its birth. If the mother is not well enough to return to work eight weeks after confinement, she receives an additional eight weeks' vacation with full pay, during which time her job must be held for her. Maternity relief covers not only women who are working but also those who are unemployed or who are receiving insurance benefits for other reasons. It also covers the wives of workers, both employed and unemployed, as well as the wives of workers on insurance relief. Women in these categories receive all the maternity benefits except wages. The supplementary sums paid for the nursing and care of infants vary from 16 to 30 rubles a month for nursing, and 4 to 8 rubles a month for care, depending on the wage-level and living costs in the region.

Invalid pensions under the social-insurance law cover two categories of employees: those who have lost their capacity to work as a result of occupational accident or disease, and those who have become incapacitated from causes outside their occupation. In the Soviet Union the term "industrial accident" is broad in scope. An accident is considered an industrial accident if it is in any way connected with wage-labor. It includes those accidents which occur while an employee is performing his job, or carrying out his employer's instructions, or doing something in the interests of the enterprise on his own initiative, as would be the case with a member of a "shock-brigade." But the term "industrial accident" also includes any accident which takes place in the neighborhood of the enterprise during working hours, even if the worker is not on his job at the time. The term also includes accidents which befall a worker in the fulfillment of his public duties, or in carrying out the instructions of a public organization. Cases of illness among persons engaged in medical or veterinary work during epidemics are also considered "industrial accidents." Similarly, the term "occupational disease" has a wide meaning. The decree of the All-Union Council of Social Insurance on this subject, issued January 4, 1929, contains a broad definition, but even this definition was not intended to be exhaustive and serves merely as a guide to the insurance bodies.

Invalids are divided into six groups according to the degree to which they have lost their ability to work. In the first group are those who have not only lost their capacity to work but also require the care of others, such as employees who have become blind or lame. In the second group are those who have become totally disabled but do not require care. The third includes those who have lost the capacity for heavy work but are still able to do light work now and then, so that they earn something, but have lost more than 50 per cent of their previous earning capacity. The fourth group includes persons who have lost between 30 and 50 per cent of their earning capacity; the fifth, 15 to 30 per cent and the sixth 15 per cent or less.

All Soviet employees are entitled to a pension in case of disability due to an industrial accident or an occupational disease, regardless of whether they are fully or partially insured. Pensions for disability due to other causes are given only to fully insured employees and to the administrative, technical and office personnel engaged in partially insured work. Persons who have lost their capacity to work because of an industrial accident or occupational disease are entitled to a pension regardless of length of service. Those whose disability is due to other causes are entitled to a pension only if they can show that they have worked a certain length of time. The requisite period of service is graduated according to trade and age, as shown in the following table:

Age of Invalid	Length of service required of workers (manual)	Length of service required of employees (clerks, etc.)
20-25 years	2 years	2 years
25-30	3	4
30-40	5	6
40-50	7	9
50 and over	8	12

The period of employment required need not be uninterrupted. Interruptions of this period are not counted unless they last five years or more; they are also not counted, regardless of their duration, if the worker or employee was engaged in military service during this period, or was at school or engaged in partially insured work. Incapacitated workers under 20 are entitled to a pension regardless of how brief a period they have worked. The amount of the invalid pension depends on the cause and degree of disability. Fully insured persons receive the equivalent of their full wages before becoming disabled. The pension is, as a rule, reckoned on the basis of the invalid's earnings during the last 12 months of his employment. But if the worker received a higher wage at any time within five years preceding his disability, his pension equals that higher wage. In cases of disability resulting from an occupational accident or disease, the pension cannot exceed 225 rubles a month. In addition to this sum obtained from the social insurance fund, a worker who has become incapacitated as a result of an industrial accident is entitled to obtain from the enterprise where he is employed further compensation amounting to the difference between his lost earnings and the pension granted by the social insurance fund. Pensions due to persons incapacitated by industrial accident or disease are paid regardless of their financial situation, the amount of their income, etc. On the other hand, persons incapacitated from other causes who have an income or wages, are granted pensions to an amount that makes the sum total of their income equal to their former earnings.

Old age pensions were first introduced in 1928 for workers in the textile, mining, and electro-technical industries and in railway transport. In January 1930 the system was extended to include workers in water transport, the chemical industry, the printing trades, and the tobacco, porcelain and glass industries. The program of the social insurance organizations calls for extending old age pensions to all wage-earners toward the end of the Five-Year Plan period. Male employees in the industries mentioned are entitled to old age pensions after 60 years of age if they have worked for at least 25 years. Women after 55 years of age, if they have worked at least 20 years, are also entitled to old age pensions. Underground workers are entitled to pensions after 50 years of age if they worked at least 20 years. A worker is counted in the group entitled to the old age pension if he has worked for one year prior to his sixtieth birthday in one of the enumerated industries. Thus, a worker 59 years of age who has behind him a service record of 24 years as a wage-earner and who then enters a steel plant or tobacco factory for one year is entitled to the old age pension. The pension is equivalent to 50 per cent of the worker's wages, regardless of his capacity to work. As a rule, the pension is based on the worker's wages during the year preceding his retirement. The maximum pension is 112 rubles a month.

In 1927 a special pension was established for "heroes of labor." If a person has rendered outstanding service in industrial or agricultural production, or in scientific work or service to the state or community he is raised to the rank of a "hero of labor" by a special decision of the Central Executive Committee of the U.S.S.R. at the request of a trade union. As a rule persons are awarded this rank if they have a record of 35 years of service, irrespective of their age; but in exceptional cases the period of service may be shorter. Heroes of labor with a 35-year period of service to their credit receive a pension equaling 75 per cent of their earnings, regardless of their capacity to work or their economic situation. If the recipient continues to work for wages, his pension is cut in half. There is another kind of pension granted to individuals who have rendered special services to the republic but have not been designated "heroes of labor." These pensions may be granted by the special Commissions for the Granting of Personal Pensions which exist in the seven republics, or by the councils of people's commissars either of the Soviet Union or of the republics, or by local soviets. These pensions are paid half by the state or local treasury and half by the social insurance fund. They range from 1,800 to 3,000 rubles a year.

The insurance offices carry out the Soviet policy of preventing disease by actively participating in various measures to safeguard and improve the worker's health. The insurance fund appropriates large sums to the building of workers' homes. Insured employees receive free treatment in rest homes, sanatoria and health resorts located in the former palaces of princes and nobles in the Crimea, the Caucasus and similar regions. The stay in rest homes varies between two weeks and a month, in sanatoria between four weeks and three and a half months. An employee in need of a rest cure receives not only free treatment, free maintenance and free transportation to and from these resorts, but obtains from the insurance funds a sum equivalent to his full wages for the entire period. For workers actually on the job who require special care and diet there are "night sanatoria" where such attention is given free of charge.

Unemployment insurance has been abandoned in the Soviet Union since October 11, 1930, because of the acute shortage of workers and the complete elimination of unemployment. Prior to that date all wage-earners were entitled to unemployment relief if they had worked for a specified period of time and were registered at the labor exchange. For trade union members the period of service required was two years; for non-members it was three. In this connection, however, it must be kept in mind that about 90 per cent of all Soviet wage-earners are trade union members. Unemployment relief was paid in the form of a main payment and family supplements. The amount varied in accordance with whether the worker was skilled, semi-skilled or unskilled and in accordance with the average of wages and the living costs in the six zones into which the country was divided for this purpose. A family supplement was paid for every child under 16, for mothers over 50 and fathers over 55. The scale of unemployment relief started with 23 rubles for skilled workers in the most expensive zone and was less for other workers. The family supplement amounted to 15 per cent of the unemployment benefit for one dependent, 25 per cent for two and 35 per cent for three.

The maximum period for which unemployment relief was paid was 18 months, but payments did not cease if the worker obtained temporary employment for less than six months, or if he belonged to an "unemployed collective" or an artel. Persons who had drawn employment relief for 18 months were entitled to draw relief for another 18 months if they had resumed work for at least six months. Unemployment relief did not deprive the worker of his right to other social insurance benefits, such as payments for temporary incapacity, maternity benefits, etc. He continued to receive free medical care for himself and family when necessary. In addition, the situation of the unemployed was relieved by reducing their rent to almost nothing—a maximum of 5.5 kopeks per month per square meter. They were relieved completely of the payment of community taxes; and the labor exchanges issued free or reduced rate tickets for meals. In addition to unemployment relief from the insurance funds, the unemployed worker also received money payments from his trade union. At the same time, the labor exchanges organized collective enterprises (the "unemployed collectives") and emergency work where the unemployed worker could draw wages for his labor, while remaining registered with the labor exchange and drawing unemployment relief. In 1929 there were about 2,000 such "unemployed collectives" where some 150,000 workers out of jobs found employment. The wages averaged 2.17 rubles per day. In addition to this wage and the unemployment relief, the worker in such a collective could learn a new trade or improve his skill at his old trade. While the system of aid for the unemployed has been abolished with the elimination of unemployment, it remains interesting as an example of the worker's status in the Soviet system.

The overhead for social insurance was reduced to one per cent of the total expenditure in 1931, as compared with 10 per cent in Germany. On the other hand, the expenditures per person insured were 131.57 rubles in the Soviet Union as compared with 53.78 rubles in England and 47.75 rubles in France. Also, the proportion of the wage-earners embraced by social insurance privileges is much greater in the U.S.S.R. than in other countries. For the improvement of medical facilities, the Soviet social insurance funds spent 22.10 rubles per person insured in 1927-28. This figure rose to 37 rubles in 1931. The number of persons in rest homes rose from 437,200 in 1927-28 to 800,000 in 1931, due to the increase in the number of workers and the increased facilities provided by the social insurance funds. In 1929-30 a total of 306,100,000 rubles was appropriated out of the insurance funds for the care of invalids, orphans and old people. The total allocated for these purposes in 1931 was 371,400,000 rubles. During that year 1,234,200 persons received insurance benefits of various kinds. Of these 680,000 were incapacitated by general illness, and 54,900 by industrial accidents or occupational diseases. The total also included 426,000 persons whose bread-winner had died of an occupational accident or disease. Social insurance allocated during 1931 for such items as the care and nursing of infants, the feeding of school children and burial totaled 60,000,000 rubles. For housing construction the social insurance organizations allocated 331,600,000 in 1931; for nurseries and milk centers, 22,000,000 rubles; for kindergartens and the feeding of children, 20,000,000 rubles; and for the training of skilled workers, 100,000,000 rubles. For vacations with pay the social insurance funds paid out a total of 364,000,000 rubles in 1931 as compared with 107,000,000 rubles in 1927-28. Since 1928 the social insurance funds have increased 150 per cent. The total appropriation for social insurance in 1931 was 2,500,000,000 rubles, or about 2.5 per cent above the figure set by the Five-Year Plan for the final year of the five-year period.[1]

The increase in expenditures for benefits to workers disabled by industrial accidents and occupational disease is due to the increase in the number of workers and the steady rise in wages; for the number of accidents has decreased in the Soviet Union as a result of strictly enforced labor laws and the activities of the trade unions. In considering the Labor Code, reference was made to the labor laws regarding sanitation, hygiene and shop rules in general. Here it may be added that in reconstructing old factories and building new ones, Soviet industry pays special attention to such matters as proper lighting, ventilation, working clothes, safety devices, and sanitation. In the Moscow region, for instance, where the textile industry is particularly developed, only 71 textile mills had ventilation systems under the old régime. In the six years from 1925 to 1931 a total of 1,080 new ventilation systems were installed in that region. Every enterprise is obliged to appropriate part of its budget for safety and sanitary devices; in addition the industrial-financial plan for the whole of national economy provides special funds each year for this purpose. Thus in 1928-29 the government spent 54,500,000 rubles for safety and sanitation in industry, and for 1931 planned to spend for that purpose a total of 124,000,000 rubles in industry and 30,000,000 rubles in transportation. The enterprises themselves also spend large sums for labor protection and sanitation. As a result of such measures accidents and illness have been declining. Soviet insurance organizations reported that in 1925-26 there were 10.7 days of illness per worker, while in 1931 there were 9.0 days per worker.

[1] A. Nelepin, *op. cit.*, pp. 38-48; *Social Economic Planning, op. cit.*, pp. 142-143; *Trud*, May 4, 1932.

In recording industrial accidents, Soviet organizations are required to consider every case. There is no tendency to conceal or minimize industrial accidents or to shift the burden to the hospitals. It is difficult to compare the accident rate in Soviet industry with the rate in other countries, since the system of private insurance in other countries leads to incomplete statistics; nevertheless, even on this basis the index of fatal industrial accidents for 1929 was lower in the Soviet Union than in Germany or the United States. In Germany the figure was 0.45 fatal accidents for 1,000 fully insured persons; in the United States 0.40, while in the Soviet Union it was only 0.26. The same holds true of serious, though not fatal, accidents. The systematic and steady improvement of Soviet labor conditions has resulted not only in a lower percentage of accidents as compared with other countries, but also a reduction in the total number of accidents. A recent survey of large enterprises in Leningrad showed that accidents in the "Red Putilov" plant had decreased 8.6 per cent in one year; at the Electrosila plant accidents decreased 16.6 per cent; at the Electric plant by 25.1 per cent; at the Baltic shipyards by 34.4 per cent; at the Optical works by 36.6 per cent; and in some other plants by as much as 50 per cent.[2]

It is interesting to note that industrial accidents decreased in these plants despite the fact that they are on the piece-work system. This is attributed partly to the fact that Soviet labor legislation prevents the piece-work system from being misused so as to fatigue the worker, and partly to the interest in work which the Soviet system stimulates in the worker. In addition, some 80 scientific institutions and laboratories are engaged in research on labor conditions. These, and the worker-inventors, supply industry with numerous safety and sanitation devices and suggestions. The joint budget of these 80 institutions is 7,500,000 rubles a year. They work in close coöperation with the factory laboratories and research departments, and with an extensive network of special technical research institutes which are subsidized independently.

[2] *Ibid.*, pp. 141-142.

The elaborate system of labor protection and the many measures for safeguarding and improving the well-being of the worker have had a profound effect on vital statistics. The gains in this respect are all the more striking since the population of the Soviet Union has had to overcome unusual handicaps. Their miserable existence under the old régime left its impress on their health. They were further exhausted by the sufferings of the world war and the civil war; by the famine and destruction which accompanied foreign intervention; and by extremely backward factory and housing conditions. But the rapid expansion of industry and the general improvement in living standards have greatly increased the worker's stamina. As a result the death rate compares more than favorably with Germany, for instance. German factory insurance fund statistics show that for every 1,000 workers insured in 1928 the annual death rate was 6.3 and in 1929 6.7. In the Soviet Union the respective averages were 5.1 and 4.8. Since the war, the average age of the German worker in industry has declined; nevertheless the death rate among German industrial workers has tended to increase. In the Soviet Union, on the other hand, there has been a marked decrease. From 1913 to 1916 the death rate among Russian factory workers was 8.0 per 1,000 men, 5.1 per 1,000 women, and 6.9 per 1,000 of both sexes. Prior to the revolution factory workers were practically the only workers entitled to insurance; hence in comparing the prerevolutionary death rate just cited with the present rate, only industrial workers can be included. On this basis, the changes in the death rate per thousand have been as follows:

	1913-16	1924-5	1925-6	1926-7	1927-8	1928-9	1929-30
U.S.S.R.	6.9	6.0	6.0	5.4	5.1	4.8	4.3
R.S.F.S.R.	...	6.2	6.2	5.4	5.2	4.9	4.4
Ukraine	...	5.0	4.9	4.3	4.3	4.0	3.5 [3]

The decrease in the death rate and the general improvement in the workers' health is partly due to the complete reorganization of medicine under the Soviet régime. Health service is con-

[3] *Ibid.*, p. 146.

sidered a public utility in the Soviet Union. The physician is in the service of society and his job is not only to cure the sick but to keep those who are healthy from becoming sick. For this reason prophylaxis is one of the main functions of Soviet medicine. In this respect great strides have been made in comparison with the prewar period. In 1913 there were less than 13,000 physicians in the whole of Russia. The majority of these were in the cities, so that the peasant population received little medical attention. In some rural districts there was only one physician to 30,000 or 40,000 people. Semi-trained men and women known as *feldschers* took care of emergencies, performed minor operations, and handled the commoner ailments. Outside the urban centers trained nurses were rare. The death rate in the hospitals was high, and the infant mortality rate was the highest of any civilized country, being more than twice that of England and more than four times that of Norway. There was no central health organization. Private institutions and practitioners did not work according to accepted standards.[4]

In 1918 medical institutions and the treatment of disease were nationalized and made a function of the state. The socialization of medicine involves making medical aid accessible to persons covered by social insurance free of charge, training a highly qualified medical personnel, and stressing the prevention of disease. Hospitals, sanatoria and pharmacies became state institutions, and doctors, *feldschers*, nurses and druggists became employees of the state. All persons connected with the practice of medicine, including physicians, nurses, druggists, clinical workers, laundresses and chauffeurs employed by hospitals and clinics, were organized in the Medical Workers' Union. However, private medical practice has not been entirely abolished. After his six-hour day as a civil servant, the physician is free to treat private patients for a fee. But even this practice is rapidly disappearing with the rapid development of state hospitals and clinics, and the increasing

---

[4] See *Medical and Other Conditions in Soviet Russia*, by Dr. Lewellys F. Barker, Johns Hopkins University.

tendency of physicians to devote their spare time to research work, for which the government supplies them with facilities.

Since the chief object of Soviet medicine is to raise the health standards of the population, medical students are kept in close contact with the mass of workers and peasants. They are taken to factories, schools and homes to study the sanitary conditions of the population at first hand. Social factors of disease and measures for the prevention of disease receive the greatest attention. In order to work out suitable preventive methods, the Soviet health service studies the working conditions of various occupations and the living conditions in the homes of the people. It also carries on a constant educational campaign to instruct the population in the elements of hygiene.

The program for disease prevention includes the widespread organization of state dispensaries and prophylactoria. The so-called "unitary dispensaries" serve districts of about 30,000 people each, and take care of about 1,000 patients a day. Every person in the district must report at specified periods to the dispensary for a physical examination. The growth in the number of hospitals and physicians in the R.S.F.S.R. (Russia proper) and the Ukraine since the establishment of the Soviet régime is indicated in the tables on the following page. A similar growth has taken place in the other federated republics.

As a result of improved living conditions and of the extension of the health service, the death rate in the European part of the Soviet Union declined from an average of 28.6 per thousand in the period from 1911 to 1913 to 20.8 per thousand in 1927. Infant mortality has declined from 300 per thousand in 1910 to 164 per thousand in 1928. Since 1928 there have been still further declines in general and infant mortality.[6]

One of the most important sources of "socialized wages" is connected with housing and rents. The growth of the population in the past decade, the destruction caused by war and the rise in living standards have made housing one of the most acute problems in the Soviet Union. In 1913 Russia proper

[6] *Economic Handbook of the Soviet Union, op. cit.,* p. 138; *Foreign Office Information Bulletin, No. 60* (479), December 25, 1931, pp. 4-6.

HEALTH INSTITUTIONS AND MEDICAL PERSONNEL IN THE R.S.F.S.R.[5]

Year	No. of medical districts	Rural pop. per med. dist.	Hospitals		No. of out-patient depts.	No. of dispen-saries*	Inst. for Motherhood and Infancy		No. of doctors	Doctors per 10,000 population
			Number	No. of beds			No. of pre- and post-natal clinics	No. of medical nurseries		
1913	3,226	36,300	....	....	....	...	...	...	15,935	1.15
1924	3,938	20,200	3,553	146,058	5,735	188	548	536	17,251	1.83
1927	5,097	16,400	4,286	189,258	7,574	527	...	793	28,594	2.84
1930	6,922	12,800	4,906	195,476	8,947	561	1,534	1,574	46,127	4.23

IN THE UKRAINE

Year	No. of medical districts	Rural pop. per med. dist.	Hospitals		No. of out-patient depts.	No. of dispen-saries*	Inst. for Motherhood and Infancy		No. of doctors	Doctors per 10,000 population
			Number	No. of beds			No. of pre- and post-natal clinics	No. of medical nurseries		
1924	1,313	17,300	883	26,236	.....	141	201	105	6,276	2.32
1927	1,574	15,000	954	33,166	.....	219	513	200	9,898	3.43
1930	2,157	11,400	1,190	39,204	2,001	232	577	327	15,503	4.61

[5] *The National Economy of the U.S.S.R.* [Russian], Moscow, 1932, p. 554.
* Includes clinics, visiting nurse-service, over-night sanatoria and general health and family follow-up.

had a total population of 139,700,000 of which 25,700,000 or 18.4 per cent lived in the cities. By 1922-23, at the end of the civil war and the beginning of economic reconstruction, the total population of the Soviet Union had been reduced 4.6 per cent as compared with 1913 and the urban population 14.8 per cent. The depopulation of the cities was due to the wartime destruction of industry and the difficulty of supplying the cities with food.

The reconstruction of industry during NEP was accompanied by a flow of population to urban centers. By 1927-28 the cities had a population of 27,900,000 or 18.4 per cent of a total population of 151,300,000. During the NEP period the urban population increased at an annual rate of 5 to 6 per cent as compared with Germany's annual rate for the same period of 1.05 per cent, the British annual rate of 1.04 per cent and the annual rate in the United States of 2.5 per cent. The Soviet Union had at this time few big cities. Moscow was the only city with a population of over 2,000,000 among the 1,924 urban settlements of the country. Leningrad had 1,800,000, and Kharkov, Kiev, and Tiflis each over 500,000. Leading cities like Odessa, Dniepropetrovsk, Baku and Rostov had populations of over 200,000. Altogether there were 31 cities with populations of over 100,000, and 60 cities with over 50,000. The remaining towns were small and their housing conditions and public utilities primitive. The situation was aggravated by the fact that for more than six years, during the world war, civil war, blockade, and intervention, no new houses had been built and old houses had not been repaired.[7]

As a result of the rapid growth of the urban population under these conditions, there was during the period from 1921 to 1928 a steady reduction in the housing space per capita. The decline was finally checked in 1927-28 when the average floor space available per person of the urban population was only 5.9 square meters (63.5 square feet), while the average floor space available per person of the working population was even less, being 4.9 square meters (53 square feet) per person.

[7] Grinko, *op. cit.*, pp. 223-224.

At the begining of the Five-Year Plan almost 75 per cent of all industrial workers living in urban settlements had about 6 square meters (64.5 square feet) of floor space each. In many industrial regions and for many industrial workers the average floor space available for living quarters was 3 square meters (32 square feet) per person. Accordingly, one of the most important problems which had to be solved under the Five-Year Plan was that of housing which Soviet authorities considered "the gravest heritage of the capitalist order." [8] The conditions of the cities under the old régime have been described as follows by G. T. Grinko, former vice-chairman of the State Planning Commission of the Soviet Union:

"It should be noted that the Russian pre-revolutionary cities bore the strong impress of the feudal-commercial-capitalistic and bureaucratic régime. The typical plan of the pre-revolutionary Russian city consisted of a more or less well arranged central part devoted to administrative and commercial enterprises and institutions, and a few streets consisting of mansions literally drowned in flowers and surrounded by gardens giving evidence of exceptional luxury, and belonging to the feudal, bureaucratic, commercial and industrial aristocracy; but all the other parts of the town consisted of hopelessly gray, poor, and dirty streets and suburbs where the toiling people in general and the proletariat in particular lived. In all the cities of the pre-revolutionary Russian empire, the working class sections never had any general sewer or water supply system. Neither did they have electric lights, trolleys, or even sidewalks. The slums of the city of feudal-capitalistic Russia in all their unattractiveness have been many times described in Russian literature. This horrible condition of the cities, left over from pre-revolutionary days, underwent further deterioration during the years of civil war.[9]

The government approached the housing problem during the first stages of economic rehabilitation by nationalizing part of the urban living quarters. By 1927-28 about 74,000,000

[8] *Ibid.,* p. 225.
[9] See Chapter 1, pp. 15-17; and *Ibid.,* pp. 225-226.

square meters (800,000,000 square feet) out of a total of
160,000,000 square meters (1.73 billion square feet) of housing
floor space had been nationalized. Individual owners and tenants retained the remaining housing space, which consisted
mainly of small buildings.

Nationalized housing is used either directly for state, social
and coöperative enterprises or is under municipal management.
More and more nationalized housing is being transferred to
the housing coöperatives, or is being rented to individual
families. In the construction of houses, the lead has been taken
by the building coöperatives whose superiority in this field
has been generally recognized. These coöperatives construct
entire new residential sections in the cities and have created
new urban settlements near big plants. Industrial enterprises
often build houses and settlements directly, constructing types
of living quarters which are best adapted to the needs and
interests of their workers. These are located near the plant
and are provided with all necessary facilities. Some of these
enterprises have built or are building entire cities, as in the
case of the Baku oil industry, Magnitogorsk, Kuznetsk, Nizhni
Novgorod, the Stalingrad tractor plant, Dnieprostroy, etc.
These cities have modern municipal and cultural facilities and
the best technical equipment.

Housing construction on a large scale began in 1926 when
292,000,000 rubles were spent for this purpose. In 1927-28 all
Soviet industries jointly invested 419,700,000 rubles in housing
construction, and in 1931 a total of 1,117,000,000 rubles. The
increase in the rate of investment in housing construction
greatly exceeded the rate of increase in the number of workers.
The housing space per worker rose from 4.9 square meters in
1928 to 5.2 square meters in 1930. Investment in housing for
industrial workers in 1931 totaled 575,000,000 rubles as compared with 300,000,000 in 1930 and 63,000,000 in 1929. In the
coal regions alone housing investments amounted to 201,-
000,000 rubles as compared with 95,000,000 in the previous
year. The total dwelling space for wage-earners in socialized
industry increased from 8,500,000 square meters in January

1931 to 14,000,000 in January 1932. In the coal regions the total dwelling space increased from 2,200,000 square meters at the beginning of 1931 to 4,000,000 at the beginning of 1932. During the first three years of the Five-Year Plan the workers obtained a total of 16,800,000 square meters of new dwelling space. It was planned to increase the new dwelling space for all workers to 33,000,000 square meters by the end of 1932, but housing facilities are still far from adequate. The present extensive program of housing construction will have to be maintained and intensified for a number of years before housing difficulties are overcome.

Fifty-seven per cent of the 1931 expenditures for housing construction were spent on building new settlements. One of the chief aims in erecting new houses and new settlements is to allow a larger percentage of workers to live close to the enterprises where they work. This places at their own disposal the time previously spent in traveling to and from work. In the Donetz basin, for example, the number of houses situated within one kilometer from the place of work in 1929 constituted 41 per cent of the total number of workers' houses as compared with 15.8 per cent in 1923. Thirty per cent of the workers' houses were located within two kilometers of their work place in 1929 as against 14 per cent in 1923; and one per cent within three kilometers as against 29.7 per cent.[10]

Tenancy in the Soviet Union is based on conditions which have no counterpart anywhere else in the world. A family living in a house owned by the municipality does not rent it for a limited period but may remain there indefinitely. No worker can be ejected from his home when he ceases to work for the enterprise which owns it. Rent is not based on contracts; nor is it determined by the amount of ground rent. The amount of rent which a tenant pays depends upon his income and the number of his dependents. Preferential rates for workers are widespread. Certain categories of workers enjoy rebates which run as high as eighty per cent of their rent. The lower the income of the worker and the greater the number of his de-

[10] *Social Economic Planning, op. cit.,* pp. 144-145.

pendents, the lower is his rent. In many industrial enterprises, the workers receive housing, light and fuel free of charge. Even where rents are paid, they constitute only a small fraction of the total expenditures of the worker's family. In 1929-30, the average rate paid by workers' families amounted to only 6.4 per cent of the total family expenditures, compared with about 20 per cent, which is considered the normal rate in other countries. Under this system of tenancy, even the workers receiving low wages can live in the better apartments.[11] This part of the worker's "socialized wage" greatly increases his real wage.

An ordinance issued by the Council of People's Commissars at the end of 1930 stressed the fact that despite the improvements in workers' housing and municipal services, these developments were inadequate and not in accordance with the requirements of an industrialized country. The ordinance declared that housing and municipal services were to be among the most important tasks to be carried out by the country. In regard to municipal services, the Soviet heritage from the previous régime was especially poor. Only 19 out of 1,063 cities had sewage systems before the war; about 200 had central waterworks; only 34 had street car lines, and 32 had municipal gas works. Even these backward facilities deteriorated as a result of the world war and civil war. Furthermore, such facilities were confined almost exclusively to the better residential sections, while the workers' districts were almost entirely neglected.

Little progress was made in municipal services during the early stages of the Soviet régime. Only the most serious problems in this field could receive any attention. Municipal economy and housing received more attention with the inauguration of the Five-Year Plan, under which over 1,000,000 workers' families moved from old quarters to new dwellings. New street car lines, water supply systems and sewage systems have been built or extended in a number of cities. From 1927 to 1931 about 5,000 new houses were built in Moscow alone; the number of street cars doubled; and the water supply and

[11] *Ibid.*, pp. 144-145.

sewage system were greatly extended. This progress, however, does not yet meet the requirements of the rapidly growing population of Moscow, which in 1931 was nearly 3,000,000 or over 70 per cent above the prewar level.[12]

From 1917 to 1931 a total of 114 new water supply systems were installed throughout the Soviet Union, bringing the total for the country up to 333. By the middle of 1931 the per capita water supply in cities was 22.5 liters. It is planned to raise this to a per capita minimum of 35 liters by the end of the Five-Year Plan. By 1931 there were 32 cities with sewage systems as compared with 19 before the war. In the same year 43 cities had street car systems as compared with 34 cities before the war. New street car systems are being built in centers like Cheliabinsk in the Urals; Grozny in the North Caucasus; Shakhty in the Donetz Basin; Zaporozyhe in the Ukraine; and Erivan in Armenia. The extension of the tramway systems is one of the most serious problems confronting Soviet municipal service. By 1931 the number of passengers had increased 85 per cent compared with the prewar period while the number of cars in use increased only 46 per cent.[13]

To meet the present housing shortage in industrial and agricultural centers, new buildings are being erected everywhere. Some of these are apartment houses, others are communal houses which are adapted to the new mode of life developing in the Soviet Union. Of greatest interest, perhaps, are the new socialist cities and settlements which are to be built along new lines based on the type of industry which such centers are intended to serve. It is planned to adapt these socialist cities to the requirements of collective living, and the climate of the district. They are to contain all the necessary domestic, cultural and educational buildings. Adequate provision is to be made for vegetation, parks and open spaces. Each new socialist city is to be organized around the basic industrial or agricultural center, and is to be equipped with proper facilities for transportation, collective preparation of food, and cultural activities.

[12] *Economic Review*, August 15, 1931, p. 364.   [13] *Ibid.*

The planning of socialist cities seeks to avoid errors of the old methods in which workers' houses were first built and only subsequently the various communal features provided, as if these were adjuncts and not integral parts of every residential settlement. The basic principles on which the new socialist cities will be built will be the same, but in each case there will be considerable variety in detail, depending on the nature of the locale. On the basis of Soviet experience in city planning, the new socialist cities will be of three general types: purely industrial cities or settlements; agrarian settlements; and industrial-agrarian cities, a hybrid type which will seek to unite city and country life. Coast, mountain and health resort cities and settlements will be of a specific type.

Soviet city planning provides for the construction of socialist cities and settlements in many districts. These include a minimum of six cities in the Donetz Basin; four in the Stalingrad region, in addition to the complete readaptation of the existing city of Stalingrad; and one city each at Magnitogorsk, Nizhni Novgorod, Dnieprostroy, in the Khopersk region, etc. In addition, proposals are being considered for the thorough reconstruction of Novo-Sibirsk, Briansk, Odessa, Rostov-on-Don, and numerous other centers now in the process of industrial development.

Stalingrad may be taken as an example of the principles involved in Soviet city planning. The fact that Stalingrad is situated on the banks of the Volga may bring in certain features inapplicable to other socialist centers; nevertheless, the general principles are likely to be similar. The Five-Year Plan provides that Stalingrad shall be converted into a center with numerous new factories, mills and power stations. This plan also provides for the construction of entirely new houses, cultural centers and institutes. This new industrial center is to be constructed in such a way as to link up all the elements of national economy on the basis of their utility and inter-relationship. The Stalingrad tractor plant, already completed, is part of this plan.

According to recent plans for this region, it is proposed to build a socialist city consisting of five sections. The new plans call for a rational grouping of industrial enterprises, based on their technological inter-relation in the process of production. There will thus be four industrial combinations: a metal manufacturing combine, including a maximum of twenty metal manufacturing mills with 80,000 employees; a timber combine; a chemical combine and a combine for light industries. These enterprises will be centralized, instead of being scattered over the wide area occupied by Stalingrad along the Volga. Accordingly, production costs will be greatly reduced because of the proximity to each other of the mills and factories dependent on one another for raw materials or semi-manufactured goods.

This vast organization of industrial enterprises will be accompanied by the construction of socialist·cities to house the working population of each industrial center. The present city of Stalingrad—formerly called Tzaritzin—is to be rebuilt on new lines, and in addition four new socialist cities are to be constructed, so that the Stalingrad of the future will consist of five separate cities.

In regard to living quarters, it is planned to diminish the rôle of the one-family house. Large buildings are to be erected to house the adult working population from sixteen years of age upward. Every individual will be entitled to at least one large furnished room. All the most modern conveniences will be privided in these communal houses. Every house will have its own swimming pool, showers, gymnasium, mechanized laundry, as well as the necessary equipment for mechanized house-cleaning. Electricity and steam will be supplied from the nearest heat and power station. Every building will have communal rooms, such as a library, a study hall, and a dining hall built along the lines of an American cafeteria. In addition every house will be provided with a buffet supplying sandwiches, candy, and mineral waters which will be open after the dining hall has closed. It is an essential part of socialist city planning that every house be surrounded by land for communal vegetable, fruit and flower gardens, which will be in the care of the residents. Every building will also contain distribution centers for wares which are not provided for in the collective program.

The former practice of housing the administrative and technical staff in special buildings will be discontinued. In the future they will be allotted quarters in those houses where the general working staff resides. When necessary members of the administrative staff will be given extra rooms. Hotels will be available for temporary residents. Children up to three years of age will have special nurseries connected with the main buildings by heated passages. Older children will have kindergartens.

In the center of the socialist cities there will be a zone in which all the social-cultural buildings will be located; around these will stretch the housing units. Every city will have its own central heating system, operated either by the industry involved or by a special heating station. Around the residential section there will be parks containing schools with open spaces for games. Separating the residential section from the industrial section will be a belt of vegetation varying from half a kilometer to a kilometer in width.

A big central food combine, according to the plan, will supply the entire population of the five cities of Stalingrad with food, which will be prepared with the aid of modern technical appliances. To make up for the present shortage of skilled cooks, special schools are to be established for training cooks, which will also run a model restaurant. These activities are to be under the supervision of specialists from the All-Union Food Trust (Narpit). Restaurants will be situated conveniently near all social and cultural institutions as well as in the various houses. These are intended to save the workers' time. The various plants will be supplied with buffets which will supply the workers with good food at cost prices. A special section will prepare food for children. It will include a milk kitchen and a department to prepare special diets.

Auxiliary agricultural enterprises are planned to supply foodstuffs which cannot conveniently be transported over long distances. Similarly there will be facilities for preparing agricultural products such as milk, butter, cheese, etc.

The educational facilities of the socialist cities will be devoted to the needs of the entire population. The education of children is to be entirely on a collective basis. Pre-school education will be linked up with simple working processes, and centers for children will be provided with simple agricultural enterprises where children may become acquainted with the processes of nature in the course of their recreation. The socialist school is planned to be continuous all the year round and will run the entire day. Educational facilities will also include theaters, auditoriums, public squares, parks, stadiums, and country resorts. Advanced scientific work will be centered in separate institutes, such as libraries, and laboratories which will be located in the central park of culture, rest and science.

In building the transportation systems of the socialist cities of Stalingrad, every consideration will be given to the convenience of the residents, so that in no case will a worker be more than a quarter of a mile from a station. Along the belt separating the industrial from the residential section of the city, electric railways will be built. Within the boundaries of the city it is proposed to have electric cars below the surface. Automobile roads will be built outside the town.

These general principles are expected to underlie the construction of all socialist cities. Along these lines, for instance, there will be a socialist city at Magnitogorsk in the southern part of the Urals. It is estimated that the population of this industrial center will be 50,000. The entire adult population, with the exception of the ill, infirm and aged, will participate in productive work of some kind. The life of the workers, except those engaged in productive and other enterprises of general municipal importance, will be centered in communal dwellings in which workers will be free from household cares inherent in individual dwellings. Children up to sixteen are to be educated along socialist lines in nurseries and kindergartens and live in residential halls adjoining the adult residential quarters. In other centers, notably Nizhni Novgorod, there are both dormitory types of dwellings and individual apartments, with kitchenettes, etc., where the children live at home. A special central institute will be built for defective children. A central enterprise will provide all the food required by the population, by means of food combines in all enterprises, social centers and residential communes. A large central general store will supply the population with all articles of a personal nature. Distribution will be arranged through chain stores in the various residential communes. Motor transport will be organized for the convenience of workers employed in outlying institutions as well as for out of town excursions. A street car line will be constructed along one of the main streets. Communal residences will be either state or coöperatively owned. One centrally located square is to be equipped for holding meetings and public demonstrations. The land adjoining the city is to be utilized for market gardening, dairies, etc. Around the schools provision will be made for adequate open space for vegetation and the maintenance of animals.

At Nizhni Novgorod the "first model socialist city" is being constructed under the supervision of the Austin Company of Cleveland. It is designed to accommodate about 60,000 persons, chiefly workers in the new automobile plant and their families. The buildings will be grouped around a central square, where the municipal government offices, the "palace of culture," the stores, hotels and museum will be located. There will be wide boulevards and a park taking up one-third of the total area of the city. At one end near the automobile plant are located the kitchen factory, packing and refrigerator plants, bakery, laundry and other service units. In other parts of the city there are a hospital, crematorium, athletic fields, a stadium, and sites for a university and other buildings. The houses face east and west, affording the maximum sunlight and air. They are separated by wide, grassy spaces. There will eventually be 60 units of 8 houses each. Five of these eight will be apartments and dormitories, the other three a club, a nursery, and a kindergarten. The dormitories are four stories high and are connected by inclosed passage-ways. Each unit has ten acres of ground, one-fifth of which is occupied by the buildings and the rest by park and play space. The houses are of brick and concrete and are fire-proof; the walls are sound-proof and the roofs are equipped for sun-bathing. The building which serves as a club contains large enclosed and open-air dining rooms which serve the food sent out by the central kitchen factory, a gymnasium and auditorium for movies and theatrical performances, lockers and showers, a library, a study, a reading room, laboratories and rooms for scientific research, etc. Workers who do not wish to live in the dormitories may live in apartment houses, similar in construction but divided into three-room apartments with kitchenettes and baths. Most of the houses built first will be apartment houses. By the end of 1931 about half of the 60 units planned for were completed.[14]

Commenting on Soviet city planning, Mr. Jacob Crane, Chicago consulting engineer who recently visited the Soviet Union, said that "Russian city planning is at this moment perhaps the most interesting and most significant in the world. To begin with, the entire city-building project, when viewed over a period of the next forty years, is so vast as to both stagger and greatly stimulate the imagination of a city planning technician. The Giprogor (State Commission for Planning Cities), which handles city planning throughout the U.S.S.R. with the exception of the Ukraine, had on its drafting boards when I was in Moscow something like sixty city planning projects, ranging all the way from Leningrad to Sakhalin Island in the Pacific and Tiflis in Transcaucasia, and designed for a total population of probably 35,000,000." [15]

Similarly, Mr. John Nolen, president of the International Federation for Housing and Town Planning, has expressed the following views on the reconstruction of Moscow: "Never has there been a chance in the history of the world to replan

---

[14] *Economic Review,* January 15, 1932, p. 39.
[15] *Ibid.,* January 15, 1932, p. 36.

an old city and make it fit for the life not only of to-day but of the future, such as exists in the case of Moscow. I have met many of their city planners and was much impressed by their grasp and comprehension of the nature of their problems, by both the technique and spirit of their work. Taken as a whole, there is nothing like it anywhere, in the original, progressive, active attack on the problem presented. . . . Sound planning begins with the largest elements, the proper placing of industries and transport for the state or nation; in this, as is well known, the U.S.S.R. goes further than any other country. This leads logically to regional planning of large economic units. In all other countries there is one uncontrollable factor—that of size of cities. No one can determine how large a city will be, for no one knows when some individual capitalist will come along and start a factory, or when some new 'suburban subdivision' will upset all traffic. In the U.S.S.R. they can determine these matters; they can therefore control all the elements of their problem, at least in the new cities. Even in the older cities, they can search for permanent solutions which will not breed new difficulties for the future. . . . Russia has definite ideas about the size of cities and intends to regulate them on the basis of social, economic and industrial efficiency. It has decided that Moscow, for example, shall not be permitted to grow to more than four millions of population, a size much in excess of the average but allowable on account of exceptional circumstances. Fifty thousand is considered necessary to social efficiency; a city that size provides proper industrial, agricultural, educational, and recreational facilities." [16]

Space does not permit a detailed description of all the factors which enter into the Soviet workers' real wage. Some of them, however, will be considered in the next chapter.

[16] *Ibid.*, pp. 37-38.

CHAPTER VIII

DISTRIBUTION AND CONSUMPTION

ONE of the most important factors entering into the worker's real wage is the distribution and consumption of commodities. Under Czarism comparatively few, perhaps from three to five million out of the 139,000,000 people in Russia proper, lived well or luxuriously. The working class and the poor and middle peasantry lived a life of privation and even semi-starvation. After the revolution, the problem of consumption was complicated by the severe decline in output caused by war and by changes in the agricultural system. Agricultural production fell to 50 per cent of the prewar level. Furthermore, as a result of the breaking up of the large estates into small farms immediately after the revolution, agriculture was, until a few years ago, in the hands of the small peasant-farmer who cultivated his land by primitive methods and with his family consumed the greater part of his agricultural output. Industry presented similar problems, its output being reduced, as a result of the military conflicts, to about 20 per cent of the prewar level.

Although consumption before and after the war was very low for the great mass of the population, the disrupted manufacturing enterprises which the Soviet régime inherited were unable to supply even this low demand. Consequently, the first step required in order to increase consumption was the rehabilitation and expansion of industry and agriculture. Under NEP the industries were restored to the prewar level of production, and under the Five-Year Plan efforts were concentrated on building up the heavy industries as the indispensable base for the subsequent expansion of those enterprises which manufacture consumers' goods. Until recently, light industry developed at a much slower tempo than heavy industry; but as a result of the advances made under the Five-Year Plan it was possible toward the end of 1931 to work out plans for greatly increasing the output of light industry, which is to be given greater emphasis in the next few years.

In developing both heavy and light industry, the Soviet Union exports certain goods in order to be able to import machinery, equipment, raw materials, semi-manufactured products and technical assistance from abroad. Most of the exports have consisted of such commodities as petroleum, lumber, furs, flax and other raw materials; but some foodstuffs and manufactured goods have also been exported. Furthermore, in 1930, after an absence of several years, the Soviet Union entered the world market as a large exporter of grain, due to the successful reorganization of agriculture on a large-scale mechanized basis. Because there has been a shortage of certain items of foodstuffs in the Soviet Union during recent years, it has been said that exportation and the "dumping" of goods on the world markets have greatly retarded the living standards of the Soviet worker. Actually, foreign trade has not reduced the level of the worker's consumption. Soviet exports and imports are still considerably below the prewar levels although the output of national economy has increased by 82 per cent. The foreign trade turnover in 1930 and 1931 was only about two-thirds the 1913 total. If this is considered in connection with the greatly increased output of Soviet economy, it is obvious that a much larger volume and a much larger proportion of the output goes for domestic consumption than ever before in Russian history. The ratio of exports to total production was thus about 2.5 times lower in 1931 than in 1913. Furthermore, a smaller share of the output of foodstuffs has been exported under Soviet economy than under the old régime. Before the war, foodstuffs made up over 50 per cent of the total exports. At present, foodstuff shipments are less than half the prewar volume. Grain exports in 1930 and 1931, for instance, were only about one-half of the 1913 exports, although in 1930 the grain crop was the largest in Russian history. In regard to wheat, in particular, although per capita production in 1930-1931 was 22 per cent and consumption 36 per cent greater than in the prewar years 1909-1913, the exports per person were 33 per cent less. Similarly, exports of butter and eggs have been far less in the past few years than the prewar exports.[1]

The basic explanation for the shortage of certain foodstuffs, particularly meat and dairy products, in recent years must therefore be sought not in the exports. It is due chiefly to insufficient production; to difficulties of transportation and distribution; to the increased purchasing power of the population, which has created a great demand for the higher grade food products among large sections of the population who could not afford them before the war; to the more equal distribution of the available supplies, especially through socialized restaurants and factory kitchens; and to the necessity of supplying large quantities of food to the workers at new construction projects.

Similarly, the shortage of manufactured goods is due not to the relatively small exports of these products, but to the urgent need of rapidly developing heavy industry, and more particularly to the increased wages and higher living standards of the Soviet worker and peasant, whose demands and the possibilities of satisfying them are considerably above those of the prewar period. The total output of factory-made shoes, for example, increased from 5,500,000 pairs in 1913 to 76,800,000 pairs in 1931. Despite this great increase, there is still a tremendous shortage because in recent years the peasants, for the first time, have begun to purchase factory-made shoes in substantial quantities. A similar situation exists in regard to ready-made clothing, which the peasants are also beginning to wear for the first time. The manufacture of ready-made clothing is almost a new industry in the Soviet Union. Production in this field increased from 365,000,000 rubles in 1927-28 to

[1] U.S.S.R. Chamber of Commerce, Five-Day Bulletin of Economic Information, Nos. 20-21, April 20-28, 1932.

1,170,000,000 rubles in 1930 and 1,800,000,000 rubles in 1931.[2]

The increase in consumption in the Soviet Union is proceeding apace with the increase in production. The growth of industrial output under the Five-Year Plan of consumers' goods amounted to 65 per cent from 1928 to 1931; to this must be added the expansion of agricultural output, due to the growth of collectivized and state farming. As a result of the mechanization of agriculture, the marketable output of grain, for instance, increased 47.4 per cent in 1929-30, as compared with the previous year, and 44.5 per cent in 1930-31. The marketable output of potatoes in 1931 showed an increase of 76 per cent; meat 61.3 per cent; butter 97.8 per cent; and eggs 33.8 per cent. The output of the food industry as a whole in 1931 totaled 5.1 billion rubles (1926-27 prices), a gain of 26.4 per cent over 1930. The production of consumers' goods in 1931 amounted to 13.9 billion rubles, a gain of 19 per cent over 1930.[3]

The rapid growth of the socialized sector of agriculture has been an important factor in increasing the marketable volume of foodstuffs. The share of the individual peasant in grain procurements is steadily declining. In 1929-30 collective farms supplied only 11 per cent of the marketable grain, while the state farms supplied only 3 per cent. In 1930-31 the share of the collective farms rose to 33.7 per cent, and that of the state farms to 6.4 per cent, so that more than 40 per cent of the grain came from the socialized sector of agriculture. It was planned that during 1931 and 1932 about two-thirds of the marketable grain would come from the socialized sector, about 50 per cent from the collective farms and 15 per cent from the state farms.

Other agricultural products are also supplied chiefly by state and collective farms, as for example 87 per cent of the total marketable output of sugar beets, 60 per cent of cotton, and from 50 to 60 per cent of milk. This is accounted for by

[2] Report of G. K. Ordzhonikidze, Commissar for Heavy Industry, *Economic Review*, March 15, 1932, p. 123.

[3] Central Bureau of National Economic Accounting; *The National Economy of the U.S.S.R.*, pp. 338, 343, 347; *Pravda*, February 17, 1932.

the fact that the percentage of the total output available for the general market is much higher in the socialized than in the private sector. Thus in 1931 about 37 per cent of the total agricultural output was marketable; of the total output of the state farms, 67.5 per cent was marketable; of the collective farms, 40 per cent; and of the individual farms, 30 per cent.[4]

Closely bound up with consumption is the system of distributing consumers' goods, i.e., the organization of internal trade. Under the Czarist régime large sections of the country were practically cut off from the distribution of goods. About 94 per cent of the entire trade and industrial turnover of the country, and 68 per cent of the total number of commercial and industrial enterprises were concentrated in districts which included only 25 per cent of the population. The whole of Transcaucasia, Siberia and Central Asia contained only 20 per cent of the total number of stores in the empire. A large part of European Russia and the vast Asiatic part of the empire, comprising together about 75 per cent of the population, shared only 6 per cent of the total turnover of manufactured goods.[5] The supply of goods to the distant regions of European Russia and to Asia amounted to less than a half a kopek per day per capita.[6]

The situation in this respect began to show marked improvement in 1926, when the period of rehabilitation was completed, and the period of the reconstruction of national economy began. In 1925-26 the retail trade turnover was over 13 billion rubles; in 1926-27 it rose to 14.5 billion; in 1927-28 to 15.4 billion; in 1928-29 to 17.5 billion; in 1930 to 18.9 billion; and in 1931 to 27 billion rubles. Thus during the period of five years there was an increase of 170 per cent in the retail turnover.[7] The greatest increase in the turnover of goods has occurred in those regions where in prewar days the goods turnover was practically negligible. For instance, compared with 1930 the goods turnover in the North Caucasus and Bash-

---

[4] S. I. Turetzky, *op. cit.*, p. 6.
[5] *Social Economic Planning, op. cit.*, pp. 83-84.
[6] *Ibid.*, p. 2.
[7] *Ibid.*, p. 84.

kiria increased 40 per cent in 1931; in Khirgizia, 114 per cent; and in Yakutia, 62 per cent.[8]

The expansion in the retail trade turnover has been due to the increase in the output of consumers' goods and in the marketable volume of agricultural products. As pointed out above, from 1928 to 1931 the output of consumers' goods increased 65 per cent. During this period the output of clothing increased 5 times; the output of shoes 3.2 times; and the output of canned goods eightfold.

Apart from the production of consumers' goods by large-scale industry, the small and handicraft industries still play an important rôle in consumption. In prewar Russia, the output of the *kustarni* or handicraft industries was of exceptional importance. More workers were engaged in handicraft industry than in census industry. Over one-third of the total industrial output before the war was turned out by the *kustarni*. At present the number of handicraft workers and the amount of their production are greater than in the prewar period; but large-scale industry has developed so rapidly that handicrafts now constitute less than one-fifth of total production. However, in certain light industries, such as textiles, clothing, food and woodwork, handicraft output still plays an important rôle, furnishing from 40 to 100 per cent of the total output.[9]

The socialized sector of the handicraft industries is organized in the producers' coöperatives which are assuming increasing importance in Soviet national economy. Under the Five-Year Plan, these producers' coöperatives have made important advances. They have contributed millions of rubles to the building up of socialized production, and have been an important factor in the industrialization of the country and in increasing the output of consumers' goods. According to a recent report of the All-Union Council of Producers' Coöperatives, the total output of these organizations during 1931 amounted to 4,320,000,000 rubles, or more than four times the

---

[8] See Turetzky, *op. cit.*, p. 304; *Social Economic Planning, op. cit.*, p. 85, and Aluf, *op. cit.*, p. 13.

[9] *Economic Review,* April 15, 1932, p. 172.

output in 1927-28, the year preceding the inauguration of the Five-Year Plan. From October 1, 1928 to January 1, 1932 the membership of these producers' coöperatives increased from 1,064,000 to 2,321,000. There are altogether some 5,000,-000 handicraft workers in the Soviet Union; of these about 45 per cent are organized in the coöperatives. However, the share of the coöperatives in the total output of the handicraft industries now amounts to over 75 per cent.[10]

The rôle of the handicraft industries in Soviet economy may be gauged from the following figures: In prewar Russia, within the present boundaries of the Soviet Union, there were a total of 4,000,000 handicraft workers. By 1920, as a result of the world war and the civil war, their number declined to 1,600,-000. In 1922 the producers' coöperatives were organized on a broad scale, and the number of handicraft workers began to rise steadily so that at present it exceeds the prewar figure by about 25 per cent. By 1929-30 the gross output of the handicraft industries slightly exceeded the prewar output. By 1931 the output of the producers' coöperatives alone showed an increase of 70 per cent over 1929-30; so that the total output of the handicraft industries is now considerably above the prewar level. Among the goods produced for the handicraft industries are certain articles of general consumption such as mats, rugs, barrels, baskets, wooden and metal dishes and utensils, toys, musical instruments, lace, rope, felt boots, harness, hardware, fishing equipment, buttons, combs, brushes, mirrors, etc. They also produce small parts of tools for state enterprises, various building materials, chemical fertilizers, and small agricultural implements.

The 1932 program of the producers' coöperatives calls for a large gain in the output of consumers' goods. The output of pottery is to increase 90 per cent over 1931; of woodwork, 68 per cent; soap and fats, etc., 55 per cent. The total output of food products by the producers' coöperatives during 1932 is to total 711,000,000 rubles. The number of stores conducted by these coöperatives is to increase to 1,000 compared with

[10] *Ibid.,* p. 172.

698 in 1931, and the number of stands to 1,400 compared with 330.[11]

The great bulk, probably over 95 per cent, of the food and other necessities consumed by workers and their families is obtained in state or coöperative stores—usually the latter—by a card system. A card entitles the holder to a certain quantity of commodities at fixed low prices. There are also "closed" coöperatives in the various enterprises which are open only to workers and their families. In the general process of socializing trade, the consumers' coöperatives play a leading rôle. Coöperatives are controlled and operated by their members. They aim to supply commodities at cost plus a small amount for overhead. At the beginning of 1931 about 67 per cent of the entire population of the Soviet Union were members of consumers' coöperatives.[12] This included 88.6 per cent of the urban and 59 per cent of the rural population, a considerable increase over 1927 when 38 per cent of the urban and 15.5 per cent of the rural population belonged to coöperatives. By July, 1931, virtually the entire urban population of the Soviet Union between the ages of 16 and 59 were members of coöperatives. At the beginning of 1931 the number of shareholders in the consumers' coöperatives was 63,000,000 as compared with 13,-400,000 in 1926 and only 1,400,000 in 1913. The number of co-operative societies in 1931 was 47,000 as compared with 10,000 in 1913. The average number of shareholders per coöperative group in 1931 was twelve times as great as in 1913. At the beginning of 1931 the capital contributed by shareholders amounted to 12 billion rubles as compared with 9.9 billion rubles in 1929. The growth of the coöperatives has been so rapid that by 1931 they handled 76 per cent of the total retail turnover of the Soviet Union, showing an increase of 50 per cent in the cities and of 29 per cent in the villages as compared with 1930.

The expansion of retail trade, making consumers' goods accessible to workers and peasants in every part of the country, is due in large part to the growth of the coöperatives which

[11] *Ibid.*, pp. 174-5.   [12] *Ibid.*, p. 4.

have superseded the private trader. The coöperatives played an important rôle in maintaining the "smytchka"—the alliance of the workers and peasants—by selling goods to both at lower prices. Between 1927 and 1930, when the consumers' coöperatives handled about 80 per cent of the workers' consuming budget, the general index of retail prices in the urban coöperatives declined about 8 per cent and in the village coöperatives about 10 per cent. The collectivization of agriculture and the growth of the coöperatives has reduced private trading to an insignificant rôle, as indicated in the following table: [13]

RELATIVE SHARES OF SOCIALIZED AND PRIVATE SECTORS IN WHOLESALE AND RETAIL TRADE IN THE U.S.S.R (*in per cent*)

Years	*Share of Socialized Sector in*			*Share of Private Sector in*		
	Wholesale Trade	*Retail Trade*	*Total Trade (in per cent)*	*Wholesale Trade*	*Retail Trade*	*Total Trade*
1923-24	82.0	35.5	55.1	18.0	64.5	44.9
1924-25	91.5	52.0	72.0	8.5	48.0	28.0
1925-26	92.6	59.8	78.1	7.4	40.2	21.9
1926-27	95.5	63.7	83.1	4.5	36.3	16.9
1927-28	98.2	74.6	89.8	1.8	25.4	10.2
1928-29	99.6	84.0	94.9	0.4	16.0	5.1
1929-30	100.0	93.5	98.1	....	6.5	1.9

The increase in production, wages and retail trade has been accompanied by an increase in the nutrition of the Soviet worker. From 1926 to 1928 the consumption of rye bread and flour decreased 18 per cent for the three years, while the consumption of wheat bread and flour increased 7 per cent. The consumption of grits and potatoes fell 13 per cent; while that of highly nutritive foods such as eggs, meat, butter and sugar increased 120, 17, 26, and 20 per cent respectively. In 1930 and 1931 the annual per capita consumption of wheat averaged 330 pounds as against 242 pounds in 1909-1913, a gain of over 36 per cent. The following table shows the consumption in workers' homes of the chief foods during the first half of 1928-29 and 1929-30. These figures do not include expenditures

[13] *Social Economic Planning, op. cit.,* p. 86.

for food outside the home. In 1929-30 only four per cent of the total expenditures for food went to restaurants; but the recent growth in the number and size of socialized restaurants has been an important factor in providing workers with good food at low cost.

MONTHLY AVERAGE CONSUMPTION OF WORKER'S FAMILY [14]

Per Capita

	1928-29 Quantity (grams *)	Cost (kopeks †)	1929-30 Quantity (grams)	Cost (kopeks)	Per Cent Change Quantity	Cost
Grain products.	14,626	326	13,973	361	− 2.8	+ 7.5
Potatoes	5,835	41	8,604	58	+ 47.5	+ 41.5
Vegetables	2,296	31	2,520	38	+ 9.8	+ 22.6
Meats and fats	4,344	315	3,895	355	− 10.1	+ 12.7
Fish	784	46	1,090	74	+ 39.0	+ 60.9
Milk	2,815	73	2,954	97	+ 4.9	+ 32.9
Butter	171	45	169	53	− 1.2	+ 17.8
Eggs	130	18	144	21	+ 10.8	+ 16.7
Vegetable oils..	252	16	320	21	+ 27.0	+ 31.0
Sugar	1,376	91	1,180	81	− 14.2	− 11.0

* 1,000 grams = 2.2 lbs.   † 1 kopek = 0.5 cents.

In the past few years, as the table indicates, the supply of meat and dairy products has fallen short of satisfying the requirements of the population. This shortage was brought about by several factors. To begin with, prewar Russia never produced a sufficient amount of meat and dairy products to satisfy even the meager demands of the great mass of the population. The peasant, and even the average worker in the urban centers, consumed very little meat and butter, living chiefly on bread, dried fish, cabbage and other vegetables. The consumption of meat and dairy products was further reduced by the great loss of livestock during the world war and the civil war. In the periods of rehabilitation and reconstruction, the amount of livestock was gradually built up to and beyond the prewar level. This was accompanied by an increase in the consumption of meat and fats, which amounted to 49.4 pounds per capita for the rural population in 1928-29, as compared with about 26 pounds before the war. The rapid develop-

[14] *Economic Review,* Oct. 15, 1931, p. 463.

ment of the movement for the collectivization of agriculture created a different situation. Many peasants were influenced by kulak propaganda, wholly without foundation, that livestock would be taken over by the collectives; others were resentful against the attempts made in some cases to achieve collectivization by coercive methods. As a result, there was a widespread slaughter of cattle. Another reason for the shortage of foodstuffs were the difficulties which burdened the transport and distribution systems. The extensive growth of urban and industrial centers strained the existing transport system and aggravated the difficulties of carrying foodstuffs from the rural to the urban centers. Similarly, the distribution system could hardly keep pace with the rapid development of the industrial areas. This problem was complicated by the "growing pains" attending the reorganization of distribution on a broad socialized basis.

In 1931 the food situation showed marked improvement. The 1930 grain crop was 87.4 million metric tons as against 71.7 million in 1929; and the sugar beet crop was also exceptionally good, being 15.2 million tons as against 6.3 million in 1929. This placed an adequate supply of grain and sugar at the disposal of the population during 1931. At the same time there was an increase in 1931 of 45 per cent in the vegetable and potato output as compared with 1930.[15]

The prevailing difficulties in food supply are being overcome in various ways. Attention is being concentrated on the extension and improvement of the transportation system, and on the development of distribution through coöperatives, socialized restaurants, etc. The program for the development of agriculture now centers largely around solving the problem of animal husbandry in the same manner as the grain problem has been solved. Plans call for doubling the per capita consumption of meat and dairy products. Per capita consumption of meat is to be raised to 88-132 pounds and of dairy products to 660-770 pounds. To further this program, the plans for 1931 and 1932 provided 400,000,000 rubles for the construc-

[15] *Ibid.*, October 15, 1931, p. 463.

tion of four central packing plants and 35 smaller plants.[16]

On July 30, 1931 the Council of People's Commissars and the Central Committee of the Communist Party issued a joint announcement outlining the program for the development of large-scale socialized livestock farms. The system of such farms was inaugurated early in 1930 as a means of overcoming the shortage in meat and dairy products. By October 1, 1931, the four livestock trusts under the Commissariat for Agriculture increased the number of livestock farms to 957 covering 123,500,000 acres. From January 1 to October 1, 1931 the number of beef cattle and sheep on these farms increased 60-68 per cent and the number of hogs threefold.[17] In 1932 the Central Union of Consumers' Coöperatives (Centrosoyuz) took steps to organize dairy establishments throughout the country. It was planned to build in the Moscow region alone 100 milk stations, 160 cheese factories and 20 refrigeration plants. In West Siberia it was planned to build 10 new cheese factories and 20 creameries; and in the Urals 120 milk stations, 14 creameries, 2 cheese factories, and 42 cream-separating plants.[18]

Similarly, steps are being taken to increase the supply of poultry and eggs. By the end of 1931 the Poultry-Breeding Trust had organized 120 state farms with 2,000,000 fowl. During the year these farms supplied 90 carloads of eggs and 400 metric tons of dressed poultry.[19] Measures are also being taken to employ the most modern methods of cattle raising, so as to increase the quantity and improve the quality of meat and dairy products.

The campaign to increase the supply of foodstuffs has involved increased activity on the part of the industries under the control of the Commissariat of Internal Supply (Narkomsnab). These include trusts engaged in the production of bread, meat, fruits and vegetables, milk, canned goods, tobacco, fish, vegetable oils, sugar, poultry, etc. During 1931 the industries

[16] *Economic Review,* September 1, 1931, p. 387.
[17] *Ibid.,* p. 562.
[18] *Economic Review,* March 1, 1932, p. 117.
[19] *Economic Review,* May 1, 1932, p. 214.

under Narkomsnab increased their output 26.4 per cent over the preceding year; labor productivity in these industries increased 15 per cent; wages, 9 per cent; and the number of workers increased by 50,000.[20] The plans for 1932 provided that the production of the food industries was to increase 36.6 per cent over 1931. Narkomsnab production was to amount to 17 billion rubles. According to plans, 13 new margarine factories were to be completed in 1932, and the output of margarine was to be tripled. At the beginning of 1932 there were three small plants for canning milk; four large ones were in construction and were scheduled for completion during the year. Fifty-six pasteurizing stations were to be built, and it was provided that during the second Five-Year Plan the supply of whole pasteurized milk would increase eighteen fold as compared with the first. The 1932 plans also called for the construction of 74 butter and cheese factories, twenty of them costing over a million rubles each; as well as twelve "giant-combines" for poultry and egg production. Twenty-two large canning factories were scheduled for construction during 1932 at a cost of 2,000,000 rubles each.[21] During 1931 about 500,000,000 cans of canned food were produced. This was about five times the prewar output. Plans for 1932 provided for one billion cans. Canned pork and beans, produced in the North Caucasus, have become extremely popular throughout the Soviet Union. A chain of special fruit and vegetable state farms has been established to provide for the canneries. It was also planned to increase the vegetable and potato area in 1932 to 9,072,000 hectares, an increase of 937,200 hectares over 1931.[22]

In addition to increasing the food supply, steps were taken, toward the end of 1931, to reorganize the system of food and commodity distribution. A statement issued jointly by V. M. Molotov, Chairman of the Council of People's Commissars; Joseph Stalin, Secretary of the Communist Party; and I.

[20] *Trud,* February 24, 1932.
[21] *Izvestia,* April 12, 1932.
[22] *Ibid.,* March 4, 1932; April 12, 1932.

Zelensky, chairman of the Centrosoyuz (Central Union of Consumers' Coöperatives), pointed out first, the growing importance of the coöperatives, as shown in the enormous increase of their turnover, and their virtual monopoly in the distribution of the commodities they handle; and second, their backwardness in organization, bureaucratic tendencies, lack of strict economic accounting, detachment from the masses, and indifference toward the basic needs of the consumer. The statement suggested the following measures to further the development of the coöperatives: (1) A chain of specialized stores should be established in order to increase the efficiency of the coöperatives. These stores are to function as branches of companies operating over the entire country and covering the following industries: ready-to-wear clothing; rubbers, shoes, and leather goods; drygoods, knitgoods and underwear; cotton and woolen cloth; goods for cultural needs; silicate products; hardware; handicraft products; groceries and delicatessen products; fruits, vegetables and dairy products. Corresponding companies for retail sales are to be organized in the various republics and regions which in addition to the commodities enumerated above will also handle furniture, meat and poultry, confectionery, and children's wear. All existing coöperative stores are to be turned over to new retail companies in the various republics and regions. (2) The system of rationing by card is to be gradually abolished. The ration-card system will be resorted to temporarily only in cases where there is an acute shortage of a commodity. The reservation of large supplies for special occasions is also to be abolished except for seasonal workers such as lumbermen or fishermen. (3) Sales by the state-operated urban retail stores are not to exceed 30 per cent of the total retail trade of the city. In exceptional cases this share may be increased to 35 per cent by permission of the Council of Labor and Defense. (4) The Centrosoyuz was instructed to open a number of stores in the fall of 1931 for the sale of bread, meat, fish, vegetables, fruit and dairy products. No less than 200 such stores were to be opened in Moscow; 150 stores each in Leningrad and the Donetz

Basin; 100 each in Kharkov, Kiev, Rostov, Baku, Tiflis, Nizhni Novgorod, Ivanovo-Voznesensk, Stalingrad, Sverdlovsk, Odessa, and Tashkent; and at least 80 stores each in the other large cities and industrial centers of the country. The statement further recommended the organization within the consumers' coöperatives of producing enterprises for the output of various commodities. Large bakeries are to be organized into special trusts within the regional or republican coöperatives and affiliated with the Centrosoyuz; and large vegetable, dairy, poultry and hog farms are to be organized as independent trusts. The local soviets and trade unions are to participate actively in the management of these farms. At the same time, the coöperatives are to be relieved of certain functions. All large industrial enterprises under their control are to be turned over to the Commissariat of Internal Supply; barber shops and similar stores are to become part of the producers' coöperatives; laundries are to be turned over to the municipal soviets. Cultural and educational institutions now run by the coöperatives, such as movies, libraries and radio stations, are to be turned over to the cinema industry, and the Commissariats of Education and Posts and Telegraphs respectively. Children's institutions are to be turned over to the Commissariats of Health and Education. The Commissariat of Internal Supply and the Centrosoyuz are to agree on the procurements for which coöperatives will be chiefly responsible in specified localities. Socialized restaurants are to be an autonomous section within Centrosoyuz. The Centrosoyuz is also to organize autonomous coöperative sections, similar to those of the railway and water transport workers, for fishermen, lumbermen, and peat workers. An increase in wages for coöperative workers was recommended, remuneration to be based on the business turnover of the coöperative. The bonus system is to be introduced in order to encourage greater efficiency. In addition the Centrosoyuz is to develop a system of short courses for training 150,000 coöperative workers, including managers of stores and branches, salesmen,

23 *Economic Review*, July 15, 1931, p. 319.

managers and workers in socialized restaurants; cooks, bakers, accountants, etc.[23]

This reorganization of retail trade is, like the reorganization of industry, intended to increase efficiency and thereby improve service to the mass of the population. In this case the change was necessary because the old coöperative machinery was no longer adequate to meet the increased needs of the workers in a country where unemployment has disappeared, wages have increased and living standards have gone up considerably in a short time.

In spite of certain shortcomings, due to lack of experience and the unprecedented problems involved in operating retail trading enterprises larger than those existing anywhere else in the world, Soviet socialized trade, planned as part of a coördinated economy, has the great advantage of eliminating wasteful expenditures for overhead and advertising which result in higher prices to the consumer. In the United States, for example, over $1,600,000,000 was spent for advertising in 1927. The total expenditure for hospital and health services (the so-called free social services) was only a small proportion of the amount spent for advertising. Operating costs in American department stores during 1927 amounted to 31.4 per cent of the total income from sales. For many articles the cost of retail merchandising is 50 to 60 per cent of the original cost. The expenditures and profits in the retail trade of the United States amount to about one-third of the price charged the consumer.

In the Soviet Union, the total expenditures in 1930 of the consumers' coöperatives, which handled about 80 per cent of the total retail trade, amounted to 1.5 billion rubles, or less than one-half of the expenditures in the United States on advertising alone. The overhead expenses of the consumers' coöperatives during 1930 were only 12.78 per cent of the value of the gross sales; and for 1931 it was planned to reduce this figure to 11.6 per cent, resulting in additional savings to the worker-consumer.[24]

[24] Turetzky, *op. cit.*, p. 10.

Contributing to the increase in the worker's real wages, is the growth of socialized restaurants. These restaurants are maintained by the coöperatives, often in the enterprises themselves, so that workers may obtain good food at the minimum prices without loss of time. In 1931 the turnover of socialized restaurants within the system of urban coöperatives amounted to 2.6 billion rubles or 54 per cent higher than in 1930. In 1927 an average of 2,500,000 meals were served per day in these restaurants; by 1929 the total had risen to 5,000,000 meals; and by 1931 to 23,000,000. It is planned to have these restaurants serve 62,000,000 meals a day in 1932.[25]

In conjunction with a decree issued in 1931 to improve socialized feeding, the Soviet Food Combine (Soyuznarpit) is speeding up the completion of large factory kitchens and restaurants in various industrial enterprises. One large factory kitchen, built to prepare 30,000 meals a day, is being built at Stalino; another to serve 25,000 meals at Alchevsk; and 45 dining rooms with a total capacity of 225,000 meals in various other industrial centers in the Donetz Basin. A large factory-kitchen is to be opened in Leningrad to serve 100,000 meals to the workers in the several metallurgical plants of that city. New factory kitchens with a capacity of 100,000 meals are now under construction at the Cheliabinsk tractor plant. A similar one is being built at the Ural machine-construction plant in Sverdlovsk, and a factory kitchen supplying 30,000 meals a day at Berezniky in the Urals. Dining rooms are, in addition, being constructed in connection with the following enterprises:

Plant	Number of Meals Daily
Kharkov Tractor Plant	165,000
Kuznetz Steel Plant	150,000
Sormovo Locomotive Works	150,000
Stalingrad Tractor Plant	100,000
Rostov Agricultural Machinery Plant	60,000
Grozny Oil Fields	60,000
Karaganda Coal Mines	26,000 [26]

[25] Nelepin, op. cit., pp. 54-58.
[26] Economic Review, November 1, 1931, p. 501.

During 1931 a total of 46,616,000 rubles was appropriated for the construction of factory kitchens. About 40-50 per cent of the urban population was accommodated by socialized restaurants in 1931 as against 13.16 per cent in 1929-30. These restaurants have altered the status of the woman worker, releasing her to a great extent from household drudgery, and enabling her to become a more active participant in production. Soviet economists have estimated that socialized housekeeping will increase the total number of adult urban workers by about 30 per cent. Of these about 40-50 per cent will be employed in socialized housekeeping institutions, and about 50-60 per cent will be released for industry, so that an additional 15-18 per cent of the urban population will be engaged in production on this basis. The number of workers would be increased by about 50 per cent without an increase in the urban population. Socialized housekeeping also increases the productivity of labor, since it organizes and coördinates supplies of food, fuel, etc. Standards of living are further increased because women, released from the burden of household duties to enter production, are able to increase the family income.

The three main factors involved in socialized housekeeping are socialized restaurants, communal laundries and the public educ tion of children. The public feeding and education of the child does not involve separation from his parents. Parents may take their children home whenever they wish, but the tendency, particularly in the construction of new settlements, is to organize the life of the community so that woman's domestic burdens are transferred to the community. The residential sections of the cities and the new cities which have been built in connection with various industrial enterprises contain in addition to dwellings, public dining rooms and adjoining rooms for libraries, billiards, chess, etc.; also nurseries and kindergartens for children of preschool age, living quarters for school children and houses of "culture and rest" with libraries, athletic fields, etc.

In considering the real wage of the Soviet worker, account

must be taken of the large sums spent by the government and various social organizations on crêches, kindergartens and children's playgrounds; on schools and workers' training courses; on workers' clubs with their own theatrical cinema, musical and scientific groups; on the abolition of illiteracy and other educational activities which will be dealt with in greater detail in the chapter on the cultural revolution. Other factors which enter into the Soviet worker's real wage include free working clothes which the enterprises are required to furnish to the workers in various occupations, such as mining, steel-making, etc. Similarly, enterprises must furnish the worker with free tools and instruments. Where the worker uses his own tools, the enterprise compensates him for their use.

CHAPTER IX

"FORCED" AND CONVICT LABOR

FROM what has been said in the preceding pages, it is clear that labor conditions in the Soviet Union have changed radically as compared with conditions in the Czarist empire; and that at present they compare favorably with conditions in most other countries of the world. The Soviet system is based primarily on the interests of those who work with hand or brain, and the labor laws of the country, as well as its administrative machinery, make every provision for fostering the economic, social and political interests of the wage-earner.

Nevertheless, despite the privileged status of the Soviet worker, charges of convict and "forced" labor have been made in various countries against the Soviet Union. Such charges have never been supported by credible evidence; yet, from time to time, misinformed or interested individuals or groups reiterate these charges and publish alleged descriptions of how Soviet employees work and live. The actual facts have been obscured either by misrepresentation or misunderstanding, and much of the discussion has been based on hearsay and propaganda.

Often the only "proofs" are "atrocity" stories from Riga, Helsingfors, Bucharest, and other centers of anti-Soviet agitation. News about the Soviet Union emanating from these sources has been characterized as follows by Mr. Karl A. Bickel, president of the United Press Associations:

"A conservative estimate on the part of the United Press cable editor places ninety-five per cent of all alleged Russian news bearing the Riga, Helsingfors, Bucharest or Warsaw dateline as incorrect and misleading. Bucharest and Riga probably take the leadership in being most uniformly incorrect. Any item coming from any of these points on any Russian subject should never be accepted with anything but the greatest reserve—the same reserve in regard to facts that you would normally extend to anything written for nursery consumption by the late Hans Christian Andersen—plus the fact that in many cases the governments of the countries in which are located the points of origination of these dispatches are actively anti-Russian, and that often the correspondents themselves are known to enjoy a marked anti-Soviet bias." [1]

A typical example of the "forced labor" charges made against the Soviet Union is the book recently published by the Duchess of Atholl, Conservative member of Parliament, in which the author seeks to explain every Soviet decision and decree as a means of obtaining "forced labor." [2] The book cites as victims of "forced labor" students who take on work upon completing their studies, and women who, upon being released from their domestic burdens, enter industry as wage-earners. [3] The author's attempts to prove the existence of "forced labor" in the Soviet Union often result in obvious contradictions. Thus she maintains, on the one hand, that "the presence of armed guards in the factories ... will be the main factors in keeping workers tied to their posts." [4] On the other hand she charges that "from April 1928 onwards, the execution of the year's plan had become more uncertain than had been hoped ... the chief cause lay in the absenteeism of the workers." Similarly, the author states that "in the three sum-

[1] Karl A. Bickel, "How the Outside World Gets Its Information Concerning Events in Russia," address delivered before the Institute of Politics, Williamstown, Mass., August 2, 1930. Proceedings of General Conference on the Internal and External Problems of Russia, p. 14.

[2] The Duchess of Atholl, M.P., The *Conscription of a People*, Columbia University Press, New York, 1931.

[3] *Ibid.*, pp. 119-20, 141.

[4] *Ibid.*, p. 175.

mer months (1930) the Leningrad factories engaged no less than 225,000 new workers, and lost 134,000." [5]

As a matter of simple logic, it is difficult to reconcile "armed guards" with an absenteeism so great that it endangers the "execution of the year's plan." The tremendous labor turnover in Soviet industry—about 150 per cent a year—would seem in itself to be a refutation of the "forced labor" charges. It is impossible for labor to be "conscripted" and yet to move from job to job at so rapid a rate. The fact is, that the special interests which circulate "forced labor" charges make little effort to be either accurate or consistent. The Duchess of Atholl, for instance, publishes alleged affidavits by "refugees from Soviet labor camps" which have been discredited even in the British conservative press as manifest forgeries. These affidavits state that "on Solovetzky Island are the whole Russian intelligentsia," felling wood in night shifts. The intellectuals are able to perform this feat because "snow throws up a certain degree of light" in the darkness.[6] Apart from the fact—apparently unknown to Her Grace—that the millions of Soviet intellectuals are engaged in every field of activity throughout the country, anyone familiar with the processes of timber felling will at once see the absurdity of the lighting arrangement provided by the Duchess of Atholl.

In the United States, charges of "forced labor" against the Soviet Union have been made chiefly by professional "patriots," anti-Soviet propagandists and "white" Russian emigrés, and by producers of manganese, anthracite and lumber. These have attempted to invoke Article 307 of the tariff law, forbidding the importation of goods made by convict or forced labor, to exclude Soviet manganese, coal and timber. The tariff law defines forced labor as "all work or service which is exacted from any person under the menace of any penalty for its non-performance and for which the worker does not offer himself voluntarily." Groups interested in the exclusion of Soviet goods have submitted alleged evidence of the existence

---

[5] *Ibid.*, pp. 33 and 117.   [6] *Ibid.*, pp. 68-71.

of "forced labor" in the Soviet Union. But this "evidence" failed to convince the Treasury Department, which permitted the entry of Soviet shipments.[7] The "forced labor" charges have been accompanied by sensational accusations which on their face are incredible. Such, for example, is the statement by Senator Frederick Steiwer of Oregon in a letter to Secretary of the Treasury Mills that the Soviet Union "makes all labor in Russia forced except in those cases where it is convict labor."[8] On the basis of such sensational charges and of distortions of Soviet labor laws, the groups interested in the cessation of Soviet-American trade have succeeded in having bills introduced in Congress which seek to exclude Soviet imports on the ground that all Soviet labor under the Five-Year Plan is "forced."

These groups cite as "proof" of the existence of "forced labor" those Soviet laws which establish the universal obligation to work. The obligation to work, according to the International Labor Office,[9] is "perfectly general, and is little more than the expression in legal terms of the necessity under which every human being lies of providing his own needs if they are not already provided for by the exertions of others." In the Soviet Union, "the necessity under which every human being lies of providing his own needs" finds legal expression in Article 9 of the Constitution of the R.S.F.S.R. which "recognizes labor as the duty of all citizens." The duty to perform some useful work is universal because the Soviet system is based on the absence of social classes whose needs are "provided for by the exertions of others." But this duty to labor, as we have seen, is surrounded with an elaborate system of law and practice which protects the rights and interests of employees, ranging from labor agreements and trade unions to social insurance and safety rules. The Labor Code guarantees the freedom of labor by protecting the worker against dismissal without valid cause; by granting him the right to

---

[7] See New York *Times*, March 16, 1932.
[8] See New York *Herald Tribune*, March 16, 1932.
[9] International Labor Office, *Forced Labor*, Geneva, 1929, pp. 286-87.

break an agreement concluded for an indefinite period regardless of whether he has valid cause or not; and the right to break a labor agreement without notice in case the employer violates the conditions of the agreement or the labor laws. Under such circumstances, where the worker has freedom of contract, "forced" labor is impossible.

Under Soviet law there exists a type of obligatory labor in cases of emergency common in other countries. Paragraph 11 of the Labor Code provides that under extraordinary circumstances involving natural calamities, such as fighting the elements, or in case of a shortage of labor for the fulfillment of the most important state requirements, citizens may be called upon to perform obligatory labor. There are in existence several decrees promulgated under this section of the Labor Code, involving obligatory labor on irrigation canals and road building. These decrees affect irrigation canals in such regions as Central Asia and Transcaucasia, where the welfare and safety of the community depends on keeping the canals in good repair or the building of new ones. The community as a whole undertakes to keep the irrigation works in proper shape and the individual peasant is therefore obliged to contribute his labor to this end. The population of the Kazak, Transcaucasian, Uzbek and Turcoman republics maintain their irrigation systems by such communal labor from year to year according to plan. This work includes maintenance, repairs and the building of new canals. The village soviets divide the work among the peasants of the community, who contribute their labor at times when they are free from field work. As in other countries, emergency work made necessary by storms, floods and other natural calamities, is carried out without regard to the season. Persons who share in the benefits of the irrigation system but are located too far from it to participate in the communal maintenance contribute their share in the form of a tax.[10] Similarly there is a decree under which a community interested in building a country road or keeping it in

[10] *The Principles of Labor Legislation of the U.S.S.R.*, by V. V. Schmidt, I. S. Voitinsky, and E. N. Danilova, Gosizdat, Moscow, 1931, p. 156.

proper shape may oblige the individual peasant to contribute six days and kulaks twelve days of labor a year for that purpose.

The Labor Code provision for obligatory labor in case of a shortage of labor for the fulfillment of the most important state requirements enables the Soviet system to meet extreme emergencies in which some particular kind of work is indispensable to the national safety. Emergencies of this kind occurred in 1931, when an acute need arose for specialists and technicians in railway and water transportation, and, similarly, in connection with the spring sowing campaign of 1931, when there was an urgent need for agricultural experts and technicians. To meet these emergencies the government availed itself of the Labor Code provision cited above and issued three decrees "mobilizing" specialists for the three fields of economy involved. These decrees called on specialists and technicians of various kinds to assist in the solution of pressing problems of national importance.

The decree providing for the "mobilization" of agricultural specialists for the spring sowing campaign was issued by the Council of People's Commissars on February 2, 1931. On February 10, 1931, the Commissariats of Labor and Agriculture issued a call to all organizations employing agricultural specialists to release 60 per cent of them for a period of two months, so that they might participate in the spring sowing campaign. This call affected agronomists, veterinary surgeons and agricultural engineers. A similar decree had been issued on January 16, 1931 for the mobilization of persons skilled in the various aspects of railway transportation. On April 14, 1931, the Council of Labor and Defense issued a similar decree empowering the Commissariat of Labor to "mobilize" specialists and technicians in water transportation, both maritime and river. On the basis of this decree, the Commissariat of Labor on April 24, 1931 ordered the "mobilization" of all such specialists, including ship captains, engineers, boatswains, et cetera. The decrees regarding railway and water transportation did not affect persons already employed in these fields.

They "mobilized" those formerly engaged in such transportation whose skill was needed in the emergency. Altogether several thousand skilled persons were affected by these decrees.

Agricultural experts "mobilized" for the sowing campaign were paid all traveling expenses. Since they were engaged in special work for only two months, they continued to receive their salaries from the institutions which employed them regularly and to which they returned at the conclusion of the sowing campaign. Specialists, technicians and mechanics "mobilized" for water and railway transportation entered their new work on conditions laid down for their specialties by the collective agreements then prevailing. Under Soviet law, no specialist or technician who leaves his job in order to work in railway or water transportation can receive during the first year lower pay than on the job he leaves. If his new post entails greater skill or responsibility his pay is proportionately higher. Sometimes such "mobilization" of skilled persons involves transference to another city or region. In that case, they receive certain privileges in regard to apartments, traveling expenses, and provision for their families whether these go along or not. The conditions and salaries under which "mobilized" skilled persons work make their employment fairly expensive for the government and indicates that far from seeking cheap labor the government seeks to obtain skilled technicians and mechanics in extreme emergencies even at high expense. In this connection it must be borne in mind that the term "mobilization" employed in the Soviet press in no way implies the use of force or compulsion. A person who refuses to accept a transfer may be penalized only to the extent of being discharged from his present post and being struck off the lists of the employment exchanges for a period of six months. This does not prevent him from earning a living at unskilled labor, and in no case can he be forced to accept work which he does not desire. Under present conditions—when the hiring of employees through the labor organs is no longer obligatory and when the acute shortage of labor compels enterprises to go begging for employees—being struck off the labor exchange lists cannot be considered a grave penalty.

Recent discussions regarding the use of convict labor have centered on the lumber industry. Although convict labor is used in the Soviet Union, as in other countries, in certain public works and road operations, the Soviet authorities have consistently denied that convict labor is employed in the lumber industry. Thus Mr. V. Molotov, Chairman of the Council of People's Commissars, reporting on this subject to the All-Union Congress of Soviets at Moscow on March 8, 1931, declared:

"I shall say at once that on timber work, about which so much is written abroad, this season 1,134,000 workers were engaged in our country. All these workers were engaged on the usual conditions of free labor and the labor of prisoners has nothing to do with timber work. We have, however, never attempted to conceal that on certain public works and road operations we use the labor of prisoners who are healthy and capable of labor." [11]

Mr. Dalton, British Under-Secretary of State for Foreign Affairs, in reply to a question in the House of Commons on January 16, 1931 on this subject, cited Mr. M. Litvinoff, Commissar for Foreign Affairs of the U.S.S.R., as follows:

"Mr. Litvinoff has stated to His Majesty's Ambassador in Moscow that convicts are employed in the Soviet Union, as in other countries, on work such as road building, a matter which solely concerns the Soviet Government. His Majesty's Ambassador has also been informed by the Soviet authorities that neither prison, nor in general, the labor of sentenced persons is employed in the branches of timber industry which produce for exports, including the work at ports."

The actual facts regarding the lumber industry were brought out in the report of the delegation appointed by the Russian timber committee of the Timber Trade Federation of the United Kingdom, which inspected and investigated con-

[11] See *Pravda*, March 10, 1931.

ditions in the saw mills, yards, and loading places in Northern
Russia in the summer of 1931. This report substantiates the
repeated assertions of Soviet officials that there is no convict
or "forced" labor in the lumber industry. The British delegation consisted of Mr. E. P. Tetsall, Past President of the
Timber Trade Federation; Mr. W. O. Woodward, Chairman
of the Merchants Section of the Timber Trade Federation;
and Mr. William Thompson, Vice-Chairman of the East An-
glian and South Lincolnshire Importers Section of the Timber
Trade Federation.

The delegation left England on June 24 and 25, 1931, selecting that date to coincide with the maximum pressure of labor
in the yards, mills and loading ports. No indication of the
places they intended to visit was given in advance, and their
itinerary was not arranged until after their arrival in the
Soviet Union, and was selected by themselves. "Our conditions," their report states, "were that we should proceed as we
wished, make what inquiries we liked through our own inter-
preter (an educated Englishman speaking Russian fluently),
examine personally any of the workmen or inhabitants alone,
and take what photographs we desired. These conditions were
strictly respected throughout our tour, and nothing in any way
limiting our work or inquiries took place, and no advance
notice of our coming could (in many instances) possibly have
been given, as we did not indicate where we wished to proceed until we were actually ready to leave."

The delegation went first to the port of Leningrad, this being a "point where very poor organization existed in prewar
times (and indeed down to the last few years) and where
labor conditions have been criticized." Regarding Leningrad,
the report of the British businessmen's delegation continues:

"It is the port of storage and shipment for about 100 up-
country saw mills, all more or less continuously producing,
and which at the time of our visit had about 90,000 standards
of sawn goods awaiting shipment. It ships in round figures
about 400,000 standards a year, and in addition large quantities of pitwood and pulpwood. It has dock accommodations

for 150 vessels, but only 25 were loading at the time of our visit; 11 of these with sawn wood, and the remainder pitprops and pulpwood. The mechanization of the work of handling this large quantity of wood is nearly complete, and the magnitude of the progress already achieved was a surprise to us, and it is probably the finest equipped timber loading dock in the world.... There are about 16,000 men and women employed in the season, but this number drops to about 6,000 in the winter months. Both men and women are well clad and shod.... The workmen are in excellent condition, look cheerful and contented. The rates are on a piece work basis, and the average is eight to nine rubles per day. Overtime is discouraged, and where it is agreed to be essential, rate and half is paid for the first two hours and after that double rates. The laborers work six days a week on the docks with one day off, and when loading three shifts are employed. Workers in factories work for four days and then have one day off. Our independent inquiries and observations convince us that the labor conditions are excellent and that the rates of remuneration agreed with the unions are satisfactory to the workmen. We saw Red-Cross huts, rest rooms and large dining rooms, also many more buildings in the course of erection. The most careful inquiries fail to disclose anything in the nature of forced labor now or at any time."

From Leningrad the delegation proceeded to various lumber camps and mills in Karelia, such as Kem, Soroka, Onega and Keret. About a mile from Kem they visited a prison camp regarding which their report states that "the prisoners sometimes work on roads, and deal with their own supplies, but there is not a scrap of evidence that they ever work on anything in connection with logs or sawn wood, and we are satisfied that they do not." The delegation concluded its tour with visiting various lumber centers in Archangel regarding which they reported that "there is not a scrap of evidence that forced labor ever existed." The report concludes that "the interest shown in the work, the kindly character of the people, the sufficiency of supplies, are in themselves a complete answer to the reckless charges which have been made." [12]

The absence of forced or convict labor in the Soviet lumber industry has also been attested to by a group of American observers who visited the northern lumber region in the vicinity of Archangel in the spring of 1932. The group consisted of Mr. Spencer Williams, Moscow representative of the American-Russian Chamber of Commerce; Mr. Myron G. Doll, an American engineer resident in Moscow; and the correspondent of the New York *Times*. This group reported that it found no signs of forced labor whatsoever.*

Conditions in the lumber industry have advanced considerably since the prewar period. Prior to 1917 the working day was 10 or 12 hours and even longer. Average wages for 10 hours' work were 67 kopeks for hewers, 98 kopeks for sawyers, and 57 kopeks for haulers, a kopek being equivalent to about half a cent. At present the working day is eight hours, wages are far in advance of the prewar figures, and living conditions have greatly improved. Wages, hours and working conditions in the lumber industry are regulated by the Labor Code, by supplementary regulations, and by collective and individual agreements. These oblige the lumber trust to pay the expenses of transportation of the employees to and from the place of work; to provide suitable living quarters and working clothes free of charge; and to establish facilities for first aid and medical care at the places of work.

Real wages are further increased by supplying lumber workers with goods and provisions at low prices. Prior to the war lumber workers usually lived in low mud huts without windows, floors or chimneys. There were no beds or bunks, sanitation was neglected and medical aid and supplies were lacking. At present lumber workers are furnished living quarters free of charge and the law stipulates that these quarters must be well built, lighted and of adequate size. In the north-

[12] *Russian Timber*, "Report of Delegation Appointed by the Russian Timber Committee of the Timber Trade Federation of the United Kingdom," published by "Timber and Plywood," London, September, 1931.

* New York *Times*, June 6, 1932.

ern region alone there were constructed in 1930 more than 1,700 new barracks and cottages, 355 community dining rooms, 362 bath-houses and 305 club and reading rooms. Early in 1931 there were in the 41 camps operated by the Northern Lumber Trust about 5,600 barracks, 645 community dining rooms, 305 bakeries, 571 club and reading rooms, 782 bath-houses, 42 medical centers and 497 wells supplying drinking water. In the woods where logging operations are carried on, medical and dental stations have been set up and the lumber workers are given free medical treatment. The government assigned 34,000,000 rubles in 1931 for the construction of living quarters and hospitals for lumber workers. In addition, 9,500,000 rubles were appropriated for cultural and educational work.

The question of convict labor in Russia can be understood best in the light of Soviet penology. Prisoners are treated as backward and unfortunate persons whose weaknesses must be corrected and who must be restored to society as useful and productive citizens. For this reason, every prison has a staff of trained physicians and psychiatrists who examine and treat the prisoners; schools where the prisoners are given the elements of education; and workshops where they are taught trades. No convict leaves prison illiterate or without a vocation. Work in prisons is not designed to punish the convict or to humiliate him. It seeks to divert his energy into useful channels. This is in line with the general policy expressed in the criminal code that "measures of social protection must not have as their object the infliction of physical suffering or the degradation of human dignity nor be inflicted for purposes of revenge or punishment." [13]

In line with this policy, the following measures of "social protection of a correctional character" are applied to lawbreakers: deprivation of liberty in correctional labor camps or in general places of confinement; compulsory labor without deprivation of liberty; banishment from a particular region, with or without compulsory settlement in other lo-

[13] Article 9, Paragraph 2, *Criminal Code of the R.S.F.S.R.*

calities, with or without prohibition to reside in particular localities; prohibition to engage in a particular occupation or industry; confiscation of property in whole or in part and fines. These measures are applied only to lawbreakers and are the Soviet equivalent to imprisonment or hard labor in other countries. They cannot, however, be applied to minors under 16 for whom the law provides only measures of "a medical and educational character."[14]

An analysis of the Correctional Labor Code of the R.S.F.S.R., shows that the entire system of handling lawbreakers is based upon substituting correctional labor for punishment. The aim of correctional labor establishments, according to the Code, is to adapt "the lawbreaker to social life by means of correctional labor combined with the loss of personal freedom, and deterring him from the commission of further crimes." The Code provides that "in place of the former prisons, agricultural, technical and industrial colonies and temporary correctional labor centers must be set up (preferably outside the towns)." The Code provides, further, that "the detention of an individual in a correctional labor establishment, aiming as it does at the thorough strengthening of those features of his character and habits which may preserve him from further lawbreaking, must not cause him physical suffering or lower his personal morale." Furthermore, measures must be taken "to remove the harmful influence of bad characters, especially that of dangerous inmates upon others, and develop that self-reliance which makes for the formation of individual characteristics and habits which are indispensable for a social life of labor."[15]

Convicts in the workshops attached to prisons and penal colonies are engaged chiefly in the production of small articles, such as cigarette containers, pocketbooks, knit goods and various handicraft articles. These products are never exported and are mostly for distribution locally. Convicts work eight hours a day and are entitled to all the safeguards provided by labor

[14] Articles 12 and 20 of Criminal Code.
[15] *Correctional Labor Code of the R.S.F.S.R.*, Articles 3-8.

legislation. In addition to food, clothing, schooling, vocational training and entertainment, which they receive free of charge, they also get regular wages averaging between 40 and 50 rubles a month. The convict receives his wages in a lump sum on leaving prison, so that he has a fund with which to start his free life. Because the correctional labor system uses work primarily as a means of training the prisoner for useful participation in society, the assignment of tasks in the correctional workshop is never indiscriminate. The prisoner's life as a whole is taken into account. With the assistance of physicians and psychologists, his health, education, previous experience and natural tendencies and interests are considered. As a result, the prisoner is able to select that vocation which will serve as a corrective and will restore him to society as a healthy and useful citizen.

"Criminals in the ordinary sense of the word," Mr. Walter Duranty, New York *Times* correspondent in Moscow reported in the January 19, 1931 issue of that newspaper, "are better treated in the Soviet Union than in any other country —with due allowance for the universal shortage of living quarters and commodities. They work, but they get trade union rates for their labor, the produce of which is sold exclusively within the Soviet Union, and they have 'parole' holidays yearly, which they almost never break."

These facts indicate that no convict labor is used in the production of exported goods; and that, far from free labor being turned into "forced" labor, Soviet law grants even convict labor many of the safeguards and privileges of free labor.

In connection with the charges of "forced" and convict labor, the press of various countries has published rumors that about 5,000,000 kulaks have been sent to the lumber camps. This statement is absurd since in 1931 there were only 1,134,000 workers in the lumber industry, and there were only 60,000 convicts, engaged exclusively in building new roads, in the whole northern region. This grotesque story is typical of the rumors circulated regarding the status of the kulaks. It is alleged, for instance, that kulaks are sent to concentration camps where they perform forced labor. Such statements are due to a misunderstanding of the Soviet government's treatment of the kulaks as a class.

From its inception it has been the policy of the government to effect a social reorganization by measures involving changes in the status of various social classes. At the base of the kulak's changed status is the collectivization of agriculture. As has already been pointed out, the collectivization of agriculture was undertaken because the old system of small-scale production by 25,000,000 individual households using primitive methods could not meet the requirements of national economy, and doomed the vast mass of the peasantry to poverty and want. The only group which benefited by the antiquated system were the kulaks, who constituted only about three per cent of the peasantry, and maintained their position largely through the exploitation of the poor peasants. This exploitation took the form of hiring poor peasants as laborers at a wage amounting to hardly more than a bare subsistence, and of lending them equipment, livestock, food and feed supplies at usurious rates of interest, often amounting to several times the value of the loan. The organization of 60 per cent of the peasant households into collective farms and the establishment of large state farms has solved the grain problem and given higher standards of living to the mass of peasants. The growth of large-scale socialized agriculture meant the elimination of the kulak as an economic factor and the disappearance of the economic basis of exploitation.

In this struggle between 97 per cent of the peasants whose interests lay in collectivization and the three per cent whose interests lay in the old system, the kulaks often resorted to sabotage, arson, the slaughter of cattle and even the assassination of leaders of the collective farm movement. A small proportion of the kulaks finally reconciled themselves to the new conditions and entered the collectives. The majority, however, migrated to other regions. A small proportion of the kulaks prolonged their resistance to collectivization by violent and illegal means. It was under these conditions that the

Central Executive Committee of the Soviet Union and the
Council of People's Commissars issued the decree of February
1, 1930 providing that "regional executive committees and
governing bodies of the autonomous republics have the right
to undertake all necessary measures in the struggle against
the kulaks, and if necessary to confiscate their possessions and
expel them from within the boundaries of certain regions and
districts." This decree applies not to all kulaks but to kulaks
in certain regions and districts, namely, those in which the
overwhelming majority of the peasants have entered collective farms. In these regions the local soviets decide on the
expulsion of kulaks and the confiscation of their property.
Kulaks who are expelled are assigned to certain extensive
regions which may adjoin the regions where they formerly
resided or may be distant.

The fate of a kulak expelled from a collectivized region is
determined not by law but by economic circumstances. The
law does not compel him to perform any particular kind of
work. For such a former kulak several possibilities are open.
In the region to which he is assigned he can obtain land and
become a farmer. Former kulaks who have availed themselves
of this opportunity have either formed collectives on their
own initiative or become small independent farmers. They
may choose either course without any compulsion. A kulak
who does not wish to farm free land may become an artisan
or handicraft worker, or a worker on railways, in shops or
factories. He is not barred from any industry in the new region. He is free to choose his trade, though his choice is
limited by his previous experience, general skill, and so on.
However, once a former kulak becomes a worker, the law regards him as the equal of other workers. He may enter a trade
union, usually after a period of probation, and is entitled to
all the guarantees of labor legislation regarding wages, hours,
working conditions, social insurance, ration cards, individual
and collective agreements and so forth.

There are no concentration camps and no "forced labor"
for kulaks or former kulaks; nor are there special laws against

kulaks who commit crimes in violation of the penal code. A kulak who commits acts of violence, such as murder or arson, in his resistance to collectivization is arrested, tried and sentenced not as a kulak but as a person who has violated the pepal code. Furthermore, just as a kulak who becomes a worker has the same status as other workers, so a kulak who becomes a convict has the same status as other convicts. The labor of such former kulaks properly falls into the category of convict labor which has already been described.

On July 4, 1931, the Central Executive Committee of the Soviet Union issued a decree defining the conditions under which citizenship rights may be restored to kulaks exiled for criminal acts. The decree reads as follows: "Kulaks found guilty of anti-Soviet and anti-collective activities (such as arson, banditry, and so on), and exiled from the village or town in which they resided by decree of a general meeting of the citizens of the village and local government organs, and hence deprived of citizenship rights according to the Constitution of the U.S.S.R., may be restored to full citizenship rights within five years after the date on which they were exiled on the following conditions: (a) if in the course of this period they have proved by their deeds that they have ceased their hostile actions against the peasantry organized into collectives and against the measures of the Soviet government designed to raise the level of agriculture; and (b) if they have proved themselves by their actions to be honest and conscientious workers." [16]

Most of the workers in the lumber industry, regarding which sensational "forced" and convict labor charges have been circulated, are peasant-seasonal workers. Their status has improved strikingly under the Soviet régime. Prior to the revolution seasonal employment made up a considerable portion of the peasants' income. The number of peasants engaged in seasonal employment at the beginning of the twentieth century was over 5,000,000. These were peasants who migrated from their villages to obtain temporary employment as wage-

[16] *Soviet Union Review*, Vol. IX, Nos. 9-10, 1931, p. 199.

earners in construction work on housing or railways, timber-cutting, peat-cutting, coal mining, et cetera. In some *gubernias* as much as ten per cent of the peasants were engaged in seasonal employment. In the *gubernias* of Moscow and Smolensk the percentage was as high as 40. The reasons for this widespread seasonal employment among peasants was the small landholding system, the consequent pauperization of the peasants, and the recurrence of famines.

An investigation at the end of the nineteenth century among more than 1,000 peasants engaged in the construction of the Kursk-Kharkov-Azov railway revealed that about 84 per cent of them worked outside of their villages from two to six months a year. The average wages were 38 rubles a month. Living and traveling expenses, which the peasant-seasonal workers were obliged to pay out of their own pockets, amounted to 21 rubles a month. Actual savings averaged only 4 rubles a month or 13-14 kopeks a day. Peasant-seasonal workers on landed estates in Kherson averaged from 20 to 50 rubles a month for women and from 50 to 70 rubles a month for men at the peak of the season. As in other centers, the Kherson peasant-seasonal workers were not provided with living quarters, working clothes, or medical facilities, but were left entirely to their own fate. Some lived in the open fields, others in dilapidated barracks under extremely unsanitary conditions. Sickness, especially eye-diseases, was widespread among them. The problem became so acute that the Zemstvos organized medical stations near the barracks where aid was given to the most severe cases. But this aid was meager, as evidenced by the fact that the Zemstvos spent for this purpose only 10,000 rubles in three years. The length of the workday for peasant-seasonal workers at Kherson was from 12.5 to 15 hours.[17] In the *gubernia* of Poltava the net earnings of peasant-seasonal workers averaged 15 to 20 rubles a month at the peak of the season, and in the *gubernia* of Voronezh

[17] *Encyclopedic Dictionary*, edited by F. A. Brockhaus of Leipzig and E. A. Efron of St. Petersburg, published in St. Petersburg, 1897, Vol. XXII, pp. 472-475.

20 to 30 rubles was all the seasonal worker was able to save for the whole season.

Over 50 per cent of all the seasonal workers throughout the Czarist empire were unable to pay traveling expenses and were therefore obliged to walk from their village to the place of seasonal employment, which sometimes was quite distant. About 98 per cent of seasonal workers on the Kursk-Kharkov-Azov railway—where conditions were rather better than for most seasonal workers—had no place to sleep while traveling to and from their place of work. Only four per cent of them had cooked meals while traveling, the others living on dry black bread. Only two per cent of them had an extra pair of shoes.[18]

Since there was little labor legislation under the old régime, the peasant-seasonal worker was completely unprotected. He obtained employment either by hiring himself directly to an employer or by becoming a member of a group hired by a contractor. The law placed no limits or obligations on the contractor or the employer in regard to hours, wages, hiring and firing, working conditions or sanitation, and even the government reports of the prewar period revealed grave abuses.

Poverty and unemployment were, in the past, the chief factors which compelled the peasant to leave his village and migrate to lumber, coal or shipping centers where he could supplement his meager income by seasonal labor. These factors have been largely removed by the collectivization of agriculture and the expansion of industry. Unemployment has disappeared and the living standards of the mass of peasants have risen. Accordingly, the pressure on the peasant to engage in seasonal labor has been lessened. But the problem of the peasant's employment during the time when he is not engaged in agriculture still requires solution; and a planned national economy precludes the chaotic and unregulated migration of labor from the villages to the cities.

In 1930 the Commissariat of Labor devoted special attention to this problem, rendered acute by the fact that economic

[18] *Ibid.*

expansion was accompanied by a shortage of labor. Certain industries were oversupplied with seasonal workers while others faced a shortage of such workers at the most critical moments. On the strength of a mere rumor that work was to be obtained in some distant part of the Soviet Union, peasants would trek thousands of miles across the country in search of jobs which did not exist, while passing up jobs which needed them and which were located much nearer home; or workers on an important industrial project would hear of better conditions somewhere else and the managers of the enterprise would find themselves suddenly deprived of many workers; while in another region the managers of an enterprise employing all the workers it could use would find themselves facing a vast army of new arrivals whom they could not accommodate. To solve this problem, the government adopted several measures for coördinating seasonal labor. A decree was issued that seasonal industries such as lumber, building and so on, were to organize permanent staffs of workers. During periods when workers cannot be employed at their own specialty in seasonal trades, they can secure a transfer to other jobs, for which, if necessary, short training courses are provided. All industries employing seasonal labor have worked out detailed plans for lengthening the working season. In addition, special funds have been appropriated to improve the living conditions of seasonal workers.[19]

The status of the seasonal worker has also been changed by the repeal of the law which made it obligatory to hire workers through the government labor exchanges. The Labor Code of 1922, as we have seen, established a state monopoly of labor hiring, so that all employers, whether state, coöperative or private, were obliged to engage workers exclusively through organs of the Commissariat of Labor. Subsequently, decrees were issued making it unnecessary to hire workers through government organs. On September 13, 1931, the Central Executive Committee and the Council of People's Commissars of the U.S.S.R. issued a joint decree granting permission

[19] *Soviet Union Review*, Vol. IX, No. 1, January, 1931, p. 7.

to "industrial enterprises, institutions, and organizations of the socialized sector to hire workers and employees in the cities, as well in the rural districts, directly, without applying to the labor offices." The law of June 30, 1931 on "Hiring Peasants for Seasonal Work in the Socialized Sector" [20] approached the problem of peasant migration for seasonal work by providing that seasonal workers be hired by agreements concluded between the enterprise employing seasonal workers and the collective farms from which they come. The object of this type of agreement is to systematize the flow of seasonal workers from the villages to the urban centers by securing the coöperation of the collective farms in the hiring of such workers.

The law of June 30 grants a number of benefits and privileges for peasant-seasonal workers hired by industries from the collective farms. These incentives are established, the decree states, "in order to encourage collective farm members and also individual peasants to engage in seasonal work in the socialized sector." The various privileges are allowed to "those collective farm members who sign contracts to work in state industry (including timber-cutting, timber-floating, peat-cutting, fisheries, etc.), in transportation, on state farms, and also on state construction work and construction work carried on by consumers' and housing coöperatives." The privileges granted are as follows:

"(1) Peasant-seasonal workers shall be entirely exempt from any deductions from their wages for the socialized funds of the collective farms.

"(2) In order to make certain that peasant-seasonal workers receive their share of the income, both in cash and in kind, of the collective farm, they shall, after their return from their wage-earning work, be given preference in the assignment of work on the collective farm.

"(3) In dividing up the harvest on the collective farm, part of the harvest must be set aside for the peasant-seasonal workers at the established prices, and in the same amount as

[20] *Izvestia*, July 1, 1931, No. 179, and September 19, 1931, No. 259.

is allowed the other collective farm members who remain on the collective farm and work conscientiously.

"(4) Those members of the peasant-seasonal worker's family who remain on the collective farm and are capable of work shall participate in the work of the collective farm in accordance with the general regulations. If on the basis of the number of working days contributed the family of the peasant-seasonal worker is unable to obtain an adequate amount of food and stock feed, or if there are in the family none capable of labor, the management of the collective farm must, in dividing the harvest, provide this family with food and stock feed in the same amount and at the same cash prices as allowed the collective farm members who work conscientiously on the collective farm.

"(5) The fixed percentage of the collective farms income distributed among the members of the collective farm in proportion to the amount of socialized property they contributed is to be distributed to the peasant-seasonal workers on the same basis as to the other collective farm members.

"(6) Families of peasant-seasonal workers are recipients in like measure as the other members of the collective farm of health benefits and of goods of which there is a deficiency. Members of such families are given preference in admission to schools, courses, etc., for vocational training or for increasing their skill.

"(7) Families of peasant-seasonal workers receive the aid of the collective farm (such as loan of tools for cultivating kitchen gardens, loan of carts, etc.) to the same extent as do other members of the collective farm.

"(8) Peasant-seasonal workers are exempt from the agricultural tax on the non-socialized part of their property including their non-agricultural earnings.

"(9) Contracts made by economic organizations with peasant-seasonal workers must provide: (a) Housing and food for the peasant-seasonal workers; (b) payment in full by the economic organization of the expenses incurred by the peasant-seasonal workers in traveling from their place of residence to the place of work (upon expiration of the agreement); (c) payment to the peasant-seasonal worker of a daily allowance of 2.50 rubles while traveling."

In order to encourage collective farms to conclude agreements with economic organizations with regard to peasant-seasonal workers or to coöperate in selecting their members for such work, the decree of June 30 provides the following privileges for such collective farms:

"(12) In agreements between economic organizations and the collective farms with regard to the selection of peasant-seasonal workers or their coöperation in hiring, provisions must be made whereby the economic organizations supply these collective farms with special means for improving their production, such means to be in proportion to the number of collective farm members who have concluded contracts for work with economic organizations.

"(13) The People's Commissariat for Agriculture of the U.S.S.R. and the Councils of People's Commissars of the constituent republics are instructed to give preference in supplying agricultural machinery to those collective farms which select a considerable number of their members as peasant-seasonal workers.

"(14) The Councils of People's Commissars of the constituent republics are instructed to give such collective farms preference in organizing schools and other cultural and educational institutions, nurseries, children's homes, etc.

"(15) Consumers' coöperatives must give preference, when assigning funds and equipment for the organization of social and communal institutions (restaurants, etc.) to those collective farms which provide the greatest number of peasant-seasonal workers.

"(16) The enumerated benefits are granted to those collective farms which actually carry out their agreements with economic organizations in regard to selecting peasant-seasonal workers or to coöperating in hiring such workers."

The decree then proceeds to extend similar benefits to peasant-seasonal workers from individual farms. The agricultural tax on non-agricultural earnings is reduced by half for those peasant-seasonal workers from individual farms who conscientiously fulfill their obligations in their work for economic organizations, which, in turn, are obliged to provide such workers with housing, food, traveling expenses and a daily allowance of 2.50 rubles while traveling.[21]

For the management of a collective farm, the decree prescribes that in working out its production program special note must be taken of those collective farm members who have trades such as coal-mining, peat-cutting, bricklaying, cabinet-making, etc. To such persons, the collective farm must grant an opportunity to work in industry, transportation, on state farms, or on construction work, retaining such workers on the collective farms only when absolutely necessary. Managers of collective farms are subject to penalties for detaining collective farm members who desire to leave for seasonal work. Managers of collective farms are also forbidden to recall collective farm members from their seasonal work in industry prior to the termination of their contracts.[22]

This decree is the result of conditions produced by a rapid expansion of industry and an acute shortage of labor. An attempt is here made to overcome the labor shortage, to halt the rapid labor turnover, and to regulate the migration of labor by drawing peasants into the various seasonal industries. But, instead of attempting to solve this problem by resorting to "forced" or convict labor, as has been charged, the method applied has been just the reverse. Peasants are drawn into state industry employing seasonal labor on the basis of voluntary contracts. Each peasant-seasonal worker signs an individual agreement with the economic organization for which he works. At the same time, the government holds out privileges first to the individual peasant-seasonal worker, and secondly to the collective farm to which he belongs. No penalty awaits the peasant who refuses to leave his collective or individual farm for seasonal work in lumber, building or transportation. The

[21] Articles 17-18.
[22] Articles 19-21.

only reference to penalties is in the case of collective farm managers attempting to retain peasants who desire to enter seasonal employment. This, as will be seen later, is the basis of all such measures in labor planning. It obliges managers and directors not to interfere with a proper distribution of labor power, without infringing on the worker's right to accept or refuse any specific job.

On July 9, 1931, a decree was issued on "measures for selecting collective farm members for seasonal work in the socialized sector and for coöperating with the economic organizations in hiring peasant-seasonal workers" which supplemented the decree of June 30 by providing that "besides the agreement with the collective farm, an agreement is also concluded individually with each collective farm member, fixing the duration of employment and the conditions upon which the collective farm member undertakes the work." [23]

On August 28, 1931, the Presidium of the Central Control Commission of the Communist Party and the Collegium of the People's Commissariat of Workers' and Peasants' Inspection issued a joint decree on the organization of selecting collective farm members for temporary work in other economic units and on the conclusion of agreements between economic organizations and collective farms. This decree contained the following significant passages:

"Section I, Paragraph 3: Control figures for the labor forces required are to be drawn up with the general district as the smallest unit. It is categorically forbidden to draw up control figures for separate villages and collective farms.

"Section II, Paragraph 1: The economic organizations are to conclude agreements with the managements of collective farms for their active assistance in the selection of labor forces. Agreements are to be concluded directly only with collective farms. No collective agreements are to be concluded between economic organizations and regional or district collective farm organizations.

"Section II, Paragraph 3: Agreements between economic

[23] *Bulletin of Financial and Economic Legislation*, July 27, 1931, No. 21.

organizations and collective farms should bear the character of productive assistance and should include concrete obligations to be fulfilled by the economic organizations and the collective farms. It is forbidden to include in the agreements purely commercial conditions in the form of fines for breach of contract, etc.

"Section II, Paragraph 4: It will be regarded as incorrect and as a gross distortion of the Government's decree [of June 30] to conclude agreements whereby collective farm members are selected in an obligatory manner or whereby wages for collective farm members leaving for temporary work are received not by the collective farm member himself but by the collective farm which then settles with the collective farm member on the basis of labor-days. The Peoples' Commissariat of Labor, the Collective Farm Center and the economic organizations are to revoke all such agreements immediately." [24]

Thus, the planned regulation of hiring labor in the Soviet Union is carried out on the basis of a direct voluntary agreement between the management and the workers, and by stimulating the personal interest of the workers by means of economic incentives. It is impossible to discern the elements of compulsion in conditions where the acceptance of employment is a matter of the worker's own choice, where refusal to accept work involves no administrative penalty and where special economic privileges are held out as stimuli to the worker.

The favorable status of the worker in the Soviet system and the free nature of his labor have been described by a number of American observers who have had occasion to acquaint themselves with the life of the Soviet worker at first hand. Thus, General William N. Haskell, former head of the American Relief Administration from 1921 to 1923, made the following statement after an extended visit to the Soviet Union in the summer of 1930:

"I was led to the conclusion that the Russian worker is as a rule more willing and enthusiastic than the American....

[24] *Izvestia*, September 10, 1931, No. 250.

The factory means something closer to him than to his American brother.... There is no gainsaying the fact that the life of the workers in Russia to-day is better than it was before the revolution.... To-day the worker has a feeling that he counts—and a vast hope for the future. In Czarist days he had nothing. The worker's attitude toward his work and toward the government must be set down as 'interested and favorable.' ...What the workman gets that makes him relatively better off than any other class and more satisfied, is his feeling of importance in the socialistic order. He is the element most favored by the government, and his voice is the controlling factor in industry and politics." [25]

Similarly, Mr. Sherwood Eddy, who has made six visits to Russia, some in recent years, has declared: "There is a healthy trade union democracy among the workers. Economically free, independent of any individual employer, apprehensive of no arbitrary discharge or neglected employment, the laboring class at least is encouraged in the freedom of expression and the right of criticism of the industry of the government.... The propaganda that these (Soviet) products are the results of convict or forced labor may serve some special interest in the United States, but is not substantiated by facts. There is very little convict labor in Russia and no need for its use on the small fraction of any products they export." [26]

Representative Henry T. Rainey of Illinois, who visited the Soviet Union in 1931, declared in an interview with the *United States Daily:* "I particularly investigated the question of forced labor in Russia and there isn't any there. Labor is freer in Russia than in any other country in the world. There is one disadvantage under which Russia now operates—that the workers in Russia have more money than ever before, and they are spending it liberally in traveling, literally by tens of thousands of people, from one job to another. They are sure

[25] New York *Times,* July 5, 1931.
[26] Sherwood Eddy, *The Challenge of Russia,* New York, Farrar & Rinehart, 1931, pp. viii, 76 and New York *American,* November 16, 1930.

of their employment wherever they stop, and they can go back to their original employment any time." [27]

Mr. H. R. Knickerbocker, correspondent of the New York *Evening Post* and Philadelphia *Public Ledger,* in a speech over the Columbia Broadcasting system on June 21, 1931 said: "I worked as a correspondent in Moscow for two years and last year I traveled about 10,000 miles through the Soviet Union to make a report on the Five-Year Plan for the New York *Evening Post* and the Philadelphia *Public Ledger.* If the Russian people are in chains, they have put them on since I was there. You can see a great many people on a 10,000-mile trip, but I saw no signs of forced labor under police compulsion. The only thing of the kind I saw was in one place out in the Iraks where I passed a road-gang of convicts, who had been working on highway construction. In the twenty-odd factories and mines I visited, many of them away off the beaten track, my chief impression of the workers was that they were a cocky lot; you would think they owned the country. Maybe they do, and maybe they don't, but they think so, and I have never seen a slave who thought he was the boss."

On March 13, 1931, the *Moscow News* published an open letter signed by twenty American and Canadian engineers and specialists employed in various Soviet enterprises declaring that although they are working in the midst of Soviet industry, "nobody has seen anything which could in the slightest degree resemble compulsory labor."

Mr. Walter Arnold Rukeyser, American consulting engineer in charge of the asbestos plant at Asbest, in the Urals, writes: "There seems to be a commonly accepted idea in this country that the Russian workman is kept in virtual bondage—that he cannot change his employment or move from place to place. I have been asked over here if it were true that 'squads of workers were watched by the military equipped with guns to prevent them from quitting their jobs.' Nothing could be farther from the truth. I am not attempting to describe conditions under which the former kulaks are employed. I know

[27] United States *Daily,* October 26, 1931.

nothing at first hand about these conditions. But as for our workers at Asbest—and there are some 13,000 of them—I can vouch for the fact that there exists nothing even approximating forced labor. As nearly as I could dig out from our employment records, I should say that we have at least a 100 per cent labor turnover yearly." [28]

Similarly, Mr. Charles A. Gill, superintendent of motive power on the Baltimore and Ohio Railroad, who helped to reorganize shop operations on the Soviet railway system during 1931, has stated: "I can freely declare that there was absolutely no evidence of forced labor. From my general observation of labor conditions in the Soviet Union, I can state that, while in some respects these conditions differ from those in the United States, the Russian worker is free at all times to quit his job and apply elsewhere for work." [29]

Mr. C. M. Peter, export manager of the Black and Decker Company, after a tour of the automobile and tractor plants of the Soviet Union, wrote an article on his tour [30] in which he made the following statement on labor conditions: "Labor turnover continues to be a big factor in all these plants, as the average Russian seems inherently to crave a change, but by providing excellent housing and school accommodations, improving living conditions in the neighborhood of the plants, and installing piece-work systems, they are making progress in overcoming this handicap. It must be obvious that if labor were forced, as we are so often led to believe, this problem could not exist."

Mr. Louis Fischer, Moscow correspondent of the *Nation* and the *Baltimore Sun,* reporting on labor conditions in the Chiaturi manganese mines [31] said: "I spent two whole days in Chiaturi. I visited the mines and some of the factories. I talked

[28] Walter Arnold Rukeyser, *Working for the Soviets,* Covici-Friede, New York, 1932, p. 155.
[29] "The Russian Situation: as Observed by an American Railroad Man," address by Charles A. Gill, before the Baltimore and Ohio Section of the American Society of Mechanical Engineers, Baltimore, March 17, 1932.
[30] *Economic Review of the Soviet Union,* January 1, 1932.
[31] Baltimore *Morning Sun,* March 8, 1932.

at a workers' meeting. I interviewed workers individually. I inspected their homes, coöperative stores, restaurants, hospitals, clubs and bath-houses. I can say quite categorically, without any fear of contradiction, that there is no forced labor and could be no forced labor at Chiaturi."

These observations by American and Canadian visitors and technicians in the Soviet Union have been supported by similar statements by German, British and other foreign specialists and businessmen. Thus on February 1, 1931, the *Moskauer Rundschau* published an open letter signed by a group of foreign specialists including the well-known German architect Ernst May, at present supervising the construction of new towns and cities in the Soviet Union; Rerup Olsen, an American engineer connected with the Institute for the Organization of Metal Works; and various German, Hungarian and Swedish engineers. This letter declared: "We have never noticed anything that had the remotest appearance of forced labor. On the contrary, we have always noticed—and still do—how enthusiastically Soviet workers concentrate on building up the economic strength of their country, how they compete to raise output, and how the system of 'shock' workers gains new supporters daily."

In the light of actual labor conditions in the Soviet Union, it is no wonder that Soviet workers either laugh heartily or react indignantly to the utterances of their self-appointed "protectors," such prominent champions of the interests of labor as the Duchess of Atholl and the owners of anthracite and manganese mines in this country.

CHAPTER X

THE PLANNING OF LABOR

THE decree on peasant-seasonal workers, referred to in the preceding chapter, is one of many measures in the planning of labor on a nation-wide scale which characterizes Soviet economy. This planning is a phase of the industrial-financial plan for the whole of national economy, and is linked up with the expansion of socialized industry and agriculture, the elimination of unemployment, and the consequent shortage of labor.

Under the abnormal circumstances of the civil war, when the population was on a rationed basis and enterprises were conducted along the lines of War Communism, unemployment was practically non-existent. There were only about 150,000 unemployed workers in July 1921. The introduction of NEP was followed by an increase in unemployment. This increase was due to various causes. Industry was so disrupted that it was unable to absorb more than a fraction of the former number of workers. At the same time there was a great influx of peasants from the villages seeking work in the urban centers. Since all enterprises were placed on a commercial basis, only such workers were taken on as the basic capital and the budget would allow for.

Unemployment fluctuated with seasonal variations, reaching its highest point in April 1929, when there were 1,772,500 unemployed.[1] The Control Figures for 1929-30 already pointed out that the development of industry in the coming year would result in an increased demand for labor, and therefore urged

[1] Kingsbury and Fairchild, *op. cit.*, p. 35.

the development of a better "planned system for hiring workers." By the end of 1930, due to the rapid development of national economy under the Five-Year Plan, the rise in the living standards of the village, and improvements in the system of planning labor, unemployment was eliminated. In its place industry faced a shortage of skilled and even un-skilled labor. The problem was now one of organizing sufficient facilities for training skilled workers to fill the urgent re-quirements of national economy developing under the Five-Year Plan.

The planning of labor as a component part of the planning of national economy was nothing new in Soviet policy. From the beginning labor legislation was based on the principle of planned national economy and the planned hiring of labor. This principle has been maintained throughout, changes being made from time to time in its application in order to meet specific problems.

These changes are based on certain fundamental principles which one Soviet writer has formulated as follows: "Labor cannot be an individual concern because the life of society depends upon it.... Socialism has always considered labor the basis of society's existence and has therefore always held that every member of society must work. Socialism has always aimed not only at the liberation of toiling society from the landowner and capitalist elements which have expropriated the means of production and used them for the exploitation of other people's labor; it has also sought to replace the chaotic organization of labor existing under capitalism by an organi-zation corresponding to the needs of society. Since socialism proposes to nationalize industry and to collectivize agricul-ture, i.e., to place the productive forces at the disposal of society, it could not but undertake the organization of labor. It is clear that when the use of the productive forces belong to society, their planned development requires a planned distribution of labor, and its planned mobilization and education." [2]

[2] Karl Radek, VOKS, Vol. II, No. 2, 1931.

The planned organization of labor has developed as an integral part of the planned organization of national economy as a whole. In 1922 the Labor Code established the state monopoly of labor hiring, providing that all hiring must be done through the People's Commissariat of Labor.[3] The state monopoly prevented private individuals and social organizations from acting as intermediaries in the hiring of labor; the employer could engage workers only through organs of the labor commissariat. The labor exchanges were free agencies supported by the government. They protected the worker against nepotism and favoritism in the distribution of jobs, and safeguarded the worker's rights in line with the policy that every worker was entitled either to a job or to unemployment insurance. These principles were the basis of planned organization in supplying work to those seeking employment and supplying workers to enterprises in need of labor power. But with them went the concomitant principle that the worker hires out his labor power on a voluntary basis. The labor exchange was primarily a medium for assisting the worker in getting a job.

A joint decree of the Central Executive Committee and the Council of People's Commissars announced on March 4, 1927, on "measures for regulating labor," and the amendment to it issued on June 29, 1927 and May 8, 1929 maintained these principles as part of the general policy of planning national economy. These and similar decrees ratified the principle of the state monoply of labor hiring by prohibiting "the enrollment of workers from other localities by means of utilizing private agents or of sending for this purpose special persons who have not received authority from the respective organs of the People's Commissariat of Labor of the U.S.S.R. or the People's Commissariat of Labor of a constituent republic." Furthermore, these decrees concentrated in the labor commissariat all records of the movement of labor and all estimates regarding the employment and dismissal of workers. They also established a system of coördinating the hiring of

[3] Article 5 and 7: Labor Code: 1922 edition.

groups of employees with the work of the labor commissariat.[4]

The laws affecting the hiring of labor have been recently changed to meet the requirements of national economy under the Five-Year Plan. One of these changes was directly due to the elimination of unemployment. In 1930 the Commissariat of Labor decreed that funds hitherto used for unemployment insurance should now be used in training young and unskilled workers by augmenting the efforts of the trade unions, the Commissariat of Labor and the Supreme Economic Council in this direction. But the elimination of unemployment rendered all the more acute the shortage of labor and the rapid labor turnover. The Five-Year Plan estimated that the number of wage-earners would increase from 11,350,000 in 1927-28 to 15,764,000 in 1932-33; but, as has already been pointed out, national economy expanded at a faster rate than the Plan called for, so that in 1931 there were about 18,700,000 wage-earners, and national economy was demanding an additional 4,000,000 for 1932.

The factors which have made it possible for Soviet industry to absorb more wage-earners than originally planned for include an extensive system of vocational training, the mechanization of agriculture which released peasants for industry, and the socialization of housekeeping which enabled many women to become wage-earners. Nevertheless, there still exists a great shortage of labor, particularly of skilled workers. As a result of the extraordinary demand for skilled labor created by the expansion of industry, workers tended to migrate from job to job. During 1930 the labor turnover in census industry as a whole amounted to 152.6 per cent, with 177.9 per cent labor turnover in the heavy industries and 114.3 per cent in the light industries. During the first quarter of 1931 the turnover in census industry was 31.1 per cent, and in the second quarter 32.7 per cent. The food industries were especially hard hit by the labor turnover, the total for 1930 being 307 per

[4] Collection of Laws, 1927, No. 41, Section 410, and No. 13, Section 132. Collection of Laws, 1929, No. 27, Section 248; *Izvestia* of the Commissariat of Labor, Nos. 19-20, 1927.

cent, and for the first half of 1931 over 172 per cent. Ore mining had a turnover of 280.2 per cent in 1930 and 125.3 per cent in the first half of 1931. The respective figures for coal and coke were 295.4 per cent and 108.3 per cent, and for electric stations 108.6 per cent and 50 per cent.[5]

Mr. Walter Duranty, writing in the *New York Times* of October 8, 1930, described the labor turnover as follows: "In the average Russian factory or other industrial enterprise the annual turnover of unskilled labor usually averages from 50-70 per cent and often passes the 100 per cent mark. What is more, there are continual, though largely seasonal, shortages of raw labor in almost every industry. Take the case of the Donetz Basin, which is the chief source of the Soviet coal and iron production. In the fiscal year just ended, the Donetz coal production fell short of the program set by some 4,000,-000 tons with a progressive decline since May. The coal industry required 250,000 workers and had actually at the end of September about 180,000, and a turnover for the year of more than 80 per cent. The reasons for this state of affairs are the following: First, the inchoate character of Russian labor—half way between town and village—in the present transitional period from an agricultural to an industrial state; second, the great number of new enterprises under construction; third, the varying wage-rates, food, housing and other facilities these enterprises offer; fourth, the instability of the Russian nature, inborn nomadic tendencies and the desire for change; and fifth, the good harvest."

The facts here outlined were, in greater or lesser, measure, true of many enterprises. The planning of labor, therefore, involved the solution of the following problems: meeting the requirements of agriculture for various kinds of skilled labor now needed as a result of mechanization and collectivization; finding means of keeping track of all the surplus labor released as a result of the mechanization of agriculture and distributing this surplus labor among the various branches, trades, and regions of industry; training skilled workers and

[5] *National Economy of the U.S.S.R.*, *op. cit.*, p. 450.

engineers; qualifying workers for promotion from less skilled to more skilled work; the specialized training of workers in accordance with the equipment they have to handle and the work they have to perform; regulating wages for the various categories of labor; increasing labor productivity and improving technique in order to better the general welfare of the workers; and elaborating and carrying out a program of health, sanitation and safety measures.[6]

Some of these measures are discussed in other parts of this book, particularly the training of workers. Here the fact may be noted that in recent years there has been a great increase in the number of workers entering Soviet industry. Between 1924 and 1931 more than 3,000,000 new workers entered industry. At the beginning of the latter year there were over 5,000,000 workers in the factories and mines, or 40 per cent more than in 1923-24. The total number of wage-earners increased from 7,143,000 in 1923-24 to 18,700,000 in 1931. The schedule set by the Five-Year Plan for increasing the number of wage-earners in the fifth year of the Plan was actually exceeded in 1931, the third year of the Plan, by 18 per cent in the whole of national economy, 32 per cent in the census industries, 37 per cent in construction, and 47 per cent in transportation. Workers in large enterprises constitute an increasingly large proportion of the total number of industrial workers, so that by the beginning of 1931 more than two-thirds of all workers in Soviet industry were employed in enterprises with more than 1,000 workers each. In the United States and Germany, only about one-third of the workers are employed in such enterprises.[7]

The increase in the number of wage-earners has been partly due to the new socialized forms of life, such as factory kitchens, crêches, etc., which have released millions of women from domestic drudgery and enabled them to enter various phases of national economy. The number of women wage-earners in national economy has increased from 2,400,000 in

[6] Social Economic Planning in the U.S.S.R., op. cit., p. 127.
[7] Economic Review of the Soviet Union, April 1, 1932, p. 155.

October 1928 to 3,700,000 in October 1930 and 5,859,000 in 1931. Of the latter 2,337,000 were employed in industry; 295,000 in transport; 282,000 in state and coöperative stores and restaurants; 215,000 in municipal services; 175,000 in government offices; and 1,063,300 in educational and cultural institutions.[8] Despite the great increase in women employees, the ratio of women to men in industry remains unaltered. This ratio varies from industry to industry, ranging from 63 per cent of the total number of workers in textiles to 8 per cent in mining. In 1931 there were 4,500,000 women in the trade unions.

The equality of men and women workers is maintained by various means. Equal pay for equal work removes the possibility of economic competition between the sexes, such as is prevalent in other countries. Physical differences between men and women which affect their working capacity are minimized by the elaborate system of labor protection. Sanitation and safety devices in the factories and social insurance benefits for motherhood are among the factors which place men and women workers on an equal footing economically.

One of the effects of socialized housekeeping has been to change woman's attitude toward work. Freed from domestic burdens, the Soviet woman does not look upon work as a temporary makeshift, but as a serious occupation for life, as men do. Already by 1929 there were in three leading industries—textiles, metals, and mining—large contingents of women workers whose work was their career. In the textile industry, 49.6 per cent of the women workers had come from workers' families which had completely severed their ties with agriculture. Of the women who entered industry from peasant families during the past few years, about 30 per cent have completely broken with the village.[9]

A recent survey of women workers in various branches of Soviet industry shows that women in the metal industry have an average length of service of 7.6 years as against 11.6 years

[8] *Economic Review of the Soviet Union*, May 1, 1932, p. 205.
[9] *VOKS*, Vol. II, No. 2, 1931, p. 13.

among men; in mining 4.1 as against 9.6; and in textiles 13.1 as against 14.3. However, while women are comparatively new in Russian industry, their skill is increasing. Figures for 1930 in the metal industry showed that 11.3 per cent of women were rated as skilled workers. These figures have increased since the training system for workers of both sexes has been extended on a wide scale. All political, social and cultural activities are open to women on the same basis as men, and there are many women active in the trade unions, the local soviets, and various government departments. In 1931 there were more than 300,000 women who participated actively in the local soviets and other government commissions; another 500,000 were active in other Soviet organizations; and 1,800,000 were active in the Communist Party and the Young Communist League.[10]

Organizationally, the planning of labor obliges enterprises, institutions and other economic units to submit plans to the labor commissariat for obtaining the necessary supply of workers. The government labor organs work out plans regarding the labor requirements of the various economic organizations, and assign districts for the enrollment of workers from other localities through the local representatives of the economic organizations.

The elimination of unemployment, the acute shortage of labor and the rapid labor turnover have resulted in certain modifications of this system. As has already been pointed out, the decree of June 30, 1931 on "hiring peasants for seasonal work in the socialized sector" enables economic organizations to hire peasant-seasonal workers by direct agreements with the collective farms. A similar decree issued on September 13, 1931 makes the hiring of workers through the labor organs only optional for the socialized sector of national economy. This decree grants permission to "industrial enterprises, institutions and organizations of the socialized sector to hire workers and employees in the cities as well as in the rural districts directly, without applying to the labor offices." [11]

[10] *Ibid.*, p. 206.   [11] *Izvestia*, September 19, 1931, No. 259.

At present only private enterprises, which constitute an insignificant part of national economy, are obliged to hire workers through labor offices, although this obligation also has been limited.

From these facts two conclusions may be drawn. Where so great a fluidity of labor exists, it is, on the face of it, absurd to speak of the use of "forced labor." At the same time, the fact that for the socialized enterprises the hiring of workers through the labor organs is no longer obligatory, while for the private enterprises this law remains only partially in force, clearly indicates that the obligatory nature of the state monopoly of labor hiring in the past was due solely to the necessity of effecting the most rational and satisfactory distribution of surplus labor power.[12] The labor exchanges continue to assist workers in finding employment and enterprises in finding workers; but the decree of September 13, 1931, permitting socialized enterprises to hire employees directly, is, among other things, an aid in meeting two of the main problems of Soviet industry: the labor shortage and the labor turnover.

The labor shortage is being relieved partly through the mechanization of old plants and factories. Under the system of planning labor, the employees released through mechanization are able to find employment in new plants and factories which are completely mechanized but lack workers. The planning system obliges managers to release employees whose services have been rendered superfluous by the installation of machinery so that they may go to those enterprises where their services are needed. To further the rational and efficient distribution of labor power the law also obliges managers to release skilled workers and specialists who are not working at their specialties so that they may be transferred to enterprises where work in their specialties awaits them. Thus the planning of labor is directed to the managers who must regu-

[12] Collection of Laws, 1930, No. 60, Section 641, and Collection of Laws, 1931, No. 60, Section 365.

late their demands in accordance with the requirements of
national economy as a whole; it makes possible the efficient
distribution of new employees entering industry, as well as old
employees released by the introduction of machinery, and co-
ordinates the transference of skilled workers and specialists
so that they are enabled to exercise their abilities in their
special fields.

The decree providing for the planned distribution of skilled
workers and specialists by laying down certain rules chiefly
for the management of the enterprises was issued by the Central Executive Committee of the Soviet Union and the Council
of People's Commissars on December 15, 1930. Its purposes
are stated in the preamble as follows: "The enormous success
of the socialist industrialization of the Soviet Union and the
rapid tempo of development of state and collective farms
have resulted in the complete liquidation of unemployment.
As a result a more complete and systematic utilization of
labor in all branches of national economy has become imperative, as well as the need for training new workers. The systematic utilization of labor forces will give the best results,
however, only when it is combined with measures tending to
develop to a greater extent the socialized method of work (socialist competition, the 'shock brigade' movement, etc.).
Such a systematic utilization of labor is impossible without a
decisive and systematic struggle against all factors which disorganize production." The most important provisions of the
decree are: [18]

"Paragraph 7: Skilled workers and specialists in enterprises
of the socialized sector of national economy who are employed
at work other than that for which they are especially qualified
may be transferred by the Commissariat of Labor in accordance with regulations established by the Commissariat of
Labor in agreement with the Supreme Economic Council, the
People's Commissariat of Transportation and the All-Union
Central Council of Trade Unions.

[18] *Izvestia*, December 17, 1930.

"Paragraph 8: In order to secure a supply of skilled workers and specialists for enterprises in the most important branches of national economy (the iron and steel, coal, chemical, machine-building and electrical industries, capital construction and transportation) from the less important branches of industry or the less important enterprises of these branches, the Commissariat of Labor has the right, on the basis of requests from the economic enterprises, and in agreement with the trade unions, to transfer, upon the ratification of the Council of Labor and Defense, skilled workers and specialists to other branches of national economy or to other localities to be employed at work for which they are especially qualified.

"Paragraph 15: Managers of enterprises, institutions, and economic units of the socialized sector of national economy are subject according to the established regulations to disciplinary penalties by order of higher organs or regulations of the Commissariat of Labor for the following offenses: (a) incorrect utilization of skilled labor within the enterprise, institution or economic unit; (b) exaggeration in requests for labor power and employment of workers in excess of the requirements established by the industrial-financial plan; (c) failure to carry out measures for the prompt providing of labor power for enterprises, institutions, or economic units; (d) failure to conform to the norm of wages set by the collective agreements or to the norm set for government employees; (e) the enticement of workers and administrative and technical personnel from one enterprise into other enterprises or institutions; (f) retention of workers and administrative and technical personnel assigned for transfer by the departments of labor."

As these provisions indicate, one of the aims of the decree is to reduce the labor turnover by preventing managers from "enticing" workers from other enterprises, another indication that methods quite the reverse of "forced labor" have been used. The decree is, in general, aimed at managers; only for them are penalties established for failure to comply with its provisions. The responsibility for its execution rests with

them, and not with employees, who are under no compulsion
to carry it out. In only one case does the decree establish disciplinary measures for employees. Paragraph 13 provides:

"Malicious disorganizers of production who deliberately and
without valid cause abandon their work in enterprises of the
socialized sector of national economy, in case of their subsequent application for work at the Commissariat of Labor
shall not be given work in industry or transportation for a
period of six months." [14]

This provision applies to persistent drifters floating from
job to job who have to be retrained on every new job and to
persons holding responsible jobs whose abandonment of their
posts without valid cause disrupts production. Such persons
forfeit the confidence of national economy, and while they
are given an opportunity to support themselves at some other
work, such as agriculture, construction, trade, etc., they cannot obtain work in industry and transportation until they
have shown, during their six months' probation period, that
they can once more be trusted in key branches of national
economy. This law is rarely invoked in practice.

Paragraphs 7 and 8 of the decree of December 15 obliges,
within specified limits, enterprises with a surplus of labor to
terminate their labor agreements with certain categories of
skilled workers or technicians who are no longer needed in a
given enterprise, so that they may be employed in enterprises
which do need their services, provided the workers accept the
offers of the latter. This planned distribution of labor power
imposes upon the employer the obligation of rationally utilizing the available productive forces; it places the employer
under the jurisdiction of the higher government bodies in regard to the number of workers that he requires. But it in no
way limits the right of the employee to refuse to accept the
work offered to him. A transfer from one enterprise to another
may take place only with the consent of the employee. On this
score he is protected by a number of laws. Article 36 of the
Labor Code provides that "an employer shall not require an

[14] Collection of Laws, 1930, No. 60, Section 641.

employee to perform any work not connected with the kind of activities for which the employee engaged, nor any work involving manifest risk of life, or not in accordance with the labor laws." In case the employee consents to a transfer, his wages may not be reduced. Furthermore, if the temporary work to which he is transferred pays a higher rate of wages than the job which he left, the worker must be paid according to the higher rate.[15]

On June 3, 1931, the Central Executive Committee of the Soviet Union and the Council of People's Commissars issued a decree providing that "in case the interests of production demand it, the management may transfer workers for a period of not more than one month for other work in the same or a different enterprise or institution in the same locality.[16] This decree defines the limits within which the labor power of the worker may be utilized. The employer may not assign work to the employee which does not correspond to his qualifications or specialty. At the same time, the employer retains the right to make rearrangements of duties among the workers for the purpose of best utilizing their skill, provided definite guarantees are safeguarded for the employee. The employer has the right to utilize the employee for other work temporarily; and the employee is obliged to accept such other work corresponding to his qualifications in case there is a temporary lack of the work for which he was hired. Refusal on the part of the worker to do such other work gives the employer the right to terminate the labor agreement, although he cannot compel the employee to perform such work.

Questions pertaining to the locality to which a worker may be transferred are settled on the basis of Article 37 of the Labor Code, which provides: "A wage-earning or salaried employee shall not be transferred from one undertaking to another or removed from one locality to another without his consent, even if such transfer or removal takes place in connection with that of the undertaking or institution; in default

[15] Labor Code, Article 64.
[16] Collection of Laws of the U.S.S.R., 1931, No. 35, Section 257.

of his consent the contract of work may be rescinded by either party and in such case the employee shall be paid a leaving grant under section 89" (providing for two weeks' pay). Under this law, the worker may reject the request of the employer concerning a transfer. A decree issued on April 10, 1930 provided that the dismissal of a worker because of his refusal to accept a transfer to work in another locality is permissible only in the following cases:

(1) If the transfer is caused by the partial closing down of the enterprise, by curtailment of work or staff, or by suspension of work for a period of more than one month;

(2) if the transfer is caused by the necessity of rearranging the distribution of work among the workers in connection with the rationalization of production or machinery, provided the new work corresponds to the qualifications of the workers;

(3) if the transfer takes place because the worker has been recognized by due process of law as being unfit to work in the given enterprise because of the nature of production or unsatisfactory sanitary conditions;

(4) if the transfer takes place as a result of a decision of the organs of the People's Commissariat for Workers and Peasants' Inspection classifying the given worker as among those fit to be in government service;

(5) if the transfer is caused by the entire closing down of the enterprise or institution or by its transfer to another locality.

In some of these cases, the worker receives two weeks' dismissal wages, and in others either two weeks' notice or two weeks' dismissal wages.[17]

The decree of December 15, 1930 referred to above provides for the transference of specialists and skilled workers who are safeguarded by the general rules covering the transference of labor. In addition, Paragraph 10 of this decree provides special incentives, privileges and safeguards for specialists and skilled workers transferred from one enterprise to another as follows: "The Council of People's Commissars of

[17] Izvestia of the Commissariat of Labor, 1930, No. 13.

the Soviet Union must establish guarantees for employees who
are transferred to work in other enterprises in accordance with
paragraphs 7 and 8 as regards dwelling space in their former
place of residence and providing dwelling space in the new
place of residence, securing admission for their children in
schools, kindergartens and playgrounds, payments of special
sums at the time of transfer, and the granting of a number of
other privileges." On the basis of this paragraph, a decree was
issued on June 18, 1931 granting the following rights, benefits
and privileges to employees transferred to other enterprises: [18]

(1) The right to a bonus amounting to a month's wages and
to reimbursement for traveling expenses, including baggage
charges incurred by himself and family;

(2) a guarantee that he shall draw wages while en route
and for an additional six days;

(3) the right to get living quarters for himself and family
in the new place of work;

(4) the right to retain living quarters in the former place
of work;

(5) a guarantee that the former level of his wages shall be
maintained, namely, that his wages in the new place of work
shall not be lower than in the previous place of work;

(6) retention of all privileges resulting from duration of
employment, his record being in no way impaired by reason
of his transfer to a new place of work;

(7) preference to his children when entering schools and
their provision with stipends;

(8) all these special privileges also apply in case the transfer is made to remote localities.

As has been pointed out, laws regarding the regulation of
labor are directed not against the workers but for the guidance
of the management. The dismissal of a worker is an exceptional act which may be carried out only under specified conditions in which the worker's interests are protected. Until
1930 workers could not be discharged if they refused to be
transferred from one plant to another, or even from one de-

[18] *Izvestia,* June 22, 1931, No. 170.

partment to another of the same plant. The decree of April 10 increased the power of the management to dismiss workers who refuse to be transferred. Such workers may be discharged provided the trade union consents. In practice a worker who refuses to be transferred may arrange with the trade union to find a substitute for him. This legal right of managers to dismiss workers under certain specified conditions tends to create an erroneous impression because in other countries the law does not specifically empower managers to discharge employees. Dismissal constitutes no problem in other countries, since, without specific legal sanction, managers may discharge employees at will, with or without valid cause. Even at present, Soviet managers have not the power of dismissal which managers in other countries have. Soviet law specifically gives managers the right to dismiss workers only within strict limits that apply to certain specified conditions affecting the welfare of national economy.

While the decrees which regulate the demand for labor are directed at the management of the enterprises, all regulations which aim to coördinate the labor supply through the workers, are based entirely on increased rewards and incentives. The piece-work system, in effect since 1922, has been expanded to include nearly all industries and now operates on a wide scale. The bonus system and other forms of rewarding superior efforts have also been extended. Employees also receive additional payments and special privileges, such as vacations, apartments and so on, if they remain at one job for several years. Thus the decree of December 15, 1930 contains the following provisions:

"Paragraph 11: Workers, engineers and technicians who have distinguished themselves as organizers of shock brigades, those who are members of shock brigades or participate in socialist competition, and also those who have worked in the same enterprise for a long period of time, and those who have made valuable suggestions or inventions for improving the work of the enterprise are entitled to the following privileges:

"(a) In case they live in unsatisfactory quarters they are

entitled to first choice in obtaining improved living quarters
in newly constructed houses of the enterprise.

"(b) Their children shall be the first to be enrolled in all
schools, technical institutions, short term courses, etc.

"(c) They have first choice with regard to rest homes,
sanatoria, etc.

"(d) They shall have precedence in the granting of trips to
other institutions of the U.S.S.R. or abroad for the purpose of
studying production processes and increasing their skill.

"(e) Members of-their families applying to the labor organs for work are entitled to be given first choice for jobs in
the same enterprise in which they themselves are employed.

"Paragraph 12: All workers engaged in mining, metallurgy,
chemical, textile, and building materials industries and also
in transportation and on large construction projects are entitled to an additional three days' vacation or three days' pay
if they have worked in the same enterprise or project not less
than two years following November 1, 1930."

The problems involved in the shortage of labor and the
labor turnover were discussed in detail by Stalin at a conference of industrial managers held in Moscow, June 23, 1931,
where he urged increased incentives as one means of increasing productivity and reducing the labor turnover. The task is,
he said, to organize the securing of labor in a coördinated
way, by means of agreements between industrial establishments
and collective farms and their members, and by means of
further mechanizing labor processes. He attributed the extensive turnover of labor to an incorrect wage policy which
did not allow for sufficient difference between the wages of
skilled and unskilled workers. This policy, he said, did not
stimulate the unskilled worker to improve his skill and
tempted the skilled worker to migrate from enterprise to enterprise in search of better wages. Stalin therefore urged a
new wage-scale which should take differences in skill into account more than has been the case hitherto. This, he argued,
would serve to attach skilled workers to the enterprise and
act as an incentive to unskilled workers to improve them-

selves. In addition, further improvements would have to be
made in the supply of commodities and living conditions.
Methods of work would have to be organized more efficiently,
so as to enable the worker to perform his work to the best
advantage, thereby increasing the productivity of labor from
month to month. "Our problem is," Stalin declared, "to liquidate irresponsibility, improve organization of work and properly distribute forces in our enterprises." Furthermore, the
development of working-class industrial and technical intelligentsia would have to be carried still further and a new attitude would have to be adopted toward the engineers and
technicians of the old school who have now come over completely to the Soviet régime. It is necessary, Stalin urged,
"to give them more attention and concern, to attract them
more vigorously to work." And finally, the principle of economic accounting would have to be carried out more effectively.[19]

In line with the policy expressed in this speech, a number
of measures were initiated, such as increases in wages, the
elimination of the continuous work-week where it was not
functioning successfully; improvement in the work of the co-
operatives; a stricter application of economic accounting; the
decentralization of industrial management; increased consumption and housing, and an extension of vocational training.

In carrying out the policy of increased incentives, a general
increase in wages by 30 per cent was instituted on October 1,
1931. The salaries of engineers and technicians were raised
considerably under this new scale as well as the wages of
workers in the various industries. Bonuses were increased for
employees who fulfilled the production plan. Similarly a new
decree on social insurance issued at the end of June 23, 1931
provided that in disbursing insurance funds special attention
should be given to raising the living standards of the workers
in general, and of workers in heavy industry in particular
through improving the number and quality of rest-homes,
sanatoria and preventive measures generally. In order to en-

[19] *Soviet Union Review*, Vol. IX, Nos. 7-8, July-August, 1931, pp. 146-54.

courage workers to remain at one job, thereby reducing the labor turnover, the new decree provided that in insurance payments for sickness and general disability those who have worked for three years in industry and for two years in one enterprise are to get full wages, whatever these may be, without any of the former limitations. Sickness and disability payments to members of "shock brigades" are to consist of full wages if they have been at the same enterprise for one year. On the other hand, workers who drift from job to job are to receive less than their full salary during periods of illness, and the non-union worker, who may only have just begun to work, is to receive half his salary for the first thirty days, and in case the illness lasts longer than thirty days, two-thirds of his salary for the remainder of the period of illness. The aim of this redistribution of social insurance funds was to encourage the steady worker as against the drifter, while placing more facilities at the disposal of the steady worker and the "shock brigadier." [20]

The preamble to the decree of June 23, 1931, clearly indicates that Soviet economy applies not compulsion but incentive in its struggle to overcome the fluidity of labor. Changes in the payment of insurance benefits are to be made, the preamble states, "in order to stimulate the work of the basic cadres, members of trade unions and members of shock brigades, and in order to provide further incentives for workers to remain on the same job, and also in order to combat the disorganizing activities which interrupt socialist construction."

In response to Stalin's speech urging the improved organization of labor and the reduction of the labor shortage and the labor turnover, the workers took action on their own initiative. They held mass meetings in all the enterprises; the suggestions contained in the speech were discussed, and measures were adopted for carrying them into effect. Open letters to the press sent by the workers in various enterprises revealed the concrete steps taken to improve the organization

[20] Decree of June 23, 1931, Nos. 9-438; *Izvestia*, June 30 and July 1, 1931, Nos. 178-179.

and methods of labor. The Putilov workers in Leningrad challenged the workers of the Stalingrad tractor plant and the Amo automobile plant to "socialist competition" in improving along these lines. A Podolsk factory announced a new dining-room providing special food for workers, as an example of raising living standards in order to reduce the labor turnover. The workers and technical personnel of the Stalin Metal Works of Leningrad addressed an open letter to "workers of all plants in the U.S.S.R." describing their efforts to improve the organization of labor. The letter relates how a conference of party members in the plant chose several "shock brigades," each of which was assigned to investigate a special subject under the guidance of engineers and skilled workers. They then organized departmental meetings of the workers, pre-sented questionnaires, collected information, and prepared a survey of the factory. The survey described the plant's achieve-ments, its deficiencies and its intentions in regard to improv-ing the organization of labor. The open letter which described these results concluded with a challenge to other plants to "socialist competition" along these lines.

This letter, typical of many published in the Soviet press, was signed by a "meeting of skilled workers, foremen and brigade leaders and by general mass-meetings in every de-partment of the plant." Reflecting the Soviet worker's attitude toward his work and toward national economy as a whole, the letter described how "we overfulfilled our plan last year, mak-ing 210,000 kilowatts of steam turbines, instead of 175,000. This year we set our program at 802,000 kilowatts of steam turbines, and have more than fulfilled our first half year's program at this fourfold ratio. We cut costs 10.2 per cent. We fulfilled our Five-Year Plan in two and three-quarters years, while spending for capital investment only 5,500,000 rubles in place of the 19,400,000 rubles allowed in the Plan. A short time ago we produced a steam turbine of 50,000 kilo-watts, the first in the country's history. Our plant has the first joint factory and technical college in the country. It has been in existence one year, and this year graduates 85 skilled work-

men from the ranks of the former unskilled. We have at present
391 students in the first class which trains skilled workers;
240 in the second which trains foremen and technicians; and
170 in the third which trains engineers. In response to Stalin's
suggestions, we shall add in August 740 workers as students
in this college."

Enumerating the plant's achievements in raising living
standards, the letter mentions two rest-homes and several summer cottages for the workers, a dining room serving hot meals
to all, a special dining room with diets prescribed for workers
who suffer from digestive troubles, a hotel for foreign workers, a technical college and a trade school for young workers
with 1,750 students, a moving picture theater and a radio
station; 575 acres of vegetable gardens and a hog-farm belonging to the plant. In addition to the "millions of rubles
saved for the state by our cost-cutting," the letter proposes
a "workers' counter-plan" for saving millions more. A great
reduction in breakage was achieved by placing seven departments on a strict business accounting basis under the supervision of 39 accounting brigades composed of 564 workers.
By the end of 1931 the workers of the plant proposed to have
12 departments on a basis of strict business accounting and
challenged "all other plants in the Soviet Union to be the first
in 100 per cent fulfillment of strict accounting." [21]

The counter-plan referred to in the letter has already been
described. It is one of the marked examples of workers' initiative in Soviet economy. The counter-plan is drawn up by the
workers of an enterprise who subject the control figures of
the industrial-financial plan to a rigid test at the point of
production. The idea of the counter-plan grew out of the
desire of the participants in "socialist competition" and the
"shock-brigade" movement to assure maximum efficiency in
their efforts to increase production. In the course of their
work, shock brigades frequently encountered a lack of coördination between their particular task and the plan of the
entire enterprise; hence they attempted to correlate their

[21] *Moscow News*, July 13, 1931.

work with the work of the entire enterprise by definite plans for each section of the enterprise. These so-called counter-plans were advanced on the initiative of the workers themselves. The counter-plans set definite tasks for each brigade, group, production collective and shop and finally for the entire enterprise. They are drawn up by the workers at the bench and solve in a practical fashion the problem of correlating the national plan with the plans of individual enterprises.

The counter-plan movement started in the summer of 1930. One of the pioneers in this field was the "Karl Marx" machine factory in Leningrad, which, during July and the early part of August of that year, saved about 90,000 rubles on the basis of 341 workers' suggestions, 105 of which were incorporated in the counter-plan. The workers increased the production plan in the cast iron foundry from 11,000 to 14,500 tons; and in the machine shop from 150 to 200 machines. At the "Bolshevik" plant in Kiev the workers' counter-plan increased production from 8,250,000 rubles to 18,000,000 rubles. In a number of instances the workers, more familiar with their own capacities and the resources of the enterprise than the central planning body, found that they could exceed the quota set by the Control Figures. The example of the Stalin factory in Leningrad in raising the quota of turbines set by the program for 1931 and carrying out the enlarged quota has been cited above. This system has played an important part in the fulfillment of the Five-Year Plan in two and a half years in the oil industry. During the second year of the Plan the workers in the Grozny oil fields produced 6,700,000 tons instead of the 4,500,000 called for by the Plan. The third year of the Plan called for 5,000,000, tons, but the oil workers considered this quota too low and drew up a counter-plan increasing this quota to 9,600,000 tons.[22]

The workers' counter-plan does not conflict with the planning organizations or with the principle of centralized management. It increases the participation of the masses of workers and the specialists in the planning of national economy

22 Aluf, *op. cit.,* pp. 30-33.

and of labor, and stimulates the backward workers to catch up with the more advanced workers. In many cases it is based on the limits set upon the consumption of raw materials, fuel, and so forth. It represents a higher program of work, improvement in quality, an increase in the productivity of labor and further cuts in the costs of production. These workers' plans counteract the conservative tendencies of certain branches of the economic apparatus. They disclose potential resources which had been overlooked, discover new resources which were concealed in the various enterprises, and stimulate mass inventions and the rationalization of the entire process of production. In addition to the counter-plans of the individual enterprises, there are the counter-plans of the combines, regions and republics. The combine, governmental department, or regional planning organization compares the workers' counter-plans of the individual enterprises with the limits set for all the enterprises subordinate to it. On the basis of the individual counter-plans, changes are made in the original quotas of the general plan.

The counter-plan was carried a step further by the workers and the management of the Djerjinsky factory who set aside 40,000 rubles for premiums and awards for inventions and suggestions, a step which was followed by other enterprises. Similarly, the organizations of a through brigade of 16,000, described in an earlier chapter, at Selmashstroy, spread to other plants and factories. The main task of such an interdepartmental brigade is to aid the workers' counter-plan by discovering and eliminating those factors which impede production. In carrying out their counter-plan, the workers at the Artem coal mine in the North Caucasus initiated the system of "towing in" backward enterprises, which spread to other industrial establishments. The Artem miners held a conference with the workers of the backward "October" mine to discover the causes of the latter's deficiencies and to find ways and means of eliminating it. The workers found that the technical staff of "October" was negligent. Accordingly, the manager of the mine was discharged, and production picked up.

Socialist competition, as has been explained, is competition among branches of industry, individual enterprises, various departments in the same enterprise, or individual workers which aims to increase the quantity or improve the quality of output, to reduce costs or to exceed the Five-Year Plan quotas in any respect. Shock-brigades are voluntary groups of workers who assume the initiative in setting the pace in their respective factories, mines, state or collective farms. There were toward the end of 1931 about 200,000 shock brigades throughout the country with a membership of 3,500,000 workers.

Counter-plans, "shock brigades" and the various forms of "socialist competition" illustrate the voluntary nature of labor in Soviet industry which is based not upon compulsion but upon economic incentive and enthusiastic initiative. The planning of labor is more than a phase of planned economy; the entire planned system, including the efficient distribution and improvement of labor power, must be considered as an integral part of a society in which the interests of the worker are paramount. The existence of socialist forms of labor organization is based on the conviction of the workers that they are not only producers but organizers of production; and that in their country there has taken place, in Stalin's words, "a radical change in man's attitude toward labor, transforming labor from the shameful and heavy burden it was once considered to be, into a thing of honor and glory."

These forms of voluntary activity on the part of the workers have constituted important factors in increasing labor productivity and in carrying out the production schedules. They are outside government regulations, although the government encourages such voluntary activities through decorations and awards. Workers who distinguish themselves in the work of the "shock brigades" may receive money prizes, additional vacations, better housing facilities, trips abroad, and so forth. Thus in June, 1931, for instance, 22 agricultural workers and 23 industrial workers were awarded the highest honors in the country—the Order of Lenin and the Red Banner of Toil. Five of these were women. *Izvestia*, official government organ, devoted about four pages with photographs running through several issues to the biographies and descriptions of these men and women, thereby revealing the qualities which the Soviet Union esteems. In addition to these individual awards, several collective awards were made. The entire working staff which constructed the Stalingrad electric power station in fifteen months instead of the scheduled twenty-four, "through the heroic energy of the workers "collective" was awarded the Red Banner of Toil. A shock brigade in the Lepse motor works and certain individual workers in Plant No. 22 were decorated for "finishing the Five-Year Plan in two and a half years"; eight Putilov workers for "services in the field of invention and rationalization of their plant"; and three, including one woman, for their work in organizing shock brigades.[23]

Counter-plans, socialist competition and shock brigades, these new forms peculiar to the Soviet economic system, are undoubtedly largely responsible for the important achievements of Soviet economy in the past few years.

[23] *Moscow News,* June 13, 1931.

CHAPTER XI

THE CONQUEST OF CULTURE

THE past fourteen years have witnessed in the Soviet Union a cultural revolution which has signified nothing less than the transformation of an entire nation. There has been not only an unprecedented metamorphosis in the knowledge, concepts and habits of 160,000,000 people, but the creation of new cultural values. The center and symbol of this cultural revolution is the worker who, in his advance toward new goals, lifts the peasant with him.

The cultural backwardness of the Russian masses under the old régime was so well-known that the favorite literary epithet for them was "the dark people." Czarism kept the masses at a low level of development where before the war 72 per cent of the rural population and 41 per cent of the urban population was illiterate. There were relatively few elementary schools and the handful of secondary schools and institutions of higher learning were the privilege of a small group of aristocrats and industrialists and were virtually closed to the workers and peasants. The distribution of newspapers, magazines and books was extremely limited. Consequently, the Soviet régime was obliged to accomplish in regard to the elimination of illiteracy, the popularization of elementary knowledge and the introduction of universal compulsory education what had already been achieved in the advance capitalist countries. In addition to these elementary tasks, the Soviet régime had to organize scientific work and research institutions and develop groups of research workers, engineers, technicians and skilled workers to meet the needs of socialist economy. Thus the process of education and training had to proceed on all levels at once from the lowest to the highest.

Culture in the Soviet Union is evaluated according to its specific weight in the general process of socialist construction. Cultural values are transformed to express the fundamental task of the reorganization of society. The cultural revolution has, therefore, followed four general lines: (1) It has raised the level of the social and political activities of the workers and peasants by drawing them into the administration of the state and of national economy. This is the base of all Soviet culture, and is the key to Soviet education and art. From this principle there follow the other lines of the cultural revolution which include; (2) the abolition of illiteracy, the introduction of compulsory education and the extension of schools and other institutions; (3) improving the skill of the workers by a thorough system of industrial education; and (4) training managers and technicians from among the ranks of the workers who are to direct the various branches of national economy.

At the basis of Soviet education lies Lenin's instruction to "unite every step of education with the workers' and peasants' labor." Accordingly, educational activities are an organic part of the coördinated plan for the building of a socialist society. Every educational unit, from the school for illiterate adults to the university and the research institution, participates actively in all phases of socialist construction. Education is an integral part of the economic, social and political life of the country. Above all, its primary aim is to raise to the highest possible degree the cultural level of the workers and peasants; and to train technical personnel from the working class for the difficult task of constructing and managing industry, upon which, in the long run, the cultural and material welfare of the workers depends. "In the last analysis," Lenin wrote in 1918, "the productivity of labor is very important, indeed it is critically important for the conquest of the new social order ... and the raising of the productivity of labor is first of all conditioned by the educational and cultural elevation of the masses." Shortly before his death, Lenin declared that "the most important condition for the building of socialism is a rapid cultural development, a cultural awakening involving the widest participation of the masses."

In carrying out this task Soviet education had to overcome the obstacles inherited from the old régime such as the cultural backwardness of the people; the scantiness of school facilities; the inadequacy of the majority of teachers for handling the problem of the new era; and the resistance by sabotage of old régime instructors in the secondary schools and universities. But with the development of the Soviet régime and the expansion of national economy, the teaching staffs accepted the viewpoint of the working class. At present there are 1,000,000 "educational workers" employed as teachers in the schools, universities and technical institutions and as librarians, curators of museums, et cetera; and, in addition, about 3,000,000 voluntary "educational workers" who participate in the nation-wide campaign to abolish illiteracy and spread universal education. These "cultural soldiers" in education are similar to the "shock brigades" in industry, and have developed new educational forms.

Until recently, the entire educational system—elementary, secondary, technical and adult—was administered by the commissariats of education in the seven federated republics, which included various boards in charge of pre-school education, technical education, scientific work, art, literature and publications, and the cinema. But the educational system was reformed following the Second All-Union Party Conference on Education in April, 1930, which led to the establishment of a uniform system of education for the entire country, and the attachment of universities and technical schools to various branches of national economy. An organic connection was established between school work and work in the enterprise. The student is thus enabled to supplement his theoretical studies by continuous practice in the work for which he is preparing. A basic seven-year general school education was established for the entire country. The secondary schools were reorganized into technical schools directly connected with industrial or agricultural enterprises. The educational system is based on polytechnic studies which aim to train the workers and peasants in modern scientific knowledge. It is divided into two main groups: The first includes fundamental institutions, such as the uniform labor schools, the technical schools, the universities, and their intermediate links. The second includes institutions created to meet the transitory demands of the present period of economic expansion which urgently requires new contingents of skilled workers and technicians. Preparatory courses for the universities and workers' colleges belong to the first group; classes for the liquidation of illiteracy and schools for the semi-literate belong to the second. In addition, there has recently developed the so-called "scholastic combine" organized for workers in the enterprises which include factory-schools and factory-colleges.

Prior to the revolution, there was practically no pre-school education in Russia. This type of education and care of children is the product of the Soviet régime, and has played an important rôle in emancipating women from household drudgery and releasing them for active participation in production and in social life. Pre-school education includes crêches, which take care of children under three years of age, while their mothers are at work in the factory or on the collective farm; kindergartens for children from four to seven years of age, who spend five or six hours in play or study suitable for their age; and children's homes for children from four to seven where they may stay longer hours. In addition, there are summer and winter playgrounds in the cities and villages, and special children's rooms in workers' and peasants' clubs and coöperative dwelling houses. In 1924-25 there were 1,139 kindergartens and children's homes taking care of 60,196 children; in 1930-31 there were 5,690 such institutions taking care of 331,623 children. In 1930 there were 2,000,000 children in the various summer kindergartens, and children's summer homes and playgrounds; by 1931 this number had risen to over 5,000,000.

Until 1930 children went from pre-school education to the

uniform labor schools which were divided into primary schools for children of eight to eleven, and secondary schools for boys and girls from twelve to seventeen. The educational reform of April, 1930, reorganized the last grades of the uniform labor school into technical schools. It also introduced universal elementary education, impossible up to that time for lack of resources. Nevertheless, even prior to this step the number of pupils increased steadily with the expansion of national economy as indicated in the following table:

NUMBER OF PUPILS IN THE GENERAL EDUCATIONAL INSTITUTIONS OF THE U.S.S.R.[1]

Type of Institution	1914	1923	1924	1925	1926	1927
			(In thousands as at the end of each year)			
Kindergartens and crêches	....	59.1	60.2	72.7	86.5	103.8
Children's playgrounds	....	....	....	....	....	204.0
Elementary Schools (four-year course)	7,235.9	7,093.8	8,307.3	9,197.4	9,498.3	9,942.0
Secondary Schools (three- to five-year course)	564.6	734.7	832.6	996.5	1,203.2	1,430.8

Type of Institution	1928	1929	1930	1931	Per Cent Increase 1931 over 1923
Kindergartens and crêches	128.4	173.2	318.2	620.7	950.3
Children's playgrounds..	323.6	581.2	1,753.5	4,222.8	....
Elementary Schools (four-year course) ...	10,375.0	10,452.2	11,775.5	17,342.3	144.5
Secondary Schools (three- to five-year course)	1,436.0	1,444.9	1,599.2	1,980.2	169.5

There has been a constant increase in the appropriations for education which amounted to about 4,000,000,000 rubles in

[1] *Social Economic Planning in the U.S.S.R.*, op. cit., p. 131.

1931 as against 381,000,000 rubles before the war. While industrial production has been increasing at an average rate of 15 per cent a year, expenditures for education have increased at an average rate of 80 per cent a year. Expenditures for social and cultural activities under the financial plan for the Soviet Union come second only to the financing of national economy, as indicated by the 1931 financial plan given in the following table:

FINANCIAL PLAN FOR 1931 [2]

(*in millions of rubles*)

(1) Financing of national economy................	21,099
(2) Financing of social and cultural activities......	5,785
(3) Expenditures for defense....................	1,310
(4) Other expenses (administration, reserve funds, payments on loans, state insurance, etc.)......	2,224
(5) Reserves	1,500
TOTAL	31,918

Appropriations for social and cultural activities in the financial plan are more than four times as large as the amount spent for defense. Educational and cultural expenditures constitute more than 18 per cent of the financial plan; and expenditures for defense amount to 4.1 per cent. These figures include expenditures under the state budget, which makes up 69 per cent of the financial plan, the other 31 per cent covering expenditures from local budgets, and by insurance organizations, trade unions and other federal and local bodies.

Elementary education is based on the seven-year school, divided into the four-year elementary school and the three-year high school. Universal compulsory education, introduced October 1, 1930, applies at present only to the four-year course and embraces all children from 8 to 11 and all those from 11 to 15 who have had no primary course. By 1932 compulsory education was to include three years' additional

[2] See *Economic Review*, February 1, 1931, p. 51.

schooling for children in urban and industrial districts. Eventually the full seven-year course is to be compulsory throughout the entire country.[3] The tendency now is to develop the full seven-year school instead of the four- and three-year schools. The three varieties of the seven-year school are the factory schools in the industrial cities and districts; the collective farm school in the villages; and the communal school in the non-industrial cities and districts. The secondary schools are being coördinated into a uniform system of polytechnic training.

Every elementary school in an industrial district is attached to an enterprise. The factory management, the local trade union, the Communist Party local and the cells of the local Young Communist League coöperate with the school authorities. In this way the enterprise assists the school in organizing labor courses and acquainting the pupils with the processes of production. Pupils in the higher grades are allowed to work in the enterprise under the guidance of skilled workers and engineers. The school teachers are also brought close to the processes of production; and, on the other hand, the school administration includes workers. The factory supports the school materially, organizing workshops in the school, and providing tools, lathes, and often instructors. It also takes care of the feeding and clothing of poorer school children. The school, in turn, assumes the task of eliminating illiteracy and semi-illiteracy among the workers in the factory through the efforts of the school faculty and senior students. Similar methods are followed in the villages where the school is combined with the collective farms. In this way, the school becomes an integral part of the factory or farm, and thus prepares the child for his place in society.

Soviet educators maintain that this system of polytechnic education fosters new qualities in the youth. They believe that the factory, which in other countries is "a center of slavery and the corruption of human dignity," becomes under

[3] American-Russian Chamber of Commerce, *Economic Handbook of the Soviet Union, op. cit.*, p. 132.

Soviet conditions "a center of human progress." Among the
workers in the enterprise, the student is regarded and treated
as an equal, learns to identify himself with his social group
and to lead a continuously creative life which is bound up
with the life around him.[4]

The rapid expansion of Soviet industry has resulted in an
urgent need of skilled workers, able to carry out the program of production. At the beginning of the period covered
by the Five-Year Plan, skilled workers constituted only 41.8
per cent of the total number of workers, as compared with
Germany, where the percentage of skilled workers in 1925 was
62.6. In addition to creating new contingents of skilled workers, it was necessary to raise the technical level of all the
workers, since these had had little experience with modern
industry. The Five-Year Plan therefore had to provide for the
rapid training of millions of workers for new and rebuilt
enterprises. The reorganization of agriculture on a large-scale
mechanical basis also required large numbers of skilled workers with industrial training, such as tractor drivers, mechanics,
electricians, and so on. To meet these needs an elaborate system of workers' education was developed beginning with the
type of factory school just described and ending with workers'
universities.

One of these workers' institutions is the factory school for
apprentices, in which workers are trained for the basic industries and for special trades. The apprentices spend half a day
in work at the factories and half a day in class. There are
also special schools for training workers for the light industries and handicraft trades, trade schools for training foremen,
and technical institutes and colleges for industrial managers.
The worker is encouraged to continue his technical education.
There are "workers' faculties" which give regular day and
evening courses for workers who wish to prepare themselves
for colleges and universities. There are also various courses for
the training of adults, including correspondence courses and

[4] I. Pistrak, *VOKS*, Vol. II, No. 4, 1931, p. 15.

classes in the Central Institute of Labor, where large numbers of workers are given six months' intensive training courses
for definite trades. Young workers trained in factory trade
schools numbered 1,016,000 in 1931; and 240,000,000 rubles
were spent in operating expenses for these schools. Students
in all higher institutions receive not only free tuition but are
paid stipends ranging from 55 to 175 rubles a month, depending upon the student's advancement in his studies and his
general economic condition. About 70 per cent of the students
in the higher schools receive stipends, and in the factory trade
schools all students receive wages. All students in the Soviet
Union are provided with dormitories, textbooks, laboratory
expenses, books, and so on at nominal fees.

Some form of education is open to all workers and peasants.
Professor Susan M. Kingsbury, in her report before the annual conference of the American Economic Association held
in Cleveland in December 1930, pointed out that there is
practically no adult in the Soviet Union who does not study
something or does not attend some school or other. The
most backward have access to classes for the liquidation
of illiteracy; the most advanced to the universities. Despite
the economic difficulties of the NEP period, literacy among
men increased from 46.6 per cent in 1921 to 58.2 per cent in
1927; and among women from 27.8 to 34.4 per cent. This con-
trasts with an increase in literacy in the twenty-four year
period from 1897 to 1920 of from 33.7 to 44.6 per cent among
men, and from 11.7 to 25.8 per cent among women. Thus,
under the Soviet régime literacy has increased at a rate five
times as great as under the old régime. At the beginning of
the Five-Year Plan there were still 18,000,000 illiterates among
persons between 18 and 35 years of age, practically all of them
among the rural population. During 1929-30 about 13,000,000
illiterate adults between the ages of 16 and 50 were taught
to read and write; in 1931 an even greater number. The
growth of literacy since the prewar period is indicated in the
following table:

PERCENTAGE OF LITERATES IN TOTAL POPULATION

Year	Literate	Illiterate
1916	33	67
1926	52	48
1930	67	33
1931	75	25

Special emphasis is placed on adult education among literates through the various courses mentioned above. In addition, the universities have been opened to the sons and daughters of workers and peasants. The change in this respect is exemplified by the changes in the social composition and the number of university students. On the eve of the revolution there were in the empire 47,200 university students. Of these, eight per cent came from the ranks of the hereditary nobility; 25 per cent from the non-hereditary nobility; 10 per cent from the priesthood; 11 per cent from the merchant class; 25 per cent from the lower middle classes; 16 per cent from among the Cossacks and rich peasants; and about four per cent from among all other elements of the population, including foreign students. By 1927 there were 159,700 students in the higher institutions, of whom 25.4 per cent were children of workers; 23.3 per cent children of peasants; 41.6 per cent children of the working class intelligentsia; and 9.7 per cent of non-laboring elements.[5]

In 1931 the total enrollment in colleges and universities amounted to 236,000 students, among whom there were 60,000 first-year students in the day courses and 20,000 in the evening courses. The number of students in the technical institutes was 423,000 of whom 161,000 were first-year students. The number of students enrolled in the workers' faculties, which prepare workers for universities and colleges, was 500,000, and it was expected that 278,000 additional students would be enrolled by the end of 1931. In 1929 the number of students in the various trade, technical and evening courses for workers

5 Grinko, op. cit., p. 260.

was 67,158; by 1930 the number had risen to over 100,000. The majority of students in all universities, colleges and technical institutes are workers or the children of workers, as indicated in the following table. About three-fourths of the students in the higher institutions of learning and in the technical institutes are from workers' or peasants' families.[6]

	Universities and Colleges			Technical Institutes		
	Workers	Peasants	Others	Workers	Peasants	Others
Years		(in percentage of total no. of students)				
1927	25.4	23.9	50.7	...	...	...
1928	30.3	22.4	47.3	25.5	37.1	37.4
1929	25.2	20.9	43.9	38.5	30.6	30.9
1930	46.6	20.1	33.3	46.9	29.0	24.4
1931	51.4	22.2	26.4	50.8	28.8	20.4 [7]

Students graduating from Soviet institutions are assured of work. The complete elimination of unemployment and the constantly increasing demands of Soviet economy for skilled workers, engineers, technicians, and scientists assures the student of being absorbed into the productive process; as contrasted with the situation in the United States, Germany, Great Britain and other countries where thousands of recent graduates and even experienced technicians, scientists and engineers are vainly seeking work.

The cultural advance of the Soviet workers and peasants has proceeded on a planned basis as part of the general planning system. "The Five-Year Plan of socialist construction," the fifteenth congress of the Communist Party declared, "must recognize the necessity of the decisive raising of the cultural level of both the city and the village population, the development of national cultures among the peoples of the Union, and the inclusion of the plan of cultural construction as an inseparable part of the general plan for the socialist construction of the Soviet Union. At the basis of the program of cultural construction must be placed those tasks of public education which will insure the cultural growth of the wide

[6] Nelepin, op. cit., pp. 38-48.
[7] Aluf, op. cit., p. 37.

masses of workers and peasants." [8] This policy has been incorporated in all plans for Soviet national economy.

The general rise in the cultural level of the people has been
accompanied by a tremendous expansion in the publication
and distribution of newspapers, magazines and books. In 1913
the total newspaper circulation was 2,700,000. By the end
of 1931 newspaper circulation totaled 35,000,000. There were
5,600 newspapers as against 605 in 1928. The increase in the
total newspaper circulation since 1913 is indicated in the
following table:

Year	No. of Newspapers	Circulation
1913	...	2,700,000
1923	507	1,532,910
1924	494	2,288,000
1925	579	6,956,098
1926	591	8,281,820
1927	556	7,577,104
1928	576	8,801,000
1929	605	12,521,000
1930	3,000	27,000,000
1931	5,600	35,000,000 [9]

In the R.S.F.S.R. (Soviet Russia proper) newspapers are
published in 41 languages; in the Ukraine in seven languages;
White Russia, five; Transcaucasia, eight; and in Uzbekistan
and Turkmenistan, in three different languares each. In addition to the newspapers for general circulation, there is an
extensive press published by the trade unions, the coöperatives, the army, the collective farms, and by various factories
and shops. By 1925 the trade unions published 22 newspapers,
six of which were dailies, and 83 magazines. Of these one
newspaper and nine magazines were published by the Central

[8] *Soviet Challenge to America*, George S. Counts, John Day Company,
1931, pp. 121-122.
[9] *Soviet Union Year Book*, 1930, p. 474; *Soviet Union Review*, June,
1931, p. 137; and *VOKS*, Vol. II, Nos. 7-9, 1931, pp. 113-122; *Economic
Life*, May 5, 1932.

Council of Trade Unions; 45 by national or federal unions; and 50 by provincial trade union bodies. There were, in addition, 30 trade union bulletins and a large number of minor publications.[10]

Apart from the regular trade union publications there are in the Soviet Union thousands of wall newspapers posted in the enterprises, offices and central buildings of the state and collective farms. The first wall newspapers appeared in the Red Army barracks at the battlefront in 1920. They did not reach the villages until 1922. Demobilized Red Army soldiers, returning to their farms, rural school teachers, and industrial workers on vacation spread the wall newspaper from the city factories and offices to the agricultural sections. Workers and peasants contribute brief articles, sketches, poems and drawings to these wall newspapers dealing with their living and working conditions, their problems, aspirations, complaints and suggestions. By 1931 there were throughout the country 1,600 factory newspapers, with a circulation of about 2,000,000; 1,800 provincial newspapers, 250,000 wall newspapers, and about 600 state and collective farm newspapers.[11]

The Soviet press publishes little advertising; the bulk of its space is given over to important economic, political, and social questions and to the daily life of the workers and peasants. Over 2,000,000 worker- and peasant-correspondents scattered throughout the country keep the press in direct touch with the life of the people by contributing articles from factory and farm. The worker-correspondents' movement was developed by the Bolsheviks many years before the revolution. As far back as 1904 Lenin announced in the Bolshevik press: "We ask everybody to write us, especially the workers. Give the workers a greater possibility of writing to our paper—to write about everything, as much as possible, about their daily life, their interests, their work." In recent years the worker- and peasant-correspondents' movement has become an important medium through which the mass of the population voices its

[10] *Soviet Union Year Book*, 1930, p. 461.
[11] *Economic Life*, May 5, 1932.

views in the Soviet press, criticizing defects and offering suggestions for improvement.

The increase in the number of books published in the Soviet Union has made the State Publishing House (Gosizdat) the largest publisher in the world. The progress in this respect since the prewar period has been striking. In 1914 a record total of 130,000,000 copies of books were issued. In 1928 the Soviet publishing houses issued 250,000,000 copies; in 1929 a total of 400,000,000 copies, in 1930 about 600,000,000,[12] and in 1931 a total of 800,000,000. During 1929 the Soviet Union published over 40,000 different titles, an increase of 600 per cent over 1920, as compared with Germany which in 1929 published 27,000 titles; Great Britain, which published 14,000 titles; and the United States with 10,000. In 1931 all state publishing concerns were coördinated in the Book and Magazine Publishing Combine (OGIZ) and all book distribution was centered in an organization known as *Knigacenter*.

The greatest increase in output has taken place in the publication of books dealing with technical, economic, social and political questions. Textbooks constitute half the output of the State Publishing House which publishes more than 50 per cent of all the books issued in the Soviet Union. In the prewar period only ten per cent of all books published were textbooks; now they constitute about 24 per cent of the total output. Before the war 15 per cent of all books were *belles-lettres;* now such books constitute 11-12 per cent of the total, although the number of copies published has increased, being 11,000,000 in 1930. In addition to Russian authors, the various publishing houses issue cheap translations of foreign writers. In 1929 a total of 5,000,000 copies of 208 translated titles were issued. During the first six months of 1930 a total of 4,217,000 copies of translated books were issued, 80 per cent of which were for workers and peasants.

The largest item in publishing is the so-called "mass book," which constitutes about 75 per cent of all the books published in the Soviet Union. This type includes books, booklets and

12 *VOKS*, Vol. II, Nos. 7-9, 1931, p. 121.

pamphlets on social and political subjects which are intended for the masses of workers and peasants; popular books on technology and the processes of production; that part of creative literature which has mass circulation and deals with subjects of interest to workers and peasants; textbooks and school books. Between 1927 and 1930 the volume of such books tripled, while total publication doubled in volume. "Mass books," written in simple language, assist in campaigns for the elimination of illiteracy, for increasing the seeded area, harvesting, organizing collective farms and so on. One of these mass books, written by the Soviet engineer Ilyin, explains the Five-Year Plan and has been widely read in the United States in translation.

During the first half of 1930, Gosizdat published over 100 books explaining the Five-Year Plan, of which 15,000,000 copies were distributed. During 1931, this number greatly increased. "Mass literature" includes books for every type of reader, from information for organizers and instructors who interpret the Plan, to the simplest workers. Over 1,000,000 copies of books were published in 1930 summing up the results of the first year of the Five-Year Plan and explaining the control figures for 1929-30. In the 1930 spring sowing campaign Gosizdat alone issued over 25,000,000 books or pamphlets on the subject, as compared with 1929, when all the publishing houses together issued only 2,200,000 copies of books on spring sowing. Most of these books came off the presses in January and February, so that they reached the most distant regions of the Soviet Union well in advance of the actual sowing season.

In addition to this method of raising the cultural level of the people and helping them to participate intelligently in public affairs, efforts have been made to bring the masses of the people into closer contact with the actual making of books, so that the contents of these books might correspond more and more closely with the daily needs of the workers and peasants. Gosizdat has created "workers' editorial councils" which discuss and criticize books already published and manuscripts submitted for publication. Meetings are held in which books and manuscripts are read aloud to groups of workers and peasants for their criticism. Book exhibitions are held in the factories and villages. The number of book stands in the factories has been greatly increased in the past few years. In 1928 over 2,500,000 books were published for the schools engaged in eliminating adult illiteracy; in 1929 over 10,000,000 copies were published; in 1931 more than double that amount was issued for the same purpose. In 1928 about 15,500,000 school-books for children were published; in 1929 this number rose to 21,000,000; and a far greater number in 1930 and 1931.

The output of textbooks for specialists was increased by 25 per cent in 1929 over the previous year, and in 1930 by 150 per cent. Tens of thousands of books on scientific subjects, such as mechanics, road-building, automobiles, differential and integral calculus, radio and aëronautics are issued every year. There is a heavy demand for books dealing with the industrialization of agriculture, the organization of state and collective farms, and the uses of new types of agricultural machinery. To make books accessible to the mass of workers and peasants, book prices were lowered by 25 per cent during 1929-30. Special editions are published at 50 kopeks (25 cents) a copy of Russian and foreign classics, modern literature, social and economic books and special children's books. The reduction in prices was made possible by the reorganization of the publishing industry, and the reorganization of the entire printing industry. A new printing plant has been built for the State Publishing House and two new sections have been added to the old plant.

As part of their cultural work, the trade unions have developed a factory unit known as the "Red Corner." Every factory, mill and plant throughout the country has a workers' club or "Red Corner" where cultural activities go on. Workers' clubs have their own theaters, cinema, radio circles, and scientific groups. In 1930 there were 1,400 literary circles composed of 28,000 novice worker and peasant writers, who contributed poems, stories, sketches and feature articles to wall newspapers. There are peasant cultural organizations corresponding to the workers' club. In 1930, for example, there were in the Ukraine alone 16,000 performances by professional theaters; 17,760 performances by workers' clubs; and 9,720 by peasant theaters. Apart from the peasant theaters, various village circles gave an additional 50,000 theatrical performances. Thus out of approximately 94,000 performances in the Ukraine about 78,000 were given by amateur worker and peasant groups. Throughout the Soviet Union a total of 500,000 theatrical and musical performances were given chiefly for workers and peasants, the majority of them by workers and peasants.[13]

In addition to amateur groups, the professional theater and the cinema industry orient themselves on the cultural needs of the workers. Not only do workers get free or inexpensive tickets to movie houses and theaters, but the artistic talent of the country devotes its energies to expressing the achievements and aspirations of the workers and peasants. Movie directors like Eisenstein and Pudovkin and theatrical producers like Meyerhold and Tairov base their work on the creative ideas of the Soviet proletariat. Plays and movies interpret the struggles of the workers both in the military campaigns during War Communism and in the present peaceful construction of a new society. The workers furnish the heroes and themes of art and literature and participate actively in its creation. They do this as critical audiences and as creators. Before being produced, plays and scenarios are often read to workers in the factory and revised on the basis of their suggestions enriched by the experience of their own lives.

The Art Department of the Commissariat of Education regulates the financial affairs of the central theaters. Similarly the educational commissariats of the provinces regulate the financial affairs of the provincial theaters. This regulation, however, is limited entirely to finances. In the choice and production of plays the theaters act independently. The provincial theaters are subsidized by the town Soviets, which include such subsidies in the general provincial budgets. Usually such

[13] Report by N. Skripnik, Commissar for Education of the Ukraine at Kharkov Conference, 1930.

subsidies are not over 20 per cent of the budget. But the demand for the theater by the workers is so great that most of the provincial theaters run without losses. In the same way, most theaters in the large cities run without losses, and some even with profit. In the Soviet Union, however, profit is not an important consideration with the theater, which is primarily an instrument of the cultural revolution. Such profits as may accrue are used for the extension and improvement of the theaters' work. In order to enable the Soviet theater to work out new methods, the Commissariat of Education subsidizes a number of experimental theaters. Subsidies are also given to the theaters of the national minorities and to amateur theatrical groups of workers and peasants.

The Soviet Government has from the beginning looked upon the cinema as one of the most important forms of art in raising the cultural level of the people. The heritage from prewar days in this as in other fields was poor. There were only eleven producing studios in prewar Russia, all centered in Moscow, Leningrad, Yalta and Odessa. There were relatively few movie theaters. By 1930 there were 15 producing studios scattered over the country in cities as far apart as Moscow, Leningrad, Odessa, Kiev, Tiflis, Tashkent, Baku, Erivan, and Yalta. Movies are shown not only in regular theaters whose number had greatly increased since 1917, but also in workers' clubs, schools, rural settlements, et cetera. By October 1930 there were in the R.S.F.S.R. alone 9,603 movie centers including the following:

Type of Movie Establishment	No.	Percentage
Cinema theaters (in towns, cities and urban settlements)	860	8.8
Workers' clubs	1,997	20.6
Schools, children's homes, etc.	224	2.3
Theatrical clubs	888	9.2
Rural cinema theaters	1,114	11.4
Traveling cinemas for rural districts	3,873	40.4 [14]

[14] L. I. Monosson, "The Soviet Cinematography," *Journal of the Society of Motion Picture Engineers,* Vol. XV, No. 4, 1930, pp. 509-527.

The radio, like the cinema and the theater, is not a commercial enterprise but a cultural instrument in the Soviet Union. There are now 55 broadcasting stations, four of which have a power of 100 kilowatts. Most of these are under the direction of the Commissariat of Posts and Telegraphs, and several under the control of the trade unions. The programs of these radio stations are directed by a Central Radio Council, consisting of representatives of the Commissariat, of the Society of Friends of the Radio and representatives of the worker and peasant correspondents. Radio programs are transmitted in about 50 languages to accommodate the various races and nationalities within the Soviet Union. In addition to concerts, the radio broadcasts news, lectures and study courses. Occasionally radio meetings and discussions are organized on subjects of general interest in which several cities participate at the same time. In 1931 there were almost 1,500,000 receiving sets in the country, many of them in trade unions and workers' clubs.

The revolution has transformed Russian literature both in regard to the men who create it and in regard to its themes. "Into literature," writes Vyacheslav Polonsky, a leading Soviet critic, "are coming men from the very depths of the working class, from the lathe, from the furrow, from the tractor, the mine, the village collective. Yesterday an unskilled laborer, a metal worker, a glazier, a tailor, a farm hand, a shepherd, and even an inn waiter—to-day, having overcome tremendous obstacles, he acquires the technique of the writing craft (with difficulties, to be sure, and with interruptions); he stubbornly masters the art, he carries his conceptions, his tastes, his habits into a field which only recently was inaccessible to him." [15]

Mr. Louis Fischer, Moscow correspondent of the *Nation* and the *Baltimore Sun*, reports a conversation with Polonsky in which the Soviet critic explained the new themes and the new

[15] Louis Fischer, *Machines and Men in Russia,* Cape and Ballou, pp. 253-254.

heroes which the proletariat has brought into Russian literature, its new basis and its new goals:

"We are pulling up the roots of capitalism in our country,
and creating new social relations, new cultural forms and a
new art. Every feature of our daily lives is being renewed.
The old, to be sure, has not yet disappeared. But it is dying,
falling to pieces." This does not mean, however, that the Soviet
Union is dispensing with the classics. "Nothing could be
further from the truth. We grow from the past.... The proletariat takes whatever it needs from the past and then departs
on its own path.... Old Russian literature was the work of
the Russian intelligentsia—the nobility, the bourgeoisie and
petty officials. It was by the few and for the few.... To-day
the proletariat and the peasantry are ceasing to be the objects
of artistic creation and becoming its subjects. The 'mujhik' is
no longer merely a reader. He has stretched out his hand for
the pen.... Who were the heroes of Russian literature before
the revolution? Tchatsky, Eugene Onegin, Pechorin, Rudin,
Nekhliudov, Bolkonsky, Bezhkov, Levin, Raskolnikov, Ivan
Karamazov. There is a characteristic that unites them all. They
are intellectuals, individualists. They philosophize. They intro-
spect. They seek their place in life. They wish to justify the
world and to find its *raison d'être*. Later the philosopher and
the grumbler gave way to the soft intellectual of Chekov, mys-
tics, dreamers, vain protestants, egoists, Hamlets, anarchists,
soul-hunters." In contrast, the new human being whom the
Soviet régime is evolving is characterized primarily by activity. "He does big deeds and engages in work that may remain
unnoticed. He builds plants and collectives, railways and blast
furnaces. He destroys illiteracy, eradicates religion, banishes
the dirt of ages, and uproots the advocates of private property.
He loves work. He hates phrases.... He identifies himself
with society. His aim is to understand the world in order to
remold it. His personal responses are secondary. Social interests dominate over the egoistic. Indeed, his social and individual interests coincide." [16]

[16] *Ibid.*, pp. 258-267.

Another Soviet writer, Vladimir Lidin, has described the change in Russian literature as follows: "In place of the old type of man there has appeared a new man. The illiterate peasant of yesterday is now the transmitter of new forms of life. The former idealistic intellectual, who never possessed any definite foundations, has been replaced by the worker-intellectual of a new type. The worker in the factory is not only a man doing his job, but is also a man who can think politically; a man who declares himself a member of a 'shock-brigade' in order to fulfill the great tasks set before the country. It is precisely this man whom our literature must portray. Furthermore, our literature must reflect in some way or other the new social relations established in the family, the new school, and the new youth."

The fusion of labor and literature has proceeded rapidly since the formation of "shock brigades." On the one hand, leading writers have abandoned the professional attitude, and have gone to the industrial centers, state and collective farms and distant races in the smaller republics, there to live the life of workers and farmers, and to describe it not as outside observers, but as active participants.[17] On the other hand, manual workers and peasants have taken to literature, describing their experiences in the "shock brigades." The relation between labor and literature is illustrated by the joint decision of the Association of Proletarian Writers and the Central Council of Trade Unions, taken in September, 1930, for drawing workers into literature. A call was issued for the formation of literary "shock brigades" among workers. By March, 1931, there were in Moscow alone 1,500 workers in these literary "shock brigades"; in Leningrad over 1,000; in the Urals 400; in Ivanovo-Voznesensk 400, and so on. A similar movement among peasants was started by the Union of Peasant Authors. These literary "shock brigaders" combine work with writing; they do not become "professional" authors, but make their writing a continuation of their life at the bench in the field.

[17] One of these writers is Sergei Tretyakov, whose "Roar China" was produced in New York in 1930.

The workers' and peasants' literary movement is an advance over the workers' and peasants' correspondents' movement, which of necessity confined itself to factual reports contributed to the newspapers. The change was taken into consideration in a recent decision of the Central Committee of the Communist Party on the "reorganization of the workers' and peasants' correspondents' movement." This decision declared that the workers' and peasants' correspondents must now become "commanding officers of proletarian public opinion, doing their utmost to direct the inexhaustible forces of this great factor to the aid of the Party and the Soviet Government in the laborious task of socialist construction. If in the first period of this development, the main task of the workers' and peasants' correspondents' movement was limited to revealing and unmasking petty defects of the apparatus, in the present period the workers' and peasants' correspondents must enter deeper into all the important problems of socialist construction, revealing the defects and illustrating simultaneously the more outstanding, positive sides of the achievements of socialist construction in all its spheres of work." [18]

At present the workers' and peasants' correspondents' movement, which includes over 2,000,000 members, is looked upon as a source of literary talent. Those correspondents who are capable of proceeding from factual reporting to thinking in images, from partial and casual journalism to creative writing will become the worker and peasant authors of the future. They will not, however, abandon the factory or farm or their participation in production.

The practice of submitting artistic productions to the criticism of workers is prevalent throughout the country, and holds good for all the arts. It is the practice of cinema directors, for instance, to show a film upon its completion first to the workers on the movie lot, then to the members of the Association of the Friends of the Revolutionary Film, and finally to a meeting of workers in a factory. The director notes all criticisms and suggestions and changes his film accordingly. In

[18] *VOKS*, Vol. II, No. 4, 1931, p. 27-28.

this way, Soviet movie directors claim, they are able to keep in close touch with their audience and to produce films vast in scope and powerful in appeal. The worker, they say, may know little about the art of the film, but he knows more than any movie director about his own conditions, and can thus infuse the technical skill of the director and actors with the breath of life, with the aspirations and struggles of the working class toward a classless society.

What is true of literature and the arts is true also of science. In order to coördinate economic development the Soviet Union has found it indispensable to plan the development of scientific technique upon which increased labor productivity depends. Mastering and developing technique involves the planning of scientific research and invention. For a number of reasons this was impossible until recently. However, an important step in this field was taken in April, 1931 at the All-Union Conference for the Planning of Scientific Research Work, where plans were discussed for training scientists from among the working class and developing the already tremendous interest of the workers in science and invention.

"Socialist science," declared the noted physicist, A. F. Joffe, at this conference, "must be created not only by thousands of specialists but by millions of inventors." The scientists gathered at the conference agreed that the organized inventive activities of the workers in the factories and on the state farms, the improvement of technology on the collective farms, and the general improvement of living conditions were laying the foundations for the development of science and technology on a wide scale, provided that the experience of the workers was consciously directed and systematized. The workers themselves play an important rôle in improving technology. Work in the factory, studies in classes and courses in technical subjects, and actual inventions which solve concrete technical problems interact and supplement each other. One aim of the conference was to make the scientific institutes organized centers for improving the skill and the inventive activities of the workers. Teaching science to millions of workers involves the employment of new methods of instruction, including the radio and the movies. The latter is especially adapted to scientific demonstration, since small parts of machines can be enlarged; movement and speed slowed down; complicated parts dissected, and theoretical schemes graphically illustrated.[19]

The conviction of the Soviet worker that he is working for himself and that he is actively participating in the management and control of production has resulted in an enormous number of inventions by workers, chiefly inventions concerned with improving production and increasing the output of those branches of industry which were unable to cope with their vast tasks. Invention has become a mass movement which enjoys public and official support. It includes tens of thousands of members and has its own journal, "The Inventor." Regarding this movement the Central Committee of the Communist Party passed a resolution on October 26, 1930 declaring that "in this period of an unprecedented rise in socialist construction and in the creative initiative of the working class, mass inventions acquire extreme importance as one of the main forms of the direct participation of the workers in the socialist rationalization of production."[20]

By a decision of the Supreme Economic Councils all enterprises employing more than 500 workers have established special bureaus for the application of inventions. These bureaus assist inventors, whether they are workers or technicians, and direct the activities of inventors toward those technical problems which are most pressing at the moment. The bureaus furnish books and legal and scientific advice, and see to it that good inventions are utilized. Under the law, the management of the enterprise is obliged to consider every invention and to report on it within a specified time. Workers whose inventions are accepted receive bonuses. The bureaus also stimulate "socialist competition" among inventors, cooperating with interested economic organizations who offer

[19] *Ibid.*, Vol. II, No. 4, 1931, p. 6.
[20] *Ibid.*, Vol. II, No. 4, 1931, p. 23.

prizes and bonuses for needed inventions. Such campaigns
have been extremely productive. During one month, for instance, 2,751 suggestions and inventions were submitted by the
workers and technicians at the Elektrozavod plant in Leningrad; 1,200 at the Dynamo plant; 4,000 at the Electrosila
plant in Leningrad; and 2,000 at the Baltic plant.

A recent campaign for elimination of waste brought 60,000
proposals from the workers of 150 factories in Leningrad.
In 1929 the aggregate number of accepted proposals at 550
factories throughout the country reached 110,000. The Supreme Economic Council coördinates the inventions of thousands of workers by means of a card-index system which
records all new inventions and proposals. These are printed
and distributed to enterprises which request them. Any factory
which wishes to improve its technical operations may receive
exhaustive information on all inventions and suggestions in
its branch of industry from the Supreme Economic Council.
This information is kept up to date and new cards are added
to the index as the invention bureaus of the various enterprises send in new lists of inventions and proposals. No
inventions are considered secret or hidden from enterprises
interested in them.

As a result of the worker-inventors movement, great economies and improvements have been effected in industry. Thus,
in the enterprises of 19 Ukrainian trusts in 1928-29 a total
of 11,800 suggestions were handed in. Only part of these
were used, yet the resulting economies were estimated at
5,000,000 rubles. During the same year the Moscow trusts
received a total of 5,420 proposals. The resulting economies
amounted to 7,500,000 rubles in 1928-29, and an additional
5,000,000 rubles in the first half of 1929-30. During 1931 a
campaign against waste lasting only one month in the Tula
machine construction plant No. 1 resulted in 5,000 workers'
proposals and economies amounting to 1,500,000 rubles. The
year 1930 marked a rise in the quality of inventions. The trend
was away from small improvements and inventions toward
more important ones, each of which gave immediate and

considerable results. Thus, a new make of rheostat invented by a group of Elektrozavod workers gives that plant an annual economy of 180,000 rubles.[21]

One of the most important aspects of the cultural revolution has been the change in the status of the minor nationalities and their extraordinary economic and cultural advance. Under the old régime, the so-called Great Russians constituted only 43 per cent of the total population of the empire, while 57 per cent consisted of various nationalities and races, including other slavic peoples, Caucasians, Turco-Tartars, Mongols, Finns, etc. The imperial government deprived these national and racial groups of the opportunity to grow economically and culturally. They were forbidden to develop autonomous cultures in their native tongues, in line with the imperial policy of Russification. The government sent Great Russians to colonize land taken from the native races in the North Caucasus, the Volga region, Central Asia and other conquered areas. It deliberately incited hostility among the subject races, instigating Jewish pogroms, Tartar-Armenian massacres, and punitive expeditions against other races. The minor nationalities were not permitted to develop their own industries and received very little of the goods produced in Russia proper. They served chiefly as sources of raw materials for Great Russian industry.

At its inception, the Soviet régime proclaimed the right of self-determination and equality of rights for all nationalities; the abolition of all national privileges and restrictions; and the free cultural development of the national minorities and races. The Constitution of the R.S.F.S.R. adopted June 19, 1918, declared that "the Russian Soviet Republic is established on the principle of a free union of free nations as a federation of national republics," and that "the soviets of the regions with a distinctive mode of life of a given nationality can unite to form autonomous regional unions," these unions to "join the R.S.F.S.R. as members of the federation." [22]

[21] *Ibid.*, Vol. II, No. 4, 1931, p. 25.
[22] Articles 2 and 11 of the Constitution of the R.S.F.S.R.

On June 3, 1926, a constitution was adopted by the republics comprised within the Union of Socialist Soviet Republics, which, among other things, declared that "this union is a voluntary union of equal peoples," and that "to each republic is secured the right of freely withdrawing from the union." [23] At present the Soviet Union consists of the following republics:

Republic	Total Area (sq. kil'm'trs)	Per Cent of Union Area	Population	Per Cent of of Union population
Russian Socialist Federative Soviet Republic	20,000,000	92.7	111,000,000	68.9
Ukrainian S.S.R.	452,000	2.1	31,500,000	19.5
White Russian S.S.R..	127,000	0.6	5,200,000	3.3
Transcaucasian S.F.S.R.	185,500	0.9	6,400,000	4.8
Uzbek S.S.R.	168,134	0.8	4,700,000	2.1
Turcoman S.S.R.	491,000	2.3	1,100,000	0.7
Tadzhik S.S.R.	145,100	0.6	1,174,000	0.7 [24]

Each of the seven constituent republics contains various racial and national groups which enjoy equal rights under Soviet law. In the R.S.F.S.R., the Russians constitute 73 per cent of the total population; the Ukrainians constitute 80 per cent of the population in the Ukraine; and the Turcomans, 70 per cent; the Uzbeks, 74 per cent; and the Tadzhiks, 75 per cent of the populations of these respective republics. The Transcaucasian republic is a federation of three national republics: Georgia, in which the Georgians constitute 68 per cent of the population; Armenia, in which the Armenians make up 85 per cent of the population, and Azerbaidzhan, in which the Turco-Tartars constitute 63 per cent of the population. Despite differences in the size of territory and population, the Soviet constitution emphasizes the full equality of these republics, and of all races and groups within these republics. Each of the republican states has an independent administration modeled on the state structure of the Soviet Union, and its own budgets. Within these republics there are

[23] Section I of Constitution of the U.S.S.R., *Soviet Union Year Book*,
[24] *Soviet Union Year Book*, 1930, pp. 20 ff.

autonomous republics of various smaller national groups. The
R.S.F.S.R., for example, contains the Bashkir, Daghestan,
Karelian, Crimean, Tartar, Kazak, Kirghiz, Yakut, Chuvash,
Buriat-Mongolian and the Volga German autonomous republics. Such autonomous republics have their own governments and budgets. Questions affecting the various nationalities are under the jurisdiction of the All-Union Council
of Nationalities, elected by the Soviet Congress. Each republic
and autonomous republic has five representatives on the
council, irrespective of size or population.

The Soviet Government has paid special attention to the
economic and cultural development of the minor nationalities
and races within the Union. While the 1931 planned budget
of the Soviet Union as a whole showed an increase of 45.8
per cent over the previous year, the appropriations for the
various republics showed greater increases for the more backward regions. Thus, the budget of the R.S.F.S.R. showed an
increase of 31.2 per cent; the Ukraine 32.9 per cent, White
Russia 35.6 per cent; Transcaucasia, 50.9 per cent; Turkmenistan, 87.1 per cent; Uzbekistan, 61.8 per cent; and
Tadzhikistan, 180.5 per cent.[25] Industrial development in these
regions has shown marked advances over the prewar period.
The gross production of the census industries in Uzbekistan
in 1929-30 was 150 per cent above the prewar level; electric
power production was 600 per cent greater. Capital investment
in Transcaucasian industry in 1928-29 amounted to 166,000,000
rubles; in 1929-30 it rose to 320,000,000 of which 36,000,000
rubles was spent on the electrification of the region. In
Tadzhikistan the total amount of capital investments increased 3,900 per cent in the period from 1928 to 1930. By
the middle of 1931 about 38 per cent of the peasant farms
in White Russia had been collectivized; in the Ukraine 66
per cent; in Transcaucasia, 41 per cent; in Uzbekistan, 64
per cent; in Turkmenistan, 55 per cent; and in Tadzhikistan,
28 per cent. The development of the metallurgical industries
in the Ural-Kuznetzk Region is transforming the Bashkir and

25 *VOKS*, Vol. II, No. 5, p. 15.

Kazak republics. The growth of the oil industry in Baku has given great impetus to the development of the Azerbaidzhan republic in which it is located; the Chechen autonomous region has been similarly affected by the development of the Grozny oil fields. Coal mining is being developed at Karaganda in Kazakstan and in Tkvarchely, Georgia; lead, zinc, and copper in Kazakstan; and copper in Armenia. Textile plants, using local cotton, have been developed in Central Asia and Transcaucasia; and a leather industry is being developed in Khirghizia and Buriat-Mongolia. Powerful electric stations are being erected in these republics, such as Dnieperstory in the Ukraine, Zages and Rionges in Georgia and Dzorages in Armenia. An extensive railway building program is being carried out, an example of which is the Turksib railway in Turkmenistan, completed in 1930.

This economic development has been accompanied by great cultural advances. Prior to the revolution most of the minor nationalities were practically illiterate, as is indicated by the following table: [26]

Nationality	Literate	Illiterate
		(in per cent)
Chuvash	7.1	92.9
Tartar	19.7	80.3
Maris	3.3	96.7
Mordavians	8.4	91.6
Armenians	7.5	92.5
Tadzhiks	3.9	96.1
Kazaks	1.0	99.0
Uzbeks	1.6	98.4
Khirghiz	0.6	99.4
Turcomans	0.7	99.3
Buriat-Mongolians	8.4	91.6
Karelians	10.4	89.6
Ukrainians	13.0	87.0
White Russians	11.3	88.7
Yakuts	0.7	99.3

[26] Ibid., p. 32.

The problem of literacy among certain of the minor races was complicated by the fact that there were a number of languages without a script. Since 1917 Soviet scholars have invented 30 scripts on the basis of the Latin alphabet. In this way the Soviet régime increased the number of written languages and opened social and political life to races and nationalities to whom these were formerly denied. Of exceptional importance was the Latinization of the Arabic script among the nationalities of the Soviet East. This had important social as well as educational results. Arabic script, which takes several years to master, was virtually the monopoly of the sheiks and mullahs. The technical difficulties of the Arabic text made it not only inaccessible to the mass of the people but presented great difficulties to the typesetter. It was for this reason that Lenin urged the Latinization of the Arabic alphabet as a "great revolution." Now throughout the Soviet East, the 37 languages which were formerly written and printed in Arabic and similar script are written and printed in Latin letters, an example which has been followed by Turkey. The Latinization of the alphabet and the invention of new scripts were useful aids in the diminution of illiteracy.

By 1927-28 over 33 per cent of the Tartars in the R.S.F.S.R. were literate; 23 per cent of the Mordovians; 57 per cent of the Germans; 81 per cent of the Jews; 76 per cent of the Finns; 68 per cent of the Poles; 38 per cent of the White Russians; 9 per cent of the Ingushes; 40 per cent of the Ukrainians.[27]

In 1930-31 universal compulsory education was introduced among minor races and nationalities on the basis of a three-year program ending 1932-33, at the end of which there will be universal compulsory education throughout the Soviet Union, including the most backward regions. Already there has been a great increase in the number of schools and students of the minor nationalities. In Turkmenistan, for instance, the number of pupils has increased from 77,000 in 1929 to 120,000 in 1931. The number of rural schools in the

[27] *Ibid.*, p. 33.

Uzbek republic has increased from 581 in 1926 to 2,034 in 1930. In 1927 only 27 per cent of the students were members of local races; in 1930 the local races furnished 70 per cent of the students. The number of students in higher and technical schools in Uzbekistan increased from 6,700 in 1925 to 19,400 in 1930. The number of students in the classes for the elimination of illiteracy reached 360,000. By the end of 1930 nearly 98 per cent of the children between 8 and 11 years of age in Georgia were attending school. In Armenia all city children and 78 per cent of the rural children were attending school. In Azerbaidzhan 86 per cent of the city children and 56 per cent of the rural children were attending school. An example of how schools are distributed in proportion to racial minorities may be taken from the Ukraine where in 1929 there were 16,506 Ukrainian schools; 1,342 Russian; 486 Jewish; 581 German; 344 Polish; 120 Moldavian; and 661 schools for the other national minorities. By 1930 the number of Ukrainian schools had increased 174 per cent; Jewish, 225 per cent; German, 364 per cent; Polish, 227 per cent; Moldavian, 222 per cent.[28]

The cultural emancipation of the minor nationalities and races has resulted in a great increase in the number of books, magazines and newspapers published in their native languages. Thus, from 1798 to 1916, a period of 118 years, there were published in the Ukrainian language 2,804 titles; while from 1917 to 1927 there were published 10,218 titles in Ukrainian. In 1930 alone 7,000 titles were published. In the latter year there were 155 newspapers, 226 factory newspapers and a great number of wall newspapers in the Ukrainian language. The total circulation of the daily newspapers was 4,500,000 copies. In Central Asia the number of books published rose from 260 titles and 1,936,950 copies in 1925 to 2,186 titles and 25,408,200 copies in 1931. In 1925 there were in Central Asia 13 newspapers with a circulation of 50,000; in 1931 the number had risen to 38 papers with a circulation of 280,000. Similar progress has been made among all the other races

[28] *Ibid.*, pp. 35-36.

and nationalities in education, the press, science, literature and the arts. This cultural advance may be considered both from the viewpoint of Soviet policy on the question of nationalities, and as a cultural advance by the workers and peasants of the entire country, since the overwhelming majority of the people in the minor republics and autonomous regions are workers and peasants.

The cultural revolution, involving as it does every aspect of life, has resulted in a profound transformation in the daily habits of the people. For example, one of the worst evils inherited from the Czarist régime was the prevalence of drunkenness. Against this symptom of backwardness the Soviet Union has been waging a persistent struggle in which the principal weapons have been improvement in the workers' living standards and in opportunities for spending their leisure time in superior ways. For serious cases of alcoholism there are special clinics. An educational campaign against excessive drinking is conducted by the "Society for the Prevention of Drunkenness," which publishes pamphlets, organizes study circles in the factories and plants, and arranges lectures and exhibits. The government has contributed to the campaign against alcoholism by limiting the sale of intoxicating liquors. In districts where workers live such sales have been almost eliminated; and intoxicating beverages are never sold in workers' clubs. The government supports the Society for the Prevention of Drunkenness and has assisted it in closing down a number of places where intoxicants are sold. The government has also limited the production of alcoholic beverages.

The transformation of social and personal relations, of modes, habits, concepts and values which accompanies the cultural revolution in the Soviet Union, has profoundly changed the status of women and children, the nature of marriage and divorce, and with these the very basis of family life. Mrs. Alice Withrow Field, an American writer who studied the conditions of women and children in the Soviet Union during 1929 and 1931, has made the following observation:

"Communism holds, in common with democracy, that children represent the power of the future and consequently they must be given the best possible care and education. Communism also maintains that a woman who is bearing and rearing children is a worker and is entitled to all the benefits accorded to any worker. In addition, Communism maintains that a woman, in performing her biological function, need not deprive herself of the social life which is the due of every working individual, i.e., she should not suffer, either economically or socially, any privations because she is a mother. She must be given every opportunity to support her family and herself, and she must have at her command—no matter how poor she may be—the best that society can give her because the workers of the future are in her care. All socially enlightened thinkers for ages past have held this view, at least in part, but until now few have advocated such wholesale methods in regard to fulfilling it as those which the Soviets have put into practice." [29]

In undertaking the emancipation of women, the Soviet system has sought to overcome those factors which in other countries prevent the vast majority of women from participating in the social, political and economic life of their community. Some of these factors are physical. Women experience brief but regular periods of physical and psychic depression during their active life, and suffer general disability before, during and after childbirth. Household duties and the care of children bind most women down to the mechanics of the home so that they have no time to study and are unable even to maintain the cultural level they may have achieved before marriage. In case of need, women are in most cases unable to support themselves and their families while taking care of their homes and children. They are compelled to choose between becoming objects of charity or neglecting their family and home duties. These factors prevent the vast majority of women with families—wives of workers or farmers—from participating

[29] Alice Withrow Field, *Protection of Women and Children in Soviet Russia*, E. P. Dutton and Company, 1932, p. 19.

in political, social or administrative work. The Soviet system, therefore, set itself the goal of emancipating women by aiding them in the mechanics of running the home and managing their families and with medical care for themselves and their children. The object was to make woman the social equal of man by relieving her from domestic drudgery.[30]

Various measures for the protection of women and children have been discussed in previous chapters. Such are the special vacations with pay for all pregnant women employees; the right of the mother during the first year after her child is born to leave her work every three hours to nurse her baby; the socialized restaurants and mechanized laundries which lighten the domestic burdens of women; and the day and night nurseries where mothers may leave their children while they work or participate in social and political activities. The factory nurseries for children of pre-kindergarten age, which supply the child with food, clothing and expert care free of charge, were founded by the Institute for the Protection of Mother and Child. The Institute has a wide variety of functions. Its Medical Section concerns itself with hospitals, maternity homes and neighborhood clinics known as consultation points. Its Social Section, by far the largest, deals with such problems as the liquidation of illiteracy and the education of women in the care of children. The Legal Section provides judicial councils where women may obtain legal advice free. Usually such advice is given by special departments in the clinics which care for the health of women and children. This section of the Institute is in constant contact with the marriage and divorce bureaus. Certain functions of the Institute require the combined attention of the social and medical sections; some are in part under the jurisdiction of the Commissariat of Education. Thus the social and medical sections and the Commissariat jointly conduct the children's nurseries and the gynecological clinics which deal with birth control, abortion, and pregnancy.[31]

The equality of women with men under the law, the entrance

[30] *Ibid.*, pp. 23 *ff.*   [31] *Ibid.*, pp. 45 *ff.*

of millions of women into productive work as wage-earners, and their emancipation from the monotonous mechanics of household drudgery, has contributed to the elimination of those factors which tend to disrupt the family. The economic motive does not enter into marriage since women are by and large not economically dependent upon their husbands. A man and a woman are married by registering at the State Registry Office or by merely living together. Registration is urged on all citizens in order to facilitate the records which are important in protecting the rights of children; but a man and woman who live together incur all the social responsibilities of marriage under the law. For purposes of registration only three things are necessary; the mutual consent of the parties contracting the marriage; the attainment of marriageable age; and a declaration that each of the parties is aware of the other's state of health. The law thus leaves the individual free in his personal relations.

Divorce is as easy as marriage, requiring only the request of either of the parties involved. However, the welfare of the child must not be jeopardized by a rupture in the relations between his parents. It is for this reason that Soviet law considers cohabitation and marriage synonymous. Parents are responsible for their children whether or not their marriage is registered. There is no such thing as an "illegitimate" child in the Soviet Union. All children have equal social and legal standing in this respect. The responsibility of parents for their children curbs promiscuity, despite the fact that marriage and divorce are easy. In case of divorce, the father must contribute to the support of the children if they live with their mother; the mother must contribute to their support if they live with their father. If a woman is unavoidably unemployed after the divorce, her former husband must contribute to her support for six months; if she is incapacitated for work, he must contribute to her support for one year. The wife has similar obligations; after divorce she must contribute to her former husband's support on the same terms.[32]

[32] *Ibid.*, pp. 67 ff.

Apart from such payments, there is no alimony in the Soviet Union. The family has been placed on a new basis in which the economic motive is minimized. As a result, Soviet workers tend to marry young and to stay married. The rise in wages and living conditions which have accompanied the expansion of national economy have resulted in a declining divorce rate.

The emancipation of women, the liberation of the national minorities, the industrialization of agriculture and the collectivization of the peasantry have changed the social and historic rôle of these groups of the population. Soviet spokesmen point out that strata of society which were formerly passive objects of the historic process have now become active participants. Women, peasants, and members of the many minor races and nationalities which inhabit the Soviet Union are active in all spheres of life. They are to be found in factories, trade unions, government posts, scientific institutions, political organizations, literature, etc. Women, for instance, constituted 41 per cent of the total number of students who enrolled in Soviet universities during 1931, and 75 per cent of the total number of students who enrolled in the medical courses. Of the total number of students who were preparing for teaching careers, 51 per cent were women.

Women and members of the minor nationalities have considerable representation on the Central Executive Committee of the U.S.S.R., the highest government organ in the country. Out of a total of 611 members, the Committee contains 96 women, 62 Ukrainians, 55 Jews, 22 Georgians, 18 White Russians, 16 Armenians, 16 Tiurks, 9 Germans, 9 Poles, 9 Uzbeks, 9 Tadzhiks, 6 Turcomans, and so on.

In inaugurating the cultural revolution, Soviet spokesmen maintain, the working class had to deal with a given structure; it had to pursue its aims on the basis of industries, geographic arrangements and social mores inherited from the preceding historic period. It had to advance toward its objectives in a society where the various national groups were on widely different levels of development, and where the general cultural level was not very high. But it is characteristic of the Soviet system that as it achieves its aims it changes the structure on which it operates; it transforms the very basis on which it works.[33]

The Soviet system began with extremely backward conditions economically, socially and culturally. Great progress has been made in all fields, but serious problems still remain. Many houses, for instance, have been built under the Five-Year Plan, but the tremendous increase in the number of urban workers has made it impossible for the construction program to keep up with the housing demand, and in many of the industrial centers there continues to be an acute housing shortage. This is particularly true of such large cities as Moscow. Even where new houses are built, the sanitation facilities are inadequate. The per capita consumption of food has increased in comparison with Czarist times, particularly since 1930, but it is still below that of some of the advanced western countries, and even though the quantity has increased, there still remains the problem of improving the quality. The same holds true of shoes and clothing. Similarly, although illiteracy has been greatly reduced, there are still large numbers who must be taught to read and write, and those who have already learned to read and write have only taken the first step; much remains to be done to raise their cultural level. Indeed, in regard to all cultural activities a great deal of work still lies ahead of the Soviet Union to meet the growing demands of the awakened population. Yet this increased demand is itself an indication of the extent to which the cultural revolution has already succeeded, and the broad basis which already exists for further advances.

When one measures the status of the Soviet worker today against his status fifteen years ago, it is obvious that he has made tremendous progress; and that the Soviet planning system, under which that progress was made, guarantees the possibilities of further advance at an accelerated pace. This fact is the key to the Second Five-Year Plan, which, on the

[33] Address by Peter A. Bogdanov, Academy of Political and Social Science, Philadelphia, April 15.

basis of the success of the first Five-Year Plan, aims to continue the building up of the heavy industries in order to make it possible to increase the production of consumers' goods, and consequently per capita consumption, to two or three times the present amount during the five-year period. The technical advances planned for the next five-year period will involve not only further mechanization of industry and agriculture, but a further rise in the cultural level of the population in all fields.

"It is not only gigantic factories and powerful machines that are being created here," Romain Rolland writes in his impressions of the Soviet Union, "but—and this I regard as the highest and finest achievement of all—millions of new people are being created, a whole generation of fearless, strong, healthy disinterested people, inspired by a burning faith in the new world."

In this cultural revolution the Soviet worker has been the leader. He has raised himself from the position of pariah in the Czarist state to a position which made it possible for the head of the Soviet trade unions to say that "in our state the most honorable title is the title of worker; to be a worker, to be a member of a trade union, is to be a privileged citizen in the Soviet Union." [34]

[34] *Soviet Russia*, by William Henry Chamberlain, Little Brown and Company, 1930, p. 163.

APPENDICES

APPENDIX I

MODEL OF COLLECTIVE AGREEMENT ISSUED BY THE ALL-UNION CENTRAL COUNCIL OF TRADE UNIONS [AUCCTU] AND THE SUPREME ECONOMIC COUNCIL OF THE U.S.S.R. FOR 1932 [1]

Date.........................

THIS collective agreement is concluded between the workers and employees of.....................(name of organization) represented by the Factory Committee of the........................ uary 25, 1932.
(name of trade union), and the administration of.................
(name of enterprise) which forms part of the...........(industry).

I. MUTUAL OBLIGATIONS CONCERNING THE FULFILLMENT OF THE INDUSTRIAL-FINANCAL PLAN:

§ 1. The collective agreement aims, through the fulfillment of the six conditions outlined by Comrade Stalin, to guarantee the most successful fulfillment of the industrial-economic problems of the fourth and conclusive year of the Five-Year Plan confronting the working class and the laboring masses with regard to the further reconstruction of national economy, the industrialization of the country, the socialist reconstruction of agriculture; and, on the basis of these, the further constant improvement of the material, cultural and living conditions of the working class and of the laboring masses of the U.S.S.R.

§ 2. In accordance with this, the Administration, the Factory Committee, the workers, the engineering and technical personnel, and the employees agree to fulfill the following quantitative and qualitative indicators of the industrial-financial plan set for 1932, as well as the assignments resulting from the workers' counter-plan of this enterprise as accepted by the Administration:

(a) To attain a total volume of production valued at............ rubles.

[1] *Biulleten Finansovovo i Khozyaistvennovo Zakonodatelstva*, No. 5, January 25, 1932.

347

(b) To increase the productivity of labor ...... per cent.

(c) To increase wages ...... per cent as compared with the annual average for 1931.

(d) The total number of workers to be ....

The different departments are to fulfill these indicators, as follows:

Name of Department	Volume of Production	Number of Workers	Production per Worker	Wages per Worker	Reduction of Costs

(1932 in per cent of 1931)   (in per cent)

The agreement is to be concluded between the Administration of the department and the departmental committee of the trade union not later than .... (date) specifying concretely the basic measures providing for the fulfillment of the industrial-financial plan of this department for 1932.

§ 3. We undertake to fulfill the assignments specified in Paragraph 2 by means of strict observance of the principles of single control and economic accounting; the proper organization of production processes based on reconstruction; mechanization and rationalization; the development of socialist forms of labor organization; increase in labor discipline by means of: socialist competition and shock-brigade work which are to be further developed into higher forms, *viz.*, the shift counter-plan and economic accounting brigades; liquidating petit bourgeois equalization of wages; liquidating irresponsibility; mastering technique; fully developing workers' inventions; introducing a strict régime of economy in utilizing metal, fuel, power, raw materials and semi-manufactures; finding and utilizing to a maximum degree internal resources of the enterprise including the full use of technical equipment; care in using machine and hand tools; actively struggling for improved quality of production, reducing stoppages and waste, organized hire of workers; liquidating the fluidity of labor and discovering superfluous labor.

§ 4. *The Administration agrees:*

(a) To apportion the assigned program for 1932 among the departments, units, groups and machines by .... (date).

(b) To hand out the industrial assignments to departments for each month not later than the .... day of the preceding month.

(c) To set the norms for raw materials, supplies, fuel, power, etc. for each type of production; to organize the daily departmental control for the fulfillment of these norms and the quality of the output.

(d) To insure the continuous supply of raw materials, fuel, tools, spare parts, etc., and to organize constant control over the quality of the raw materials, fuel and tools received by the enterprise, this control to be carried out by responsible individuals. In case of discovery of poor quality of supplies, the administration is to take the necessary measures with regard to the suppliers of the materials in accordance with the laws concerning economic accounting, and anyone guilty of accepting inferior supplies will be held responsible.

(e) To carry on an organized hiring of workers, to discover superfluous labor and redistribute it in a planned manner.

(f) To utilize labor in the proper manner by means of attaching workers to definite machines or units.

(g) To carry out a planned maintenance of equipment.

(h) To further apply direct and progressive piece rates and other encouraging systems of pay (incentives), and increase the number of operations included in the technical rate-setting, as well as establishing the proper system of keeping account of the production and earnings of workers.

(i) To carry out all measures in connection with safety devices and better working conditions, for sanitation and health.

(j) To present to the Factory Committee at least once per quarter an analysis of labor productivity and wages at the enterprise by type of operation, and data concerning the effectiveness of the various systems of wage payment.

(k) To assist in every way the development of the socialist forms of labor—shock brigades, brigades of model production, cost accounting brigades, shift counter-planning, etc. To present to the factory and departmental committees every ten days data concerning the development of the quantitative and qualitative tasks of the industrial-financial plan by the entire enterprise and departments, and separately for the following units.......................................
(indicate the separate large units and dates for presenting data).

(1) To assist in every possible way the improvement of socialized feeding, housing, cultural and living conditions of the workers.

(m) To assist in raising the technical level of the workers by organizing mass technical propaganda.

(n) To insure for night workers the facilities and services accorded to day workers.

§ 5. *The workers, engineering-technical personnel, and the employees agree:*

(a) To liquidate completely all absences for unsatisfactory reasons, to adopt all measures for preventing and reducing the number of stoppages, to utilize to the maximum the working day, to strive to fulfill and exceed the assigned production tasks, at the same time improving the quality of production and eliminating waste.

(b) To handle with all possible care equipment and tools; to exercise economy in the use of raw materials and supplies; and to keep within the norms set by the plan for power, supplies, raw materials, etc.

(c) To improve their own skill systematically by means of attending polytechnical schools, study circles, etc.

(d) To partcipate actively in production conferences, in improving production processes, and the organization of labor.

(e) To assist Party and trade union organizations in providing cultural and political education to new workers.

(f) To assist in the organized hiring of workers, to draw into industry members of workers' families, to aid in discovering superfluous labor and redistribute it in a planned manner.

(g) The engineering-technical and skilled workers agree to transmit their production experience and knowledge to the new workers.

(h) Foreign workers and specialists also agree to transmit their industrial and technical experience to the workers, engineers and technicians of the enterprise.

§ 6. *The Factory Committee agrees:*

(a) To mobilize the workers, engineering and technical personnel, and the employees of the enterprise for the fulfillment of the industrial-financial plan by means of further development of socialist competition and shock-brigade work, inventions, strengthening the work of production conferences and increasing their attention to questions of the organization of labor.

(b) To organize through the workers a systematic checkup of the fulfillment of quantitative and qualitative indicators of the industrial-financial plan.

(c) To participate in the drawing into industry of members of workers' families and in concluding socialist agreements with collective farms, at the same time assisting through patronage in improving the organization of labor on collective farms and freeing superfluous labor from these farms; to insure the fulfillment of socialist agreements with the collective farms in regard to cultural, material, and political service to the workers hired under these agreements.

(d) To assist in strengthening labor discipline by developing cultural-political work and by applying measures of social influence to shifting, irresponsible workers who break labor discipline.

(e) To participate actively in the organization of labor in the discovery of superfluous labor and redistributing it in a planned manner; to participate in the work connected with the technical rate-setting and resetting of wage scales.

(f) To strive for the improvement of supplies of goods to workers, to organize model cultural facilities, and to insure control and practical aid in the building of houses, crêches, parks, bath-houses, etç.

(g) To organize together with the administration of the enterprise the systematic dissemination of information to the workers concerning the fulfillment of the production program and the results of socialist competition and shock-brigade work.

(h) To develop at the enterprise a network of courses and study circles for the training and retraining of workers.

(i) To organize all necessary services and facilities for workers on the night shift.

(j) To assist the administration in every possible way in carrying out measures for fire prevention and insuring the active participation of members of trade unions and other workers in fire-fighting brigades.

II. THE ORGANIZED HIRING OF WORKERS, TRAINING OF PERSONNEL AND MASTERING TECHNIQUE:

§ 7. The hiring of workers is carried on by the Administration in an organized manner. It takes place by means of agreements with collective farms or labor organizations and through drawing into industry members of the families of workers, engineers, technicians, and employees.

The Administration is to appoint individuals responsible for the hiring and discharge of workers. The Factory Committee is also to appoint one of its members to check the hiring of workers.

The Administration must inform the Factory Committee about each newly hired worker within three days, and the Factory Committee has the right to refuse admission to the new worker within three days after receiving notice from the administration, giving its reason for such action.

§ 8. The hiring by the administration of persons discharged for breaking labor discipline may take place only after the approval of the Factory Committee.

§ 9. For the purpose of wider introduction of the labor of women, the administration agrees to hire during 1932 .... women (enumerate by occupation). Prior to their hire these women are to attend short-term courses. The administration also agrees to carry out the instructions of the Commissariat for Labor of the U.S.S.R. of May 19, 1931, specifying that certain positions and occupations are to be filled by women only.

§ 10. *The Administration agrees:*

(a) To conduct systematic checkups of superfluous labor and redistribute it in a planned manner among departments of the given enterprise, as well as among other enterprises and branches of the national economy in accordance with directions of the higher organs.

(b) In filling vacancies and hiring for new positions, to give first preference to the most skilled members of shock-brigades, youths and women prepared for these positions, and to persons with longest record of work at the plant, as well as workers who have graduated from military and technical courses.

The Administration must prepare a concrete plan each quarter for the advancement of workers to higher positions, indicating the number of workers and types of work, and forward these plans to the Factory Committee.

(c) To organize a technical station, providing the necessary headquarters and assign .... rubles for maintaining a mass technical library and other additional expenditures connected with mass technical propaganda (laboratories, experimental shops, technical museums, etc.).

(d) To begin (in large enterprises) the building of a House of Technique, by appropriating .... rubles and providing the necessary building materials.

(e) To assume all expenditures connected with workers' excursions to a total of .... rubles. The places to which excursions are to be made and list of participants must in each case be submitted to the Factory Committee.

(f) To pay for the training of .... workers in correspondence courses.

(g) To organization technical consultation points for all workers.

(h) To subscribe to technical literature in foreign languages in all enterprises employing foreign workers, and provide for the participation of foreign workers and specialists in production conferences by supplying the necessary interpreters; and to provide leaders for clubs and circles of foreign workers.

§ 11. *The Administration agrees during 1932:*

(a) To train and retrain at the factory technical courses .... persons, and in the evening workers' schools .... persons.

(b) To organize courses for rate-setting not later than .... (date) and train .... per sons; to send workers for training outside the enterprise as follows:

Courses	*Persons*
....	....
....	....

The selecton of these workers is to be done in conjunction with the Factory Committee.

§ 12. The Administration agrees to organize two-weeks' courses for new workers in order to acquaint them with conditions in the enterprise, in the use of safety devices, etc. The workers on their part agree to attend these courses.

§ 13. During 1932 the Administration agrees to enroll in the Factory and other schools .... per sons (indicate number by sections and date of enrollment).

The Administration agrees to organize not later than ....
1932 a school for working youths for .... persons in order
to improve the skill of young workers.

Note: Places in the factory training schools are reserved first for
the children of members of shock brigades and of workers with the
longest working record at the enterprise, for children from children's
homes, and children of collective farm members employed at the
enterprise through agreement with the collective farm.

The appropriations provided in the industrial-financial plan for the
building (or enlargement) of the factory training schools are to be
spent by the administration during .... (indicate time).
The Administration agrees to complete the building (or enlargement)
and equipping of the school and to supply the school with all necessary equipment, curricula, etc.

§ 14. The Administration agrees to employ the graduates of these
schools in the enterprise in their specialty, and provide for them
working conditions which would help them gain additional schooling,
and systematically to advance them as their skill increases.

The students of the factory training school agree to improve their
theoretical and practical training, to exercise care in the handling of
equipment, tools, and materials, to participate in the productive life
of the enterprise (rationalization, inventions) and abide by the regulations of the enterprise.

The Administration agrees to set up a study-work day for the
factory training schools with a strict régime of both theoretical and
practical training.

§ 15. Graduates of the schools for the training and retraining of
workers agree to work at the enterprise not less than ....
(indicate time). Persons trained or retrained for a special trade at
the expense of the enterprise who leave without sufficient reason, or
are discharged for breach of discipline prior to the date indicated
above, must repay to the enterprise all educational expenditures for
the balance of the time of the agreement.

§ 16. The Administration agrees to create all the necessary conditions for the successful completion of productive practical work by
the students, placing the responsibility for this upon especially assigned engineers and technical workers of the enterprise. At the same
time, the administration agrees to provide facilities for practice for
the higher groups in the seven-year factory training schools.

III. SOCIALIST ORGANIZATION OF LABOR:

§ 17. *The Factory Administration agrees:*
(a) To examine all suggestions for rationalization resulting from
production conferences or received from workers, engineering and

technical personnel and employees within a period of five days and announce the results to the author of the suggestion. In case a suggestion or invention is accepted and its economic effect determined, the premiums are to be awarded to persons who made the suggestion or invention in accordance with the existing regulations concerning premiums. The accepted suggestion must be put into effect within a specified time. The recommendations concerning the practicability of suggestions are to be handed over for final decision to the higher administrative and trade union organizations.

(b) To assure the prompt study by experts of the practicability of workers' suggestions, improvements, and inventions by organizing the necessary production base (experimental shops, laboratories, technical consultations, etc.).

(c) To assist actively in the work of production conferences by providing them with speakers from among the technical personnel (to render reports), and also provide the production conferences with the necessary facilities.

(d) To keep a systematic record of the work of the shock brigades and competing groups and furnish information to the Factory Committee not later than the 5th of each month concerning the work of the shock brigades and competing groups and individuals. Special persons are to be designated in each department for the purpose of keeping this record (indicate how many persons for each department).

(e) To solve the problems concerning the adoption of economic accounting, within five days from the time a brigade expresses its desire to adopt this system, to work out the necessary indicators for the work of the brigade or individuals, and to sign an economic accounting agreement with the brigade (in accordance with the decision of the Supreme Economic Council and the All-Union Central Council of Trade Unions of September 11, 1931).

(f) To insure a regular supply to the economic accounting brigades of raw materials, tools, etc., as well as the prompt repair of equipment, and to introduce the proper methods of keeping records of the fulfillment of the tasks of the cost accounting brigade and, on the basis of this, award premiums to brigades for achievements in production.

(g) From the funds provided for socialist competition (as specified in the instructions of the Central Executive Committee and the Council of People's Commissars of August 13, 1931), to develop a system of prizes for the best shock brigadiers, engineering and technical personnel, shock brigades and economic accounting brigades in each department, etc., for the best production results (fulfillment and over-fulfillment of quantitative and qualitative assignments), for exercising initiative in developing socialist competition and new forms of labor organization which aid in the fulfillment and overfulfillment of the industrial-financial plan.

The awarding of premiums to the best student shock brigadiers is to take place on the same basis as adult workers for the best qualitative achievements in school and shop, for accomplishing the study and production program ahead of schedule, for maintaining proper discipline, etc. Student candidates for premiums are to be proposed by the Administration and factory school committee, or by the production conference, and are to be discussed at the meetings of the workers of each department (factory conferences).

§ 18. *The Factory Committee agrees* to insure systematic guidance and instruction for organizers of shock and cost accounting brigades, to organize technical assistance on the part of the engineering technical personnel to the shock and cost accounting brigades and competing groups; to organize production conferences by groups and occupations and insure the wide participation in these conferences by workers, engineering-technical personnel, and the Administration.

§ 19. *The Administration, the Factory Committee, the workers, the engineering-technical personnel, and the employees agree* to insure the strengthening of labor discipline on the basis of strict observance of the principle of single control, together with mass cultural-political work to achieve unconditional fulfillment of internal regulations of the enterprise, and through the imposition of fines and the application of social influence upon those who break labor discipline.

§ 20. *The Administration and the Factory Committee agree* to create suitable conditions for the holding of production-comradely trials (providing the necessary rooms for such trials, instruction and leadership on the part of the Factory Committee, to assist in putting into effect the decisions of these trials, etc.).

§ 21. The transfer of a worker to permanent work requiring less skill is permitted in case the workers' Conflict Committee or the Medical Committee establishes the unsuitability of the worker for his present work, and also if a worker systematically fails to attain the norm set for the given operation or exceeds the established percentage of waste. The worker who has been transferred to lower-paid work due to production needs is to receive first consideration for occupying his former position in case of renewal of the former operation within three months after his transfer. A similar right is reserved by a worker transferred to easier work because of illness (after his recovery).

IV. WAGES AND TECHNICAL RATE-SETTING:

§ 22. The wage of the first category is established for piece workers at...........kopeks per hour,...........per day, and for time workers at.............kopeks per hour,............per day. The problem of setting two schedules for piece and time workers and abolishing calculated percentages of additional earnings is permissible depending upon whether or not the given enterprise is introducing new scales and regulations in accordance with the decision of the All-Union Central Council of Trade Unions and the Supreme Economic Council concerning the signing of collective agreements for 1932.

Hourly rates for piece and time workers are to be set in accordance with the following table:

Categories	1	2	3	4	5	6	7	8
Coefficients								
Hourly rates for piece workers								
Hourly rates for time workers								

§ 23. The distribution of workers into categories is to be effected in accordance with the instructions given in the Rate-Skill Handbook of each industry, by the heads of departments. Disagreements between workers and heads of departments concerning rates are to be settled by the Rate Conflict Committee of the department, and in case of failure to reach an agreement, is to be referred to the factory Rate Conflict Committee.

§ 24. The existing guaranteed additional earnings for time workers are to be abolished and in their stead premiums are to be awarded for these groups of workers for completing work ahead of schedules set by the Administration as well as for fulfilling qualitative assignments. The awarding of premiums is to be carried out in accordance with regulations set by the Administration and the Factory Committee (these regulations must be attached to this collective agreement).

§ 25. Highly skilled workers, paid in accordance with rates for ....categories and whose work is of decisive importance in the fulfillment of the industrial-financial plan (enumerate leading positions in each department), are to receive pay higher than the rate set for the given category by........per cent (enumerate occupations and the percentage each is to receive).

Note: This paragraph does not apply to enterprises where the new rates are in effect.

§ 26. Students in the factory training school, in individual or brigade groups are to be paid in accordance with the following four-category scale of daily wages:

Wages Category	1	2	3	4
Coefficients	1.0	1.2	1.5	1.9
Daily rates				

Note: In cases of 3 and 2½ year courses the students of the fifth semester are to be transferred to the workers' scale and are to be paid in accordance with actual work performed.

§ 27. For students working in excessive heat, in underground work, and in hazardous occupations, rates are to be 10-25 per cent higher than those of students working in normal occupations.

While conforming with the existing regulations relative to the transfer of students from one category to another (every six months) there is to be a wider introduction of the practice of quicker promotion of students from category to category in accordance with their achievements in school and in the factory.

§ 28. Salaries to the engineering and technical personnel are to be made in accordance with schedule of categories attached to this collective agreement (Appendix No. . . . .). Individual salaries in excess of normal are to be set by the head of each department in accordance with the maximum and minimum specified in the schedule for each category, as well as in accordance with the total wage fund. Salaries of the chief engineer and his assistants, as well as those of the engineering and technical personnel of the central administrative unit are to be set by the director of the enterprise while salaries for the engineering and technical personnel of departments are to be set by the head of each department.

§ 29. In order to stimulate material interest in fulfilling and exceeding the industrial-financial plan, in increasing the productivity of labor on the basis of proper distribution and utilization of labor power, in reducing costs and improving quality of production, the Administration agrees to introduce:

(a) Within one month a system of premiums for the engineering and technical workers of the various departments and the enterprise as a whole; such premiums to be awarded for the fulfillment and overfulfillment of assignments relative to quantity, quality, and cost.

§ 30. The awarding of premiums to the engineering and technical personnel must be carried on on a strictly individual basis, *i.e.,* the premiums are to be awarded to each worker in accordance with the results of his individual work regardless of the results shown by the department as a whole in the fulfillment of the plan, quantitatively and qualitatively. Heads of departments and their assistants are to receive premiums based on the results of the department as a whole. The technical director and his assistants are to receive premiums based on the results of the work of the enterprise as a whole.

§ 31. Salaries of employees and workers not directly engaged in production are to be paid in accordance with salary schedules attached to this collective agreement (Appendix No. . . . .). Within the limits of the wage fund for this group of workers the salaries of individual workers are to be set as follows: for those in the central offices by the factory administration; for those in various departments by the administration of the department. Disagreements concerning salaries are to be settled in all instances by the factory Rate Conflict Committee.

§ 32. The Administration agrees to introduce within one month the direct piece rate system for the following categories of accounting and office workers (enumerate occupations to which the above is to apply). For the remaining office workers the Administration agrees to introduce within one month a system of premiums for fulfilling work ahead of schedule when this is accompanied by the requisite quality.

§ 33. *The Administration agrees* to introduce individual direct piece rates by March 1 for at least .... per cent of the workers directly engaged in production and for at least .... per cent of workers not directly engaged in production (enumerate departments and percentages for each). At the same time it agrees to introduce the progressive piece rate system for the workers of the following departments: (indicate departments, occupations and dates). The progressive increases in rates are to be introduced for production in excess of established norms, but these are not to be lower than the average of actual production for the given department, unit, or group. The increased expenditures of wages resulting from the introduction of progressive piece rates are to be offset by the reduction in overhead expenses so that in all cases the progressive piece rate system is to correspond closely with the fulfillment of the plan with regard to costs.

§ 34. The production norms are to be calculated by the Administration for the shock-brigade workers with due consideration of technically inevitable stoppages, the normal percentage of waste, and the time necessary for rest during the working day. At the same time the Administration agrees to organize technical instruction facilities for the workers so that with the introduction of each new production norm the worker receives detailed instructions concerning the method of work on the basis of which the new norms are to be fulfilled. Revised norms are established for a period of one year. Subsequent revisions are permissible only in case of change in the technological conditions of work and in case of the introduction of new technical or organizational measures which considerably increase output per worker, and also in cases where it becomes plainly apparent that the norms have been set either too high or too low. All subsequent revisions of norms and rates are to be carried out through the Rate Conflict Committee at the request of the head of the department or the departmental workers' committee.

§ 35. In occupations (enumerate) where the production norm corresponds to the production plan for the year, in case of an upward revision of the plan during the year when such change is not accompanied by a change in organization and technical conditions increasing the earnings of the workers, the production norms are to be increased correspondingly and the payment per unit remains the same.

§ 36. Piece rates are to be determined by dividing the ratio of the rate per piece worker by the amount of production. No additional payments are to be made. For workers in the leading professions enumerated in § 25 piece rates are to be increased by ...... per cent equal to that established for them as a highly qualified worker of the trade or profession.

§ 37. In regulating wages and revising production norms and piece rates in a planned manner the factory Administration is to be guided by the Control Figures as specified in § 2 of this agreement.

For the preparation of attachments, equipment and tools required for a specific operation when the time necessary for this has not been determined in the setting of norms and piece rates, the payment of this work is paid to the worker above the piece rates as additional independent work.

§ 38. *The Administration agrees* to prepare within one month a technical exhibit of production and in case of revision of the norms of production to set piece rates in accordance with grades [of the product] so that the lower grades are paid for at a lower rate than the higher grades (approximately, the second grade is 20 per cent and the third grade 40 per cent lower than the first grade).

§ 39. Disagreements concerning norms and piece rates between workers and the Administration are to be settled by the Rate Conflict Committee. Until the disagreement has been adjusted the worker has no right to refuse to perform the work assigned to him, even if he objects to the rate and norm set for the operation.

§ 40. Students beginning with the second year of their training are allowed to perform piece work in enterprise. For this they are to be paid on the same basis as adult workers and are compensated for shorter hours by additional payment in accordance with the schedules set for students. The earnings of students for piece work are to receive the average percentage of the earnings of the piece tical studies. Students who work with piece rate workers in a brigade are to receive the average percentage of the earnings of the piece rate workers or brigade as a whole above their scheduled rate.

§ 41. Skilled workers to whom students are attached for industrial training are to carry on this work in conjunction with their basic work and are to receive an additional monthly compensation equivalent to 25 per cent of the earnings of the student—15 per cent to be paid monthly and 10 per cent at the end of the semester, provided the student passes his examinations.

§ 42. In case the training takes place in a brigade of piece-rate workers, the skilled workers to whom the students are attached are to be compensated for their training in the same way. A similar manner of payment is to apply to workers who guide the training of adult workers. In case of training in a brigade, the Administration agrees to attach all students to skilled workers not lower than the .... category. Instructors in industrial training who are in charge of the training of a brigade of students are to be compensated in accordance with the prices of a piece worker of similar skill plus a 10-20 per cent additional payment.

§ 42. The wages of workers of the enterprise who are being trained for new trades or for increased skill are to be paid by the Administration on the following basis: (a) in case of the retraining of skilled workers, they are to receive wages in accordance with piece rates established for this work, but not lower than the rates set for the .... category with subsequent increases as their skill increases; (b) in case of the retraining of unskilled workers, they are to be paid in accordance with the scale set for the .... category.

§ 43. Payment of wages is to be made twice monthly, outside of working hours, by departments, on different dates for each department, namely .... (list departments and dates).

V. IMPROVEMENT OF WORKING CONDITIONS:

§ 44. *The Administration agrees:*
(a) To fulfill all measures relative to the improvement of working conditions (safety devices, industrial sanitation, etc.) in accordance with the agreement for labor inspection and the schedules specified by this agreement (Appendix No.........). The Factory Committee agrees to conduct a daily check of expenditures of the funds provided for this purpose by the Industrial-Financial Plan.

(b) Not later than the .... day of each month in 1932 the following departments (enumerate) are to be provided with dining quarters, supplied with the necessary sanitary and technical equipment, while the .... departments (enumerate) are to be provided with special dining rooms accommodating at least......... persons per shift. In conjunction with these dining rooms special refrigerators and space for storing vegetables are to be provided.

(c) Not later than .... 1932 to repair (or build) bath houses and showers for workers engaged in dirty work.

(d) Not later than .... 1932 the following departments (enumerate) are to have washstands, and each worker is to be provided with towels. Clean towels are to be furnished according to necessity, but no less than one every five days. All washstands are to be supplied with soap or else the Administration is to furnish soap to each worker individually at the rate of .... grams per month.

§ 45. For special working clothes and workers' street clothing the

Administration agrees to set up in all shops and departments individual lockers with two sections in each (one for clean and the other for soiled clothing). Regulations for using the lockers are to be agreed upon by the departmental committees of each department, and are to be made known to the workers. In case of loss of clothing the enterprise is to replace same either in kind or by payment of the full cost. The Administration agrees also to make provisions for checking, during working hours, bicycles and motorcycles belonging to individual workers and to compensate them for any loss of same.

§ 46. Special working clothes, food for counteracting occupational diseases, soap, etc., are to be furnished in accordance with the schedule set by the Commissariat for Labor. Laundering, repair and disinfection of working clothes and repair of work shoes, are to be done at the expense of the enterprise.

In addition to such clothing and shoes, the Administration also agrees to furnish to workers, in accordance with the schedule set by the Commissariat for Labor, with clothing to protect the workers' own apparel from excessive wear, and the worker is to pay for such clothing at cost. Such protective clothing and special working clothes, as well as special food and soap, are to be supplied to factory school students in the same ratio as for adult workers in the same occupations. Payment for protective clothing is to be made in instalments covering a period of .... months. In the event that the Administration is unable to furnish special clothing at the time set, it must supply the worker with an amount of money equivalent to its cost and must also compensate them in proportion to the time clothing is overdue. Protective clothing for which the worker has paid remains his property.

§ 47. The workers agree to handle with care all special clothing and shoes and to keep same in lockers in accordance with regulations adopted. When special clothing must be replaced or when a worker is discharged, the clothing and shoes must be returned. No new clothing is to be furnished unless the old is returned. For appropriating clothing or willfully destroying property belonging to the enterprise and furnished to the worker for his individual use (special clothing, respirators, glasses, tools, etc.), the worker may be fined a sum five times the cost of the supplies (less amortization). Accidental loss of or injury to such supplies due to the carelessness of the worker makes him liable to a fine up to five times the cost, minus amortization, depending upon the decision of the Rate Conflict Committee or the labor association. Deductions from wages for such fines are to be made only after a decision has been rendered by the Rate Conflict Committee and may be made from any amounts due the worker, but are not to exceed 25 per cent of each pay.

§ 48. *The Administration* is to provide quarters, as well as the

necessary equipment and facilities for transporting sick workers to
hospitals or their homes. In all departments there are to be first-aid
cabinets for which a specified person in each department is to be responsible, such persons to be appointed by the Administration and the
Factory Committee. In underground work, in hot and hazardous occupations, all workers must be supplied with individual medical kits.
The Administration and the Factory School Committee agree to subject
each new student to a medical examination prior to his enrolment
and to have systematic examinations from time to time during his
attendance at the school.

§ 49. *The Administration agrees* to introduce all measures connected
with minimum requirements for sanitation, in accordance with a fixed
schedule and based on the agreement between the Commissariat for
Health and subject to the approval of the health authorities (decree
of the Council of People's Commissars of the R.S.F.S.R. of May 20,
1930). The Factory Committee agrees to institute a systematic
check-up of the fulfillment of this agreement by both the Administration and the worker.

§ 50. *The Administration agrees* to send to sanatoriums, convales-
cent and rest homes .... shock brigadiers who are fulfilling
the task outlined by the plan, and who need special cures or rest,
appropriating for this purpose special sums from the funds set aside
for premiums.[2]

§ 51. *The Administration agrees* to establish courses for training
workers in the use of safety devices peculiar to each occupation.
The workers agree to abide by the rules concerning safety devices
and labor protection, to maintain hygienic conditions in the plant, and
to advise the administration of any shortcomings with regard to
hygienic or safety conditions.

§ 52. *The Administration agrees* to spend from the total fund of
.... rubles appropriated by the Industrial-Financial Plan for
housing construction the sum of .... rubles for the construction and repair of living quarters. The houses are to be completed
not later than .... 1932, while the repair and re-
modeling of apartments is to be completed by the .... month
of 1932. The distribution of apartments in the houses belonging to
the enterprise is to be carried on by the Administration in conjunction
with the Factory Committee. First choice is to be given to workers
and engineering and technical personnel who are members of shock
brigades, cost accounting brigades, to inventors and those who have
worked longest in the enterprise. The apartments in the houses under
construction are to be distributed among the workers beforehand in
order to carry out a social check-up for completion of the houses.
The Administration agrees to build dormitories for the factory school
out of funds appropriated by the Industrial-Financial Plan not later

than .... 1932. The Administration agrees to spend .... rubles from the housing fund for planting trees, grass, shrubs, etc., in the workers' settlements.

§ 53. The workers and employees discharged from the enterprise because of production needs (rationalization, unfitness, injury, enrolment in the Army or schools, etc.) may be requested to leave their apartments, out the Administration must provide them with other living quarters. When a worker is discharged for breach of labor discipline he may be evicted without any obligation on the part of the Administration to provide him other living quarters.

§ 54. Families of workers, engineering-technical personnel, or employees who meet death as a result of industrial accidents are entitled to receive from the Administration an amount equal to a full month's wages of the deceased.[2]

§ 55. All workers who have worked at the enterprise for at least two years by September 1, 1932, are entitled to three days' additional vacation. In case these workers leave for their vacations prior to this date the additional three days may be granted them in advance by agreement between the Administration and the departmental committee.

§ 56. *The Administration agrees* to reconstruct or establish lunch counters in the following departments .... and also organize the furnishing of hot luncheons in the factory school. The Administration also agrees to contract with the coöperative organization and the Factory School Committee to furnish hot lunches at reduced prices in all shifts for students of the factory school. The Administration further agrees to assist the coöperatives in continuously supplying workers with food products by furnishing credits to the amount of .... rubles for the development of .... (vegetable gardens, pigsties, dairy farms, etc.) and also provide quarters not later than................... for closed distribution stores on the territory of the enterprise or near by. The repair, lighting and heating expenses of the closed factory dining rooms and lunch counters are to be paid by the Administration.

Note: Night shifts are to receive the same dining room and lunch counter service as day shifts. In exceptional cases it is permissible to supply night workers with hot food kept in thermos containers at the lunch counters.

§ 57. *The Factory Committee agrees* to organize systematic mass checking of the work of the closed distribution centers, dining rooms and lunch counters, and assist continuously in a practical way in insuring an uninterrupted supply of products to the workers and the improvement of feeding facilities.

[2] This sum is separate from the payments made by the social insurance fund—J. F.

§ 58. *The Administration* agrees to furnish the funds necessary for the organization and maintenance of créches, playgrounds, pioneer groups and sports fields for the children of the workers in the enterprise, to the amount of .... rubles.

§ 59. The Administration is to provide funds for cultural work in the amount of .... per cent of the total payroll, and in addition to this *the Administration agrees:*

(a) To vacate all club and "Red Corner" quarters occupied for other uses, or provide new quarters, not later than the .... month of 1932 in the following departments..................... and dormitories and supply them with the necessary furniture and equipment (tables, chairs, blackboards, etc.) and also with lighting, heating, and cleaning services at the expense of the Administration.

(b) To pay for the heating, lighting, guarding and repair of clubs and palaces of labor, and repair all clubs and palaces of labor serving the workers of the enterprise.

(c) To begin the building of a club not later than the.......... month of 1932 and complete same not later than................. For this purpose the Administration is to appropriate during 1932 .... rubles and see to it that the necessary blueprints and building materials are supplied to the construction project.

Note: On new construction projects temporary clubs and "Red Corners" are to be built simultaneously with the building of the project.

(d) To participate in organizing and equipping a park of culture and rest to be connected with the enterprise for which purpose the Administration is to appropriate .... rubles.

(e) The Administration is also to share in the expense of building the seven-year factory school to the amount of .... rubles.

(f) The Administration is to turn over to the factory seven-year school all tools, machines, and other supplies discarded by the enterprise which may be useful for training purposes. The Administration is also to supply additional shops, laboratories, and workrooms necessary for the school, to equip the .... shops with machinery and .... motors, and to organize .... workshops (indicate necessary equipment).

(g) To appropriate .... rubles for prophylactic work among workers and their children (pioneer camps, plyagrounds) and provide the necessary space for pioneer headquarters.

(h) To furnish suitable quarters for classes in liquidating illiteracy.

(i) To set up radio facilities in the "Red Corners" of the following departments .... by .... 1932, and appropriate .... rubles for the further development of radio, and supplying the necessary electric power.

(j) To share the expenses of building the following facilities for sports: .... (stadiums, swimming facilities, etc.).

(k) To share in the financing of a factory press (newspaper) to the amount of .... rubles.

VI. Working Conditions for Engineering and Technical Personnel:

§ 60. In order to put into effect the instructions of higher bodies the Administration agrees to supply within one month each engineering and technical worker with written instructions specifying the rights and duties of the position occupied. The Administration and the Factory Committee agree within one month to make a complete check of the work performed by each engineer or technician in order to relieve him of those functions which do not pertain to his position.

The Engineering and Technical Council agrees to urge all engineering and technical workers to volunteer to sign agreements for remaining in the enterprise for a specified number of years.

§ 61. The hiring, discharge, or transfer of engineering and technical workers is to be done by the Administration upon notifying the Factory Committee (the Engineering-Technical Council). The Administration agrees to draw the Engineering and Technical Council into active participation in solving the problems relative to the fulfillment of the plan and to a rational utilization of the engineering-technical personnel.

The Engineering and Technical Council agrees to assist the Administration in selecting and properly distributing engineering and technical workers throughout the enterprise.

§ 62. In cases of dismissal, in accordance with points A and B of Article 47 of the Labor Code, engineering and technical workers must be notified in writing one month previously. The engineering and technical workers agree to notify the Administration one month in advance in case they wish to leave the employ of the enterprise. In case of the discharge of an engineering or technical worker because of activity detrimental to the material interests of the enterprise, the Administration agrees to form a committee of experts consisting of representatives of the Administration, Factory Committee, Engineering and Technical Council, and expert-specialists recommended by higher bodies of the Engineering and Technical Council (district, regional and, in more serious cases, central).

§ 63. The schedule of vacations for the technical personnel is to be determined by the Administration and is to be submitted for approval to the Factory Committee (Engineering and Technical Council) with the following provisions:

(a) The engineering and technical personnel whose wages are not subject to the daily norms as enumerated in the list attached to this collective agreement are to receive vacations of from three weeks to one month (including the usual vacation), depending upon the type of services.

(b) Engineering and technical workers employed in the .... department on .... operations, whose work is considered injurious are to receive special clothing, neutralizing foods and supplies on the same basis as industrial workers in these departments.

§ 64. The Administration agrees to provide the engineering and technical personnel with a regular day of rest in accordance with a set schedule. In case of exceptional necessity an engineer or technician may be required to work during his scheduled day of rest, but the Administration must grant him a rest day within a period of ten days.

§ 65. Engineering and technical workers are not to engage in any activity during working hours outside of their professional duties unless special permission has been granted for this by the Administration.

§ 66. The Administration is to appropriate the necessary funds in the amount of .... rubles per year for facilities necessary for increasing the skill of engineers. This includes special trips and excursions within the U.S.S.R. or abroad, the establishment of review courses, sending engineers to special courses or scientific-technical congresses and consultations, study of foreign languages, establishment of technical libraries, publications, etc. Candidates among the engineering and technical personnel for trips abroad or special assignments to increase their skill are to be nominated by the Administration and the Factory Committee (Engineering and Technical Council).

The Administration agrees to make it possible for the engineering and technical workers to carry on their studies in the factory laboratory, library, archives and workshops.

§ 67. The Administration agrees to appropriate for correspondence courses of engineering and technical workers the sum of .... rubles. The Bureau of the Engineering-Technical Council is to assist the workers in their correspondence work (organizing brigades and circles for study) and organizing consultations for them.

§ 68.

(a) The Administration agrees to provide, not later than .... 1932 the necessary living quarters for those engineering and technical workers who do not have such quarters.

(b) In all newly constructed houses 10 per cent of the space is to be reserved for those engineering and technical workers who are in need of living quarters, upon agreement with the Engineering and Technical Council. This space is to be in addition to that provided in the special houses for specialists.

(c) Upon agreement between the Factory Committee and the Engineering and Technical Council .... places are to be reserved for the children of engineering and technical workers in the factory schools, and technical institutes functioning at the enterprise.

§ 69. The Administration and the Factory Committee (Engineering and Technical Council) agree to organize the proper utilization of the services of foreign specialists in their own specialties through the creation of satisfactory conditions of work and giving proper attention to developing cultural-political work among them, as well as services in connection with cultural and living conditions.

The Administration of the enterprise agrees to provide .... rubles for the purchase of foreign language literature for the foreign specialists.

VII. PRIVILEGES FOR MEMBERS OF TRADE UNIONS:

§ 70. Members of trade unions, in addition to having the same rights and privileges as all other workers, are entitled to the following privileges:

(a) To be retained at the enterprise when superfluous labor is being discharged, and to be transferred to other occupations within the enterprise.

(b) To advance to occupations requiring more skill.

(c) To enter special courses for increasing skill.

(d) To first choice of living quarters in houses belonging to the enterprise.

(e) To enroll their children in factory schools, factory 7-year schools, children's playgrounds, kindergartens, crêches, etc.

(f) To be among the first to be sent to rest homes, sanatoriums and for special cures.

VIII. APPROPRIATIONS FOR THE TRADE UNION ORGANIZATION:

§ 71. For the maintenance of the Factory Committee the Administration agrees to appropriate funds amounting to .... per cent of the total payroll. The Administration agrees to provide the Factory Committee and the departmental committees with suitable quarters and equipment for their proper functioning and pay for the necessary services (telephone, heat, light, repair, watchman, etc.)

§ 72. For the purpose of checking the fulfillment of the conditions of this agreement and adjusting labor disputes, factory and departmenal rate conflict committees are to be organized at the enterprise, and these are to function in accordance with the regulations of the Commissariat for Labor. When the Rate Conflict Committee

has a case under consideration involving a worker of a national
minority or from a foreign country, the Administration must provide
interpreters.

IX. PROCEDURE IN CONTROLLING THE FULFILLMENT OF THIS COLLECTIVE AGREEMENT:

§ 73. The Administration and the Factory Committee agree to
organize a continuous systematic check-up of the fulfillment of their
mutual obligations. In case of a breach of agreement, the Administration and the Factory Committee are to take immediate steps
to eliminate the breach.

§ 74. The Factory Committee and the Administration are to conduct a mass check-up of the fulfillment of the collective agreement
once every three months. Administrative workers directly responsible
for a breach of this agreement are liable to prosecution under Article
134 of the Criminal Code. Every worker, engineer, technical worker,
or employee is subject to discipline in accordance with the schedule
of fines, and is also responsible to trials by comrades-courts of his
fellow workers, and, if a member of a trade union, to his trade union
organization.

§ 75. The Administration agrees to publish this collective agreement, together with all appendices, not later than.................
1932, in .... copies, and furnish the same free of charge to
all workers.

APPENDIX II

CONCERNING THE PARTICIPATION OF WORKERS AND ENGINEERING AND TECHNICAL PERSONNEL IN THE PREPARATION OF THE SECOND FIVE-YEAR PLAN [1]

(Directive instructions of the All-Union Central Council of Trade Unions and the State Planning Commission of the USSR.)

I

The All-Union Central Council of Trade Unions [AUCCTU] and the State Planning Commission of the USSR attach exceptional importance to the drawing in of millions of workers, youth, engineers, technicians, and scientific workers into the preparation of the second five-year plan for the building of socialist society on the basis of the directives of the XVII All-Union Party conference. In the preparation of the second five-year plan the trade unions must utilize to the fullest extent the experiences, activities and creativeness of millions of men and women workers gained in the struggle for the fulfillment of the first five-year plan.

The entire work of the trade unions and the participation of the working masses in the preparation of the second five-year plan must take place under the slogan of unconditional fulfillment by each enterprise, by each productive section, and brigade of the plan for 1932, the concluding year of the first five-year period, accompanied by a struggle for higher productivity, better organization of labor on the basis of the six conditions outlined by Comrade Stalin, stricter economy, the mobilization of internal resources and the improvement of the quality of production.

In accordance with the decision of the IX All-Union Congress of Trade Unions, the AUCCTU and the State Planning Commission of the USSR propose to the trade unions and planning organizations:

1. To organize a mass collection of suggestions among workers and engineering and technical personnel for the second five-year plan

---

[1] *Izvestia*, May 25, 1932.

dealing with all sides of the work of the given enterprise, and to develop mass work in the following directions:

(a) Solution of the problems of labor organization; the elimination of irresponsibility; the proper distribution of workers and utilization of equipment; elimination of accidents and production difficulties; mechanization of labor and the rationalization of production processes; determination of the full productive capacity of each department and the entire equipment under the three-shift system; determination of the possible output and type of goods to be produced; the possible increase in productivity of labor by years and for the last year of the second five-year period; determination of the conditions of technical reconstruction (the building of new departments, the installation of additional equipment of the most modern type) which will make it possible to increase the productivity of labor and the industrial output during the second five-year period.

On the basis of the work performed by the best cost-accounting and shock-brigades, outline the concrete measures to be taken in order to increase the productivity of labor and reduce costs.

(b) To organize among the working masses and the engineering and technical personnel mass discussions and the drafting of perspectives for the development of each department and the enterprise as a whole, based on the introduction of the best technical methods of production, the wide application of standardization, and uniformity of products and the maximum utilization of existing equipment.

(c) To discuss widely the possibilities of organizing at the enterprises the production of new kinds of goods, freeing the USSR of dependence upon capitalist countries, and also the wide application of scientific discoveries and the latest technical inventions, such as electrical welding, electro-chemistry, pouring under high pressure, etc.

(d) Find ways of utilizing new types of domestic materials in productive processes and foster all efforts toward the utilization of waste and by-products.

(e) Concentrate the special attention of the working masses and the engineering and technical workers upon solving the problems of the technical-industrial-financial plan, upon the radical improvement of internal plant planning, especially internal transport and warehouse organization (economy).

(f) In the plan for the second five-year period, particular consideration is to be given to the problem of specialization and coöperating of enterprises, tying this up with the plan for the reconstruction and the wide conversion of enterprises to large-scale mass production.

(g) To direct the rationalization work of enterprises to the study and decisive elimination of stoppages of equipment and the non-productive loss of working time.

(h) Organize a systematic struggle for cleaning the plants of waste

and dirt, and for maintaining the proper standards of cleanliness with
regard to the shops, tools and equipment.

(j) Organize the preparation of plans concerning safety devices,
labor protection, better working conditions in the shops and the enterprise as a whole and secure the active participation of all in this work.

(i) Concentrate the attention upon the fight against over-expendi-
tures of wage funds. The decisive elimination of the petty-bourgeois
equalization of wages by means of the wide introduction of piece-
rates and other incentive forms of wage payment for work; the organization of true technical piece-rate setting by drawing into this work
old skilled workers—all this must take a prominent place in the work
of the economic and trade union organizations, which must draw
from the experience of the best enterprises, departments, and cost-
accounting brigades which have fully mastered the technique of production.

2. To devote special attention to planning the training of skilled
workers and specialists without taking them off their work. In accordance with this:

(a) Outline a network of permanent educational institutions and
forms of technical instruction; and increase the technical knowledge
and the skill of the workers and specialists through a system of
correspondence courses, special skill courses, etc.

(b) To provide for the establishment in the enterprises of the
material base for the development of all types of instruction: the
building of new quarters for school combines, factory schools, supplying them with proper equipment, etc.

3. The trade unions and the planning organizations must provide
for the inclusion in all plans of new construction in enterprises, the
building of establishments and institutions connected with the improvement of working conditions, cultural provisions and living conditions
of the worker; provide the workers with living quarters, improve the
facilities for socialized feeding and distribution of consumers' goods,
etc. In accordance with this it is necessary:

(a) To outline a plan of construction of living quarters for workers
in the basis of the perspective development of the enterprise and the
expected increase in the number of workers. These plans are to be
drawn up in such a way as to insure a radical improvement of living
conditions for workers toward the end of the second five-year, first
of all for the workers in the basic industrial regions and in the leading branches of the national economy of the USSR. Organize the
wide utilization of local building materials and the introduction of
standardized housing construction.

(b) For the purpose of the quickest possible drawing in of women
into industry, it is necessary to provide in the plans the maximum

development of the building of crêches, laundries, dining rooms, etc.

(c) Prepare separately the plan for building and developing suburban workers' settlements, factories, vegetable gardens, dairy and hog breeding farms. rabbit breeding stations and fisheries. It is necessary that each enterprise utilize fully all the possibilities for the improvement of supplying the workers with food products from the enterprise's own suburban establishments or from other local sources (purchasing from nearby farms).

4. To make provisions in the second five-year plan for raising the quality and standard of cultural work in order to insure the fulfillment of the most important problems of the cultural revolution: the raising of the cultural-technical level of the country and to provide for the cultural-political reëducation of the working masses on the basis of the scientific Marxist-Leninist viewpoint and the development of a conscious Communist attitude to labor. On the basis of this:

(a) Prepare measures insuring the full utilization of the existing network of cultural institutions: introduce the shift system, better utilization of building funds, etc.

(b) Prepare a plan for the building of cultural institutions and schools in accordance with the perspectives of the enterprise, keeping in mind the national composition of the working force, conditions of work, and the growth of cultural demands and problems of preparing cultural groups.

(c) Make provisions in the plan for the second five-year period for the further development of the material base of cultural and recreational measures (schools, training of personnel, crêches, playgrounds, building of libraries, theaters, clubs, cinemas, red corners, etc.), basing this on the funds to be provided by state enterprises, trade unions, coöperatives and other social organizations.

(d) Provide for the necessary measures toward the polytechnization of the school: increase the funds for polytechnical equipment, school laboratories, shops, work rooms, institutions for the organization of work with children, etc.

— (e) Provide for the maximum development of the network of institutions of workers' education and correspondence courses, insuring the improvement of the general cultural and technical level of the workers (equivalent to seven-year schools in the basic industries and four-year schools for all others), and also the complete elimination of illiteracy and poor literacy during the second five-year period.

II

1. The Central Committees of the trade unions must participate directly in the working out of the problems of the second five-year

period in the corresponding economic and planning organizations, basing their work on materials worked out for the second five-year period by enterprises, factory committees and also district trade union and intra-trade union organizations.

2. The CC of trade unions must participate actively in brigades of social assistance functioning in conjunction with planning organizations, and together with the planning and economic organizations they are to organize branch and regional conferences dealing with problems of the second five-year period.

3. The planning organizations and the CC of the trade unions must draw into the preparation of the second five-year plan all-union and local scientific research institutes and scientific technical organizations, placing before them concrete problems connected with the perspectives of developing a given branch of industry.

4. The CC of the trade unions and the planning organizations are to work out with special care the problems of new capital construction in their branch of industry and the distribution of productive forces.

5. While drawing the masses of workers into the preparation of the plan for the second five-year period the CC of the trade unions, the district intra-union and union organizations together with the planning bodies must accomplish the following through setting up operative leadership and checking the fulfillment of the directives at the enterprises:

(a) Organize mass brigades of workers and engineering-technical personnel by branches of industry for determining the natural resources and also for drafting the plan for electrification, heating developments, technical reconstruction and determination of the specialization of a district, region or republic.

(b) Determine the perspectives for the maximum development of enterprises of local significance on the basis of discovering and utilizing local materials and mineral resources, fuel, building materials, and the utilization of by-products.

(c) Determine the surplus sources of local raw materials, fuel, building materials, labor power, etc., which could be used to supply enterprises of all union or republican significance.

6. Republican, regional, and district councils of trade unions, together with the planning organizations, must be very thorough especially in preparing the problems of:

(a) Housing and municipal economy: water supply, bathhouses, laundries, sewage systems, lighting, improvements, etc.

(b) Suburban economy, a network of socialized feeding establishments, the building of factory kitchens, mechanized dining rooms calculated on the basis of the proposed development of industry and the increase in the number of workers.

(c) In the five-year plan special attention is to be devoted to problems of cultural and recreational services, developing a network of schools, clubs, palaces of socialist culture, theaters, libraries, the building of workers' settlements, planting of parks, shrubs, grass, and the proper organization of leisure for workers.

(d) Indicate ways of reorganizing health work; a plan for the building of hospitals, sanatoria, crêches, health centers at the enterprises; indicate ways of developing prophylactic work with a view of utilizing to a maximum degree the facilities of a given district, region or republic.

7. The district, regional and republican councils of trade unions, in addition to combining the materials of the trade unions for the second five-year plan, must insure active participation of the district trade union bodies in the adoption of their proposals by the planning and leading organizations in the given locality; and also, wherever necessary, organize a series of intra-union conferences, and meetings concerning problems arising in the preparation of the second five-year plan.

III

1. The AUCCTU and the State Planning Commission of the USSR in stressing the immensity of the problems of the second five-year plan and the importance of the participation of the wide masses in its preparation, point out that the practical work in this connection is to be especially concentrated in and placed upon the producers' unions and the factory committees.

2. The intra-union local organizations (district and regional councils of trade unions) must organize daily checks upon the fulfillment by all trade union organizations of the directives of the AUCCTU and the CC of the trade unions in organizing mass work in the enterprises, insuring the active participation of the workers in the preparation of the second five-year plan.

3. For the purpose of working out the solution of special problems of each enterprise, the factory and departmental committees must organize a wide network of special brigades consisting of shock-brigade workers, engineers and technicians, with the necessary drawing into this work of the Comsomols;[2] they must also utilize widely for the same purpose the production conferences, planning-operative groups, engineering-technical sections and the active body of inventors.

4. The AUCCTU and the State Planning Commission of the USSR draw the special attention of all trade union and planning organizations to the exceptional political significance of the participa-

[2] Communist Youth League.

tion in the drafting of the second five-year plan of the millions of workers, youth, women workers, employees and engineering and technical personnel. Only the experience of millions of workers will make it possible to use to the fullest extent all available resources, the growing activity and socialist competition, shock-brigade work of the laboring masses in the struggle for the building of a classless socialist society. As a result of preparing the second five-year plan, the trade unions must achieve new successes in the direction of drawing workers into socialist construction.

VEINBERG
Secretary of the All-Union Central Council of Trade Unions

V. KUIBYSHEV
Chairman of the State Planning Commission of the USSR.

May 22, 1932.

APPENDIX III

EXCERPTS FORM THE RESOLUTION OF THE NINTH CONGRESS OF TRADE UNIONS ON THE REPORT OF THE ALL-UNION CENTRAL COUNCIL OF TRADE UNIONS [AUCCTU].[1]

THE trade unions must mobilize all the forces of the working class for the complete fulfillment and overfulfillment of the national economic plans of the present and final year of the Five-Year Plan in all branches, this being the necessary prerequisite for the fulfillment of the problems of the Second Five-Year Plan. Special attention must be concentrated upon the fulfillment of the plans for the iron, steel and non-ferrous metal industries, for coal production, machine-building and transport, the aim being to fulfill the counter-plans advanced by the workers.

The Ninth Congress stresses especially the necessity for a struggle in all trade unions for the counter-plan in iron and steel, calling for the production of 10 million tons of pig iron. The Ninth Congress of Trade Unions proposes to all trade union organizations to strengthen the explanatory work among the wide masses of workers, particularly among those recently drawn into industry who have not experienced the oppression of a capitalist factory, concerning the necessity of completely overcoming the difficulties of growth connected with the reconstruction of national economy, with the building of a new gigantic socialist industry, with mastering the most modern technical methods of production.

The trade unions must explain to the mass of their membership in all their daily work that the radical reconstruction of national economy now being carried out by the Party and the working class; the building of Magnitogorsk, Dnieprostroy, the Stalingrad and Kharkov tractor plants, the Kuznetz iron and steel mill and other giants of industry; the organization of state and collective farms and machine and tractor stations, constitute the transformation of the USSR into an advanced industrial country and form the sole basis for a real rise in the material and cultural living standards of all who work.

The trade union organizations must strive that each worker, each

[1] *Pravda*, May 7, 1932.

member of a trade union should understand the policy of the Party and should actively fight for the successful fulfillment of the industrial-financial plan, for an increase in the productivity of labor, for the reduction of costs and model quality of production.

Socialist competition forms the basic method in the entire work of the trade unions.

The basic problem of developing socialist competition is to furnish concrete leadership and aid for each member of a shock brigade, for each shock brigade; and on this basis to raise the quality of leadership for competition and shock-brigade work on the part of trade unions.

A determined fight is to be declared against exaggerated figures, misleading reports, pseudo shock-brigadiers in socialist competition.

The trade unions are to utilize to the fullest extent those forms of socialist competition which have been proved most successful in the practical work of the masses and are to concentrate the greatest amount of attention upon the work of cost-accounting brigades, shift-counter-planning, which have been models of mass struggle for increasing the productivity of labor, reducing costs and improving the quality of production.

Only the systematic and persistent work of the trade unions in keeping proper records of the results of socialist competition and actual accomplishments in fulfilling the industrial-financial plan, will make it possible to insure the further development of socialist competition and shock-brigade work and raise these to a higher level.

The Congress considers it necessary to improve the entire matter of awards to individual members of shock-brigades as well as to enterprises for the best results in fulfilling the industrial-financial plan and for setting the higher standards of work.

The rôle and practical work of production conferences must be raised to a new level.

The industrial conferences of a brigade, a department, a plant must concentrate their attention upon the realization of workers' proposals, upon the mobilization of the experience and initiative of the wide mass of workers for the better organization of labor and production, upon the proper distribution of the working force at each enterprise, upon the discovery of internal resources, upon participation in the drafting and checking of the fulfillment of the technical-industrial-financial plan.

Specialists are to be more widely drawn into the work of the production conferences which are to concentrate still more attention upon problems of mastering new technological processes, upon discussion of plans for rationalization and the struggle for the mechanization of labor processes. This work is to be combined with extensive explanation of the most advanced technical experience and best ways and methods of organizing production.

It is necessary to raise the rôle of assistant directors (of enterprises) in the work of production conferences, and to advance to this work the best groups of organizers of socialist competition and shock-brigade work, insuring for them the necessary authority and support from both trade union and administrative organizations, and free them from the performance of extraneous functions.

The Congress considers that the administrative and planning organizations must reorganize the practice of preparing and passing the industrial-financial plan, so as to insure the greatest possible reflection of the counter plans advanced by the workers in the industrial-financial plans of the enterprises and the various branches of industry; and must create the necessary conditions for the realization of the most important directives of the XVI Party Congress stating that "the trade unions, in preparing the economic plan, must come forward with concrete proposals based upon a consideration of all remarks and indications of the working masses and trade union organizations concerning the plans of individual branches of industry as well as the plan as a whole."

Since the Congress considers as the most important problem of the proletariat the question of the growth and strengthening of state farms (livestock, grain and industrial crops) and the organizational-economic strengthening of the collective farms, the Congress makes it obligatory for all trade union organizations to offer decisive assistance to state and Party organizations in the fulfillment of this most important task, bringing to the state and collective farms and machine and tractor stations the experience gained in socialist competition, shock-brigade work, the struggle for cost accounting, the introduction of piece-rate work and the elimination of petty bourgeois equalization in wages.

The Congress considers that the slogan "face production" remains the basic slogan of the trade union movement. The major tasks in realizing this slogan at the present stage are the completion of the radical reorganization of the wage payment system and the organization of technical rate-setting, a widespread struggle for the systematic improvement of the material and cultural living standards of the working masses.

The Congress notes in the work of a number of trade union organizations the presence of a formal-bureaucratic attitude toward the problems of the daily needs and requests of their members, and that this represents an opportunistic misconstruction of the slogan "face production." This slogan demands the most careful and attentive attitude on the part of the trade union organizations toward the worker, his concrete needs, necessities, and demands. Only opportunists, only persons dominated by Menshevik ideology can believe that the slogan "face production" in any way contradicts the Bolshevik defense by the trade union organizations of their members against bureaucratic abuses which still take place in the work of the administrative, state and coöperative apparatus.

The Congress categorically demands from all trade union organizations, beginning with the central committees of the trade unions, down to the departmental (shop) committees, that they carry on a determined struggle against any tendency to ignore or disregard the material and cultural needs of the workers, the "trifles" of the workers' daily life; against the careless and bureaucratic attitude to the complaints of workers concerning shortcomings in the factory, living conditions, coöperatives, state organizations, etc.

The trade unions, as mass organizations of the proletariat, must learn to combine the working out of the most important problems of labor organization and industry, the organization of distributing consumers' goods, the cultural development, etc., within each branch of industry, plant, shop, and the exercise of daily care concerning each worker with the ability to offer concrete aid to each worker and his family. The degree of success attained by the trade unions in their work must be checked on the basis of the concrete aid furnished by them both to groups of workers and to individual workers.

The struggle for the systematic rise in the productivity of labor is the most important problem of each worker and of each trade union organization. Productivity of labor, according to Comrade Lenin—"is, in the final account, the most important and most significant factor for the victory of the new social order."

The trade unions must pay exceptional attention to the question of regulating wages and setting rates. The socialist reconstruction of the whole of national economy, the elimination of unemployment, the problems of mastering new technique have brought to the fore in the most acute manner the problem of reorganizing the system and forms of wage payments so as to insure the organized influx of workers who would remain in the industry for extended periods of time, a correct organization of labor and a maximum increase in the productivity of labor. Since the correct organization of the system of wages is considered by the Congress to be the major level in raising the productivity of labor, the Congress approves of the reorganization of the system of wages on the basis of the six points of Comrade Stalin which has been begun by the trade unions and enterprises under the leadership of the Central Committee of the Communist Party. The Congress makes it obligatory for all trade unions to eliminate the petty bourgeois equalization of wages and interfere in the most determined manner with all attempts to misconstrue the line of the party with regard to wage payments.

The Congress delegates to the AUCCTU the task of completing in 1933 the introduction of the new rate schedules and qualification directories for all branches of industry, transport and agriculture, introducing higher pay for the leading and highly skilled trades among workers engaged in difficult labor processes, thus putting into effect the socialist principle of payment in accordance with quantity and quality of labor and stimulating the workers to attain higher skill in their work. In considering the piece-rate system of wage payment as the system which is most suited to meet the problem of raising the productivity of labor and the further improvement in the material conditions for workers, the Congress proposes that all trade union organizations should strive to introduce to the maximum extent direct and unlimited piece-rate wages; and, in those branches where it is advisable from the production point of view, to introduce progressive piece rates.

One of the major conditions of a correct system of wages and the full utilization of the technical capacity of equipment, the raising of the productivity of labor and the better organization of labor is found in technical rate-setting and the strengthening of the technical rate-setting bureaus and the conflict committees, especially those of the individual shops. The trade unions must make it one of their major objectives to master the technique of rate-setting as the most important link in their entire production work.

The trade unions and the administrative organizations must strengthen the rate-setting bureaus with trained workers, create around them active groups of volunteers from the ranks of the skilled workers and the engineering and technical personnel, and organize, together with the administration, facilities for the training of these volunteers, drawing the scientific research institutes into the training work.

The Congress approves the introduction of higher wage increases for the workers in the leading branches of industry—steel and iron, machine building, coal, basic chemistry, transport—in accordance with the decisions of the Party, and considers it necessary to further insure a higher tempo of wage increases for the workers of these branches of industry and for the leading trades.

The Congress makes it obligatory for all trade union organizations to insure the necessary conditions for the work of the engineering and technical workers at the enterprise and to organize the proper provisions for their material, living and cultural needs.

* * *

The growth of socialist economy is creating a solid basis for a further improvement in the material and cultural standards and living conditions of the working class. On the other hand, "The worker to-day, our Soviet worker, wants to satisfy his material and cultural needs relative to food supplies, as well as living quarters, cultural requirements and all other needs. He has a right to this and we must guarantee him these conditions" (Stalin).

The increased demands of the workers, the necessity of proper distribution of the increased volume of supplies in accordance with the interests of socialist construction and the widening of the trading system require stronger attention on the part of the trade unions to the entire system of workers' supplies, distribution of consumers' goods, and the improvement of the work of the trade-coöperative apparatus.

The responsibility of trade union organizations with regard to supplies (the work of the closed workers' coöperatives, dining rooms, vegetable gardens, hog breeding and rabbit breeding establishments) is increasing considerably. The trade union apparatus which does not fight against all cases of abuse regarding questions of workers' supplies, should be replaced as an apparatus incapable of insuring the carrying out of the Party line in the struggle for a constant rise in the material well-being of the working masses.

The trade unions must organize mass control (check-ups), carry on a determined fight against bureaucratic practices in the administrative and coöperative apparatus, strive for the maximum development of Soviet trade and at the same time carry on a merciless fight against trafficking in consumers' goods intended for the workers. The trade unions are to take special care in seeing to it that every kilogram of bread, every meter of textiles should be promptly distributed to the consumers in accordance with the distribution plan.

"The recording and checking of the amount of labor and the distribution of products—herein lies the essence of the socialist transformation, once the political domination of the proletariat is set up and assured" (Lenin).

At the same time the trade unions must actively assist in the development of the procurement of supplies by the coöperatives themselves, in the organization of collective farm markets based on the widening of Soviet trade.

The Congress makes it obligatory for all trade union organizations and especially for the trade unions in the food and light industries, the state livestock and grain farms to insure the unconditional fulfillment by these branches of national economy of their industrial-financial plan for 1932, at the same time improving the quality of consumers' goods and food products.

In order to intensify the struggle of the trade unions for the widening of the raw material base for industry (cotton, wool, flax, leather, silk, etc.) the Congress proposes that the central committees of the trade unions in light industry should develop the practice of patronage of the workers over the industrial crop regions, primarily over the state and collective farms in these regions.

The trade unions of the districts and republics which are the backbone of the country in the production of industrial crops and raw materials (Central Asia, Transcaucasia, Kazakstan, etc.) must concentrate their attention upon the development of the raw material and industrial crops base.

The trade unions must strive to achieve a widening of the network of suburban enterprises (vegetable gardens, dairy and livestock farms, rabbit breeding stations, fisheries, etc.) in the vicinity of large factory centers; they must assist in the struggle for higher yields and improved methods in the suburban enterprises in order to insure a development of these enterprises within the next two years to a point where they will be able to supply the basic needs of these centers with regard to vegetables, dairy products, and to a considerable extent meat and fish.

It is necessary to achieve the elimination of the chief shortcomings in the organization of socialized feeding (unsanitary condition of dining rooms, poor preparation of food, impolite handling of clients, trafficking of products, etc.), to improve the quality of meals and to increase the number of dining rooms, tea-rooms, cafés and factory kitchens which furnish meals for the workers and their families.

The Congress obligates each trade union organization to exert all its efforts for the further development and completion of the plan of housing and municipal construction; the mobilization of local building materials; the full utilization of appropriated funds, reducing the cost and improving the quality of construction work, striving especially to extend the building of the lower cost type of standardized houses; the organization of the proper distribution of living space, giving preference to members of shock-brigades and old staff workers.

The trade unions are, at the same time, to lay stress upon the development of crêches, kindergartens, laundries, municipal establishments for the use of leisure time, thus insuring a wider possibility of drawing women into industry.

The Congress obligates each trade union to pay maximum attention to questions of improving working and living conditions for workers (ventilation, cleanliness both in the enterprise and in dormitories for workers, the development of a network of health units at the enterprises, clinics, hospitals, the development of sports and physical culture systems which tend to prevent occupational diseases).

It is necessary that trade union organizations pay increased attention to the Pioneer movement, supporting in every possible way all measures tending to provide healthier and better living conditions for workers' children and improving their bringing up.

During the second five-year plan there is to be a rapid improvement in the standard of living of the working masses, "by the end of the second five-year plan the supply of consumers' goods, including food, is to increase to two or three times that at the end of the present five-year plan" (XVII Party Conference).

The IX Congress of Trade Unions proposes that all trade union organizations begin a determined struggle for the realization of this most important Party directive.

* * *

The trade unions must strengthen their attack upon any bureaucratic disregard of the daily needs of the workers by the administrative, government, coöperative or trade union apparatus.

In order to combat bureaucratic errors in the Soviet apparatus and to improve the quality of services for the working masses, the trade unions must coöperate even more closely with the Workers' and Peasants' Inspection departments (establishing nuclei of coöperation with the complaint bureaus, checking campaigns, etc.).

It is necessary further to develop the practice of patronage on the part of enterprises over government institutions, and to aid in the establishment of assistance for persons combining social and government functions, and to carry on tireless work for improving the staff and raising the qualifications of government employees.

The IX Congress stresses the fact that the trade unions will be able to fulfill their rôle as the driving belt from the Party to the masses only on condition that the entire trade union apparatus, and primarily the leadership of the trade union organizations, will "live the worker's life, will know it thoroughly, will be able to determine unerringly in connection with any problem at any moment the mood of the masses, their actual aspirations, needs and thoughts; will be able to determine without any shadow of false idealization the degree of the consciousness of the masses and the extent of the influence exerted over them by certain preconceived notions and hangovers from the past; will be able to gain for themselves the unlimited confidence of the masses through a comradely attitude to them, a careful provision for their needs." (XV Party Congress).

* * *

In connection with the rapid influx into industry of new workers who come to the factories for the first time, there has been a tremendous increase in the educational problems of the trade unions. These new strata of workers, especially those who have come from the villages and the youth who have not yet mastered proletarian discipline, who are not acquainted with large-scale socialist production, the majority of whom have not yet been liberated from petty bourgeois habits, practices and outlook, demand the particularly careful attention of the trade union organization. The trade unions, while constantly and systematically raising the class consciousness of all the workers, must make it their primary task to draw these new strata into the trade unions and provide Communist education for them, inculcating at the same time the new labor discipline.

At times elements foreign to the working class find their way into socialist enterprises: kulaks, petty traders, declassed elements, etc. They carry on their undermining work at the socialist enterprises, disorganize production and attempt to exercise a corrupting influence upon the new strata of workers. The trade unions must repel these class enemies mercilessly. With the support of the shock-brigadiers and the old experienced workers the trade unions must carry on a determined struggle for the new labor discipline, against petty bourgeois laxity, grafting, petty proprietary hangovers "of those small groups and strata of workers which hold on obstinately to the traditions and habits of capitalism and continue to look upon the Soviet state as formerly: give 'it' as little work as possible and get from 'it' as much money as possible" (Lenin). The trade unions must inculcate the consciousness of these workers with the understanding that the worker is the boss of the country, that he is working for himself, for his own class.

The Congress proposes that all trade unions strive in a determined manner for the further development of Marxist-Leninist education at the enterprises, in the brigades, in the shops, the dormitories, the military barracks, spreading this among the widest strata of workers and stressing as the major probem in the cultural and political work the development of a conscious attitude of the worker toward socialist production, the overcoming of petty bourgeois hangovers, the transformation of the workers into "conscious and active builders of the classless, socialist society."

One of the most important tasks of the trade unions is to satisfy the growing desire of workers for more schooling.

The radical reconstruction of national economy has brought to the fore the most important problem of training staffs of skilled workers and specialists for socialist construction. The Congress considers the factory training schools the basic units for the training of skilled workers, and obligates the trade union organizations to work for the further development of these schools and for the improvement of the work in them in accordance with new techniques, stressing especially the training of skilled personnel from the midst of the nationals of each national region or republic. It is also necessary to develop the training of skilled workers and proletarian-technical intellectuals in the school combines, evening shift technical schools, school enterprises, and many other ways, without having the workers leave their present jobs.

The Congress proposes that all trade union organizations together with the administrative organizations and the Commissariat for Education should strive for further improvement in the quality of schooling in the higher and secondary technical schools, for the better organization of productive practice in the enterprises, and better provisions by trade unions for proletarian students. The trade unions are to utilize all the levers for their cultural-mass work (clubs, red corners, radio, circles, courses, study combines, factory press), and at the same time strengthen technical propaganda, imparting to all workers, especially the newcomers, a knowledge of their machines, the technological processes of the entire enterprise and the basic elements of political science.

The trade unions are to eliminate all illiteracy among workers and at the same time strive for the inculcation of cultural habits in the worker's home: the reading of newspapers, the use of libraries, the attendance at clubs, red corners, the striving for cultural surroundings in the enterprise, the home, for a workers' cultural settlement.

It is necessary to achieve a radical improvement in the entire question of organizing rest and entertainment (the use of leisure) by means of an organized spending of leisure (rest days), excursions to suburbs, parks, cinemas, museums, theaters, the development of a wide network of cultural units, sport and physical culture grounds, shooting galleries, swimming, boating and skiing stations, parks of culture and rest, and also through the creation of appropriate conditions for rest in the workers' clubs.

* * *

The transfer of the center of gravity of the trade union work to the enterprises, shops and brigades and the wider development of mass work demand a determined strengthening of the trade union units at the factory. The careful selection of group organizers and provisions for constantly training them, their political enlightenment and Bolshevik temper must become the primary concern of all trade union organizations.

It is also necessary to strengthen the factory and workers' committees choosing, on the basis of proletarian democracy and the elective principle, for trade union work persons capable of leadership among the mass of workers, persons who know the needs and desires of the workers. It is necessary to take all steps toward improving the quality of work of the entire system of training trade union workers, especially strengthening the factory trade union units.

The Congress takes note of the fact that in the scientific-theoretical work there are still remnants of "craft-unionism" tendencies and Men-

shevik points of view concerning the trade union movement, and
instructs the AUCCTU to organize together with the Communist
Academy an extensive working out of the basic problems in the work
of the trade unions on the basis of the teachings of Marx-Lenin-Stalin
with special reference to the problems of the second five-year plan
and to strengthen the work upon the central questions of the history of
the trade union movement.

The Congress requests the AUCCTU to strengthen the instruction
work for trade union organizations of the national republics and regions,
aiding the latter by supplying funds and workers for the development
and education of local workers of each nationality.

The Congress considers absolutely correct the decision of the Central
Committee of the Party and the Fifth Plenum of the AUCCTU regarding the increase in the number of trade unions for the purpose of
attaining "a more concrete participation of the trade unions in the
leadership in socialist industry, the organization of the growing activity
of the working masses around concrete problems of production, and a
more thorough consideration of the production and living peculiarities
of separate groups of workers, the improved services to workers and
the struggle with bureaucracy." The IX Congress notes that these decisions have been put into effect only in so far as the breaking up of the
large unions into smaller ones is concerned, while with regard to raising
the rôle of industrial unions these decisions have not been sufficiently
realized and not all trade union workers have fully grasped them. The
Congress therefore considers it necessary to stress the importance of
realizing to the fullest extent the decisions concerning the strengthening
of the rôle of the central committees of the unions.

The central committees of the unions must concentrate their efforts
primarily upon questions of regulating wages and setting rates and categories, upon the organization of labor and production, upon housing
construction, upon the improvement of the working and living conditions of their members. The intra-union organizations must concentrate
their attention chiefly upon questions of workers' supplies, municipal
construction, cultural-political work, labor legislation, etc. This, however, does not exempt the central committees and their district branches
from exercising care and responsibility for the many-sided services for
the members of the trade unions, including the improvement of supplies, the raising of the cultural level and political education. On the
other hand, the republican, regional, district councils of trade unions,
while not renouncing responsibility for problems of wages, production,
etc., must give up the duplication and replacement of union organizations, and concentrate their major attention upon checking the fulfillment of the directives of the Party, the government and the AUCCTU.
The AUCCTU must base all its work directly upon the work of the
central committees of the trade unions, furnishing them with concrete

aid and constantly checking and providing concrete leadership for their activity.

The Congress instructs the AUCCTU to specify clearly the functions of its apparatus and those of the intra-union organizations on the one hand, and the central committees and their district departments on the other, specifying clearly their responsibilities and duties.

The Congress considers that the decision of the Fifth Plenum of the AUCCTU concerning the creation of production sections and the work with the leading trades has been put into effect in a very weak manner and by some trade union organizations it has not even been started. The Congress proposes that the AUCCTU should take immediate steps toward putting into effect these decisions of the Plenum, and carry on a determined fight against the formal, bureaucratic attitude to this most important directive.

The Congress instructs the AUCCTU to take all necessary measures toward improving financial discipline, insisting on prompt payment of membership dues and improving the financial relations between the central committees of the trade unions and the AUCCTU in the direction of increasing independence of the industrial unions.

The Congress considers that the leadership of the trade union organizations must be concrete and operative, and based upon a differentiated approach to the individual ranks of the working class, to individual strata and groups, especially to the leading trades. The necessary prerequisites for such leadership is the determined stopping of futile conferences, a transition from the method of paper leadership (leadership through the issuing of resolutions, decisions, etc.) to the organization of live assistance for the factory trade union units, the wider drawing in of voluntary active workers into trade union activity and the development of a systematic struggle of the trade unions for the fulfillment of the decisions of the Party and government, for checking the fulfillment of union decisions.

In noting the growing rôle of working youths and the Communist youths (Comsomols) in production, the Congress demands that the trade union organizations strive toward the further strengthening of work carried on together with the Comsomols, encouraging the initiative of the young workers in improving production and in bettering the satisfaction of the needs of the members of trade unions. It is necessary to draw the largest number of young workers into leading positions in the trade union apparatus.

The struggle for the fulfillment of the second Bolshevik five-year plan demands a colossal increase in the rôle of the trade unions in socialist construction. As a school of Communism the trade unions must "be the builders of the new life, the educators of new millions who will learn by their own experience not to make any errors, who will discard old prejudices and learn by experience the business of state and industrial administration.... Only this will provide the unerring guarantee that the cause of socialism will be completely victorious and exclude any possibility of a return to the old" (Lenin).

The IX Congress appeals to all trade unions to mobilize all the forces of the entire working class and the laboring masses for the complete fulfillment of the plans of the final year of the first five-year plan and for a Bolshevik fight for the second five-year plan—the plan for the building of a classless, socialist society in the USSR.

APPENDIX IV

BUDGET OF LENINGRAD WORKER'S FAMILY [1]

An accounting at random of the family budgets of Leningrad workers and engineers has brought to light some interesting facts concerning the rise in the standard of living of Leningrad wage-earners in recent years.

This study indicated that there were on the average 3.68 members to each family. Of these there are 1.48 persons employed in each worker's family, and 1.42 persons in the family of the engineer or technician.

The average income per worker's family was 165 rubles per month in 1930, and 244.8 rubles in the beginning of 1932, an increase of 48.4 per cent. The budget of a worker's family consisted of the following income: wages—220 rubles, socialized wages—6.5 rubles, extra earnings—2.77 rubles, and various other forms of income—16.5 rubles.

The expenditures of a worker's family were distributed as follows:

	1930	1931	1932
	(in rubles)		
Rent	10.72	10.52	12.32
Heat and light..............	5.75	5.60	5.88
Food	74.94	94.30	104.21
Clothing and shoes..........	24.09	27.37	40.41
Household goods	4.62	6.02	9.09
Cultural and educ. needs.....	4.39	5.33	8.74
Hygiene and medical.........	3.42	4.52	5.00
All other expenses..........	13.11	18.92	24.58

The increase of expenditures on food exceeds 39 per cent, clothing and shoes—about 70 per cent, household goods—95 per cent as compared with 1930. It should be remembered that the major part of educational and medical facilities are provided free of charge, through a well organized system of social insurance, trade union clubs, etc.

With regard to the budget of families of the engineers and tech-

[1] Information Bulletin of the Commissariat of Foreign Affairs, May 5, 1932.

nicians there is also a considerable increase from year to year. The average income for the engineers' family reached about 465 rubles in the early part of 1932, and consisted of the following: regular wages—402 rubles, additional earnings—13 rubles, special aids—6 rubles, all other earnings (mostly premiums)—44 rubles.

This data was compiled on the basis of cases picked at random for an investigation and are typical in that they characterize fully the improvement in living standards for all Leningrad workers and engineers and their families.

GLOSSARY

GLOSSARY

Aucctu: All-Union Central Council of Trade Unions.

Census Industry: All industrial enterprises which employ 15 workers or more and use mechanical power, and all those where no mechanical power is used but where at least 30 workers are employed.

Control Figures: The annual program for the whole of national economy.

Industrial-Financial Plan: The annual plan based on the Control Figures—assigned to the individual enterprise (factory, mine, mill or farm) by the higher planning bodies. It includes definite schedules for all phases of activity of the enterprise such as the amount and quality of output, production costs, labor productivity, the working and living conditions of workers, etc.

State Large-Scale Industry: All those industries which have been nationalized and placed under the direct supervision of the state (the Supreme Economic Council and the Commissariat of Internal Supply). It now embraces about 95 per cent of large-scale industry.

Gosplan: State Planning Commission: a permanent advisory body attached to the Council of Labor and Defense, composed of experts and itself divided into specialized sub-departments and sub-committees.

Gubernia: An administrative unit or province which existed until 1929. such as Tambov, Vladimir, Moscow, etc.

Kulak: (literally "fist")—a rich peasant employing labor, making a living by trade and acting as village usurer.

NEP: The New Economic Policy.

Pood: 36.11 pounds or 16.38 kilograms.

R.S.F.S.R.: Russian Socialist Federative Republic.

Verst: .66 miles or 1.06 kilometers.

BIBLIOGRAPHY

BIBLIOGRAPHY

A. Aluf, *The Soviet Economic System.* [Russian.] (Moscow, 1931.)

M. S. Balabanov, *An Outline of the History of the Working Class in Russia.* [Russian] 3 vols. (Sorabkopa, Kiev, 1923, and Economic Life Pub. Co. Moscow, 1926.)

Dr. Llewellys F. Barker, *Medical and other Conditions in Soviet Russia,* Scientific Monthly, New York, July, 1932.

Karl A. Bickel, *How the Outside World Gets Its Information Concerning Events in Russia.* Address delivered before the Institute of Politics, Williamstown, Mass., August 2, 1930.

Peter A. Bogdanov, *Prerequisites and Aims of Soviet Planning.* Address before Academy of Political and Social Science, Philadelphia, April 15, 1932. Published in Proceedings of Session.

Saul G. Bron, *Soviet Economic Development and American Business.* (Horace Liveright, New York, 1930.)

J. M. Budish and Samuel S. Shipman, *Soviet Foreign Trade—Menace or Promise?* (Horace Liveright, New York, 1931.)

Bulletin of Financial and Economic Legislation No. 21. [Russian.] (Moscow, 1931.)

Emile Burns, *Russia's Productive System.* (E. P. Dutton & Co., New York, 1931.)

William Henry Chamberlain, *Soviet Russia—A Living Record and a History.* (Little, Brown & Co., Boston, 1930.)

Collection of Laws of the R.S.F.S.R. [Russian.] Moscow, 1930.)

Collection of Laws of the U.S.S.R. [Russian.] (Moscow, 1930.)

Col. Hugh L. Cooper. *Russia.* Article in Engineers and Engineering, April, 1931.

Correctional Labor Code of the R.S.F.S.R. [Russian.]

George S. Counts, *The Soviet Challenge to America.* (John Day Company, New York, 1931.)

Criminal Code of the R.S.F.S.R. [Russian.] (Moscow.)

Maurice Dobb, *Russian Economic Development Since the Revolution.* (E. P. Dutton & Co., New York, 1928.)

Robert W. Dunn, *Soviet Trade Unions.* (Vanguard Press, New York, 1928.)

Economic Conditions in the U.S.S.R. (Handbook.) [English.] Issued by the U.S.S.R. Chamber of Commerce (Vneshtorgizdat, Moscow, 1931.)

Economic Handbook of the Soviet Union. Issued by the American-Russian Chamber of Commerce, New York, 1931.

Economic Review of the Soviet Union. Published by the Amtorg Trading Corporation, Information Department, New York.

Sherwood Eddy, *The Challenge of Russia* (Farrar and Rinehart, New York, 1931.)

Alice Withrow Field, *Protection of Women and Children in Soviet Russia.* (E. P. Dutton & Co., New York, 1932.)

Louis Fischer, *Machines and Men in Russia.* (Harrison Smith, New York, 1932.)

Forced Labour. Issued by International Labour Office, Geneva, 1929.

Forced Labour Report, second discussion. Issued by International Labour Conference, International Labour Office, Geneva, 1930.

Joseph Freeman, Joshua Kunitz and Louis Lozowick, *Voices of October —A Survey of Literature and Art in the Soviet Union.* (Vanguard Press, New York, 1930.)

G. T. Grinko, *The Five-Year Plan of the Soviet Union.* (International Publishers, New York, 1930.)

I. M. Gubkin, *The Natural Wealth of the Soviet Union and Its Exploitation,* Cooperative Publishing Society of Foreign Workers in the U.S.S.R., Moscow, 1932.

Calvin B. Hoover, *The Economic Life of Soviet Russia.* (Macmillan, New York, 1931.)

Information Bulletin of the Commissariat for Foreign Affairs. [Russian.] (Moscow, March 5, 1932.)

Interpretations of the Supreme Court of the U.S.S.R., 2nd ed. [Russian.] (Moscow, 1931.)

Kaploun, S., *Theory and Practice of Labor Protection.* [Russian.] (Moscow, 1927.)

Susan M. Kingsbury and Mildred Fairchild, *Employment and Unemployment in Pre-War and Soviet Russia.* Report submitted to the World Social Economic Congress, Amsterdam, August 23-29, 1931. Issued by International Industrial Relations Association (I.R.I.), The Hague, Holland, 1932.

Labor Code of the R.S.F.S.R. of 1922, with changes and amendments up to June 15, 1929; [Russian]; published by "Voprosy Truda," Moscow, 1929.

L. Lapidus and K. Ostrovityanov, *An Outline of Political Economy.* (International Publishers, New York, 1930.)

V. I. Lenin, *The Development of Capitalism in Russia,* Vol. VII, Collected Works. [Russian.] State Publishing House, Moscow.

Margaret S. Miller, *The Economic Development of Russia, 1905-1914.* (London, 1926.)

V. M. Molotov, *The Success of the Five-Year Plan*. (International Publishers, New York, 1931.)

L. I. Monosson, *The Soviet Cinematography*, in the Journal of the Society of Motion Picture Engineers, Vol. XV, 1930.

Monthly Labor Review, issued by U. S. Department of Labor, Washington, D. C.

National Economy of the U.S.S.R. (Handbook.) [Russian.] Central Bureau of National Economic Accounting, Moscow, 1932.

A. Nelepin, *Wages in the U.S.S.R.* [Russian.] (Moscow, 1931.)

Official Bulletin of the International Labour Office, supplement to Vol. XV, No. 2, Geneva, 1929.

Moissaye J. Olgin, *The Soul of the Russian Revolution*. (Henry Holt and Company, New York, 1917.)

K. A. Pazhitnov, *Collection of Decrees and Decisions on National Economy*. [Russian.] (Moscow, 1918.)

K. A. Pazhitnov, *The Working Class in Russia*. [Russian.] (Kniga Izdatelstvo Put i Znanyu, Leningrad, 1924-25.)

Albert P. Pinkevich, *The New Education in the Soviet Republic*. (John Day Company, New York, 1929.)

Walter Polakov, *How Efficient Are the Russians?*, In Harper's Monthly Magazine, December, 1931.

George M. Price, *Labor Protection in Soviet Russia*. (International Publishers, New York, 1927.)

Report of the All-Union Central Council of Trade Unions, Pravda, April 12, 1932.

Rote Arbeit, edited by Jurgen Kuczynski. Historia-Foto, G. m. b. H., Berlin, 1931.

Walter Arnold Rukeyser, *Working for the Soviets*. (Covici-Friede, New York, 1932.)

Russia After Ten Years, Report of the American Trade Union Delegation to the Soviet Union. (International Publishers, New York, 1927.)

Russian Timber. Report of Delegation Appointed by the Russian Timber Trade Federation of the United Kingdom. Reprinted from *Timber and Plywood*, London, September 19, 1931.

V. V. Schmidt, I. S. Voitinsky, E. N. Danilova, *Principles of Labor Legislation in the Soviet Union*. (Moscow, 1931.)

Selection of Documents Relative to Labor Legislation in Force in the U.S.S.R. Printed by H. M. Stationery Office, London, 1931.

N. M. Shvernik, *Trade Union Problems in the Reconstruction Period*. [Russian.] (Moscow, 1930.)

N. M. Shvernik, *Further Improvement in the Work of the Trade Unions*. [Russian.] (Moscow, 1931.)

Social-Economic Planning in the U.S.S.R. Report of Soviet Delegation at the World Social-Economic Congress, Amsterdam, August 23-

29, 1931. Issued by International Industrial Relations Association (I.R.I.), The Hague, Holland, 1932.

Soviet Culture Review. [English.] Published by the Soviet Union Society for Cultural Relations with Foreign Countries (VOKS), Moscow.

Soviet Russia in the Second Decade: A Joint Survey by the Technical Staff of the First American Trade Union Delegation to the Soviet Union. Edited by Stuart Chase, Robert W. Dunn and Rexford Guy Tugwell. (John Day Co., New York, 1928.)

Soviet Union Review. Published by Soviet Union Information Bureau, Washington, D. C.

Soviet Union Year Book. Compiled and edited by A. A. Santalov and Louis Segal. (George Allen & Unwin, Ltd., London, 1930.)

M. I. Tugan-Baranovski, *The Russian Factory.* [Russian.] (St. Petersburg, 1898.)

S. I. Turetzky, *Soviet Trade and the Welfare of the Workers.* [Russian.] (Moscow, 1931.)

N. N. Vanag and S. Tomsinsky, *The Economic Development of Russia.* [Russian.] (Gosizdat, Moscow, 1928.)

VOKS Bulletin, Published by the Soviet Union Society for Cultural Relations with Foreign Countries, Moscow.

I. Voitinsky, *Legal Aspects of Labor Relations According to Present-Day Soviet Legislation.* [Russian.] (Moscow, 1931.)

Y. A. Yakovlev, *Red Villages.* (International Publishers, New York, 1931.)

Clara Zetkin, *Reminiscences of Lenin.* (London, 1929.)

INDEX

INDEX

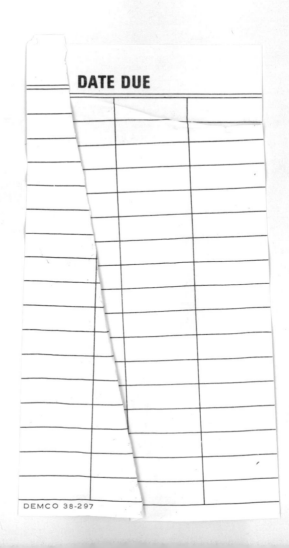